POSTPONING AUTUMN

"The great Gaels of Ireland are the men that God made mad,

For all their wars are merry, and all their songs are sad."

—G.K. Chesterton

By

MARY MATHIAS

i

ISBN 978-1-969201-75-2

Synopsis

When Berta Ronan purchases a stately Victorian home in Dorchester—the very same house where her mother once worked as a maid in the early 1900s—she unknowingly inherits not just a property, but a tapestry of secrets that will unravel both her family's past and her own carefully constructed worldview. Set against the backdrop of Boston's changing social landscape during the 1950s and '60s, the story follows Berta, her alcoholic husband Tim, and her maiden sister Mae as they navigate the challenges of raising three distinctly different daughters in a de facto segregated city.

As the youngest daughter, Colleen forms an unlikely friendship with a Jewish boy from a neighboring community—the family's long-held beliefs and prejudices are put to the test. Through their eyes, we witness a city in transition, where old boundaries are beginning to blur and traditional values clash with social change.

Weaving together themes of family loyalty, religious identity, and social transformation, "Postponing Autumn" combines rich historical detail with touches of supernatural mystery and unexpected humor. Like Dorothy's journey through Oz, the characters must navigate their own yellow brick road of self-discovery, though not all will find their way home.

Dedication

To a time, a town, and a community that make dreams come true.

And for Dennis, who never found Oz.

Acknowledgement

Special thanks to my beta readers: Diane and Teresa Walsh, Priscilla Flannery, and Patricia Gravalese. Deepest gratitude to Brian Ebert for his technical assistance

About the Author

Mary Mathias is a Dorchester native and longtime resident of East Boston. A member of the Grub Street writing community, this is Mary's debut novel. Her intimate knowledge of Boston's changing landscape and its diverse communities brings authenticity to her storytelling. She currently works in the medical field and resides in Dorchester,

Chapter One

They said the house was haunted. Bejeweled in stained glass, crowned with a cupola, and trimmed by a lonely widow's walk, number thirteen Mount Nottingham reigned supreme over a dominion of Gothic, Queen Anne, and Second Empire homes surrounding the Mounts' park, forming a tranquil cul-de-sac. Mrs. Lindsey died intestate. Lacking relations, her estate lingered in probate; the house doomed to become the first victim of urban blight. Enter the Ronan family, remission.

Mae watched her mother skulk through the main floor of the hollow house as if in fear of coming face to face with her late employer. Soiled kitchen cupboards clung to the aroma of Genevieve's French cuisine long after the cook moved to France before the First World War. After a forty-year absence, only the cursed staircase, the bewitched piano, and the memory of Robert remained.

"Mother, are you well?" Mae asked.

Nuala batted her lids. "I'm fine... memories."

Blond, with deep-set green eyes, Mavis was the prettier of Nuala's two daughters. Yet it was the twice-wed Berta who had given Nuala two granddaughters, Rosaria and Margo.

"I can't manage these stairs," Mae puffed, following her mother to the second floor.

"Poppycock, your sister is eight months along and hasn't trouble with the climb. It's those blasted cigarettes. This was Robert's room," Nuala reminisced in a voice cracked by age and emotion. Mae placed a comforting hand on her mother's shoulder.

"You were meant to live here. Pity it took so long." Nuala looked out at the backyard's maple tree through a window framed in frost. "Many a summer's day, Annabel and I would lie beneath that tree. Never cared for Annabel, but 'twas just the two of us who worked the house. There was Genevieve, the cook, she only spoke French. Mrs. Lindsey was born in France, spoke the language. Annabel was dismissed; the girl was a thief."

"Tim, come over here," Berta called to her husband in the carriage house, inspecting a car left by Mrs. Lindsey. Berta's tall, slender figure resembled her mother's. Her brown eyes and black hair were passed down from her father.

"What's the problem?" Tim asked while making his way across autumn leaves, now a mushy mulch. Berta shielded her eyes from November's sun to look up at the maple tree. "That branch will come down with the next ice storm and cripple someone."

"'Fraid there's nothing we can do, Berta. The tree's rooted in the neighbor's yard."

"'Tis a maple, that branch won't come down in our lifetime. A swing is what's needed," Nuala voiced from behind. Tim, a redhead Navy veteran who had been orphaned as a child, always referred to Nuala as mother. If alcohol is a good man's weakness, Timothy Ronan was a saint.

"Are you happy, Mother?" Tim asked.

"Oh yes, Tim, 'tis a dream come true."

"Then I'm happy. The swing goes up tomorrow."

Berta watched her mother giggle and flirt with Tim. No white bun or hairnet on Nuala's bleached, brassy blond hair in a circa 1920s permanent wave. Most

2

women didn't wear lipstick once their lips collapsed into their chin. Nuala's lips were painted ruby red. Berta showed her mother the respect required by the fifth commandment, suspecting her mother had broken all ten.

Rosaria and Margo chased one another around the second floor's circular balcony. The thump from their loafered feet set the player piano's musical scroll in motion.

"What in blazes?" Tim blurted.

Nuala clutched his arm. "'Tis The Weeping Willow Rag. All rags are a celebration of life."

"It's morbid."

Berta shook her head. "The willow can do its weeping in the carriage house. We can't have it playing willy-nilly with every slamming door, or 'The Celebration of Life' will be the death of me."

"Margo, Rosaria," Nuala shouted up to her granddaughters. "Watch yourselves, the railing is loose. Tim, you'll have to secure it—the third spindle on the right 'tis a poor fit, not original to the banister."

Tim let out a long whistle. "That's one hell of a staircase. They don't make 'em like that anymore." Brass cherub lamps rested on the newels of the deep mahogany staircase. Its landing is highlighted by a stained-glass fleur de lis. A circular balcony gave the impression that the masterpiece was crowned with a halo.

"We each get our own bedroom; I'm picking mine first," insisted the fair-haired Margo. Only her mother and the nuns at Saint Regina's Elementary School dare call her by her birth name – Nuala. The eight-year-old preferred her middle name. Ice blue eyes concealed a smoldering temper equal only to her mother's. Margo was Tim's little fairy with lips kissed by the angels.

"The angels better like the taste of soap. They'll be getting a steady diet of it," Berta would say. Long-legged with long dark hair, ten-year-old Rosaria flew down the stairs into her father's arms.

"Oh, Poppy, I love this house."

"You can thank your grandmother and the V.A.," Tim turned to Nuala. "What's the story on the old jalopy in the carriage house?"

"That's not a jalopy, 'tis a 1908 Stevens-Duryea Model S. It's to remain garaged."

Margo's eyes widened. "You can drive, Grandma?"

"Not a jalopy like your father, but I can drive a Duryea."

Berta stood on the front porch looking over at the park. "Dear lord, here comes Himself." He was Martin, Berta's hot-headed brother. Tim never passed up the opportunity to poke fun at the disabled fireman. "He threw his back out picking up his paycheck, now he's trying to pick up a wealthy widow." Bald and bowlegged, Marty lived far from Boston's inner city to get away from "them." Everyone knew who "they" were. Throbbing red worms rippled under his sweaty temples, and his necktie hung around his throat like a noose.

"Are you outta your mind, Bertie? Buying a house on the Mount?"

"Mother finds it enchanting."

"Right, right, enchanting. Take my advice. Clean the place up and put it back on the market. The old lady is wrapped up in some kind of fantasy. This is 1948, not 1908—things change. She'll be dead, and you'll be stuck with this house she dropped on you."

"I like it," Berta lied. "We're still in the parish. I didn't want to take the girls out of Saint Regina's; they have friends living nearby."

"Not for long, all you see around here are Jews and coloreds." Marty waved his hand at his sister. "Ah, do as you please, you're as pig-headed as your mother."

***

The siblings walked arm in arm from their mother's open grave. "It feels strange to be an orphan. I don't remember Pop yet, I've always felt the loss," Mae said, snapping open her pocketbook to retrieve a tissue.

Marty chuckled. "Do you really believe the old man was killed by a trolley car? That's a bucket of blarney."

4

"We'll never know now, will we?" Berta snarled. In an overripe brogue, Marty mimicked his late mother.

"The poor dear, not in the country more than a day, he sees his first trolley car coming down the road and doesn't the good lord give him a closer look."

"That's ancient history," Berta scoffed.

Marty stopped to light up a Corona. "What are you going to do with the house?" he asked between puffs.

"What about it?"

"You're gonna sell it, right?"

"I'll do no such thing."

"It's haunted."

"You're talking through your hat."

"Am I, Bertie, am I? That house scared the bejesus out of me. I was a kid when the old lady snuck me into that place. I couldn't wait to get back to the shithole room we were living in. The old lady spent more time with that Lindsey gimp than she did with us. She was always going on about 'Master Robert,' how he was a brave army officer. The guy was a freak, missing a leg and half his face."

"He had a facial scar," Mae corrected.

"You never got a good look at the guy, I did. Ugly as sin, but he was loaded. Money, that's what made him so appealing to her."

"God forgive you."

"No, Bertie, you had a different upbringing than Maize and me. By the time she popped you out, she was shittin' in high cotton. Working for the church, she claimed. Give me a break, the priests don't pay the kinda dough she was raking in. Suddenly, we got our own apartment. You went to a sister school. Mazie and me didn't get a good education. We were eatin' sawdust in that stinkin' room yet, she wouldn't sell that rock."

5

"Pop gave her that ring. It was all she had to remember him by."

"Come on, the old man didn't have a pot to piss in and he's gonna buy her The Hope Diamond?" Marty's face lost all color. "Bertie, please don't tell me the ring is in that hole 'cuz if it is, I'm diving in after it."

"Good, save us a trip back to bury you. I blame Tim for this."

Mae defended her brother-in-law. "Please, Berta, don't blame him. Tim's beside himself with grief."

"He should have been beside her when she took the fall. Leave it to Tim to do a half-ass job replacing a banister spindle. Thank God it wasn't one of the girls who fell over the railing."

"Blame's on you, Bertie, for saddling yourself to a drunk."

"Marty!"

"I'm deaf to him, Mae."

"Open your ears for this—Mazie's right; it wasn't Tim's fault. The old lady didn't fall; she was pushed."

Chapter Two

The house was cold, January cold. The four-legged Glenwood gas stove could only accommodate one backside pressing against its warm door; this morning, it was Margo's.

"You shouldn't brush that chimp's hair in the kitchen. I don't want cooties floating in my tea." Rosaria ignored Margo's insult and continued to tug on Colleen's coarse red locks with a horsehair brush more familiar with the seven-year-old's backside than her scalp.

"OOWW!"

"I'm sorry, sweetheart," Rosaria apologized. Slipping into a Navy-blue blazer bearing Saint Regina's school emblem, Margo returned to the breakfast table. "No one ever said being beautiful was easy."

"You ought to know, you're beautiful and easy," Colleen cracked. Berta's threatening stare silenced the table.

"Finish your breakfast. I'm in no mood for a lecture on tardiness from Sister Superior."

"I can't sleep in my bedroom; it's inhabited by a ghost," Margo grumbled. "I want Grandma's room."

"A ghost?"

"Yes. At night, when the moon is full and the house eerily silent, a spirit comes to my bed and howls, 'I'm in search of a pus-filled pig.' I told him Colleen's room is down the hall, but he keeps coming back."

"That's because he means the other kind of pig, pig."

"Not another word from either of you," their mother warned. Margo stuck her tongue out at her fat, freckled nemesis.

"What did I just say?"

"That wasn't a word."

"Keep it up, Nuala, and I'll cut your hair off."

"Her hair will grow back, cut her face," Colleen said, sliding a butter knife across the table to her mother.

"As for you, Miss I-Can't-Find-My-Way-Out-of-The-Third-Grade-with-a-Map. If you don't get a passing grade in arithmetic, the nuns won't keep you back again; they'll throw you out."

"Please don't scold her," Rosaria pleaded in Colleen's defense. "She tries. I'm helping her with her lessons."

"You're on a fool's errand. If the nuns can't knock some sense into her, I doubt you can. Time, ladies."

"Yes, Mom," the three girls sang out. Colleen tugged the drawstring to her dark blue canvas bookbag, slinging it over her shoulder like a sailor coming ashore. Berta wore her "Let's get this ritual over with" face as her daughters kissed her cheek.

Reaching the foot of Mount Nottingham, Margo ran ahead, completing the trek in the company of gossiping girlfriends. Rosaria and Colleen swung their hands as they walked.

"Did you remember your homework?"

"Yup," Colleen answered with a skip. "Rosaria, do you like high school?"

"Perhaps next year, when Margo's a freshman."

"That's all she talks about, how when she gets to high school, she's going to wear silk stockings and date anyone in pants."

"Oh no, she won't, Mom won't allow it."

"Ya, but she'll change out of her bobby socks once she gets to school. She's a sneak. I hate her guts."

"Margo's not a bad person; she's just determined to have her way."

"Are you waiting for Margo to make friends for you? Ma says it doesn't pay to be shy. I don't have friends because I hate everyone, and they hate me."

"You mustn't entertain such thoughts."

"It's true."

"I won't stand for your self-pity act. Let's not dally or you'll be late."

The two raced to the iron gate surrounding Saint Regina's Elementary School. Rosaria waited for Colleen's class to file into the yellow brick building. "Margo!" Rosaria called out to a bobbing blond ponytail. Laughter and school bells muffled her cry. Her head lowered, Rosaria mumbled, "See you after school."

The last seat in the last row was relegated to scholastic lepers, untouchables, the iceberg carrying off the old, sick, unwanted, to Dante's fifth level of hell. To a daydreamer, it was nirvana, a cozy corner warmed by a steam-spitting radiator. Colleen's eyelids grew heavy, her head bowed forward, her arithmetic book slid from its grocery bag cover onto the floor. Black-robed and mute, Sister Leonard Josephine pointed to the detention room like the ghost of Christmas Future directing Scrooge to the cemetery. There'd be no plea for leniency, no groveling for a second chance with a promise of redemption.

Colleen marched down the macabre corridor lined with statues of heroic saints and noble martyrs. Saint Rita weeping tears of blood; Saint Joan burning at the stake; Saint Veronica holding out a bloody shroud, as Saint Lucille offers a tray of eyeball hors d'oeuvres and the crowd favorite, Saint Lawrence, who the pagans roasted over an open spit, turning him like a rotisserie chicken, garnering him the title "Patron

Saint of Culinary Arts." Detention may break fellow detainees, not Colleen, for whom physical pain and psychological torture were constant companions.

Frightened children, their folded hands bound by invisible cuffs, awaited their punishment. Lightly tapping a wooden ruler on her palm, Sister Xavier slowly proceeded down the row of desks. Like a Japanese GI in a Philippine jungle hearing the snap of a twig, Sister spun around, riddling her captives with a battery of questions.

"One forty-eight divided by four equals? Forty-two times thirteen equals? Three hundred and forty plus seven minus twenty-four equals?" At that moment, Colleen was an American Mata Hari tied to a chair, being interrogated by a Japanese General. Holding a riding crop under her chin, he'd ask, "Do the numbers one hundred and forty-eight divided by four, forty-two times thirteen, three hundred minus twenty-four plus eighty-two mean anything to you? You American dog." Having stored her saliva, Mata would spit in the General's face. "Take her away!" he'd order. Oh, to spit in Sister Xavier's face would be worth having bamboo spikes shoved under her nails. As for the other Catholic cons, they'd crack, give out more than their name, grade, and homeroom number. The General would get his answers. Thirty-seven. Five fifty-nine. Four hundred and five... the war was lost.

***

Like a marathoner crossing the finish line, Margo swung open the back door, its tight spring snapped with a shotgun blast.

"I've told you time and again not to slam that door!" Berta hollered from the living room.

"Yell at me later," a breathless Margo wheezed, waving a manila envelope in her mother's face. "Colleen messed up again, this time it's Art. Nobody flunks out of Art! It must be real bad because Iggie... Sister Ignatius called me to her office and told me to see that you and Poppy, got this. Open it. I bet it's a drawing of Jesus going to the bathroom."

"Where's van Gogh now?"

"Kept after. You going to cut her ear off?"

"After I cut out your tongue."

"Come on, open it."

"It's addressed to your father and me. We'll open it when he gets home."

"That's not fair."

"To whom?"

"To me!"

"You have homework. Go do it."

It wasn't every day Colleen met Poppy's bus. He wasn't regularly employed, and she rarely came home from school on time. Tim stepped off the bus wearing beige khakis and a smile.

"We've got to stop meeting like this," Tim said.

Colleen's wide grin barely covered her oversized teeth.

"Kept after?"

"Yeah."

"What was it this time?"

"I don't know."

"I bet your mother does."

Tim opened the old oak door, allowing Colleen to enter first. "Honey, we're home!" The two snickered, knowing Berta wouldn't find the greeting amusing.

"Hold it right there," Berta said, flapping the large envelope. "I received this Special Delivery from Sister Ignatius."

Tim looked down at Colleen. "Who's that?"

"Iggie, Art."

Keeping one eye on the duo, Berta slid out the artwork as if she were about to announce an Academy Award winner. In her hand, she held a drawing entitled

"When I Grow Up, I Want to Be..." In the blank was written "Just Like My Dad." Below the phrase, a cartoon figure of a man, one arm hugging a lamppost, in the other a jug labeled XXX. Tim examined the potent portrait.

"The kid can draw."

"THAT'S YOU, YOU HORSE'S ASS!" Berta wagged the drawing in her husband's face as a master would to discipline a dog.

"Do you know why you're hanging from that post? Because you lack a backbone. You're not only spineless, you're useless. You give in to the girls the way you give in to your demons. You haven't a care in the world. It's up to me to keep this family in line. In other homes, it's, 'Wait till your father gets home.' In this house, it's, 'let's see if your father makes it home.' You're not a man, you're a cartoon, a clown, the town drunk." Throwing the crinkled drawing in her husband's face, Berta stormed into the kitchen with Colleen in tow. Unfolding the crumpled artwork, Tim scratched the back of his head.

"Still think she's talented."

***

Tim's red-rimmed eyes matched his ruddy complexion. "Please, Berta, let me call my sister. She works with delinquent boys; she'll straighten Colleen out."

"Great, just what we need, Sister Fruitcake of the Most Precious Blood of Jesus. God, does that woman get my goat." Tim placed his arm around his wife, who pushed him away.

"Please, Berta, Colleen's not a bad kid; she doesn't mean any harm. She doesn't understand what happens when you do something without thinking."

"A fire, Tim. She set a fire roasting marshmallows in her bedroom. The girl is an idiot. Call your wacky sister, maybe she can understand her."

"Sister Virginia's train comes in at two-thirty; we better get a move on, Sport." Tim poked his head into the parlor. "You girls want to come along?"

"Sorry, Poppy," Rosaria said, holding a set of curtain rods. "I promised Mom I'd help with the windows."

Tim turned to a lounging Margo. "I suppose you're waiting for a phone call."

"Yeah, right, a phone call," replied the fifteen-year-old from behind a Seventeen Magazine.

"Looks like it's just you and me, Sport," Tim turned to find Colleen sitting on the car's hood.

Margo lowered her fashion rag. "Psst, Rosaria, I bet that nun will make them say a rosary on the ride home."

South Station was a glass and gold leaf palace. Colleen never missed an opportunity to visit. Walking through its lobby made her feel like somebody among the penniless nobodies who called the train station home. Newspaper hawkers, flower shops, shoeshine stands, and grown-ups running with suitcases in hand reminded her of the Chattanooga song. She envisioned a young soldier standing in the doorway of a departing train, its whistle drowning out his "I love you" to his beloved, waving from the hectic platform. As the train pulls away, we see our hero run from window to window for one last fleeting look at the only woman he ever loved, ever would love. The Hun and a wooden cross wait for him in the blood-soaked French countryside. Colleen laughed to herself, imagining her father chasing after his sister's train, reaching the end of the platform, he falls to his knees, head in hands, he sobs, "Why, why?"

"There she is!" Tim called out, jolting his daughter from her MGM daydream. The two-ton nun waddled toward Tim with open arms like a panda bear trained to walk on its hind legs.

"Don't we look spiffy, Mister Ronan," said the jolly nun, ruffling her blushing brother's hair. "Colleen, right?"

"Yes, Sister Immaculata," she answered with a curtsy.

"It's Aunt Virginia, I'm off the clock." The message was delivered with a hearty laugh and backslap, nearly knocking Colleen to her knees. The car bounced under the weight of its portly passenger, whose perspiration saturated the upholstery. Tim mopped his forehead with a farmworker's hankie.

"How the hell can you wear that penguin costume in ninety-degree heat?"

"You want me to take it off?"

"Yes!" Colleen chirped.

"Don't put it past her, Sport." Resigned to the fact there wouldn't be a flabby floorshow, Colleen resumed looking out the hand-me-down Ford's window as it snaked through Chinatown to the South End's Bowery.

"Is you-know-who as hot-tempered as I remember?" Sister asked.

"Does a bear..."

"Good, I look forward to a spirited exchange."

Tim cranked the emergency brake, announcing, "Home sweet home." Colleen bolted from the car, intent on warning her sisters of the impending fight.

"Steady now," Tim advised his sister as he pried her from the car like a child from the womb. The nun braced herself, placing one hand on Tim's shoulder, the other on the car's hood.

"The limp's new," Tim noted.

"The knee's old."

"Forty is old?"

"It's an act. I figure Berta will go easy on a cripple."

"Sorry, Daniel, my money is on the lion."

"How do I look?" the nun asked, adjusting her stiff white bib.

"Like you just stepped off the set of 'The Bells of Saint Mary.'"

"Wiseass."

Berta greeted her sister-in-law with a miserly smile. Virginia responded with a silent nod. The girls delighted in watching their mother struggle to control her disdain for the nun. Once small talk ceased, Sister proceeded to make herself at home.

Delving into her habit's deep pocket, she removed a handkerchief, keys, a wooden signal, and rosary beads.

"What are they doing there?"

Tim laughed at his sister's theatrics, knowing she was putting on a show for the girls who wanted to laugh but feared the repercussions. "Did you rent that habit from a magician?"

"No, Timmy boy, I—ah, that's what I was looking for." Sister slapped a pack of Winstons on the coffee table. "Light me up." Berta cracked a frozen smile. The girls huddled at one end of the sofa. Everyone knew what that smile meant except Sister Virginia. Berta was itching to reach into the hall closet to call on her partner in punishment, the leather belt.

"Your father ever tell you how I hung him out the window by his feet when he was a baby?" Sister asked with a cigarette dangling from her lips.

Colleen sat up. "Did you drop him?"

"Don't think I wasn't tempted. To this day, he cries whenever he sees clothes drying on the line. Did you know about Uncle Darby?"

Berta had heard enough. "If this is the one-eyed Uncle Darby story, I'd prefer my daughters not hear it." Tim gave his sister the "Now you've done it" look. Having tussled with Berta in the past, Sister prepared for the inevitable. The nun snuffed out her cigarette in a small commemorative plate bearing the image of the Holy Father, one of Margo's trophies for selling the most Christmas cards in her class.

"Looks like Ash Wednesday came early for Pope Pius," Tim said with a wink.

The girls were ordered out of the room so the grown-ups could talk. Everyone knew they'd be discussing Colleen's fate but pretended they didn't. Berta cleared her throat.

"You met Colleen on the ride over. I'd appreciate your opinion. Her grades are atrocious, and she can't keep up with her classmates. We're considering enrolling in a public school. We hoped it wouldn't come to this," Berta said, casting a threatening eye on Tim, knowing what camp he was in.

"Come on, Berta," Tim grumbled. "You got Rosaria and Margo in public school."

"That's high school, that's different, don't you agree, Sister?"

"Is Colleen open to the idea of leaving Saint Regina's?"

Tim cut off his wife's answer. "She don't like sister school."

"Are the public schools in this town that bad?"

Berta's voice slowly and evenly began to rise. "I'm not concerned with the education she'll receive. Colleen is not overburdened with brains. I wouldn't want her to fall in with the wrong crowd—those schools are breeding grounds for hoods and hooligans. I fear she'll easily adapt to that environment. My daughter is no angel."

"She gets it from our side of the family," the nun joked.

"Colleen, get in here. Now." Following her mother's order, a downcast Colleen shuffled into the living room. Berta shot a menacing look at the nun. "I think you and your aunt should have a serious conversation. I'll leave the two of you to chat. Come along, Tim."

Slamming the kitchen door open with the heel of her hand, Berta vented. "Doesn't that woman gall me. I should never have let you talk me into this."

"You don't have to take her advice but hear her out."

"Then I'll throw her out." Tim paced. "I feel like a defendant waiting for the jury to return." Laughter from the other side of the door seeped through the walls. Berta drummed her nails on the Formica kitchen table. "Do you hear that? This is a very important decision in Colleen's life, and that nun is telling jokes. I want to know if I should put my child in a public school, not a vaudeville. Go in there and break it up."

"So, Sport, whatddya think of my sister?"

"She's not like any nun I know."

"You got that right," came a voice from the kitchen. Berta made her entrance. "So, what's the verdict?" The nun's casual smile signaled to her sister-in-law that the question didn't merit an in-depth response.

"Were it up to Colleen, she'd choose to attend a public school."

"It's not up to Colleen. If all I had to do was ask her, I wouldn't have invited you here."

Tim hustled Colleen out of the room. He'd taken her to the movies the previous week to see Frankenstein Meets the Wolfman and didn't want her sitting through a second showing. Berta stiffened. Sister bristled. Tim took cover.

"Since you value my opinion, I think Colleen should be placed in a public school."

"Do you?"

"Yes, Berta, I do. Colleen should study in a class where she feels safe, not threatened, able to concentrate on her studies, not preoccupied with the prospect of being punished or ridiculed."

"She brings it on herself. The school doesn't need to change; she does. She's ridiculed for her behavior and punished for her failing grades."

"If her grades and behavior haven't improved in four years at Saint Regina's, why send her back?"

"Here I thought you would knock some sense into Colleen, tell her to smarten up. You were raised by nuns; it's your duty to promote a Catholic education. You're supposed to be the backbone of the order." Sister's anger surged. She was not going to allow Berta to define her role in The Order.

"I'm not its backbone; it's mine. I don't support the order; it supports me. I could have taken a very different path if the nuns hadn't taken me in; that's a debt I can never repay. They molded me into the woman I am, and I love what I do. I didn't have what Colleen has, a family to come home to, one that loves, cares, and fights for me." Sister's voice softened. "Allow her the opportunity to expand her horizons, interact with children of other faiths and cultures. All Tim and I had was one another, and they split us up. Berta, I know you have your own painful past."

17

With each syllable, Berta poked her finger into the nun's bib. "You—know—nothing. The flu took your parents, well, boo-hoo. Don't tell me about the pain I've endured; this isn't Queen for a Day. All you counseled Colleen on was how to be the class clown. I'll have none of it under my roof."

"It's my roof, Berta," Tim said. "She's my sister. Treat her with the same respect you'd give any woman in the order."

Sister Virginia snuffed out a second cigarette. "I can see I've overstayed my welcome."

"Please, you needn't go. Tim's right, I'm sorry I spoke out of turn."

"I have a few old chums I'd like to look up while I'm in town. It was wonderful to see the girls again. Tim, I'll wait for you in the car."

Chapter Three

The slam from a car door sent Frieda scurrying to the parlor window. At last, a parking spot opened. Her son set the ground rules.

"If I don't get a space where I can see my car, I won't come in for dinner." Frieda watched over both the vacant spot and her overcooked chicken. "Please hurry," she pleaded as if her son could telepathically receive the message.

Were Aaron's white Fiat a centimeter longer, he'd have the evening to himself. The surgeon was as skilled with a wheel as he was with a scalpel. He shoehorned his car to the curb. At six foot three, he'd normally race up the apartment building's cement steps like a gazelle—get in, get out. For some reason, tonight was different.

Six-thirty-two Blue Hill Ave was a generic brick building, one of many attached to the next, distinguishable only from those with street-level apartments that had been converted to variety stores or laundromats. His boyhood bedroom once looked out on an elm tree. Now, the view was of a billboard advertising cigarettes and brandy. An unexpected wave of nostalgia carried him back to the first time he ran up those steps. At ten, he was a king entering his castle. The houses in his Ukrainian village were made of wood and mudstone, some had thatched roofs. That was Russia, this is America. Twenty years later, his stomach turned at the thought of walking into the crumbling fortress. The neurosurgeon's free time was at a premium—why waste it making small talk with his doting mother? Was it guilt, a sense of duty, or another opportunity to prove how far he'd come on his own?

"All this mail is addressed to you," said his mother. Frieda was Russian, from her high cheekbones and broad shoulders to her braided hair and gapped-tooth smile. Her reemergence from war's rubble was a reminder of his heritage, one he wasn't ashamed of but didn't embrace.

"The Bermans are moving at the end of the month," Frieda said as she laid out the china. "I thought maybe you should want to take their apartment. You would be one flight up, and when you find a nice girl and marry, you'd have a home until you buy one of your own."

"Are you nuts? The Bermans and anyone else who can afford to are leaving the area. I've been offered a position at The Peter Bent Brigham. I'll be living across town. How did the kid make out on the Latin entrance exam?"

"The kid has a name."

"Did Leon pass the exam?"

Frieda hesitated. "I didn't allow him to take it."

Aaron slammed the stack of envelopes on the table. "You didn't allow him? Allow him!"

"He'd be an underclassman; the other boys will tease him."

"Better now than later."

From behind his bedroom door, Leon listened to his mother and brother converse in Russian. Aaron only spoke the language when the subject was Leon, who wasn't fluent. The nine-year-old resented being treated like a baby, yet was relieved he'd be returning to The Edwin Talbot Elementary School for the next three years. Aaron would often recount his glory days at The Boston Latin School. Tall and handsome, Aaron was both a genius and a jock. Leon was intelligent, but that's where the similarity ended.

"Either my wife is having an affair with Mario Andretti or Doctor Hirsh has blessed us with his presence." The voice was followed by a closing door. "What's that? A T-Bird?"

Aaron corrected his aged stepfather in a dismissive tone. "It's a Fiat V8."

"Too good for a Ford?"

"Henry Ford was an antisemite."

"So was Charles Crapper, but you use his toilet."

"Fine, Oscar, I'll buy a Ford and take a crap in it."

Frieda covered her ears. "Please, the language."

Oscar summoned his son to the table. "Leon, come to dinner."

Sulking, Leon took his seat next to his mother.

"Something wrong?" Oscar asked his son.

"Nothing," Leon grunted.

Aaron shook out his napkin. "I was just discussing the prospect of his parents allowing him to grow a set of balls." His brother never spoke to Leon, only about him, the way one speaks in front of the old and feeble-minded.

"Leave your brother be."

"Come on, Oscar, the kid doesn't have friends or play sports. His life revolves around his mother and books."

Oscar smiled across the table at his wife. "As does mine."

Walking to the window, Aaron parted the Venetian blinds.

"Please, come finish your meal," his mother pleaded.

"I will, I just want to check on the car... on second thought, fix me a plate, I'll take it with me."

21

"What happened to please and thank you? She's your mother, not some nurse or your mechanic."

"Forget the food. I'm late." Aaron kissed his mother's cheek and whacked his brother's head. "See you on the playground, kid."

***

Berta took the key from above Tim's bedroom door. The couple no longer shared a bed. Berta wouldn't tolerate her husband's drunken sexual advances. Banished to a room of his own, provided a sanctuary to drink in peace. In his absence, Berta would use the opportunity to search for liquid contraband. She never failed to confiscate a fifth of Four Roses or Old Thompson's rotgut. Tim escaped reality at the expense of his body, a body of no use to his wife or employer. As for the girls, one day they'd come to see their mother for what she is, a saint, a stern, stoic saint who'd sacrificed any future happiness to care for a weak-willed sinner who lost his soul with his first drink.

"He's locked in, the ambulance is on the way," Berta assured Mae while picking glass splinters from her sister's palm.

"No doctors," Mae insisted.

"It's begun to swell."

Mae winced. "It will heal on its own."

Pneumonia, neighbors were told. A blanket covered the long-armed jacket. Houdini may have mastered his locks, but not Timothy Ronan.

***

This wasn't Berta's first visit to the State Mental Hospital, but she'd never been to its fourth floor—one reserved for violent patients. The corridor looked and smelled like the other wards, only quiet. Its occupants were sedated, she presumed. Under the supervision of paid eyes, Tim rested his head on the visitation room's cold metal table.

"I'm sorry, Berta," he sobbed.

Hands on her hips, her bottom lip sucking in the upper, Berta looked up at the ceiling's peeling paint.

"Sorry? You're sorry? Sorry to you is like asking, How's your day? It means nothing." Dragging a heavy wooden chair over torn linoleum, Berta sat across the table from her weeping husband.

"I was in a very dark place when you came into my life. I haven't forgotten, never will. Your love overrode my pain, but I can't do the same for you, not my love, not the girls. Oh, I've tried, I've been kind when I was angry, caring when I no longer cared. It's not in my nature to bend, give in, or give up. If I thought cutting my arm off would free you from the clutches of alcohol, by God, I'd do it.

"In my darkest hour, I didn't turn to the bottle; I turned to you. The girls grew to love you long before I did, and they'll love you long after any feelings I have toward you die, and this is how you return their love, by throwing a drink in Rosaria's face, cutting Mae's hand with a broken bottle." Backing up her chair, Berta stood. "The girls will be spending the next few weeks on the Vineyard. Perhaps the sea air will carry off memories of last night. I love my daughters, keeping them safe is my priority, even if the threat is their own father."

Tim palmed his tears. "I love them too! Just when I get to my feet, I fall."

"Jesus fell three times on his ascent to Calvary. Get up."

***

The weeks leading up to Labor Day brought sun worshipers to the shore, their skin soaking up the last rays of summer, their eyes soaking in the view of a bare-backed blonde. Margo strained to clasp her swimsuit top.

"Hook me up, and no funny business." Colleen fell to her knees on the beach towel, securing the clasp across her sister's evenly tanned back.

"Why should I apologize?" Colleen whined. "He's the one who called me lobster girl."

"After you crammed a jellyfish down his trunks. This behavior is what got you thrown out of Saint Regina's. Try it in public school, and those kids will beat the crap out of you."

23

Margo grabbed Colleen's hand. "Come on, let's get this over with. You're an embarrassment."

"That boy said his father is the police chief and he'll arrest me."

"Good. You can share a cell with Poppy."

Colleen yanked her hand from Margo's. "Don't say that. He's coming home."

"Lighten up, it's a joke." Margo shook out her hair. "I'll smooth things over with my charm; let's hope Chief Jellyfish likes blondes."

"Are you going to seduce him?"

"Possibly."

"How do you seduce someone?" Colleen asked in earnest.

"Not by shoving a jellyfish down his pants, unless he asks you to."

"Come on," Colleen pestered. "How do you do it?"

"The first step is to make your presence known in a dramatic way."

"Then I just seduced that boy, and he wasn't the first."

"Do you want to hear this?" Margo continued. "The next step is to give him THE LOOK. Using your body as bait, you reel him in. You needn't like your victim; it's the satisfaction you derive from having power over another human being. Say, where is this place? My feet hurt."

Colleen pointed to a glass-fronted contemporary house jutting out over the surf, an architectural anomaly in a vacation spot where gingerbread cottages gave the town a Christmas coating.

"It looks like one of those movie star houses!" Margo gasped. "That jellyfish is living in some cool digs."

Experiencing the same awe as passengers boarding the Titanic, the sisters held on to the metal railing surrounding the modern marvel. Throwing her shoulders back, Margo tousled her hair and slid her sunglasses to the tip of her nose.

"Watch and learn." A wave of the hand signaled Colleen to ring the bell.

The door opened, standing before them the handsomest man they had ever seen on or off the silver screen. Tall, blond, and tanned, he flashed a Pepsodent smile.

"To what do I owe this visit, so I can do it again?"

Colleen nudged her starry-eyed sister.

"Oh, um, yes, I'm Margo Ronan, and this is my precocious sister Colleen."

"How do you do? I'm Ronny Kilday."

"Mister Kilday, I believe my sister had an unfortunate encounter with your brother."

"You mean Clifford? He's the local hellion, no relation. He comes by now and then to keep this lonely bachelor company."

"Nonetheless, Colleen owes him an apology."

"Unfortunately, he's out wreaking havoc down the other end of the beach. I'll pass the message on. Say, why haven't I met you before this unfortunate encounter? I pride myself on knowing all the beach bunnies in town."

"I've been busy beating up boys."

"Colleen!" Margo gently patted Colleen's tangled locks. "Forgive this little ruffian."

Ronny threw back his head in laughter. Margo fixed her eyes on the rise and fall of his Adam's apple beneath a deeply tanned throat.

"May I offer you ladies a drink?"

Margo held her hand to her chest. "Goodness no. Pater doesn't approve of partaking in spirits before the dinner hour; he's such a Puritan."

"Sounds like a sensible man. Any chance I'll run into him at the country club?"

"If he's driving, he'll run into you."

Margo's eyes flared. "Colleen! Don't listen to such nonsense. Pater won't be summering with us—the poor dear is tied up in the city."

Ronny gave a knowing nod. "Tell me about it, my dad is in real estate, banking, you name it. He wants me to go into the business. I told him, the only thing I'm working on is my tan."

Ronny bent at the waist with an outstretched arm like a doorman at the Plaza welcoming a pair of socialites. "Ladies."

Margo looked down her nose at Colleen. "Be a dear and return to our summer residence and inform Rosaria I'll arrive home posthaste."

Sharp rocks and broken clamshells were no more than an annoyance to feet carrying news of Margo's latest conquest.

"Rosaria! Where are you?" The answer came from the back porch.

"I'm hanging laundry. Why isn't Margo with you?"

Colleen bent forward, gasping to recoup her breath. "Margo has a new boyfriend. I watched her seduce him, using her body as bait; she reeled him in for the satisfaction of having power over another human being."

Rosaria shook Colleen by the shoulders. "Who? What man?"

"The one who lives in the house that looks like it belongs in Malibu... the real Malibu."

"Where is she now?"

"Having cocktails with him, even though Pater wouldn't approve, but perhaps just this once, la-di-dah."

"She's drinking with a strange man?"

"Yup, but he's real handsome."

"I knew I should have accompanied you to the beach; neither one of you can keep out of mischief." Rosaria snatched her beach jacket off the clothesline. "You stay here."

Lounging across the divan, Margo deeply inhaled. "What a lovely place you have, that ocean view is spectacular. It conjures up memories of days spent at Malibu."

"You've been to Malibu?"

"Why yes, we keep a home not far from there."

Ronny bit the inside of his cheek. Living in Milton, Dorchester's white-collar offspring, he knew she was referring to a local swimming hole.

"You needn't put on airs, Miss Margo, it's your beauty, not your pedigree, I find so intoxicating. I have to come clean. This isn't my house. The homeowner is a client of my dad's. He's overseas and needed someone to keep an eye on the place. Let's relax and enjoy the view."

"OPEN THIS DOOR!" Rosaria's voice shook with anger and fear.

Pushing past Ronny, she yanked Margo off the sofa.

"Rosaria, wait, this is Ron Kilday."

"You mean Ron Juan."

Ronny blocked the exit. "Allow me to apologize; had I known Margo's absence would cause you such distress, I would have escorted her back to your summer residence."

"That's mighty big of you."

"I know how this must look, but I assure you nothing inappropriate occurred. Say, you girls wouldn't be free Saturday night? There's a party at the yacht club. We could always use a couple of pretty girls to liven things up. What do you say?"

"Oh yes!" Margo gushed.

Rosaria put her nose in the air. "Come along, Margo."

Rosaria marched Margo back to the summer shack. "You don't know that man's intentions."

"And you know better than to listen to Colleen."

"I witnessed you drinking with my own eyes."

"It was ginger ale."

"Pater will be relieved."

"Please don't tell Mae."

A voice broke in from behind. "I will."

Margo shook her finger in Colleen's face. "You do, and I'll tell Mae that jellyfish was a crab."

***

"You thought I was crazy to pack dance dresses. I knew we'd be asked out on dates," Margo stated with authority. "Zip me up."

Rosaria sheepishly followed the order. "Gosh, Margo, I wouldn't consider this a date. Ronny merely asked if we'd like to come along."

"He's bringing his friend Victor, which means we're doubling."

"If Mom were here..."

"She's not. Mae understands; she was young once, had a social life. Ma and Grandma undermined Mae's chances to marry. She's not going to screw up my plans. I'm going to elope."

"You're only fifteen, marriage shouldn't be a priority."

"It should be for you. You graduate next year."

"I wish you had accepted Ronny's offer to drive us. My shoes will be full of pebbles."

"We can't have him know we're staying in this rat hole."

"Oh, Margo, I'm so disappointed in you. Take pride in what you've achieved despite your circumstances. There are those less fortunate, don't attempt to appear better off than you are."

"These people are rich. We have to play the part to compete. Once these guys fall for us, they won't care what town we're from or that our father is locked up in a rubber room."

"That's so unkind."

" I won't let his reputation soil mine. Are my seams straight?"

Rosaria glanced at her sister's calves. "Yes, Margo, they're straight."

"Good. Let's go."

Rosaria inhaled the sea air. "Oh, Margo, look at the sunset. This is a moment to be treasured."

"The sun will be there tomorrow; concentrate on tonight," said Margo, throwing cold water on her sister's warm emotions. "Guys don't care about poetry and sunsets. They'll say they do, but they don't. All men care about is sex."

"Margo!"

"Sorry, but someone had to clue you in. Want a husband? Tell him you've been saving yourself for him and him alone. You never had nor ever will give yourself to a man who wouldn't marry a virgin. If he's a playboy, he'll run scared. If he's a stand-up guy, he'll pursue you, let you call the shots."

"We're not out of high school, we have no business discussing sex."

"You know what's going to happen to you? You'll end up like Mae, an old maid. Ma will chase off any suitors. Once she's killed off Mae, she'll turn you into her flying monkey, shut you away. You'll be chained to that hag and that house. If we can't move out until we marry, I'll marry."

"What about love?"

"I'm marrying for money and sex. If you're waiting for love, you're in for a major disappointment. Now let's test my theory."

The bar was dressed in a nautical theme. Thick ship ropes and a fishing net canopied the bar. A uniformed bartender rang a ship's bell with every tip tossed his way. Sizing up the chiffon and taffeta crowd, Margo twisted her mouth and elbowed her sister.

"We've got this."

"Will you look what just walked in?" Victor said with a nudge to Ronny's side.

"If it ain't Betty and Veronica."

Ronny straightened his tie and posture. "Just remember, Betty's mine."

Margo rushed into Ronny's embrace. "I wasn't expecting this!" he said, jolting back.

"I'm full of surprises," Margo giggled. "Who's your friend?"

"Allow me to introduce Victor Castile, my comrade in arms."

Margo squeezed Victor's bicep. "And what an arm it is... Oh, this is my elder sister Rosaria."

Victor clicked his heels like a military officer. "A pleasure."

Rosaria was drawn to the young man's deep brown eyes and strong, dark features.

"May I escort you to our table?" Victor asked, holding his bent arm to Rosaria. "We're seated next to the band. Ronny told me you girls are great dancers."

Rosaria perked up. "Oh yes, Margo and I have won a number of competitions."

"We were invited to dance on Bandstand," Margo inserted. "But our spiteful mother blocked our path to stardom."

"Margo, not now," said Rosaria, drawing a weary sigh.

Ronny set a tray of drinks on the table. "Soft drinks all around. I wouldn't want you girls taking advantage of us."

Victor tugged on his cuffs. "So, Rosaria, are you in school?"

"I enter my senior year in the fall, as well as working part-time at Woolworth's."

Margo shuttered her eyes. "She's going to college when she graduates."

"I'm embarking on a teaching career."

Victor surveyed Rosaria's legs. "Let me guess, you're a cheerleader."

"I'm a Girl Scout leader."

Victor's expression soured. "Are you going to hit me up to buy a box of cookies?"

"The cookies don't come out until March."

"I hoped they'd come out tonight."

Ronny broke in. "Vic was the drummer in a combo he formed while living in Florida."

"FLORIDA!" Margo screeched. "I'm moving to Florida when I graduate. Where else can a girl run around in a bikini all day?"

"My place," Ronny snickered.

"My mother's Cuban," Victor explained.

"You play the bongos?"

"Sorry, Margo, I'm not Desi Arnaz."

"I tried my hand at the violin," Rosaria said, attempting to salvage the conversation. "It's a difficult instrument to master. I was unable to put in the time it required."

Margo bounced in her seat. "I want to dance."

"I want to get out of here," Victor grumbled.

Rosaria stood. "Come along, Margo, we'll go to the powder room before the band takes the stage." Behind the bathroom door, Rosaria lectured her sister. "You're an embarrassment."

"You won't speak up, so I do. I think Victor has the hots for you. Admit it, he's your type."

Rosaria bit her lip. "I don't think I'm his type."

"I know men," Margo said, reapplying her pink lipstick. "I predict you'll be dating for the remainder of the summer."

Secretly, Rosaria wished her sister's prediction would come to pass—after all, Margo knew men.

Victor craned his neck to make certain the girls weren't within earshot. "I ain't getting anywhere with that Rosaria chick."

"She's shy," Ronny assured his pal. "Why don't we take them to The Trident? My dad has an account with them. We can have dinner on the old man."

"I can't be seen around town with Rosaria."

"Since when?"

"Since I've been dating Linda. With her in Europe, I wanted to get some action, bang broads on the beach. Not listen to Mozart with a schoolmarm."

"Give her a chance, she'll let loose on the dance floor."

"The only dancing I want to do is out that door. You see what she's like. A real looker, but it's look don't touch."

"Put a sock in it, here they come."

The gentleman pulled out the ladies' chairs.

"Ronny tells me you girls are from Boston, whereabouts?"

Margo jumped in, not allowing Rosaria to state the truth. "The Hill."

"Mission Hill?"

"No, silly. Beacon Hill."

"If you're from Beacon Hill, what are you doing in Old Lady Dunlap's cottage?"

Margo's face fell.

"Mrs. Dunlap is a family friend. We're doing the poor dear a favor by helping her clean out the place before she puts it on the market. The pitiful soul has fallen on difficult times. Her late husband made several poor investments."

Victor's dark complexion ran pale watching a group of girls heading toward the table.

"Victor!" a plump teen called out. Her artificial blonde hair color didn't blend with her natural olive skin tone.

Margo signaled Rosaria with her eyes that she'd be putting the oversized interloper in her place. "Who's the cow?"

Victor answered in a stutter. "She, she..."

"She, she is coming this way."

"Victor, what are you doing here? When is Linda due back?"

Ronny abruptly came to his feet. "Rhoda, allow me to introduce my cousin Rosaria and her friend Margo. Rosaria's husband is stationed in San Diego. She plans to join him in a few weeks."

Rhoda's eyes wandered from Rosaria's bare ring finger to Ronny's steady eyes. "Ronald Kilday, I'm ashamed of you, putting your cousin up in the dilapidated Dunlap dump. I thought your father was heading a committee to have that eyesore demolished. It decreases our property values. Rundown houses and commoners will do that. It was a pleasure to meet you two hardy souls. Toodles." Rhoda parted, wearing a self-satisfied grin.

"Don't listen to that sow. Linda is Victor's sister," Ronny lied.

Rosaria kept her head lowered. Margo kept her chin up. "Why lie?"

"Our business is none of hers. As a matter of fact, we were about to ask you to dinner. There's a restaurant called The Trident, it's high-class. There's more to the Vineyard than clam shacks."

"Like the Dunlap shack?" Margo asked in a huff.

"Those girls got nothing better to do than gossip about good-looking rivals."

"I don't feel well," Rosaria mumbled, twisting the hem of her dress. "I'm returning to the shack."

Ronny took her hand from her dress. "If you're uncomfortable, we'll go somewhere else."

"You're very kind, but I'd like to get back."

The red Camaro pulled up to the ramshackle cottage Rosaria had romanticized as the white picket-fenced house she'd own one day. Now she viewed it as a mirror image of herself, old and homely, a house people pass by without notice.

"You're not sick, are you?" Ronny asked with a sympathetic smile. "Don't blame Vic. I told him he shouldn't sit at home waiting for Linda to return. I suggested we take a couple of pretty girls out to dine and dance. Then that herd of bison showed up."

"You're very kind," Rosaria complimented in a wobbly voice. "You had better get back before Victor steals your girl."

Ronny ran around to the passenger door and escorted Rosaria up a set of rickety steps. "I misjudged you, Ronny, you're a very nice fellow."

Mae sat sorting through a pile of sea glass she and Colleen had collected over the past week.

"Back so soon? Where's Margo?"

"I didn't feel well, Ronny drove me back. I'm going to bed."

"Rosaria, sit and tell me what happened."

"Oh, Mae," she said with a sniffle. "The boys were only interested in Margo. She cluttered the conversation, telling them where she'd been, what she wants, thinks, and believes. Victor has a steady, she's in Europe. He was just being kind. A girl showed up who knew his girlfriend; he was uncomfortable, so was I." Rosaria rested her head on Mae's shoulder, knowing her aunt would soothe her wounded pride.

"You're a very attractive girl, but you're shy. Margo is outgoing. If fellas met you without her around, I'm sure they'd ask you out."

"I'm not cross with her. She doesn't mean any harm."

"You're headed for college next year; you'll meet new friends who don't know your sister. They'll like you for you. It's time you stood on your own two feet. Stop using Margo as a crutch. You'll meet the right boy. The best miracles take the longest to arrive."

Chapter Four

Leon had been awarded a window seat in his sixth-grade classroom. He could be trusted not to spend the school day staring out at autumn leaves, freshly fallen snow, or the '56 sedan in the auto showroom across the street. Only two weeks into the school year, he'd already abused the privilege by gazing out at the redhead girl on the schoolyard swing, always alone, always on the swing. Volunteering to stay after to help Miss Burgess gave Leon time alone with his beloved teacher.

"It's good of you to stay after. I'm grateful for your help."

"I like sticking around," Leon said, wiping down the blackboard.

"How are things at home?"

"Okay, I guess. Why?"

"Most students have one foot out the door before the dismissal bell, yet you lag behind."

"I, um, like being around you, adults, I mean. The kids only want to be my friend so they can cheat off me."

"Do you allow them?"

"Do I have friends?"

"You're a delightful boy, witty as well as wise. Share your talent with others, take a chance, don't anticipate rejection. Say hello to someone you've been wanting to meet. You may find a lifelong friend."

Leon rendered an unenthusiastic smile. "Yes, Miss Burgess."

The echo from metal stairs—normally muffled by a herd of children running for freedom—clanged with each slow, solitary step from Leon's Buster Brown shoes, the same ones he'd busted out of the previous school year. His mother's amateur cobbling skills didn't go unnoticed by mocking classmates. There she sat, his muse on her throne. Heavy rain had fallen, yet she sat on the wet seat. Here was his chance to complete Miss Burgess's assignment.

Sneaking up from behind, he tugged on her ponytail as if summoning a servant. The swing swiftly spun around. Confronting him was a face redder than her hair.

"Who the hell are you?" snarled the Goliath of a girl, taking a visual inventory of her David. His light-colored curls were as tight as hers. Mended wire-rimmed eyeglasses accentuated his root beer barrel candy brown eyes.

"I'm Leon Hirsch, but everyone calls me Lee," he innocently answered with a smile and extended hand.

"No, they don't... but I will. Doofus."

"What's your name?"

Colleen squeezed her eyes into narrow slits. "None of your big fat business."

"Why would your parents name you that?" A textbook rocketed toward his head. The projectile was worthy of both the space program and the arms race. A piece of paper parachuted from between the math book's pages; he snatched it up.

"Colleen Ronan, what the...? You only got three out of ten questions correct on this test!"

"And they were guesses," she boasted. Leon returned the bound weapon.

"Why do you always sit out here alone?"

"Are you spying on me?"

"Yeah, I'm spying. I see you take recess with the little kids. You look old enough to be a teacher."

"I'm in the third grade."

"The third grade!"

"I'm big for my age."

"I'll say! Why do you hang around after school?"

Colleen rolled her eyes, not letting on that she enjoyed the attention. "I'm supposed to be at the library. I'll give it another twenty minutes, then head home."

"Do you think that's wise?"

"Yeah, chucklehead, I do."

"Do you have homework?"

"Some arithmetic."

"Mathematics can be fun, once you understand it." He pulled Colleen off the swing.

"Hey! Where are you taking me?"

"To the library to do your homework."

"Isn't that called cheating?"

"It's called getting you out of the third grade."

The low granite wall surrounding the library was a remnant of the antebellum estate that once stood on the site. Colleen propped her battle-scarred leg on the wall. "Hang on, I've got to tie my shoe."

"You're stalling," Lee hollered from the arched portal entrance.

Colleen barreled up the broad stone steps. "I'm only staying for a couple of minutes."

"The library is open till six."

"Like I care." Colleen sluggishly shuffled toward the children's reading room. Lee turned her in the direction of a marble staircase.

"That's the adult floor. We're not allowed up there."

"I am." Her companion led her past the librarian's desk with all the confidence of a gangster ushering his moll into a backstreet speakeasy. The rumble of wooden chairs pulled from their table prompted heads to turn.

"Sit," Lee whispered.

Colleen looked up at the ceiling's cupola. "We have one of those in my house, only smaller."

"Right."

"Honest, we do... who's that?" she asked, pointing to a toga-wearing bust.

"How should I know?"

"Let's find out."

"Sit down."

Returning to her seat, Colleen opened her physically abused textbook only to slam it shut. "Those are word problems. I don't do word problems."

"You don't?"

"No, I do not," she answered with her arms folded across her chest.

"Then let's move on to fractions."

"Miss Harris won't teach fractions till March."

"Then you'll be ahead of your classmates."

Colleen defiantly tore a page from her marble notebook.

"What are you doing?"

"Drawing," she snipped.

Lee snatched the pencil from the artist's hand. "If you're just killing time, do it in the schoolyard. When you're at this table, it's to study."

"This is my time, I'm not in school, and you're not my teacher. If I want to draw, I'll draw." Colleen rose from the table. "I'm leaving."

"See that dictionary," Lee said, motioning to a Webster on a pedestal.

"What about it?"

"How many words are in it?"

Colleen shrugged. "A couple of hundred thousand."

"You can read them, spell them, use them in a sentence, yet you'll let ten numbers keep you from getting promoted. Come on, Colleen, you can do this, not on your own, but you will."

"Goodbye," she stated with an exaggerated turn.

"I dare you." The fugitive froze in place, craning her neck around, she locked eyes with his.

"You what?"

"Dare you." Lee saw-sawed a pencil between his index and middle fingers. "I dare you to complete this assignment on your own."

"If I stay, what do I win?"

"A passing grade."

"If you win?"

"We come here after school, make it a regular thing."

"I may be a dope, but I can put two and two together. If you want me as a friend, why don't you ask?"

"I'm asking."

"Get lost, I don't need friends."

"You need to get out of the third grade."

Colleen returned to the table, opening her book, and she mumbled, "I won."

***

"You're late, I was worried," Frieda said, wearing a stern expression to mask her relief.

"When I'm late, you worry; when I'm early, you worry."

Frieda's maternal instinct clued her to a change in her son. "Leon, what's happened?"

With a nonchalant shrug, he snapped on the TV. "I helped some girl with her homework, no big deal."

"Oooh, a girl," said his mother with a sly curl of her lip. "This girl, she's in your class?"

The question was ignored. Frieda stepped in front of Tarzan, leading a herd of elephants on a rampage.

"The girl, is she in your class?"

"Old enough, but she was kept back a couple of times."

"What's her name?"

"Colleen something, she's from the Mount."

"The Mount, and she's not in a Catholic school?"

"She was, but the nuns gave her the boot."

"Just one?"

Lee got a sneaking satisfaction from confusing his immigrant mother with hip slang; his mother was the only person who thought he was hip.

"Miss Burgess asked me to help this Colleen girl with math, and I didn't want to disappoint Miss Burgess. So, I'll be getting home late for a while."

***

He was sitting on her swing. HER SWING! A peculiar stirring cramped her gut, tangling her intestines. She savored the high she'd experienced in his company; now she was left piecing together the previous day's events. Had she exposed her soft side, her quest for companionship? Head held high, and books tightly pressed to her chest, she sucked in a lungful of air as she exited the schoolyard without acknowledging his watchful eyes.

The swing's chain rattled. "What grade did you get?"

Casually turning, Colleen faced his self-righteous smile. "Miss Harris accused me of cheating."

"Then you got them all correct," Lee said, approaching her with a cavalier swagger.

"I'm a good guesser."

"Do you have homework?"

"Some."

"You want to go to the library?"

"It's on the way."

Fearing their business arrangement would be interpreted as a budding friendship, the two strolled in silence until the other students fanned off.

"You look kinda pretty," Lee confessed, rapidly sliding his eyes from her torso to the pavement.

Anticipating another chance encounter, Colleen had taken care when dressing for school. "My sister likes to dress me."

"She dresses you?"

"She picks out my clothes, she doesn't put them on me."

Colleen tilted her head. "Do you always go to the library after school?"

"Most days."

"We have a library in my house. We made it into a TV room. My mother said my grandmother would roll over in her grave if she knew what we had done to that room. Do you have a TV?"

"Yes, but my father doesn't let me watch it much. I only get to watch what I want when he's not home. He's retired, so he's always home."

"My dad is sorta retired. He's not that old, but he doesn't work much. Do you have a dog or a cat?"

"No."

"Me neither. There are a bunch of wild cats living in our carriage house."

"You have a carriage house?"

"Honest. It's more like a barn; there's an old car in it. My dad said it's an antique, but my mother calls it a hunk of tin. She said my grandmother had an unhealthy attachment to it. My mother doesn't want those cats living in the car. She wants my father to round them up and club them to death. My mother is sick that way. She said that's what they did to jackrabbits in the Midwest. She threatened to lock the cats in and turn the car engine on, killing them with the fumes. She said during the war, the Germans..."

"SHUT UP! JUST SHUT UP!"

Colleen never had a kid yell at her like a grown-up. She didn't know where his anger stemmed from. Bewildered, she mumbled an apology. "I'm sorry. Sometimes I talk too much."

Embarrassed by his outburst and fearing he may have lost his new friend, Lee slowly smiled. "You don't talk too much, you're too stupid to know what you're talking about. I have to take that into account."

Colleen whacked his arm. "Bully."

"That's the first time I've been accused of that! I'm kinda sorry too."

He was tutoring a different girl now. She came to the library prepared, never forgot her books, and looked him in the eyes when he spoke. She'd tug on his sleeve and whisper, "I got that one right."

He loved it when she got one right. Once outside the library, she'd tease him, but within its walls, she looked up to him. He was needed by a girl who claimed she didn't need anyone.

Chapter Five

"You sure are quiet, big mouth. What's bugging you aside from bugs?" Lee asked as the two left the library.

"You have to come home with me."

"Aww gee Colleen, my mother expects me to come home... alive."

"This is your fault."

"Mine!"

"After I got an A in math, my mother wants to meet you to see if you're some kind of a jerk."

"Tell her I am."

"She wants to see for herself."

Lee pictured Mrs. Ronan, whom Colleen had described as looking like Abe Lincoln in a dress, sitting on a stoop, smoking from a corncob pipe while goats roam freely throughout the house.

"Tell her I'm sick."

"I'm telling her nothing. You're coming with me."

Lee had never ventured to the top of Mount Nottingham; at its summit lay a well-maintained park, not the kind where children play but where adults go to admire the panoramic view of Boston Harbor. All the homes on the Mount were built before the turn of the century, none grander than number thirteen.

"Come on, it's over here," Colleen yelled, running across the park.

On tiptoes, Lee peeked through the leaded glass window of the oak door. Colleen jerked her head like a prison guard returning an inmate to his cell.

"Get in."

Lee was awestruck by the home's grandeur. The atmosphere made him uneasy. Perhaps the Ronans were squatters like American G.I.s in war movies who set up camp in a small Italian village, making the local Catholic church their headquarters, using the baptismal font to wash out their underwear, throwing them over the outstretched arms of a Jesus statue to dry.

Fortunately, the Celtic Visigoths hadn't defiled the original structure. Fourteen-foot-high coffered ceilings with plaster crown molding, pocket doors, built-in china cabinets, and a player piano had been retained out of neglect, not appreciation. The Ronan's left their stamp in their choice of furnishings, more suited for a third-rate Vegas motel than a proud urban Victorian mansion. Lee's heart sank on entering the former library, reduced to a tacky TV room. Years of dragging wrought-iron furniture left deep scars across parquet floors. The burnt orange vinyl sofa cushions made for easy clean-up after an assault from a water-filled vase or a tumbler of amber-colored liquid thrown from across the room. The built-in bookcases housed religious knick-knacks and a half set of World Book Encyclopedia ending with M. He suspected the bindings would crack if opened.

"Don't you think you ought to introduce me to your mother so I can get out of here?"

Colleen fiddled with the television's coat hanger antenna. "I will, but she's on the phone yelling at someone. You know how to fix a TV?"

"No, Colleen, I don't. Maybe I should come back some other time."

The sound of girlish laughter lured him to the window. Pulling back a set of prickly fiberglass curtains, he looked out at the walkway. His heart raced watching two tantalizing teenage girls take a seat on the porch swing, singing "Run to Him" along with Bobby Vee over a transistor radio. Colleen looked over Lee's shoulder.

"Those are my sisters," she said in a "party's over" voice.

He hoped the party had just begun. Rosaria was the first to enter the house. Margo lagged behind to change from silk stockings to Bobby socks. The tall brunette with delicate features moved across the room like a beautiful ghost. This couldn't be a sister to the oafish redhead he'd befriended.

"Colleen, are you going to introduce your young man?"

She called him a man!

"That's Lee," Colleen answered without taking her eyes off the rotating television screen.

"Forgive my sister for the half introduction. I'm Rosaria."

"A pleasure to meet you, Rosaria."

"A gentleman, how refreshing. You're all Colleen talks about."

Colleen stood behind Lee, mouthing, "I'll kill you."

Then she appeared. Were he in heaven, and he may be, the cherubim and seraphim would sing on high. She was Venus, Aphrodite, Tuesday Weld, rolled into one. Lee audibly gasped. He'd seen plenty of pretty girls in the movies, but this one was looking into his eyes, smiling, holding out her hand to him.

"The name's Margo. You must be Mr. Hirsch."

She called him Mister!

"The pleasure is all mine, Margo," he said, pretending to be a suitor.

Her shrill voice broke the spell she'd cast. "Hey, Ma, get out of here. The Princess of Pus found a prince."

Berta emerged from the kitchen. She was the type of woman other women called handsome. Her stiff posture gave him the sensation of being small and vulnerable. Her nose was sharp, almost beaked, in contrast to Colleen's freckled pug. Widow-peaked, her hair was blue-black like a raven's wings. He feared she'd greet him with a vampire's "Good evening, Mister Hirsch."

"Colleen, the TV off," she crowed in an accent more Beantown than Balkan. "We finally meet the famous Lee Hirsch. I don't know how to thank you for helping Colleen pass math."

His ears were listening to Mrs. Ronan, but his eyes were on Margo as she inspected a couple of 45s, she and Rosaria had purchased on the way home from school. Berta continued to voice her gratitude.

"You've done more to raise Colleen's grades than any teacher or nun could. We'd love to have you stay for dinner."

Colleen had told him Margo let a gas station attendant kiss her for an eight-piece set of plastic cups and feel her up for the matching dishes the Esso station gave away with each fill-up. Lee wondered what she would do for Waterford.

"Oh, um, no, thank you. My mother doesn't know I'm here. She'll be worried."

"You're always welcome."

Lee indulged in one last look at Margo, who rewarded his adoration with a seductive stare.

"Bye-bye, Lee. It was swell to meet you. You deserve a medal or something."

The compliment came with a flirtatious nose crinkle.

"I'll take the or something."

Margo ran her index finger along his smooth jawline. "You're fresh."

The sisters dashed upstairs.

"They're going upstairs to practice dancing. They win all kinds of competitions."

"Are you sure they're your sisters?"

***

Oscar's voice thundered. His arms flailed. "Where have you been!"

"Colleen asked me to meet her family," Lee meekly answered.

"You couldn't ask to use the phone? They do have a phone?"

"Yes, but—"

"But you don't think of your mother, how can a smart boy be so stupid?"

"Please, Oscar, no arguments."

"This is not an argument. You don't argue with a dummkopf. Ten minutes ago, you were having a heart attack, now you defend the boy."

"He's home, he's safe."

Frieda turned to her son. "Colleen's family, what are they like?"

Oscar threw his arms in the air and left the kitchen.

"Not all that bad. I mean, nobody was killed."

"Were they impressed with you?"

"The Ronans are impressed with anyone who walks upright."

"Leon," his mother shamed. "You should ask Colleen to dinner."

"Colleen? Here? In this house, eating our food? You don't ask for that kind of trouble. She's a savage. Wasn't the war enough? Don't put us through this."

Oscar called out from the living room, "Leon, you heard your mother, ask the girl."

Running down the hall to the bathroom, Lee rocked himself on the edge of the bathtub, covering his ears like a hostage listening to a comrade being tortured in the next room.

"Leon, come out," Frieda ordered with a knock. "I spoke to Mrs. Ronan, she's a lovely lady."

"You got the wrong number."

"You're bringing Colleen home on Tuesday. We'll finally meet your little friend."

***

"I have to wash up before I go to your house, my mother doesn't want me to look like a pig." He could have had fun with that line, but was too nervous to joke.

"Coming in?" Colleen asked rather than ordered.

"Nah, I'll wait for you at the park."

Colleen entered the house as Rosaria was leaving. The sisters exchanged words. Colleen pointed over to Lee, seated on a park bench, hands tucked under his thighs, his eyes on his shoes. Looking up, he was captivated by the sight of Rosaria gracefully crossing the street; he longed to see her dance.

"Are you waiting for Colleen?" she asked, taking a seat next to the petrified schoolboy.

"Yes, she's having dinner at my house."

"Oh my, do your parents know what they're in for?"

"They think they do."

"If your parents are like you, they'll find her amusing."

"They're not. I'm scared."

Rosaria laughed and rubbed his arm. "My sister has a strong dislike for people, but she likes you. Colleen protects those she loves."

Rosaria curled her fingers and swatted the air. "She's a wild tiger. Cats don't take responsibility for their actions; they can't be shamed like a dog. Cats don't need people to survive. If you offer them food or a saucer of milk, they'll eat, drink, and be on their way. If the cat returns, you've been accepted. Tame the tiger, and you'll have a friend for life. Here she comes."

Rosaria pressed her finger to her lips. "Not a word, it's our secret."

He'd never had a teenager speak with him like he was a grown-up. Lee stood as Colleen came closer. She was car wash clean. It was apparent someone else had taken soap and water to her.

"Your sister is neat," Lee said as he watched Rosaria walk away.

"If you don't like Rosaria, you're not human."

Very few members of Colleen's parish ventured over to Blue Hill Avenue on foot. It wasn't that they weren't welcomed, there just wasn't any reason to be over there. Colleen had a reason. It was home to her best friend. Her dad would drive past Lee's block on their way to The Franklin Park Zoo. She'd never had the opportunity to peer into shop windows, hear people speak in a language foreign to her. The men wore suits; they were merchants, not khaki-clad laborers. The bustling boulevard was laced with restaurants, jewelry stores, and soda-fountained pharmacies. She was filled with wonder. Lee was her Aladdin, the fairytale prince who whisked the princess away on his magic carpet to an exotic land existing just blocks from the Mount.

"Are you coming or what?" her prince hollered back at Colleen, whose nose was pressed against a butcher shop window.

"Lee, get over here, you gotta see this."

"It's a butcher shop, big deal."

"I've never seen dead animals with their heads still on, gruesome. Let's go in."

The rotund butcher in an apron tied above his belly pounded a rough cut of beef with a tenderizing mallet the way Nikita Khrushchev hammered out, "WE WILL BURY YOU!" with his shoe. Realizing he had an audience, the butcher welcomed the curious couple in with a broad, Soviet smile. His belly jiggled as he and Lee exchanged greetings in a shared language. Colleen tugged at Lee's sleeve.

"What did he say?" she whispered.

"He said he'd give me a good price for the fat cow I'm with. Now come on, the sooner you get to my house, the sooner you leave."

"Do you have weapons at your house?" she asked, trying to keep pace with her companion.

"No."

"What are you going to do when the Chinese invade? Hide behind me?"

"The Chinese invented gunpowder; they won't be afraid of your crummy bow and arrow made out of a stick and pastry string."

"What about the Russians?"

"They have the bomb."

"Antarcticians?"

"Have you ever been pelted with penguin eggs?"

"You have colored people living around here."

"What of it?"

"Just saying. Do you think a dog knows his master is colored?"

"Sure, they do, but they don't care. Dogs are kinda like retarded people, they like anyone who's kind to them."

"What if they're mean to the dog?"

"The dog runs off."

"We had a mean runaway dog on the Mount. I named her Molly, spelled M-A-U-L-Y. This dog got hold of our mailman, ripped his guts out and ran around the park with them. My mother said it was all in the spirit of fun until she realized the bitch ate Poppy's unemployment check."

"Colleen, you are such a liar. You better not tell those stories to my parents, and don't blab about what Margo does on dates, or how your parents' marriage is a sham, and they don't want to hear how Saint Joan ran a sword through some guy's eye. This is where I live."

Colleen looked up at the three-story brick building with cement steps leading to a stone porch.

Lee reluctantly opened the door to what was considered a large apartment by most standards, but seemed cramped to Colleen. There wasn't a wide foyer, but rather a long hallway giving one the sensation of being in a railway car. Lee introduced Colleen to his parents. Like the little teapot, Mrs. Hirsch was short and stout. Without speaking a word, her homespun dress and graying braids wrapped around her head like a crown of thorns made it clear she was from The Old Country. Mr. Hirsch was spindly and bearded, and could easily be mistaken for a grandfather.

In a thick Russian accent, Frieda welcomed Colleen into a dimly lit dining room. The table was set for five, no sign of plastic. Oscar nodded to his son, who rolled his eyes as he pulled out Colleen's chair.

"I've looked forward to our meeting, Miss Ronan," Oscar said in an accent different from his wife's. "My son speaks of nothing else but who listens?"

Colleen knew she was in the company of a kindred spirit.

"My son described you as adventurous," Frieda said, wearing a wide grin. "I usually don't make such a meal unless it's a holiday, but having you at our table is a special occasion."

"Did Lee have a hand in the dinner menu?"

Lee's lips curled. "I may have."

"Then I know I'll enjoy it."

Colleen feared they would say grace in some weird language, but they didn't. Mrs. Hirsch disappeared into the kitchen, returning with her "special salad."

"We call this selyodka pod shuboy; it's very healthy, has herring, potatoes, beets, and carrots. You try?"

"Oh yes!"

Lee dry-rubbed his hands; surely this would be a spit out for a girl who ate grape jelly and butter on white bread every day for lunch. Colleen closed her eyes and pursed her lips.

"Humm, heavenly," she moaned. Taking a moment to allow her stomach time to warn her bowels that there would be fire in the hole, she dug in.

"Save room for the appetizer," Lee warned with a lowered head, unable to look up for fear he'd break into hysterics.

"This took much time to prepare," Frieda explained.

One look and Colleen knew it would take less than five seconds to throw up the gelatin blob resembling a giant fisheye. Its yellow yolk pupil, glossed over by a cloudy cataract, glared up at her.

"I told my mother you like jelly."

"Jellyfish?"

"Kholodet," Frieda explained. "It's an aspic."

"Ass pick," Lee mumbled.

Their eyes were fixed on one another like gunslingers with both hands hovering over their weapons. Knowing her sacrifice would guarantee the release of a poor soul from purgatory, Colleen closed her eyes and gulped. The slimy creature slithered back up her esophagus. Putting her napkin to her lips, she forced it back down her gut.

"I'd love to have the recipe. My family should share this experience," she choked.

"There's very little cooking involved."

"Good, I'm not allowed around fire."

"Her family just discovered it," Lee cracked.

"If you like, I can teach you."

"Oh, Mrs. Hirsch, I wouldn't want to put you to all that trouble."

"What trouble?"

Colleen looked across the table at Lee. "Gee, that would be swell." Her eyes traveled from Lee to a basket of warm bread, probably homemade, not from a plastic bag. Frieda handed the basket to Colleen. "Essen." Colleen snapped up two slices.

"Fet chaze," Lee insulted in a low voice.

"He called me a fat pig!"

Oscar raised his brow. "You know Yiddish?"

"No, but I know your son. I'll swear at him tomorrow, in English."

Oscar's shoulders shook from a silent laugh. Lee sheepishly smiled. His father never laughed at his jokes.

"Now you taste a favorite dish my sons love. I think you should like it too." Frieda held a covered casserole dish between two burnt but functioning oven mitts. With great fanfare, she lifted the cover. To Colleen's dismay, a dove didn't take flight. "Kishka. It's an acquired taste."

"Don't inquire what's in it," Lee said, wearing a smirk.

Oscar didn't see the humor. "Leon, your mother spent all day preparing this meal. Show respect for both your mother and our guest."

Lee stewed, knowing that if Colleen made the remark, his father would have laughed.

"It's a variety of meats, mostly organ meat," Frieda explained.

"My mother loves to cook organs," Colleen informed.

"Your mother keeps kosher?" Oscar asked.

"No, she throws everything out. She threw her back out once, and my sister out twice."

Any doubt Lee had of his parents finding Colleen crude and obnoxious melted in the laughter she brought to the table. A deep voice entered from the hallway.

"If that's laughter I hear, I'm in the wrong house."

The table's attention turned to the tall, slender man in doctor's whites. The name "Aaron Hirsh, M.D" was stitched above the jacket's pocket. Colleen took note of the surname's spelling and advantage of the interruption to slide a piece of mangled meat from her mouth into her pocket. The lighting was dim; Colleen strained to see any resemblance the doctor had to anyone at the table. The doctor's hair was dark, Lee's light. His facial features were strong, rough, and chiseled. Lee's soft and doughy.

"I'm Aaron," he said with an extended hand.

"A pleasure to meet you, Doctor."

"Please, it's Aaron."

"My mother told me to always address a doctor as Doctor; they earned the title."

"I like your mother."

"That's because you've never met my ill-tempered mother."

"Kholodet, Kishka! You're a mighty brave girl."

Lee looked across the table at his brother. "Brave? You're looking at a girl who swallowed a caterpillar to see if a butterfly would fly out of her butt."

"Leon!"

"Sorry, Mom."

Aaron leaned into Colleen's ear. "You do realize my little brother is smitten with you."

Lee simmered. Aaron always spoke as if Lee wasn't present, but why did he have to do it in front of Colleen?

"Your brother is an impressionable young man. I try not to toy with his affections."

Lee rolled his eyes. "Give me a break."

"My, my," Aaron commented. "You're a wit as well as a wordsmith."

"The credit belongs to my sister Rosaria. She aspires to become a teacher."

Frieda nodded in Lee's direction. "My son also aspires to teach."

"Since meeting Colleen's sister Margo, I now aspire to pump gas."

The dueling duo laughed over their private joke.

"My sister has an active social life."

"Aaron, you've got to see her sister Margo, what a knockout."

Aaron lowered his fork. "That's not a term one uses to describe a young lady."

"You needn't castigate your brother. My sister is a knockout; my mother's knocked her out on more than one occasion."

"Tell us about your family," Aaron asked.

Panic pressed on Lee's chest, reminding him of the time a group of Irish boys held him underwater at the YMCA pool.

"I won't bore you with details of my parents' turbulent marriage."

Lee removed his eyeglasses and rubbed the bridge of his nose with his middle finger. Colleen squinted at him and continued.

"Aside from my two sisters, my aunt Mae lives with us." Colleen turned to Frieda. "My aunt asked if you know Elba Raskind; they work together at Bloomfields."

"Why yes! Elba is a dear friend. She moved away a few years ago but comes to visit from time to time."

Colleen's eyes zeroed in on a glass jar at the end of the table. "What's that?" she asked with a curled lip.

Lee held up the jar containing grayish, yellowish spongy clumps floating in a milky liquid. "Gefilte fish."

"That's fish from the ocean? What did they use for bait?"

"Your picture. Dare you to eat it."

"I want to save room for the rugelach before Margo arrives to walk me back home."

"I won't hear of it," Aaron insisted. "Call your mother and tell her I'm giving you a ride back."

"My mother is out burying someone."

Her comment was followed by a knock on the door. Aaron pushed his chair from the table. "I'll answer it."

The doctor's mouth fell open with the door. Margo offered her hand in a manner that left him wondering if she wanted it shaken or kissed.

"I don't believe we've met," Margo said, knowing it was unlikely the two would ever have crossed paths.

"I'm Aaron."

"So, your jacket says."

Frieda welcomed Margo to the table. "Come, sit, eat."

"Thank you, but I shan't be staying," she said, casting an affectionate eye on Lee, causing a bashful blush. "I want you to know you've raised a fine, young man."

"Too bad Lee's not more like him."

Margo wagged her finger in Colleen's face. "Colleen! Save your wise cracks for the schoolyard."

Margo turned to the table. "You must forgive my sister. Colleen has a limited brain capacity, as I'm sure you've noticed."

Aaron came to Colleen's defense. "She makes up for any shortcomings with her contagious humor."

"She is contagious, isn't she, doctor. We're deeply indebted to Lee."

Frieda beamed with pride. "Our door is always open, and don't forget about our cooking class or your rugelach."

The hostess handed Colleen the dessert wrapped in wax paper. Lee held up the jar of pickled fish.

"Oh, Colleen, aren't you forgetting something?"

She snatched the jar from his hand. "Why, thank you, my family will enjoy it."

Aaron hastily grabbed his coat. "Come along. My car is out front."

Margo shook her head. "No, thank you, Doctor, we'll return on foot. I need the fresh air, and Colleen needs the exercise."

"The neighborhood's not safe after dark. Please, I insist."

"I promise we'll call to inform you of our safe return."

Margo stroked Colleen's hair as Aaron escorted them to the door. "Thank you for the kindness you've shown this misguided outcast."

Once on the street, Margo took her hand from Colleen's head and wiped it on her coat.

"You're disgusting, and that food smells."

"Why did you turn down a ride in a sports car?"

Margo's face lit up from the flame in her cupped hand. Shaking the match out, she tossed it into the street.

"This is why," she answered with a cigarette dangling from her lips.

"Ma's gonna kill you!"

"Eventually." Looking down the street, Margo closed her coat collar around her throat. "Let's get out of here. This part of town gives me the creeps."

Aaron looked out to the street at the departing girls. "What a knockout."

"She's got lots of boyfriends."

"She's a teenager, I don't rob cradles, but there's no crime in looking."

Colleen climbed to the attic's turret, the highest point in the house, with the only view of Aladdin's Empire. An old oriental rug, a remnant of the Lindseys' reign, served as her magic carpet. Accompanied by her Gefilte genie in a jar, she looked up at the ceiling's cupola to the night sky. Using the constellations as their guide, they were airborne. The carpet knew where they wanted to go, back to her prince's mysterious kingdom.

***

The house was drafty, the mornings dark. The sisters sat down to a breakfast of hot tea and their mother's signature burnt-bottom corn muffins.

"What time did you get in from the wake last night?" Margo asked her mother.

"Sometime after ten, we lingered a bit. Poor Howard, he's lost without Bernice. He was never right in the head. Bernice blamed the war, but they say he drank bleach as a child. I don't doubt that contributed to it. He'll be dead in six months, that's the way it is when the wife dies first."

"I merely asked what time you got in, not what all your bleach-drinking friends are dying from."

Colleen waved her tea-soaked muffin. "Ma, Ma, Mrs. Hirsch cooks worse than you. She wants to give me lessons. Can I?"

"May I?" Rosaria corrected.

"Just don't burn her house down; the entire block will go up. That neighborhood is a slum."

"Aside from the meal, did you enjoy yourself?" Rosaria asked.

"Yeah, his parents are kinda strange. He has a brother who's a doctor."

Berta shook her head. "Aren't they all."

"He's really handsome," Colleen added, looking to Margo for confirmation.

60

She weighed in with a shrug. "He's okay looking."

"Better looking than Ronny, what a dink he turned out to be."

Berta stood. "Save it; you'll be late for the bus."

"May I get my ears pierced?" Margo asked, admiring herself in the coat tree's mirror.

Berta answered with a sharp "No."

"All the girls at school are doing it."

"If all the girls at school jumped off a cliff, would you?"

"No."

Colleen piped up. "That's not the answer she wanted. Ma, may I get a tattoo?"

"No. Enough of this nonsense."

"Why not?"

"Girls don't get tattoos."

"Mrs. Hirsch has a tattoo."

Rosaria lowered her head. Margo bit her lip. Colleen continued, unaware of the statement's impact.

"I asked her why she had one. She said it was so she wouldn't forget. I asked, forget what? She said her phone number. Then I said, 'What if you move and your number is changed?' Ma, she sounded just like you."

Chin to chest, Colleen furrowed her brows and growled. "We go nowhere."

"You wanna know what else?"

"No time for stories, get a move on."

Berta hustled her daughters out the door. "Girls!" she called from the front steps, rubbing her bare arms.

The sisters exchanged puzzled stares as they returned to the porch.

"You left without kissing me."

Each girl pressed their lips to their mother's cold cheek.

"Now skedaddle."

"That's weird," Colleen remarked as they headed down the Mount.

"She hates kisses."

"Not today," Rosaria replied.

Berta kept watch from the front steps until her daughters faded from view. "There but for the grace of God."

Chapter Six

The tapping of a pencil on the library's table got Lee's attention. "You stuck on a question?"

"The question is: How come your brother is so much older than you?"

"If I tell you, will you hurry up and finish that worksheet? I'd like to get home before dark."

"Sissy."

"Fine, I won't tell you."

"If you tell me, I'll read to you from Margo's diary in her voice."

Lee was aware he was about to enter uncharted territory, not knowing how much, if anything, Colleen knew about the extermination of European Jewry. "My mother is from Russia, that's where Aaron was born. When the war broke out, my parents thought it was best to send him to America to live with my dad's brother, Izzy. My mother was going to join him, but the authorities took her away. It wasn't until three years later that my father found her. Aaron lived on the second floor with Uncle Izzy and his wife, Nelda. After they died, Aaron got a place of his own. He keeps some of his stuff in the back bedroom, but he's never lived with us. The only time he comes by is when he's hungry or wants to pick a fight."

"The authorities took Poppy away a couple of times, but my mother never went looking for him. The next question is, why does your brother spell his name differently from yours?"

"Aaron says it's the American spelling. I have a question for you. How come your sisters are pretty and you look like you were in a car wreck?"

"That's because they had a different father. The Japs shot him down. He died in a ball of fire. My mother doesn't talk about it, which is weird because she likes that gory stuff. She picked my father up in a bar, and here I am."

***

The screen door snapped shut behind a winded Colleen. "Rosaria! Where are you!"

Rosaria rushed into the kitchen. "What's happened?"

"Where's Ma?" Colleen gulped.

"Poppy took her to the market."

"Where's Margo?"

"She's out with Wayne."

"Which one is Wayne?"

"Black sports car, jellyroll... Will you please tell me what's going on?"

"Mister Malformed is out on his lawn. I've only seen him once. I'm riding back over for another look. The bike seats two. Are you coming?"

"Who is Mister Malformed?"

"We call him Mr. Malformed because he's a man who dresses as a woman. Lee said he's a real sicko and to stay clear of him, so I'm headed back over there." Colleen grew impatient. "Are you coming or what?"

"Perhaps she's a woman who resembles a man."

64

"This isn't a nun. He stands on his lawn and wags his thing at us."

"You are not leaving this house!"

Colleen stomped her foot. "Come on, Rosaria, what if he gets arrested and I never get to see him again?"

"You won't, because I'm informing the police."

"Don't call them." Colleen looked over Rosaria's shoulder. "Here comes Margo! Wayne will drive us."

Racing to the street, Colleen flagged down the black hot rod. Margo hung her head out the car window. "What's happened?"

Colleen paused to catch her breath. "Rosaria is calling the police on Mister Malformed, the man who dresses like a woman and shows us his thing."

Wayne bolted from behind the wheel. "Where's this asshole live?" he raged, shaking the messenger by her shoulders.

"Normandy Street," Colleen blurted.

Margo ran the back of her hand down Wayne's cheek in the hope of taming the savage beast. "Let the police handle it."

"The cops are good for nothing. Are we still on for Friday?"

Margo pointed her fingers like a gunslinger with a set of six-shooters. "You got it."

Both girls waved goodbye as the hot rod screeched out a war cry, leaving behind the scent of burning rubber. "Show off," Margo snipped. "Now what's this all about?"

"Margo!" Rosaria called from the porch. "The police are on their way. I do hope they apprehend him."

"You did the right thing," Margo assured Rosaria, who nervously twisted a handkerchief.

"We can discuss this later. I'm late for my hair appointment."

"Why didn't you have Wayne drive you?"

"Because I'm getting my hair done for my date with Ronny is why."

Rosaria spun around. "Where did Colleen go?"

Margo pointed to their sister pedaling off in the direction of Normandy Street.

Tim placed an armful of groceries on the porch. Grasping the railing to catch his breath, he gave Rosaria a hasty kiss.

"Lots of excitement going on. We had to pull over for cops and an ambulance."

"Oh God, Poppy. Colleen is over there!"

"Over where?"

"Normandy Street. We must get her!"

"Hey, hey, calm down."

Rosaria dashed to the street. "Mom! Mom!"

Knowing Rosaria wasn't given to hysterics, Berta experienced a surge of adrenaline.

"It's Colleen, Mom, she's over on Normandy Street."

"Wait till I get my hands on that..."

Spotting Colleen laboring up the hill, Rosaria breathed a sigh of relief. Bursting to announce the morbid news, Colleen dropped her Schwinn and continued on foot.

"He's dead. Malformed is dead! You shoulda seen it. Wayne drove his car up on Malformed's lawn and crushed him up against a tree. His eyeball popped out, squirting blood on everyone. You wanna know the best part? The cops pulled out their guns and ordered Wayne to get on the ground. They cuffed him and hauled him off to jail."

Berta put her palm up to halt the grisly narration. "Will someone please tell me who the hell is Mister Malformed?"

"He's an exhibitionist who masquerades as a woman," Rosaria explained.

"Then good for Wayne."

"Mom! Wayne could face the death penalty!"

Berta sympathetically shook her head. "Poor Nuala, she loved that car."

***

The slam of a door accompanied by the old player piano's ragtime tune signaled that Berta was on the warpath.

"You haven't worked in weeks; the least you could do is get out there and clean the yard."

Flying out the back door, Colleen cheerfully came to the rescue. "I'll help you, Poppy. I like to rake. You bag."

"Thanks, Sport."

The yard served as Colleen's refuge. Many a day she'd spend imagining her swing would send her flying out of the neighborhood, never to return. Aunt Mae was the only person privy to her secret fantasy. Mae said, "When God wants you to come home to Him, He lets you fly off the swing on angel's wings and into His loving embrace. If you jump off the swing and fall to the ground, He's letting you know now is not your time, you have work to do here on earth."

Tim leaned on the porch railing, sweating despite the cool fall air; his two-pack-a-day habit had caught up with him.

"Go inside, Poppy. I'll finish the lawn. Tell Ma, I was getting on your nerves. She'll understand."

"I just need a short break. I'll drive down to Elmer's Variety and pick up a couple of candy bars. I need a pack of smokes. What'll it be? Sky Bar or Snickers?"

"I can't decide."

"I'll get both." She knew he would.

Lee was going to wait until Monday to return the dog-eared math book Colleen dropped on the ground to inspect an ant hole. Oscar had instilled in his son a reverence for books; seeing Elements in Mathematics on the pavement, Lee instinctively picked up the textbook. It was still in his possession when Colleen took off for home. It wasn't until this morning that he discovered a homework assignment due on Monday. Up the mountain Lee climbed. He paused to admire the Mounts' park ablaze in a blanket of the season's foliage. The honk from a sporty car jolted him back to his mission. As expected, the wheels were for Margo, decked out in movie star sunglasses and a scarf tied under her chin to hold her platinum mane in place.

"Lee! Colleen's round back," she called to him with a parting wave. He hoped she noticed his new pair of Wrangler blue jeans.

Creeping into the yard, he was startled by the sound of his name. "Hey, Lee!" Colleen shouted. "Watch this." Letting go of the swing's ropes, her body landed into a four-foot-high pile of leaves that crackled like cellophane. It took a keen eye to distinguish her red hair from the leaves of the same color. "You could have broken a bone or ended up paralyzed," he scolded.

Standing stiff, her arms crossed over her chest like a mummy in an open sarcophagus, Colleen fell back into the pile of leaves. While submerged, she picked up a handful of cold, soggy mulch. "I've got something for you," she sang.

Lee backed away. "Don't, I'm warning you." Like a bull released into the ring, she charged toward him, tackling her friend to the ground, shoving the slop down his back, rubbing it in for good measure.

"Go inside and wash your hands," he ordered, shaking the muck out of his shirt.

Colleen strolled over to the garden hose. Knowing it was a potential weapon, Lee took off running. "Where ja go? Come out, come out, wherever you are. I won't spray you, honest."

Cautiously creeping out from behind the safety of the carriage house, a crabapple whizzed past his head. "I didn't say I wouldn't pelt you with apples."

Lee cupped his hands against the carriage house window. "You have a car in there. It looks pretty old."

"We can go inside and play in it."

"Are you sure your mother won't be sore?"

"She won't mind, she wants to junk it."

Lee's eyes widened as Colleen opened the weathered door. "Wow, she's a beauty!"

"Jump in," Colleen beckoned from the driver's seat.

"I don't want to get in trouble."

Squeezing the bulb on the car's horn, its "OOGA-OOGA" echoed in the dark, empty garage.

"Stop goofin' around."

"Get in."

"Okay, okay. What a neat car. My brother has some expensive cars, but nothing this cool. You're not driving this thing."

"Not if I can't find the key. Maybe it's under the seat. There's something stuck under here."

"Probably a dead rat. I'm getting out of here."

"Stay put, sissy, it's metal." Colleen's face fell. "It's just an old oil can."

"Don't come near me with that thing."

He ran from the carriage house. Stiff-legged, arms stretched out, Colleen marched toward him like a robot.

"You get oil on my blue jeans and I'll, I'll..."

"I'll tell you what you'll do." Dabbing a clump of decades-old motor oil on her index finger, she held it to his lips. "Lick it."

Lee slapped her finger from his face. "Not even for a set of plastic dishes. I didn't come here to be pelted with apples, have wet leaves shoved down my back, or oil smeared on my face."

"Then why did you come?"

"To return your math book. Why didn't you tell me you had an assignment due on Monday?"

"I forgot."

"Did not."

"Did so."

"Get a pencil; we'll do it now."

"I'll do it tomorrow."

"No you won't."

"You're no fun, and math's not fun."

"I said it's fun once you understand it. You don't."

Returning with a pencil and paper, she took a seat on the porch's bottom step. Lee sat behind her, entertaining himself by picking twigs and bits of dead leaves from her thick, tangled hair, unwinding each curl to make certain he hadn't missed a bug or a bud. She wondered why he would bother, and so did he.

***

There she sat, not swinging, just sitting. It wouldn't be a chance encounter, but rather a way to say goodbye without damaging her pride. Lee crossed the empty schoolyard and took a seat on the swing next to hers.

"What do you want?" she mumbled.

"Can't a guy sit on a swing?"

Colleen turned her back on him.

"The silent treatment, eh. You still have to take math in the sixth grade. I'd be willing to help you, but Aaron said they have a tough curriculum at Latin. Besides, I'm at the age where I'm developing an interest in girls, which leaves you out of the mix. Don't get me wrong, I'll acknowledge you if we meet on the street. I may even buy one of your pencils."

"You're a real prick, you know that? But of course, you do, your mother reminds you every morning when she sends you off to school."

"You know what your mother sends you to school with? A chip on your shoulder. That's what's holding you back, not math. Someday, someone is going to knock that chip off. I hope it's me."

Colleen hung her head. "I'm a bully, you can't teach that out of a person."

"Sure, you can."

"How?"

"By being kind." Lee pulled her off the swing. "Come on, I'll walk you home."

***

The heat didn't help, ninety degrees. Berta paced. Mae held the oral thermometer to the sun-drenched bedroom window.

"One hundred and three."

Berta swallowed hard. "I'll send Nuala to fetch Doctor Abbot."

Margo objected from the bathroom at the end of the hall. "Send Colleen; I'm going to the beach with Bonnie."

Mae placed her hand on Berta's shoulder. "I'll go."

Standing at the bathroom's open door, Mae watched Margo coat her face with moisturizer, preparing to battle with the sun. "Please don't be difficult, your mother has her hands full with Rosaria."

"It's her tonsils, what's the big deal? They were removed a couple of days ago. She can't be that sick." Margo fastened her high-heeled sandals. "I'll be back around three."

"Take Colleen with you," Berta hollered.

Margo clopped down to Rosaria's bedroom. "Is this some kind of punishment?"

Berta gave Margo's wardrobe a brief inspection. "You're not leaving this house in those short shorts; you'll be arrested."

"You're so old-fashioned," Margo lectured. "Get with the times; you're still living in the twentieth century."

"So are you, now put some clothes on."

The sisters trotted down the Mount's steep hill, Margo in the outlawed shorts, her blouse knotted under her breasts, and sunglasses resting on the tip of her nose. Colleen followed, burdened under the weight of an overstuffed beach bag.

"Where's Bonnie picking us up?"

"She's not. Her cousin is getting married today, so we're walking."

"You never walk or go anywhere with me. What's up?"

"You're right, I don't. We're meeting up with Mora."

"Ma hates Mora."

"That's why I like her."

The tall, slim, silky-haired brunette waved her arms. "Margo!"

Mora's welcoming smile evaporated. "What's she doing here?"

"The price I had to pay to get out of the house. Don't mind the whale, she'll be in the water all day."

Mora raised and lowered her brows. "Are we ready?"

Margo nodded. "Let's do it."

The two teens walked to the edge of the curb, each holding out a thumb and a leg. As expected, the first male driver to pass didn't.

"Where are you girls headed?" asked the middle-aged man wearing madras Bermuda shorts that exposed his hairless legs. High cotton socks and leather bedroom slippers signaled he was a lonely loser.

"The beach," Margo answered, fanning herself with a sunhat. "I want to take my clothes off and get wet."

The driver flipped his cigarette into the street. "Hop in."

Mora and Colleen squeezed into the backseat, cluttered with crushed crayons and mushed French fries.

"Sorry about the mess. This is my brother's car. My bike is in the shop."

Colleen surmised his bike was a Raleigh.

"Harley's my ride. Ever been on a motorcycle?"

"No!" Margo squealed.

"I'm going to be frank with you," he said, giving Margo a wink.

"You can be whomever you like, we don't care."

The driver scratched his throat. "Like I was saying, there's nothing like the feel of leather between your legs."

Mora rolled her eyes. Colleen wondered if Mora's expression was directed at the driver's comment, or Margo baring her soul to "Frank," who by the end of the half-mile ride knew Margo's favorite song, singer, actor, and color.

"Pink! You're a mind reader!"

"Ya wanna know what's on my mind?"

"Do tell."

"Turn here," Mora directed the driver into the beach parking lot.

The backseat passengers cordially thanked their sweaty coach. Margo showed her gratitude with a kiss to his forehead and a glimpse of cleavage. "I don't know what we would have done if you hadn't come along."

"Walk," Colleen quipped.

Margo swatted her with a towel. "We'll be heading back around three if you happen to be in the area."

The trio set up shop in front of the lifeguard station. "I can't believe you kissed that old guy," Colleen said in disgust.

"I bet he feels young now."

"Don't you move," Mora ordered Colleen with her index finger. "We'll be right back."

Watching the flirty friends head over to the bathhouse, Colleen spread out her towel and switched on Mora's transistor radio, playing a tinny "Shake Rattle and Roll." Leaning back on her elbows, she imagined herself at a dance surrounded by a group of gossiping girlfriends being looked over by a cute boy on the opposite side of a decorated gymnasium. Her daydream was interrupted by a pimple cream commercial and the sobering realization she was lonely, no longer content to tag along; she was meant to be a pack leader, yet, knowing without a female peer to act as her compass, she'd find herself lost and afraid to venture into the woods Margo so expertly navigated. A crossroads lay ahead. A change was taking place; she had one foot testing the waters of womanhood, the other buried beneath a sandcastle slowly being washed away by the tide. Soon, both feet will be wet. For now, she was an overweight twelve-year-old, in a skirted swimsuit, being babysat by a resentful sitter who needed more looking after than she did.

The two seacoast sirens sauntered back to the blanket in bikinis, not only exposing their navels but the reason for camping out in front of the lifeguard station.

"Ma's gonna kill you."

"Sorry, kiddo, if you've got blackmail in mind, it won't work. I keep this bikini at Mora's house. Her mother's brain is fully developed. If you want money for the snack bar, you'd have better luck going through the trash barrels for returnables."

The familiar screech from a lifeguard's whistle summoned a burned and buoyant Colleen to the surface.

"You, out of the water," ordered the lifeguard.

Colleen sloshed ashore like the Creature from the Black Lagoon. She squinted at the bodybuilder in orange trunks.

"You got a problem?"

"Are you with those girls?" he barked.

"What if I am?"

"The blonde, what's her name?"

"How should I know? We picked her up after some guy threw her out of his car."

"Too bad, I was going to pay a quarter for the info."

"Give her the quarter and she'll give you more than her name."

"I just might do that."

The bronzed guard turned to leave. Colleen stepped into his path. "Her name's Margo."

"Thanks, kid."

The flipped coin landed in the sand. Colleen dug it up like a dog exhuming a bone. It wasn't thirty pieces of silver, but she didn't have to kiss Margo. Sneaking spoonfuls of Rosaria's tonsillitis ice cream left Colleen craving the cold comfort only a creamsicle could provide. The gooey orange gum on the ice cream wrapper stuck to her anxious fingers. Holding the ice cream's stick between her teeth, she used the bathhouse water bubbler as a finger bowl. The sound of a profanity-laced brawl coming from the boy's bathhouse demanded her attention. Back flat against the tiled wall, she peered around the corner to investigate. Shocked by the brutality taking place, she made a beeline for the blanket, abandoning her prized ice cream in the hot sand.

"Where's the lifeguard?" Colleen puffed, collapsing on the blanket.

Mora laughed. "We told Charles Atlas to take a powder."

"You have to find him! There's a fight behind the boy's bathhouse."

Unconcerned, Mora continued to rub Sea and Ski onto Margo's bare back. "Did you hear me? There's a fight!"

"It's probably over a girl," Mora said with a shrug.

"They're beating up a colored kid!"

Margo sprang up, clutching her swimsuit top. "Hook me up, we're getting out of here."

"There's a phone booth in the parking lot, call the police," Colleen pleaded as Margo shimmed into her sandals.

"We are staying out of it."

"That kid didn't come alone," Mora added. "His friends ran off to get the rest of the tribe. Now pick up our stuff, we're going."

"But we just got here," Colleen whined.

"You don't get it, do you?"

"No, Mora, I don't."

"You stay clear of those people. This has nothing to do with us. He wouldn't have come here if he weren't looking for trouble."

Mora snuffed out a cigarette in the sand. "If he wants a suntan, let him go to his own beach."

"Where's that?" Colleen shot back.

"How should I know. It's not like I'd ever go there. Now get a move on."

Colleen sat on the steps to Mora's three-decker waiting for Margo to slip out of her bikini. Not only was Margo changing, but so was the neighborhood. Colleen couldn't escape the change taking place in herself. She'd begun to care about the plight of others. In four months, she'd be a teenager, yet she lacked an interest in clothes and cosmetics like Margo, or books and children like Rosaria. She was carving out her own path, where it would lead was the adventure that lay ahead.

Margo clopped down from the front porch. "Don't let your brother get his grubby hands or any other part of his body on my bikini."

"Let me know if that lifeguard calls."

The sisters trudged the remainder of the way home with sun in their eyes and sand in their shorts.

"Margo, are you moving out after you graduate?"

"Ronny is going to marry me, so you can have my room."

"He asked you?"

"Next year."

"How many children do you think you'll have?"

"What's with all the questions?"

"I don't know; it's just when you were my age, you were seeing boys and smoking cigarettes. I don't like that stuff."

"That's because you're a hairy-legged lesbian."

Margo covered her ears, protecting them from the high-pitched screech of an approaching ambulance.

"Look, Margo; it's going up the Mount. It's someone we know!"

Colleen desperately struggled to hold on to their beach supplies. The soft soles of her P.F. Flyers allowed the iron-hot pavement to scorch her sweaty feet.

"Hurry up," Margo called back to Colleen. "It's Poppy, I just know it. He must have fallen again."

Reaching Mounts Park, Colleen dropped their bags. "Margo, look, it's Father Onley! Poppy's dead!"

"Shut up. He's not dead. It's a slight heart attack."

"Ma is with him, Margo, she's crying!"

The ambulance roared past, carrying off their mother and a solemn priest, but for whom were they shedding tears and reciting prayers? Mae waved the girls into the house.

"Is it Poppy?" Colleen asked, teetering on the brink of tears.

Mae shook her lowered head.

"It's Rosaria!" Margo cried.

Mae clasped Margo's hands. "Doctor Abbot thought it best to have Rosaria hospitalized."

Margo tugged her hands out of Mae's. "In an ambulance? With a priest? No, Mae, it's not her tonsils."

"She has a high fever and difficulty walking."

"Is her leg broken?" Colleen innocently asked.

"It's not broken. Mae won't tell you because she's a coward. Rosaria has polio. Say it, Mae. Rosaria has polio!"

"We don't know that, dear."

"Don't you dare 'dear' me. I'm not stupid. I hate you. I hate God."

Margo stormed up to her room. The slam from her bedroom door set off an impromptu rag from the haunted piano. "Should we go up there?" Colleen timidly asked.

"No, she needs to go through this."

"But she's busting up her room."

78

"Leave her be."

Reaching down to pick up a shoe intended for her vanity mirror, Margo looked over at her turntable. On it, The Crests' recording "Step by Step." Using the heel of the shoe, she hammered the record, reducing it to sharp shards of vinyl.

Colleen curled up on the sofa next to her brave-faced aunt. "Mae, where's Poppy?"

"He went out."

"He's drinking, isn't he?"

"Everyone has their way of handling bad news."

"When we saw the ambulance, we thought it was for Poppy. I felt bad because sometimes he makes me so mad, he embarrasses me, but I promised God if he kept Poppy alive, I'd treat him with the respect he deserves. I'm going to keep that promise."

"Rosaria would want you to."

"I ate some of Rosaria's ice cream. Will I get polio?"

"No."

"Is she going to die?"

"Rosaria won't die, but life around here will never be the same."

Chapter Seven

The house was still. The calls had stopped. Mae was told not to wait by the phone. They would discuss Rosaria's condition when Berta returned. Mae waited by the phone.

Berta canvassed the crowded waiting room. Tears and terror frosted the faces of anxious souls in search of treatment or news. The metal wastebasket brimmed with Dixie cups and Kleenex. Ashtrays were full. Head bowed, Berta looked at the run in her stocking. Ugly legs, she thought. Her eyes followed a blue varicose vein snaking along her inner calf, a bulging reminder of her last pregnancy. She felt it shameful to complain about her battered limbs while Rosaria's lovely leg remained frozen. Father Onley was no stranger to hospitals, Berta was.

"I wish to hell they had taken her to a Catholic hospital," Berta grumbled.

"God is everywhere; the best doctors aren't. She's in good hands."

"Yes, Father, sorry about the hell."

"I've used more colorful language under less trying circumstances. Why don't we say a rosary?"

A voice interrupted the second decade. "Mrs. Ronan, I'm Doctor Fischer." The introduction was administered with an outstretched hand. Berta didn't shake it; Father Onley did.

"The fever broke. Our staff neurologist will be by to examine her leg."

"Examine it? One needn't hold a medical degree to examine it or diagnose its condition."

"Fortunately, the paralysis only affected her right leg."

"Fortunately? Yesterday, my daughter could walk!" The priest positioned himself between the doctor and the matriarch as a reminder to Berta of the conversation she and the cleric had just shared. "Will she be confined to a wheelchair?" Berta asked in a civil tone.

"A brace should suffice."

The priest held Berta's trembling hand. "She's alive."

"I'm upset, Doctor. I apologize. It's just ... it came on so suddenly."

"Rosaria is awake. You're welcome to visit with her."

Father Onley thanked the doctor and placed his hand on Berta's shoulder as they walked down the corridor.

"I have to appear upbeat, optimistic—it's not in my nature," Berta confessed.

Father Onley whispered in Berta's ear. "Your real self would have ripped that doctor's head off."

"Mom?" came a whimper from a room two doors down. Berta patted her hair in place, rubbed her sweating palms on the sides of her dress, and made the sign of the cross. The room was dim. Both mother and daughter wore a brave face, yet each knew the other had been crying.

"Oh, Mom, I was so worried about you. Father Onley, thank you for coming. You're the only person who can crack my mother up. I always went to your confessional knowing my penance would be listening to your jokes...Mom, please don't cry. I'll come through this. With God, all things are possible."

" Saint Mark 10:27," Father Onley remarked with a smile. "I'm glad someone listens to my sermons."

"Where's Margo?" Rosaria asked with searching eyes.

"Home."

"She'll be upset when she learns I can no longer dance." Rosaria's defenses were dissolving. "I'll never dance again, will I?

"We don't know that for a fact."

"What I do know is I can't move my leg. I know what I have and what I am."

"What you are is my daughter, and no daughter of mine wallows in self-pity."

"Berta, now is not the time."

"Mom's right, Father. If she says I'll dance one day, I'll dance one day. Mom, Father Onley, go home. I'm tired, so are you. I'm sure everyone is waiting for news. Tell them this is just a setback," she instructed in a wobbly voice.

"Very well, but I'll be back tomorrow and every day until you come home. Is there anything I can bring you?"

"Bring Margo."

The tinkling of a breakfast cart melted a dream of home to the reality of lying in a metal-framed bed. She was unsure whether the ascitic waves were a reaction to medication or the sight of the hospital's milky scrambled eggs. Using a cloth napkin, Rosaria covered the breakfast plate, resembling a body en route to the morgue. A deep voice accompanied a gentle tap on the open door's frame.

"Miss Ronan?"

Her eyes drifted from the floor to a white-clad doctor. Brown-eyed and dark-haired, he wore a nervous smile. Sitting slope-shouldered at the edge of the barrack bed, her sweaty, tangled hair hung over her eyes, veiling a gray complexion and chapped lips. She'd never been alone with such a handsome man. "*He's a doctor,*" she reminded herself. "*He wouldn't give me a second look if I were perfumed, wearing lace and lamé. He's only interested in my dead dangling leg.*"

"I'm Doctor Hirsh." Rosaria weakly shook his cold hand. "I'm a neurologist. I'll be checking in on you from time to time, taking note of your progress." Aaron looked up from her chart. "You didn't receive the polio vaccine?"

"My mother was hesitant; the vaccine is new, she feared it may have an adverse side effect." Unable to punch out a wall, Aaron flexed his knuckles. "She...you weren't...my God, some people are so damn..." Rosaria's eyes teared.

Aaron ran his fingers through his hair. "I'm sorry, I didn't mean to upset you, but the vaccine is given at school; it's mandatory."

"I've graduated."

Realizing his comments were upsetting her, his voice turned from surly to silky. "What I'd like to do is have you try some simple movements."

"Yes, Doctor," she answered without raising her head.

"You'll have to look up at me."

Rosaria lifted her eyes to meet his, wondering if he thought of her as a wallowing, weak-willed teenager, ugly, helpless, one of the "poor things" who hobble the hallways.

"Watch my hands," he directed, spreading out his arms. "On which hand am I wiggling my fingers?"

"The left."

"Very good. Now, follow my finger with your eyes." Rosaria's eyes tick-tocked to the flow of his digit. A slow smile crossed his face.

"Are you going to tap my knees with a rubber hammer?"

"I just happen to have one here in my pocket." A slight tap to her left knee produced a jerk. Their eyes met in suspense.

"I don't expect a reaction from your right leg, so don't let it upset you."

"It won't, I promise." Her leg lay limp. "I'm going to be in a wheelchair, aren't I?"

83

"Not if I can help it. Fortunately, you're in the care of the best doctor in Boston."

"My, but we're confident!" Rosaria covered her mouth with both hands, gasping at her bold remark. "I'm sorry, Doctor, I didn't mean..."

"No apology necessary. You sound like my mother. She has a way of bringing my ego back to Earth."

"My mother will put you in the earth if you don't get me walking."

"That bad?"

"That bad."

"You won't run the Boston Marathon, but with the aid of a brace and..."

"I'm frightened, Doctor. I'm frightened." Her fingers twisted the hem of her nightgown. Aaron took them into his. He was more at home in the O.R., not with a weeping girl needing comfort, not a diagnosis. Aaron lifted her chin with his index finger. "You'll walk again. Edna, our physical therapist, will exercise your leg and teach you to accomplish essential tasks and overcome the challenges you'll encounter once you return home. Each day you'll see an improvement, and each day I'll be by to check on your progress."

"I trust you, Doctor. I won't disappoint you. I was an accomplished dancer."

"Dancing is a great way to regain strength in your legs. I'll be sure to tell Edna of your talent." Aaron offered his hand; it was warm, slow to release hers.

"You're Lee's brother."

"You know Leon?"

"Yes, I'm Colleen's sister."

"Well, well, that sister of yours is quite a character."

"She sure is, and your brother is a very special boy."

"I'll be sure to tell him."

"I already have."

***

"We're here!" Colleen ran to her sister with flowers and kisses. Rosaria held out her arms to Margo.

"There's nothing to be afraid of."

Berta gave Margo a shove. "Your sister is talking to you."

Colleen broke the stalemate. "Can...may I see your leg?" Rosaria pulled back the bed sheet. "Looks fine to me."

"The problem lies on the inside. I'll be fitted for a brace tomorrow." Margo fled the room. The word "brace" invoked images of her sister's leg strapped into a cage.

"Why that..."

"Please, Mom, let her go. She needs time."

"Only because you asked."

"Where's Poppy?"

"He's out in the car. He'd only upset you."

"That's probably where Margo went."

"No, I'm here," Margo replied in a voice barely above a whisper. Rosaria held out her arms, and Margo ran to them.

"Don't cry, I'm going to dance one day. Do you have any gossip?"

"Leslie dyed her hair blond."

"How does she look?"

"Awful!" The three sisters laughed.

"Colleen, you'll never guess who my doctor is."

"Ben Casey!"

"Close. He's Lee's brother; he remembers you."

"How can anyone forget Colleen?"

Rosaria's eyes lit up. "Dr. Hirsh!"

"I see you have company."

"Allow me to introduce my family. My mother Roberta, Aunt Mae, and my sister Margo."

Aaron greeted the women with a smile and a nod. "Colleen needs no introduction," Aaron said, squeezing the twelve-year-old's shoulder.

Margo seethed; he'd met her and offered to drive her home, yet he clumped her in as one of the Trinity, sharing a patronizing nod.

"It's a comfort to know Rosaria will have plenty of support when she returns home. So many of our patients lose ground when they fail to keep up with their therapy, so don't go easy on her; she'll need a push." Aaron eyed Colleen. "And I don't mean down the stairs."

"How's Lee?" Mae asked.

"He's not thrilled with high school, but he'll adjust. I'll tell him you were asking for him. Any message from you?"

he asked Colleen.

"Yeah, give him the finger."

"Mind your tongue." Berta snapped.

"I always wanted to give my brother the finger; now's my chance." Aaron stroked Rosaria's leg, setting off a roaring furnace in Margo's stomach, compounded by her mother's smile. Not one of her exaggerated, phony smiles; this one was genuine, a seal of approval.

***

Hearing Italian leather soles on ceramic tiles, Freida hastily wheeled her antiquated washing machine with its attached wringers onto the back porch. "Aaron, how good that you come for dinner."

"Why's that back door unlocked? You'll never learn...I smell Borax."

"I was washing."

Aaron walked to the new Maytag he'd given his mother for her birthday. Lifting the lid, he ran his hand around its drum. "Dry. The instruction booklet is still inside."

Freida closed the kitchen door. "Your father is sleeping; he's not been feeling well. I don't want you to wake him."

"My father is dead."

"Please, Leon will be home any minute. I don't want you to upset him; he's doing poorly with his classes. Maybe you could help."

"I'll tell you why his grades are slipping." Hearing Oscar stir, Aaron lowered his voice. "It's not because he isn't bright, he is. But he's a social misfit."

"Your brother is not like you. He doesn't make friends so easily."

"And he never will; you know why? I was raised by Americans. That kid is tied to a couple living in the Old World. Christ, you walk through that door, and it's 1910. I bet that kid has never eaten a French fry. "

"You should take him to a hamburger joint." In a well-worn robe and soft leather slippers, Oscar shuffled across the kitchen to kiss his wife's hand.

"Are you sick?" Aaron asked.

"I'm old, I'm tired, a doctor I don't need, or a sermon from a confirmed bachelor on how to raise a child."

"Why must there always be an argument?" asked an exasperated Freida. "With all you see at the hospital, why should you upset yourself with how we wash our clothes or raise our son?" Freida pressed her lips tightly together and shook her head. "The Ronan girl, shame. One should have such heartache. Is she in your hospital?"

Aaron's stone face melted to puddy; rarely seen dimples framed his smile. "As luck would have it, Rosaria is a patient of mine."

"How is she?"

"Beautiful, intelligent, well-spoken, and wise beyond her years. I've never met a girl like her, and that family of hers is a real circus act, but they're up there every day. I'm now known as Doctor Lee's brother. How'd the kid take the news?"

"He's not to know." Freida boldly stated.

"You can't be serious."

"Why tell him?"

"Mamushka! You can't continue to shelter him from anything you deem disturbing. As long as you treat him like a child, he'll remain one, or is that what you want?"

Lee slammed the apartment door and dropped his books on the credenza his Aunt Nelda had rescued from her ancestral home prior to the outbreak of war.

Freida fumbled with placemats. "Dinner is ready." The brothers exchanged dismissive glances across the table.

"What are you doing here?" Lee cracked in a creaking adolescent voice. "If this is about Rosaria, I already know."

"Let's not talk of unpleasant news at the dinner table," Freida said.

"It's not unpleasant. Rosaria is fine; she's an optimist. It lifts my spirit to be around her. Leon, you know what a great gal she is."

"Elba Raskind came to visit," Freida said, changing the subject. "She's lost weight."

"About time. She's a prime candidate for a heart attack," Aaron stated.

"And you, an ulcer," Oscar snapped.

"I'm consumed with my patient's wellbeing, so I lose sleep, skip a meal, is that so bad? Christ, Oscar, you're the one who pushed me into medicine."

"Pushed you!"

"Don't get me wrong, I love my work, but I would have liked to have explored other options."

"Car racing? Girl chasing?"

"Law, politics."

"Enough!"

The timbre of Freida's voice silenced the adversaries. Lee got up from the table.

Aaron called after him. "You don't have to go to your room. I'm leaving. By the way, Colleen asked me to deliver a message." With the flash of a finger, Aaron was gone.

***

The weighted metal brace with stiff leather straps tugged on her leg like a prisoner's ball and chain. She'd never committed a crime, nor had Jesus; this was her Calvary. Edna waited at the end of the corridor, urging Rosaria on in a "Come to Mommy" voice.

"Look down that corridor," Aaron instructed from behind. "That's not Edna you're walking toward, but down life's yellow brick road, the pot of gold at the rainbow's end, the house on the Mount, whatever you desire awaits you there. Walk to it."

What she desired were children, if not her own, a classroom of children. Rosaria handed Aaron the elbow crutch she'd relied on for balance and hobbled to the schoolhouse.

***

Giddy. Colleen had never seen her mother giddy. "That was Doctor Hirsh on the phone. Rosaria can come home on Friday." Colleen wrapped her arms around her mother's waist, and the two hopped. On any other occasion, they would have been self-conscious of their behavior, but not today. Rosaria was coming home. Berta cocked her head at Margo, whose eyes were glued to the television screen. "Nuala, did you hear me? Rosaria is coming home. Aren't you excited?"

"Yeah, sure."

"I'll need both of you to help move the sofa; the scatter rugs have to go, and... Nuala! Get off your posterior and shut that soap opera off, or I'll put you, in a General Hospital."

"How's she going to get around without help from darling Doctor Hirsh?" Margo asked with one eye on Port Charles.

"He wouldn't discharge her if he didn't feel she was capable of doing for herself."

"Speaking of feeling, I saw him rub her leg; he had his arm around his favorite patient's waist. She was in her nightgown for Christ's sake." Berta held her tongue, allowing Margo to dig a grave with hers as she mimicked Rosaria. "I told him I danced, he said he was too old for rock 'n roll, but one day they would share a waltz."

"He can do a jig for all I care as long as he keeps her spirits up."

"If Doctor Two Left Feet steps on hers, she won't feel it." The moment had arrived.

"Why are you jealous, self-centered snot! Would you like to trade places with her? It can be arranged. I swear, Nuala, if you upset your sister with this foolishness, I'll cripple you!"

"I'm just looking out for her. He's going to break her heart."

"No, Nuala, this isn't about Rosaria or her feelings; it's about you. It's always about you. You can't stand anyone receiving attention from a man other than yourself. He's attentive to her because she's his patient; that's what good doctors do. I don't doubt he does like her; who wouldn't?"

"He doesn't just like her, he wants her, he knows it's just her leg that's lost feeling."

With the back of her hand, Berta slapped Margo across the mouth. "You feel that?" Margo shielded her eyes as if blinded by bright headlights on a dark road. Berta violently shook Margo's shoulders. "Don't you ever, ever use that language in this house."

"Who's going to rub her leg, help her dress, and tell her she's beautiful?"

"You are! You've had plenty of boyfriends, Rosaria was never jealous or vengeful."

"I don't hate her. She's been through so much; I won't stand by and allow some playboy who's used to getting what he wants to take advantage of her."

"If you have your sights set on that man, you're on a fool's errand."

***

"Here she comes!" Colleen shouted, running from the house to greet Rosaria.

"Careful, Sport, don't knock your sister over." Tim cautioned. Rosaria took hold of the porch railing.

"I can do this, Poppy." Tim rubbed his palms on his thighs, resisting the urge to carry her into the house. "I can do everything I used to, only it takes a bit longer."

"Have a seat," Mae said, patting the strategically placed sofa.

"No, Mae, I'm to walk as much as possible. If all I'm going to do is sit, I may as well be in a wheelchair." Rosaria's eyes lit up at the sight of Margo descending the staircase. "Margo! Doctor Hirsh said we can continue dance practice."

"I've got to run. I'm going to the movies with Ronny."

"I'd love to see Ronny, have him come in."

Margo inspected her lipstick in her compact mirror.

"We're late as it is, maybe when we get back." Margo kissed Rosaria's forehead. "Good to have you home. Got to run."

Rosaria's eyes dimmed. "Ronny always comes to the door; she's still upset."

Berta peered out the window to watch Margo head down the hill. "What she's upset about is the attention Doctor Hirsh has shown you."

"What would he or any other man want with a girl who can't walk?"

"You can walk, you just did, and men do find you attractive."

"Boys didn't call on me when I had the use of my leg; I doubt walking in a brace makes me desirable. She's not angry with Doctor Hirsh; she's angry at me and God."

"If she doesn't give you an apology, she'll give God his in person."

***

"Everyone," Berta announced. "I want you all at the dinner table."

"Turkey!" Colleen rejoiced, "This is just like Thanksgiving."

"It is Thanksgiving. God has returned Rosaria to us." The family held hands around the table, their heads bowed. Margo mumbled a prayer of thanks. Mae and Berta doted on Rosaria. "I know you mean well; I was told to do what I can and strive to accomplish what I can't."

"Did Doctor Hirsh tell you that?"

"No, Margo, Edna did. She's my physical therapist; she instructs me in facing challenges unique to women."

"Like putting on stockings?"

"Yes, putting on stockings."

"I bet Dr. Hirsh would be willing to make a house call to assist with that unique challenge."

Berta slammed down her fork. "That does it."

Colleen egged her mother on. "Cut her face, snap her spine."

"This is not a joke! Rosaria has enough to contend with without having to put up with your wild romantic notions."

"I was just his patient, nothing more. I won't mention him again. Ronny sent me a lovely flower arrangement. You're very fortunate. He's a great guy."

"You want him too?" Yanking Margo by the back of her head, Berta dragged her into the kitchen. Tim looked up from his plate of dark meat. "And they're off."

***

Colleen poked her head into Rosaria's bedroom. "What are you up to?' Rosaria asked.

"Who, me?"

"Yes, you."

Colleen bent her knees, her hands braided in a praying pose. "Please, please, please, teach me to dance."

"You know I can't."

"No, I don't. You're afraid."

"Perhaps in a few months' time."

"There's a Christmas dance coming up, everyone knows you're my sister, they think I can dance."

"Margo could teach you."

"Margo? Remember when you tried to teach me the stroll and she told me to keep walking, or, when we danced the pony, she said I should be sent to the glue factory."

Rosaria squinted her eyes and wagged her finger. "I know what you're up to, you little sneak."

"You want to walk, I want to dance, what do you say?"

"Select a record."

Colleen shuffled through a stack of 45s neatly piled next to the turntable in the corner of Rosaria's clutter-free room. She knew what record to put on, Rosaria's favorite, The Del Vikings "Come and Go with Me." Colleen snapped her fingers to the beat.

"Dum, dum, dum, dum, dum , dum,de,do,de, dum." The plug was yanked from the wall. "Hey!"

"That's too advanced," Rosaria said matter-of-factly.

"That's the song you danced to when you won The Bandstand Contest; it's your best." Rosaria sat on the bed with her back to Colleen, who knew she was crying.

Hunched over the once-prized record collection, Colleen cried, "Eureka!" waving the musical find over her head. "Cherry Pie!" The scent of Chantilly filled the room before the voice reached their ears. Margo stood against a tall wardrobe, looking down at her freshly polished nails. Rosaria instinctively checked Margo's footwear. Their mother insisted they not scratch the hardwood floors. Margo's feet were housed in soft ballet slippers. "You know you're wasting your time; that fat sow has two left hooves."

"With your two right feet, you'll make a great dance team," Rosaria joked, resurrecting a smile she'd lost along with the use of her leg.

"You stand in the middle," Margo instructed. "I'm not standing next to the eleventh leper." Side by side, the girls swayed to "Cherry Pie."

***

Rosaria unfolded the deeply creased letter.

Dear Rosaria,

It's a pleasure to notify you that your enrollment file is complete.

You have been accepted as a student in our Teaching Program. We look forward to having you with us as a student in the January semester.

"Rosaria!" At the sound of her mother's voice, she hastily folded the acceptance letter and returned it to her jewelry box.

"Yes, Mom, I'm on my way down." One last look in the mirror; her Peter Pan collar was free of any trace of face powder. No lipstick on her teeth. How she wished her dress were two inches longer. Her mother and Margo shared an opinion with the frequency of a Halley's Comet return, yet both agreed the dress was an appropriate length. "Don't dress for the brace," she was told.

Berta kissed her eldest daughter's cheek. "Don't be nervous."

"I'm fine, Mom."

Berta and Mae watched from the front door as father and daughter drove away. "First one in the family to go to college," Mae noted.

"First and last," Berta added.

"The other two may surprise you."

"And we'll put a man on the moon."

Uncle Marty's hand-me-down Rambler headed down Tremont Street to the Massachusetts Educational College.

"I'm proud of you, darlin'. I didn't finish high school, and look at me, never kept a job."

"Poppy, the talent you possess can't be taught. I'll take a dad with a big heart over any scholar with a big brain."

Rosaria twisted her purse strap.

"Nervous?"

"I told Mom I wasn't, but I am."

"You'll ace the interview. I'm going to drop you off in front of the school and circle around for a spot."

"You'll never find one. I can do this on my own. You needn't accompany me."

"I'll give you an hour. I'll find something to do, and it won't be drinkin', I promise. Now go get 'em."

The interview was just a formality. Today, she'd meet her counselor to explore career options. It wasn't up for discussion; she was going to teach.

Professor Fuller didn't appear much older than Rosaria, yet her tweed suit and bifocals worn like a necklace revealed her true age. "Please have a seat," the professor invited with a robotic smile. Rosaria was relieved the chair hadn't been pulled out for her. "You must be excited to start your first semester with us."

"Oh, yes, teaching has been a lifelong dream," Rosaria answered as she picked at the leather chair's nail head trim.

The prim professor looked up from a manila folder bearing Rosaria's name. "Have you given much thought to the teaching path you plan to pursue?"

"I'd like to teach the primary grades."

"A noble vocation. Any other careers that interest you?"

Rosaria thought it was best to address the elephant in the room. "Teaching is a calling. One that I plan to follow. I've never considered another career before or after my paralysis."

"We offer an extensive liberal arts program that would prepare you for any number of promising careers: librarian, administrator, counselor."

"If it's my brace, I can assure you I'm able to stand for long periods of time, maneuver around a classroom. If you require it in writing, my physician can..."

"Can you run, climb, jump? All that aside, you'll be teaching young children; having a teacher who's been struck down by polio may instill fear of this heartbreaking disease." Rosaria's jaw tightened, rage simmered in her empty stomach, as tears fought to flow. "Fall victim? Struck down? I'm not a victim; I'm a survivor. I haven't been struck down; I've been put down, but I won't be kept down."

"Sorry, poor choice of words. I apologize."

"My being a teacher will generate inspiration, not fear. The children will learn that anything is possible. We all have handicaps; mine are in full view. Let them see the brace, touch it, and explore the mechanics. My class will learn that a brace doesn't hurt, words hurt, and the most hurtful words are, 'You can't.'"

"Please, Miss Ronan, my aim is to keep you from wasting your time and your parents' money pursuing a career that wouldn't serve you in the future."

"It's not my parents' money; it's mine. You're right, it would be a waste of my time and money to attend this institution. Thank you for your guidance."

The confidence she'd shown melted in the sun while waiting for her father to return. "If I had a tin cup, I'd make a lot of money standing out here," she mumbled. Tim hadn't arrived at the allotted time, she worried, but his tardiness allowed her time to compose herself. The old Rambler chugged to the curb. Tim prepared to assist Rosaria, but she was seated next to him before he could shift into park. "How'd it go?"

Rosaria turned her head, watching a group of laughing students run up the granite steps to a college she once yearned to call her alma mater. Tim wrinkled his forehead. "You're crying. That happened in there?"

"Oh, Poppy!" she wailed. "That professor told me I wouldn't be a good teacher. My brace would frighten the children."

"That does it. I'm going in there."

"Please, Poppy, don't." Rosaria hung her head. "Perhaps she's right."

"I ain't no scholar, but that professor is talkin' through her ass and you're a fool to listen to her. Did she say you can't go to that school?"

"No, only that I'd be wasting my time and your money."

"You know what you gotta do. You gotta take your place in class, prove you're able to teach, that it ain't up to someone else to tell you what you can or can't do. Honey, don't just do it for yourself; do it for the next handicapped student who wants to teach. No one can tell them they can't because you did."

"I love you, Poppy."

"I love you, too, darlin'. I'll support whatever you decide. No one can tell you what to do. Not them, not me, your mother? Now, that's another story. When the Dragon Lady gets wind of this, she'll wring that professor's neck. Then let's see who ends up in a brace."

***

"Yoo-hoo-Mazie!" Hand on the front door, Mae closed her eyes and bit her lip. After a long, emotional day at the factory, she was in no mood to listen to Irma, the neighborhood gossip, relaying the latest census on who left the Mount and who moved in.

"I won't keep you." All Irma's reports began with that phrase and ended hours later.

"I was wondering, with Bloomfield's closing, if you might be interested in a job at the phone company. There's an opening for an operator. You like people and have a lovely voice and a sweet disposition. I do the training; we'll be joined at the hip for two weeks. The money's good. You can start right away. What do you say?"

"Thank you for keeping me in mind, Irma, but I've already lined up a job as a secretary at City Hall."

"City Hall! Who do you know?" Irma asked with a wink and a nudge.

"Eugene Bullard recommended me for the job."

"The City Councilor?"

"Yes, Councilor Bullard and I kept company before the war."

"Shame, because...say! What about Rosaria?"

"Rosaria?"

"Why not? She's a smart cookie. Oh, I forgot she's going to college."

"She put that on the back burner. What does the job entail?"

"A lot of sitting." Irma accompanied the remark with a slap to her rear end. "This is what twenty years with Ma Bell will do to ya. Hmm, let's see. She'd have to

98

work a switchboard, that's easy enough. Rosaria could go places should she decide to make a career out of it. Then again, she may find herself a fella. Lots of girls do. Rosaria fits the bill. I'll put in a good word for her. The big boys upstairs boast about how much they do for the March of Dimes. Now let them put their compassion into practice."

"Irma, you're a Godsend."

$$\sim\!\!\circ$$

Chapter Eight

Mae poked her head into the TV room. "Would you girls be interested in going to a party on Christmas Eve?" she asked with childlike excitement. "The factory closes in a few weeks. Mort's throwing a party for the workers and their families."

"Where's it being held?" asked Margo, who had no interest in attending.

"At the factory."

"A Christmas party in a garment factory? You must be joking."

"Mort is going all out. It's being catered, a live orchestra, games, and an open bar."

"Count me out."

"Margo! You must go."

"Sorry, Rosaria. I have a date with Ronny on Christmas Eve; there's a party at the country club."

"Colleen isn't over her bout with a strep throat, so it looks like it will just be the two of us," Mae said, looking over at Rosaria.

"Oh, Mae, I'd love to go, but you know."

"No, Rosaria, I don't."

"I haven't been to Bloomfield's since I was a child."

"You have to get used to going out without Margo. Come with me, test the water. You'll see it's not as frightening as you think."

"They'll all look at me like I'm Tiny Tim."

"Show them up. You can dance a little."

"I used to win competitions; now I dance a little. I can't do the twist to every song. That's if anyone besides Mort asks me to dance."

Mae took hold of her niece's hands. "Do it for me. I won't see most of these people again. You weren't born when I went to work at Bloomfield's; you girls grew up there. We'll leave the party whenever you want."

"How will we get there?"

"We'll take a cab. It will be fun, I promise."

***

Colleen burst into Rosaria's bedroom. "What are you going to wear to the party?"

"I haven't decided if I'll attend."

Margo entered the room with an armful of dresses. "Oh, you're going. I want all the dirt, who got drunk, who kissed whom, and what they were wearing."

"There will be mistletoe," Colleen teased.

Margo held out a tea-length green velvet dress. "They'll drop their drinks when you walk in wearing this number."

"I prefer the pink dress I wore to my graduation."

"Pink in winter? You're not covering your legs. It's been decided; you're wearing the green."

Berta kept one eye on her knitting, the other on *The Honeymooners: Christmas Special*. Colleen sat on the floor in a cross-legged Indian pose in front of the television set.

"They're predicting snow. Shame Mae and Rosaria had to take a cab to the party. Leave it to your father to lose his license. Just as well, he would have run off the road in this weather. Get your arse off the cold floor before you get a kidney infection."

Colleen came to her feet. "I'm going upstairs to bug Margo."

"What ja doing?" Colleen asked Margo who was posing in front of her vanity mirror.

"Preparing for my impending engagement. What expression should I wear? There's the smile and wave Miss America gives, or shall I look up at Ronny adoringly as if he were the only person in the room?"

"You really think he's going to give you a ring?"

"Why else would he take me to the country club? His family and all their rich friends will be there. Ronny will stand, tap his glass with a fork, and announce our engagement. Everyone will kiss me and say, 'Welcome to the family.'"

***

"Look at you! You've grown to be such a beauty!" Elba exclaimed to an embarrassed Rosaria, who imitated her mother's saccharine smile.

"Thank you, Mrs. Raskind."

"Freida Hirsch told me her son enjoyed having you as his patient. I don't mean he took pleasure in you being sick, you're not sick, you're..."

"I understand, and I was fortunate to have been a patient of Dr. Hirsh. Please say hello to his mother for me."

"Mae, over here!"

"Come, Rosaria, let's sit with Carla." Carlotta Travella was Mae's closest friend at work. They started at Bloomfields on the same day, Mae as a secretary, Carla as a seamstress. Rosaria wasn't certain what Carla weighed, only that she was the heaviest woman she'd ever known. It was apparent that Carla became a seamstress out of necessity.

After a few polite exchanges. "How's your mother? Has Margo gone to Hollywood, Colleen to prison?" There was nothing more to say. Carla shook her head. "Look at your aunt and Mort dancing. You'd never guess his career is over at 49."

Mae had been Mort Bloomfield's personal secretary after his father passed on. Mort would tease the Ronan sisters whenever Mae brought them in on an occasional Saturday. Rosaria choked back tears as she watched Mae and Mort on the dance floor. Those were her most treasured childhood memories. Like the factory, she was useless, obsolete. Twenty, and her life was over. Mort was headed her way as jolly as Rosaria remembered, but a shadow of the man he once was. At 49, he looked as his father had at 60.

"There's my girl!" Mort squeezed Rosaria's cheeks together as an adult would to a baby. She suspected that if she were not in a brace, he'd greet her with a wolf's whistle and a pat on the fanny. He'd booked a Guy Lombardo look-alike who thought he was the real deal, playing old standards and hokey sing-alongs. Rosaria knew the Negro teens from shipping tolerated the ballads out of respect for Mort. "Ya like the band?" Mort asked. "He's no Elvis, but don't step on his blue suede spats." Mort laughed at his own joke. Rosaria volunteered a weak smile. "Drink up. I'll check in on you girls later." Carla tapped her foot to the music. Rosaria couldn't help but notice the foot was a deep red, almost purple. "What have you been doing since you graduated?" Carla asked.

Rosaria knew Carla was informed daily by Mae on every aspect of her personal life. "I'm employed by the Telephone Company."

"Good benefits, the phone company."

Rosaria desperately wanted to leave, but Mae was having such a good time performing a comical Tango with Mort.

"I'll miss this place," Carla lamented. "Twenty-two years. We came from different parts of the city, different cultures, customs, and religions, but once we walked through that door, we were family. The young ones don't know the meaning of work. Your aunt will tell you. The old man ran this place like a gulag. He'd time how long we spent in the toilet. Not Mort, nice, nice, man. The old ones treat him like a son, the young ones like a friend." Carla eyed Rosaria, picking at her nails. "You're self-conscious."

"Wouldn't you be?"

"No and look at me."

"Yes, but ..."

"But I'm an old lady."

"Oh no, Mrs. Travella. That's not what I meant."

"Rosie, I've been very fat for a very long time. I went from being the fat kid to the fat girl, to the fat lady."

"Your appearance doesn't matter; everyone loves you."

"Exactly. When people look at you, they'll see the brace; then they'll see your beautiful face and wonder what you think of them. How old are you?"

"Twenty."

"Young people. When I was 20, I wondered what people thought of me. As I grew older, I no longer cared what they thought. Now that I'm an old lady, I realize no one was ever thinking of me. Don't waste your life trying to impress others; let them impress you."

"You're a very wise woman, Carlotta Travella."

"And a very fat one. My Louie, he never mentions my weight. He didn't see the fat: he saw the lady, and that's how he treats me, like a lady. He knew I'd make a good wife, loving mother, and great lasagna. You'll have the pleasure of meeting the pasta prince. He's going to drive you home."

"We live on the other side of town."

"It's not out of our way."

"I know why you're one of my aunt's best friends. Would you excuse me? I'm going to visit the powder room. Now don't time me," Rosaria teased.

Winded, Mae returned from the dance floor. "I need a cigarette."

"You two can still cut up the rug."

Mae playfully slapped her friend's hand. "At my age, when a gentleman asks you to dance, they're being polite or generous."

"Mort is neither. The spark's still lit."

"Ancient history. Where's Rosaria?"

"She went to the powder room. I've never heard anyone refer to that latrine as a powder room. She's such a sweet girl."

"Too sweet. I worry about her, always have. She relies on Margo for companionship. There'll come a day, soon I suspect, when Margo marries and leaves Rosaria sitting at home with the old ladies watching life pass her by. "

"Shouldn't you check on her?"

"I'll give her a few more minutes. She insists on doing for herself."

At home, the sink was situated next to the toilet, enabling her to lift herself and her underpants up together. Edna hadn't prepared her to maneuver around an antiquated bathroom stall. "What made me think I could do this alone? I won't ask for help. I refuse to be pitied," she stated in an empty restroom. Placing her right hand on the toilet tissue box, Rosaria stretched her left hand against the stall's rickety wooden door, allowing her to hoist herself up. *"I did it!"* She silently rejoiced. *"Now, if I can shimmy up my underpants."* Her arm didn't reach; Rosaria returned to the seat, defeated. The restroom door swung open. Her heart jumped. The paralysis crept from her leg to her stomach. Her nose tingled from the scent of Aqua Net. Her lungs refused to exhale. The chattering girls sounded like a room full of parakeets. Consumed with talk of boys and cosmetics, they failed to notice the braced leg tucked behind the porcelain bowl. With a chorus of laughter punctuated by toilet flushing, the group returned to the party. Rosaria covered her face with her hands, releasing the tears she'd suppressed since leaving the hospital. The life she planned—college, teaching, marriage, motherhood—gone.

"I can't live like this," she cried aloud. "I'm weeping on the toilet. I hate my leg. I hate my life." A surge of anger overtook her, and she violently yanked on the brace's leather strap. It tore off.

"Rosaria." Her aunt's voice echoed in the empty restroom.

"Mae, I'm in here. My brace strap broke. I can't unlatch the door."

Mae squirmed under the stall door. Bits of toilet tissue feathered her teal dress. The two struggled to get Rosaria to her feet. "This will never work," Mae determined as she lowered her whimpering niece back onto the toilet seat. "I'll get Mort."

"No! No! I can't have everyone know."

"I'll put an out-of-order sign on the door. Stay calm, I'll be back in a jiff." Mae approached her boss, who was in the middle of a priest, rabbi, and minister joke. "Mort," she whispered, wearing a tense smile, "We have a crisis in the ladies' room."

"Flooding toilet?"

"Flooding teen."

The bang from the door opening startled Rosaria. "The cavalry has arrived!" Mort sang out. Rosaria knew he was attempting to make light of her predicament to put her at ease, but it only served to heighten her embarrassment. "Hum," Mort said, stroking his chin. "This calls for surgical intervention. Fortunately, I come from a long line of cutters and stitchers. I'm going to remove your brace, sew the strap back on, and reinforce the other frayed one."

"I'll show you how to remove the brace, Mr. Bloomfield."

"That's Dr. Bloomfield to you, Miss. If I can figure out how to unhook a bra while blindfolded in the backseat of my old man's Caddie, I can tangle with a leg brace. Ain't that right, Mae?"

"This is no time to clown around."

"You hear that, Rosaria? She called me a clown. Mae, you're fired." Mort bent down in front of the red-eyed Rosaria. "This is just a small setback; don't try to do it all on your own. People don't help out of pity, but from past experiences. We've all found ourselves on the floor of a public toilet at one time or another. Welcome to the club. Sit tight, I'll be back in five, make that three minutes."

Mae folded her arms and tapped her toes. There was an edge in her voice. "So, you had trouble getting to your feet. You should have asked one of the girls for help. Yes, Rosaria, I saw them. Tell me something, had one of them needed help, would you walk away? Step over her? I'm disappointed in you, letting pride put you in jeopardy of injuring yourself."

"I'm back! This strap will hold for the rest of your life," Mort predicted in a Groucho Marx voice, wiggling an invisible cigar.

"And if your life is as long as those legs, you'll live to one hundred."

"Mr. Bloomfield, I'm so embarrassed. I can't pull up my panties."

"Put your arms around my neck." Mort lifted her off the seat as Mae hoisted up Rosaria's underpants. "Don't upset yourself," Mort joked. "I've seen kinkier goings on in this bathroom, ain't that right, Mae?"

"Wise ass."

"Wise ass! You're fired again. I'll see you ladies out here."

Rosaria wiped her weeping eyes with toilet tissue. "He probably can't wait for me to go home so he can enjoy the party without looking after a pathetic cripple."

"Pathetic cripple? Mort doesn't think you're pathetic. He thinks you're darn lucky."

"Me? Lucky?"

Mae removed the out-of-order sign from the door. "Mort's nephew is in an iron lung. Stop feeling sorry for yourself; it's unbecoming. I'll let Carla know we're leaving."

Rosaria timidly slid out of the bathroom. Head lowered, brooding, she took a seat at the refreshment table. Its long tablecloth provided cover for her leg. Biting her lip, she fixed her red-rimmed eyes on the ceiling. Carla tsked and shook her head. "Louie should be here soon."

"Don't pity her. If she's upset, it's her own fault."

Carla broke into a broad smile. "Will you look who's here, it's Patsy!" Carla waved her son over. The eighteen-year-old stomped snow off his pointed black boots and shook snow out of his thick, dark hair.

"Patsy? Little Patsy?" The boy blushed at Mae's description, hoping she'd mistaken his bashful blush for windburn.

"You remember Mae Rourke?"

"Sure do. I had a major crush on you when I was a kid."

Carla's eyes combed the crowded factory floor. Where's your father?"

"Papa's at the club, says he's on a winning streak, sent me to pick you up."

"I'll get our coats." Mae walked to the makeshift coatroom.

"You're giving Mae and her niece a ride home to Dorchester."

"Dorchester! That's the other side of town!"

Carla reprimanded her son with a slap to the back of his head. "Idiota."

"Who's that?"

"Who's who?"

Patsy pointed out Rosaria with his chin. "The doll in the green dress."

"The young lady is Mae's niece, Rosaria."

"Excuse me."

One hand in his pants pocket jiggling the car keys, the fingers of his other hand combing through his hair, Patsy casually strode over to the coffee urn as if he'd just happened to be passing by. "Say, aren't you Mae Rourke's niece?"

Rosaria fluttered her lashes to mask her puffy lids. His eyes were a rich brown, his hair too long, his jeans too tight, and the leather jacket was worn to impress his peers. Rosaria held out her hand. Patsy removed his from the jeans pocket. "I'm

Carla's son, Patsy." Her hand was soft, his cold. "I shoulda worn gloves. I'm giving you a lift home."

"We planned to take a taxi."

"In this weather? Wouldn't hear of it."

"Have you ever been to Dorchester?"

"Sure, I guess so. I mean, I think I might have been there... who hasn't?"

"I've never been to East Boston."

"Not even to the airport?"

"I've never flown."

Patsy dragged over a metal folding chair, turning and straddling it. "My folks sent me to Italy last year. I guess it's some rite of passage. Come to find out, they planned on marrying me off to a cousin. This bro... girl was big, sweaty, and had a mustache. They'll nevah get me on a plane again!"

Rosaria laughed into a napkin.

"You got a terrific smile, don't cover it... So, um, you go to Dorchester High?"

"No."

"Yeah, I figured you for a Catholic schoolgirl."

"I've graduated. I planned to attend college in January but had apprehensions."

"Yeah, I was apprehended once for skippin' school, but I still finished the school year."

"You have a marvelous sense of humor." Rosaria complimented, running her fingers over her pearl necklace, unknowingly directing Patsy's eyes to her chest.

"That's a pretty necklace."

Blood poured from her face to her neck. "They're imitation."

"They look real on you." Patsy turned his attention to the geriatric orchestra. "I think it's time The Royal Canadians headed back to the border. We need our dance music. I've got an idea." Patsy walked across the dance floor.

She watched as he exchanged words with a group of teens. A wave of panic drowned out the excitement Patsy had planted. "He wasn't told!" she gasped into her cupped hands.

"Hey Rosie!" Patsy called across the room. "One of those cats has a radio in his locker; he's gone to get it. Nobody is tellin' us we can't play our dance music. Let them old fogies sit it out," he said, holding his arms out to her.

Rosaria lowered her head. "I can't."

"No problem. I'll teach ya. I'm a pretty good dancer if I may say so myself." Rosaria lifted the tablecloth, exposing her caged leg. "Oh, um, well, that's okay. We can listen to the music and talk about somethin'."

The couple sat in silence, watching the other teens rock to "Little Bitty Pretty One." Patsy's foot kept time to the music. Rosaria raised her head as the air filled with the sound of Skip and Flip's "Cherry Pie." Patsy sat snapping his fingers to the swing beat. Her mind was made up. She wasn't going to deprive herself of being held in the arms of a boy who wanted to dance with her, not because she was a great dancer or Margo's sister, but in his eyes, she was pretty, interesting, and fun.

"Patsy, teach me to dance."

Carla turned to Mae. "Look at Casanova up there. I think Rosie has come out of her shell."

Mae lit a cigarette. "It's going to be a long night, one long overdue."

"It's the phone. I bet it's Ronny. Are you going to answer it?" Colleen asked, itching to witness a fight.

Margo continued to brush her hair one hundred strokes before bedtime. "Let it ring."

"No way, I'm answering it."

Margo dropped her brush. "Great, you made me lose count. Bring the phone over here." Colleen held out the pink princess phone. "Margo Ronan speaking. Yes, I understand." Margo tick-tocked her head from side to side. "I do hope it's not a case of alcohol poisoning; it's been going around." She twirled the phone cord around her index finger. "Thank you, Mrs. Kilday, and Merry Christmas to you as well." Margo slammed down the phone. "Dear Ronald, is ill. He's either drunk or with some floozie. So help me, if he were here, I'd shoot his balls off. This is the worst Christmas of my life."

"Mine too."

"Why? You have nothing to live for."

"Now that I can dance, I wanted to go to the Junior High Christmas Dance."

"Why didn't you go?"

"I wasn't asked."

"Rosaria goes to dances unescorted; plenty of girls do. No one finds it strange."

"I'd be the only one unescorted." Margo reached into her night table and took out a deck of playing cards.

"Just my luck," Colleen groused, "Spending Christmas Eve playing Go Fish with an Old Maid."

"Shut up and deal."

"Shhhh, you hear that?"

"It's Rosaria."

"Slow down, you'll break your neck on those stairs," Berta cautioned a euphoric Rosaria, who ignored the warning.

"Has Margo returned home?"

"She never went out."

The two luckless sisters scrambled out to the staircase balcony. "Margo, Colleen!" Rosaria cried out. "I met a boy. He asked me out for New Year's Eve!"

"What did you tell him?"

Margo whacked Colleen on the back of the head. "Shut up and get in my room."

Rosaria followed, closing the door, not wanting their mother to hear. "Say, why aren't you out with Ronny?"

"Long story. Let's hear about this boy." Sitting on Margo's bed, Rosaria recounted the evening to her dateless sisters.

"I had just experienced a dreadful episode trapped in the restroom with a torn brace strap. Mr. Bloomfield repaired it and assisted me in pulling up my underpants. I wanted to die. Then Carla's son arrived to drive us home, and my life changed in an instant."

"Carla? Isn't she the fat lady?" Margo asked.

"She's not only a lady but a loving wife and mother who makes a great lasagna."

"I'll be sure to let Betty Crocker know. So, what does he look like, and please don't say he's a tub of lard like his mother."

Colleen sat with her hands clasped tightly around her knees, listening intently to the Cinderella story. "Yeah, what does he look like?"

"Frankie Avalon."

Margo's voice dropped. "NO!"

"Yes! He walked right up to me and introduced himself. Carla didn't put him up to it. His name is Pasquale, but everyone calls him Patsy. He's witty and very easy to talk to." Colleen and Margo huddled together, relishing every detail. "He wasn't made aware of my paralysis, so when he asked me to dance, I declined and showed him my leg. What song do you think was playing?"

"What? What?" The two sisters sang out.

"Cherry Pie!"

Margo rejoiced, falling back on her pillow with both hands over her heart. "It's true love! I couldn't have scripted it better."

Berta's voice thundered from below. "Mass tomorrow, 7 am. Do you hear me?"

The announcement was ignored. "While we shared a slow dance, he asked if I had plans for New Year's Eve."

"Boy," Margo brooded. "I wish I'd been there instead of waiting for that idiot to call."

"But you were there."

Margo cocked her head. "I don't get it."

"When Patsy asked me to dance, I declined. Then I thought, "What would Margo do?" I got up and I danced. I may have looked foolish, but I didn't care."

"Now you know how Colleen feels every day of her life."

Colleen twisted her mouth to one side.

"Remind me to laugh."

Rosaria giggled. "Mom's right; it's late. We had better get to bed. Christmas tomorrow!"

Colleen tiptoed to the bedroom door, sneaking a peek at her jubilant sister making her way down to her bedroom, humming "Cherry Pie." Pulling her shoulders to her ears, she flashed a Cheshire smile and plunged next to Margo on the bed. "Remember when I said this was the worst Christmas ever? I changed my mind. It's the best!"

"Mine too, swamp monkey, mine too."

Chapter Nine

"I'll get the phone," Colleen hollered.

"Colleen?"

"Ronny!"

"How was your Christmas?"

"It was swell. You'll never guess what happened."

"Margo tore up my picture?"

"Besides that."

"Fill me in."

"Rosaria has a boyfriend."

"She has!"

"They met at a Christmas party."

"I want to meet this Prince Charming. Maybe we can double date."

"Only if it's for a long walk off a short pier."

"I'm in the doghouse?"

"She's sending you to the pound."

"Didn't Margo get the flowers I sent?"

"She got them and threw them in the trash. My mother took them out and threw the vase at Margo."

"Is that him?" Margo snapped. Colleen handed her the phone. "Get lost. Get out of my life and leave my family alone."

"Colleen told me the good news. Why don't the four of us go out?"

"You haven't heard a word I said. IT'S OVER!"

"One stinking mistake and it's over?"

"It wasn't one mistake. It was Christmas Eve. You were going to announce our engagement."

"I have the ring, I'll drive over. We can tell your folks and set a date."

Margo cupped her hands over the receiver and deepened her voice. "You just thank your lucky stars, brother. I could have gone to the police plenty of times. I'm not your girl or your punching bag."

"I've sworn off the booze. I'll never take another drink."

"And you'll never lay another hand on me. We're history."

"I don't want to touch your body because every other guy in town already has. You make me look like a sucker. Well, suck on this."

The phone came down hard on her ear.

"That was Ronny, wasn't it?"

"Stay out of it, Ma."

"You think you're too good for him."

"Yes, I do."

"Pride goes before a fall."

Margo wiggled her fingers at her mother. "And the fall goes before a winter."

"You'll come to regret letting that man go."

"What I regret is not going to New York or Hollywood when I got out of high school."

"Nuala, you're only eighteen, you may have looks, but you don't have two nickels to rub together. Get off your ass and get a job. Your sister has been working since she was fourteen. Rosaria could cry "Poor me, " but she has self-respect, not just a pretty face. What little money you do make goes toward clothes and makeup."

"Those clothes and makeup are like money in the bank."

"Real money is in a bank. Open an account."

"If you had allowed us to go on Bandstand, I'd be famous by now, married to some nightclub singer. We won that contest. You stole our lives, deprived Rosaria of her day in the sun, have people see her dance on national TV, have it on film."

Berta raised her hand. Margo stuck out her chin, welcoming the blow. "Don't beat me because you're angry at yourself."

***

"Help your father shovel," Vera ordered her son. Ronny took his overcoat from the hall closet. A silver flask slid out of its pocket.

"I suggest you stop drinking."

"I suggest you go sit under your albino Christmas tree." Ronny insulted with a cigarette dangling from his lips.

Stomping snow from his boots and tossing his leather gloves over the entryway's grated radiator, Conrad Kilday reprimanded his son. "Since I didn't receive a snowblower for Christmas, the least my son could do is give me a hand with the shoveling, but you're hungover."

"Conrad, speak to the boy."

"I'll give it another try, Vera," he groaned. "It's for the best, son."

"I love her. I've dated lots of girls, but Margo is special."

"Listen to your father. At your age, all you see is a pair of legs and a tight sweater. Trust me, after a few children, those assets will be a distant memory. You'll find all you have in common are the children, half Ronan."

"Meaning?"

"The girl has dollar signs in her eyes; you have stars in yours. Open them and take a good look at her family. None of them have gone further than high school, if that. Her father vacations at the funny farm, and Rosaria, that poor thing, makes people uncomfortable."

"People? No, you're uncomfortable, and Rosaria is neither poor nor a thing. You're a vain, pretentious bitch."

"Ronald!"

"No, Dad, that could be me in a brace. You may not approve of the Ronans, but they're a family I'd be proud to be a member of."

"Listen, Son, Margo doesn't want to see you. She'd rather stay behind and live the same existence as her parents. Let her go, she wants it that way, and so do we."

"If you have a problem with the neighborhood they live in, you're to blame. I'm going out."

"Ronald, wait," his father said. "We have to talk. It's not about Margo."

Ronny slumped into a blue toile-upholstered wingback chair. Vera backed out of the study, closing its pocket doors. Conrad clasped his hands behind his back and paced as he had ten years earlier, relaying the facts of life to his son, who not only knew them but had already put them into practice. "Son, I know everyone thinks bankers and realtors are the big bad wolves wanting to blow their houses down, but that's not our intention. We're here to help families like the Ronans achieve the American Dream, the same one your mother and I afforded you."

"By manipulating the market? Dad, I'm aware of what's been going on around the Mount and along Blue Hill Ave. the people who live there; they don't want to leave."

"Please, allow me to explain. Up until ten, maybe twenty years ago, there weren't many Negroes living in Boston; now they're coming up in droves for the jobs, who can blame them? They settled in the slums surrounding downtown, same as our people did when they first came over, but we got out, bought homes farther away. No one helped us. No, sir, we did it by the sweat of our brows, scrimped, saved, no handouts for us. The Negroes aren't capable of that. Our intention is to help them get out of the tenements and into good homes in safe neighborhoods."

"But not safe enough for Whites?"

"These people would have migrated eventually; we're just speeding up the process by giving them low interest rates on homes in neighborhoods Whites don't want to live in, the Jewish neighborhood."

"If the Jews won't sell?"

"They'll sell and sell cheap. You think they want to live next door to the people we're bringing in? The Irish will stick around for as long as the church does; they don't want to leave their parish. Frankly, I don't care if they stay put; most of them are carrying a mortgage. We're making money, but the Jews own their homes outright; we don't make a dime off of them; it's dead real estate. Some Jew do-gooders will throw out the welcome mat for the Negroes, while the rest of them run out the back door to the high-end suburbs. When they do move, and they've already started, they'll have to take out a mortgage. In the end, the Irish, Jews, and Negroes will all owe the banks. We're going to profit from this game of domino's by buying up the property the Negroes leave behind for pennies on the dollar."

"Slums?"

"Not for long. The city is due for a rejuvenation. When the time comes, they'll need to expand, and we'll be sitting on all that property. We can name our price, and the city will pay it. I'll tell you what happens to the Ronans. They keep their house, the girls marry and move away, leaving their mother with a big house in a bad neighborhood, and when she does decide to sell, the house won't be worth what she owes on it. I'm sorry, Ronald, the Ronans bought the wrong house at the wrong time in the wrong neighborhood."

***

The closet was orderly; dresses hung on padded hangers, light colors to dark, short sleeves to long, casual to formal. Once polished, Rosaria's shoes were returned to their tissued boxes. "I don't know how you find anything in this closet; it's so neat," Margo remarked from behind a garment bag.

"I cede to your judgment. Patsy complimented the green dress you chose."

"They all do when you first meet."

"You don't know Patsy, he's honest and sincere."

"Won't you please try on my red cocktail dress?"

"It's a lovely dress, but only you can pull off wearing it."

"And I have. So, we're back to square one. Where did he say he was taking you?" Margo asked, throwing rejected garments on the bed.

"I said, where is he ..." Margo was stopped mid-sentence by her sister's tears. "Hey, what brought this on?"

Rosaria dropped onto the bed. "He...I haven't heard from him since Christmas Day. I thought maybe this time..." Margo rocked her weeping sister in her arms. "If Mae likes him, and you love him, then he's a keeper."

"Why hasn't he called?"

"Call him. Ask him if you're still on. If he says no, put Ma on the phone."

"I would never call a boy."

"I always called Ronny to chew him out."

119

"Gee whiz, why won't you give Ronny another chance? We all like him, even Mom."

"To be honest, I've been waiting for an excuse to dump him. There's another side to Ronny, I know what I'm doing."

***

There was no mistaking Dominic Travellas' white El Dorado illegally parked in front of his parents' brick rowhouse. Patsy left his buddies on the corner and raced home. Nicky sat at the kitchen table scanning a racing form, his sports jacket slung over the back of his chair. Dominic Travella never wore an overcoat. Patsy staggered through the apartment door. "Nicky, I need a favor," he wheezed.

"No."

"I ain't even asked!"

"The answer is still no."

"I don't need your car. What I need is a reservation for New Year's Eve at a nice restaurant."

"What do I look like, a maître d'?" Nicky threw his car keys at his brother.

"It's easier to give you my car than get you a table on New Year's Eve."

"Aw, come on, you know people."

"Look, kid, the only place I can get you a table is at Rozzella's. It's owned by a couple of queers. The fat one owes me money. I'll give him a call, tell him to give my brother and his girl a real nice table on New Year's Eve, or his balls will be on the menu New Year's Day."

"That would be swell... gettin' the table, I mean." Patsy tossed the keys back to his brother, who caught them without looking up from his stats. "Say, you really like this girl."

"Sure do."

Standing, Nicky dug into his back pocket and peeled a couple of tens off a roll of bills. "You're gonna need serious cash at that place. I scored on the Celtics-Pistons game last week. Tip everyone on the way out, you got that. No, embarassin' me."

"I can't pay this back."

"Happy birthday."

"My birthday's July first."

"I might drop dead tomorrow- keep it." Patsy gave his brother a hug.

"Enough already. Save it for your girl. Now get out of here."

"Rosie, it's Patsy." Rosaria waved her sisters to the phone.

"Hello, Patsy."

"I got us a six o'clock reservation at Rozella's. I hope that's not too early for you, but it being New Year's and all ..."

"Six will be fine. I'm not familiar with that venue; it sounds posh."

"It's a restaurant. It sounds Italian."

"What do you suggest I wear?"

"You looked swell in that green dress. I'm not sayin' you should wear it, but if you did, you'd be a sight for sore eyes. I figure I'd get to your house around four-thirty; give me time to meet your family."

Margo held up five fingers. "Perhaps you should arrive at five."

"Five it is."

"I look forward to seeing you again."

"Me too, I mean, seeing you, not me seeing me."

Rosaria laughed. "I get it."

"Ya not gonna go and change your mind or anything?"

"Never."

Margo twirled in place. "Oh, my God. He's so polite. Ma is going to love him."

Colleen sprinted downstairs to the kitchen. "Ma, Ma, Rosaria's date wants to meet us when he comes to pick her up."

"He better."

"Margo's dates don't come to the door."

"Ronny did, but he was a gentleman, not Nuala's type."

***

Swaying her highly teased black hair, Salina circled her suited little brother. "Not bad. I'd even step out with you." Her father voiced his objections from the next room. "You don't see a man without my say so."

Patsy closed his bedroom door. "You gotta tell him. It's New Year's, you and Bobby ought to be spendin' it together, as husband and wife. Papa knows Bobby's a good guy. You've been alone too long."

"Not for Papa."

"Vincent's been dead three years; the twins need a father. Papa doesn't have the fight left in him."

"That's what worries me. I don't want to give him a heart attack, and Mama's got the sugar. If they get cancer, I can't go through it again."

"Here I am lookin' forward to my date, and you have to start with the cancer." Salina removed the handkerchief from Patsy's suit jacket and blew her nose. "I know," she conceded, brushing off the back of his jacket. "I'll tell them tonight."

Carla replaced the missing handkerchief with one pressed knife sharp. "She's a good girl; don't get fresh with her."

"I'm a good boy, tonight."

"I'm warning you. Now go," she said with a push to his back. Carla returned to her kitchen. "Will you be ringing in 1961 with us?"

"Yeah," Salina answered. "I'll bring the girls over around nine. How's the leg?"

"Mine or Rosaria's?" Carla asked, making light of the diabetes eating away at her foot.

"Hers."

"Bad, but she gets around. It's her heart that concerns me. Mae tells me Rosaria has never been on a date. She's very shy. If he breaks her heart, I'll rip out his."

Patsy rang the doorbell, withdrawing his finger as if he'd touched a hot stove. Colleen clamored for the door. Margo grabbed her by the hair. "OOW!"

"What did I tell you? A lady doesn't answer on the first ring."

"Go find yourself a lady." Colleen flung the door open. "Rosaria! Your date is here." Margo meandered into the room. "Forgive my little sister, she's been raised by wolves. I'm Margo, and this is Colleen."

"Nice to meet you both. I'm Patsy Travella. If your parents are at home, I'd like to meet them."

Margo flipped her hair off her shoulder. "I'll inform them of your arrival."

Once out of Patsy's sight, Margo raced into the kitchen. "Ma, he's here. Hurry up, I don't want to leave him alone with Colleen."

Berta wasn't what Pasty expected. She didn't share Mae's soft, fair features; hers were dark, strong, her authoritarian bearing was more imposing than the house. Patsy stood at attention. "Mrs. Ronan, I'm Patsy Travella," he stated, offering his hand.

"Yes," Berta responded with an open hand and a smile. "Rosaria and Mae speak highly of you. They're both a good judge of character."

"Rosaria's dad?"

"I'm on my way up." Emerging from the basement, Tim wiped his soiled hands on his pants and shook Patsy's. "I've been replacing a faulty fuse."

"You're a Navy man," Patsy noted.

"How did ja know?"

"The tattoo." Tim looked down at the anchor imprinted on his hairless bicep.

"I served on the USS Phelps. Spent most of the war off the Philippines."

"My dad was in the Merchant Marine."

"Couldn't have won it without them."

Pasty looked up at Rosaria, cautiously descending the stately staircase, a vision in the green velvet dress. His impulse was to help her down, but he took his cue from the family, who seemed not to notice her slow descent. Patsy met her at the foot of the stairs, holding her arm by the elbow and her stare with his heavy-lidded eyes, causing Rosaria to blush. "I feared you may have gotten lost."

"Not a chance."

The thrill she felt having Patsy hold open her mink-trimmed coat was snuffed out by Margo buttoning her in, a task Rosaria could perform, and Margo knew it.

"It was sure nice to meet you. Maybe next time, I mean, you know."

Rosaria came to his rescue. "We wouldn't want to lose our reservation."

Patsy awkwardly shook Berta's hand with his right and Tim's with his left. "Happy New Year."

Berta looked out of a street-facing window, watching her daughter being escorted to a shiny Chevy. "He's no more than a boy."

Margo slowly shook her head. "Boy or not, he's nice, polite, and very good-looking."

"Give him a few years, and he'll be as big as his mother."

***

124

"My, this is a very sharp automobile," Rosaria complimented.

"It's my sister's car, she bought it off her neighbor, Needles."

"Oh dear, is he an opium addict?"

"Nah, his folks died when he was a kid. His aunt got stuck with him. This Needles, he's got a car dealership and a crush on Salina."

"What a beautiful name; it's so exotic."

"She's gonna love you, that's if she lives to see tomorrow. Tonight, she's gonna break the news that she eloped. My Pa is going to deck her."

"He wouldn't do that...would he?"

"No."

"My mother would."

"Looks like I won't be needin' the ladder I got in the trunk." The thought of eloping made Rosaria feel beautiful, desirable, and loved.

"Why did Salina elope?"

"My brother-in-law Vincent died three years ago from cancer. He left twin girls, Brook and Lynn. Vincent was from New York. Salina is supposed to still be in mourning, but Vincent was so sick for so long, she deserves to be happy, and it ain't ... it isn't like Bobby and her just met; they went to high school together. My folks know he's a good guy, but Papa says it doesn't look good. I say, what's the point of them living apart? Marriage is all about sharing your life with someone you love, can't wait to get home to, and let everyone know what a lucky guy you are." Rosaria imagined Patsy coming home to her, wanting people to see them together. He was aware of Tim's condition, yet treated him with respect. "Patsy, I want to thank you for the way you behaved toward my father."

"What do you mean?"

"You know what I'm referring to."

"Hey, everyone has their weakness. Take my Pa and my brother Dominic. They like to gamble. See, with drinking, you've got a limit to how much you can drink before you kill yourself, but with gambling, you go over your limit, and someone else kills you. Pa, he plays for fun, but Nicky's in deep; that's all he does, no job, just cards and sports betting. He's wasting his life. Your dad's not violent?"

"Far from it. Poppy is a pussy cat. I'm a daddy's girl; he means the world to me."

"That must be a great world to live in, having a girl like you. He's a lucky guy."

"I'm lucky to have him."

The car pulled off the exit ramp. "Nicky says this is a great restaurant; he ought to know, he's out every night. Will ya look at this place!" said an awestruck Patsy as he drove around the circular drive to a waiting valet. Rosaria's eyes glistened. "It looks like a castle! I've never been to such an elegant restaurant," she marveled, much to her date's relief, one short-lived as the two looked up at the long, winding steps leading to the entrance. "I'm sorry, Rosie, I had no idea."

"We can dine somewhere else."

"There is nowhere else! We are dining here." Jumping out of the car, Patsy opened the passenger door and scooped her up into his arms. "Rosie, one thing you've got to know about me, I always keep my promises." Mae's prediction had come true; there was someone out there to love and protect her. She was in his arms.

Chapter Ten

"You're home early. Did they fire you?" Berta asked in a monotone voice.

Margo put her nose in the air. "I quit that measly job."

"Isn't that dandy?"

"Fear not, I am one step closer to stardom," Margo announced while dancing a calypso around her mother and aunt.

"You had a good job, good pay, and an employee discount, and you threw it away for what? A dream that won't come true?"

"That's where you're wrong. I'll no longer be selling cosmetics to old women who want to look young. I'm on television!"

"How exciting!" Mae rejoiced.

"You're looking at the WHBN weather depicter." Berta rolled up her sleeves and reached into the broom closet, home to the leather strap.

"Ma, Ma, before you beat me, just listen. This real dreamy guy comes to my counter, tells me he's a talent scout, says he's been watching me, and I'm just the girl they're looking for in the news department."

"You won't be on the news. You'll be in it."

"You haven't heard the best part; I'll be working alongside Zip DeWolf; he's a meteorologist—that's what weathermen are called in the industry. Zip predicts the weather. I, on the other hand, depict the weather. It's a concept developed by my boss, Mr. Mac Godfrey."

"McGodfrey or MacGodfrey?"

"Mac, I guess. That's the name he goes by, Mr. Mac. None of the other outlets has a depicter. That's what we in the business call TV stations, outlets. See! I've already picked up the lingo!"

"You'll be picking up your intestines if you don't march back to Filenes and beg for your job back. That man is exploiting you. I know about WHBN. Catholics are forbidden to watch that station, excuse me, outlet."

"I won't be depicting for long because some big Hollywood producer will come to town, a non-Catholic producer, see me depicting and say, "That's her! That's the girl for my next blockbuster. Look how she makes love to the camera."

Berta wagged the strap. "You can start by kissing this."

"Mr. Mac speaks French. He says I have what the French call 'An air of savoir-faire.' He used some other French words, 'Jenny says something.' It means I'm as beautiful on the inside as I am on the outside."

"Your boss can see your beautiful insides because I'm going to... what's the French word? Ah, yes, disembowel you."

"I knew you would say that, so I signed a contract."

"You did, did you?"

"Yes, I did."

"Mr. Mac, does he know your age?"

"Of course, he does. "

"Then he must know you can't enter into a contract until you're twenty-one. He'll need my consent, and I won't give it. So, tell that mountain miser he can blow that contract out of his bagpipe."

"I can work, drive, get married, have kids, but I can't sign a crummy piece of paper?"

"And you can't drink or vote because you're irresponsible. Would you, perchance, have a copy of the contract?"

"If you must know... "

"Oh, I must."

"Mr. Mac has it. He didn't want me to lose it."

"Did he give you a business card?" Reaching into her jacket pocket, Margo handed the card to her mother, who read it at arm's length. "Mangus M, MacGodfrey Jr., WHBN, Washburn Place, Boston, Mass. I'm going to pay a visit to Mr. Mangus M. MacGodfrey."

***

WHBN lay buried deep in South Boston's warehouse district. The six-story Arcadia Building housed a footwear manufacturer, a restaurant equipment wholesaler, a floundering printing company, and a colony of pigeons that left their down and droppings on the perpetually slick street.

"Good thing I know how to drive a manual," Tim said as he cranked the elevator's brass lever handle. "These old cage elevators make me feel like a canary choking my way out of a coal mine." Bouncing to a halt on the fifth floor, Tim pulled the grated accordion door open to a lobby befitting a modern-day television station. The silver call letters were affixed to the dark paneled wall above a reception desk flanked by large rubber tree plants. Uncomfortable amid the high-end surroundings, Tim rubbed his palms on his thighs. "I'll wait in the car."

"You stay put," Berta ordered in a low voice. Tim retreated to an olive-green vinyl chair situated next to a pedestal ashtray overflowing with butts and chewing gum wrappers.

"They need a cleaning lady, not a depicter," Tim mumbled.

"Not to worry, I'm going to mop the floor with this character." Wearing a threatening smile and a navy-blue pencil-skirted suit that emphasized her narrow figure, Berta approached the dowdy receptionist. The girl's stringy, light brown hair was tucked behind her oversized ears; her smile was pleasant, and her nails were immaculate. It was her eyes, Berta found intriguing, both moonstone blue, one lacking a pupil.

"Would Mr. Mac Godfrey be available to speak with me? I'm Berta... Roberta Ronan."

"You're the depicter's mother!" Without asking what business Berta had with her boss, the exuberant girl came out from behind the counter. "Wait till you meet him! You can't help but love him. I caught a glimpse of Mr. Mac over on Stage One." She motioned for Berta to follow her as if they were children sneaking under a circus tent. Berta's suspicions proved accurate as they drew closer to the Ring Master. The awestruck girl timidly tapped her idol's hunched shoulder.

If a human could be feral, Mac was a tomcat. He didn't live on earth; he roamed it carrying the scent of where he'd been. His hair was long, not beatnik long to convey a message, but from neglect. He stood slump-shouldered like a scarecrow crucified in a Kansas cornfield. Berta sized him up as a mad genius, passing as a plainspoken fool. "Mr. Mac, I hate to interrupt you." Mac slammed his pen down on his clipboard.

"Iris, what is your problem aside from the obvious?"

"This is Berta, Roberta Ronan."

"Mrs. Ronan!" he welcomed with a crooked, insincere smile. "What a pleasure to finally meet you. Iris, get lost."

"Yes, Mr. Mac. Is there anything else I can do for you?"

"You heard me, scram." Like a cow with its curd, Mac chomped on a stick of gum, watching the receptionist walk away.

"Check it out," he said with a nudge to Berta's side. "Her real name is Doris. She still doesn't get it."

Berta's face lost all expression. "I don't suffer fools gladly, Mr. Mac Godfrey."

"Ya what?"

"Saint Paul, 2 Corinthians, Chapter 19, Verse 11."

"And I don't suffer dysentery gladly. Saint Louis, 2 Corndogs, Month 7, year 53."

"You, sir, are a very sick man."

"I'm over it. So, what can I do for you?"

"What you can do is hand over any paperwork my daughter signed and take that gum out of your mouth, or you won't have a tooth left in your head."

Mac held out his hands as if straightening a picture frame. "Amazing, the resemblance is striking. Now I know where your daughter gets her good looks."

Berta squeezed her eyes like a dog about to attack. "Is that your office?" she asked through clenched teeth.

Mac turned to the frosted glass door. "That, my dear lady, is the nerve center of WHBN, but we don't want to conduct business in there," he said, crinkling his nose. "The cleaning lady passed on; the office is rather disheveled, and when I find a shovel, I'll bury her."

Berta opened the door. "Get in and tuck your shirt tails in; you look like an unmade bed."

Mac gave a mock salute. "Yes, Ma'am."

"Wipe that smirk off your face and close the door."

"Whoa, whoa, let's play nice."

Berta sniffed the air. "I smell a wet dog."

"Glad you brought the subject up, Berta. May I call you Berta?"

"No, you may not."

"In time, perhaps. As I was saying, this is a cutthroat business, Berta, dog-eat-dog. It's the blood, sweat, and tears I put into this station you smell."

Berta leaned forward, pressing her palms on the desk's ink blotter that absorbed more coffee than ink. "Listen, you mangy mutt. If you lay a paw on my daughter, I'll neuter you."

"It appears we've gotten off on the wrong foot. I want to assure you I'd never take advantage of your daughter or compromise her dignity; that would be counterproductive. I hired Nuala to bring class and respectability back to this station. When people think of WHBN, I want the word purity to come to mind."

Berta's eyes zeroed in on a girlie calendar fixed on the wall behind him. Mac jumped to his feet. "What the, I'm sorry you've been exposed to such depravity. We just moved into this space. The former tenant left it behind. I asked that it be removed, but as I explained, we lost our cleaning lady, and by golly, every time I reach up to take it down, I'm called away."

"According to Miss March, you moved in last week. Nuala will not work at a station that's been condemned by the Archdiocese."

"My point exactly. Look, I won't sugarcoat this. It's the advertisers who pay the bills. We only have two. One for jock itch, the other a laxative. 'Get Up and Go.' They may as well call it 'Get Up and Turn the Channel.' Berta, I know what you're thinking, who gives a crap? Well, I do. But once the lovely Nuala joins the WHBN family, the advertisers will beat a path to the door. We both know Nuala wasn't hired for her brains; on the contrary, the less she has, the better. I'm what's known as a female aficionado, and your daughter has the whole package. No one is going to change the channel while she's on the screen."

"I'm leaving. But not without the contract. I won't be hoodwinked by a sleazy Scot."

"Don't judge me by my surname, I'm a very generous man with an open heart and open wallet who cares for my employees and the community we serve."

"My daughter is a minor; the only thing you'll be serving is a prison sentence."

Head bowed, Mac listened and smiled. "There you have it, the mark of a kind, caring mother who looks on everyone as her child. I bet you're a great cook. Why don't I come by for dinner? Wednesday good for you? By the way, I'm allergic to shellfish."

"Mr. Mac Godfrey, I didn't come here to cook your dinner, decorate your office, or listen to jokes. What I want—"

"What you want is to discuss money." Berta took a handkerchief from her handbag and wiped down the chair's seat.

"I'm listening."

"Some things are best put in writing." Mac scribbled numbers on a coffee-stained sheet of paper and slid it across the desk.

"This is what I agree to pay your daughter."

Berta held the paper at arm's length. "You write like a Chinaman."

Mac took the agreement from her hands. "Allow me. One hundred dollars per television appearance plus monetary compensation for advertising and station promotions. That comes to roughly thirty clams an hour. You're not allergic to shellfish, are you?"

***

The car door slammed. "Margo, it's Mom!" Rosaria called out. The excitement in her voice fell. "She doesn't look pleased."

"She's never happy," Margo pouted. Mae and the girls anxiously waited at the front door.

Berta tossed her hat and gloves onto a nearby chair. "Since when am I so popular?"

"Since you hold my future in your hands," said Margo, waving crossed fingers.

"He wanted you to start out on the weekend broadcast, but I wasn't going to have you miss Mass, so you'll be on Monday through Friday."

"You signed?"

"Yes," Berta quickly snapped, not wanting to explain her decision.

"I love you, Ma," Margo squealed. "You won't regret this. I'll make you proud."

Tim passed his wife on the way to the kitchen. "She'll have that phone tied up all night."

Rosaria gave her mother a wary look. "What possessed you to sign the contract? That's not like you."

"Mr. Mac Godfrey is aware of the station's reputation. He feels that having a sweet, wholesome girl like your sister will improve its image. I was assured she wouldn't be asked to do anything inappropriate, and she'll be making more money in one year than your father made in ten."

***

"Nuala! Our star! Welcome aboard. I spoke with your mother, a force to be reckoned with, but I reckon I forced her." Mac placed a fatherly arm around Margo's shoulder. "Come into my office. I've got papers for you to fill out," Mac said as he walked over to a file cabinet. "Don't be shy, come in, take a seat. I want you to consider this office as a second home."

"If I lived in an outhouse. What's that smell?"

"Chip off the old block, you are."

Margo snatched the paper from Mac's hand and a pen from the desk. "Where do I sign? I'm going to throw up."

"Here, here, and there." Mac looked the document over and rubbed his hands. "Good, good. Now, let's mosey on over to the wardrobe. I'll introduce you to Iola; she'll be making your costumes."

"My what?"

"Costumes. Ya know the get-up you'll be wearing."

"I am an actress, not a showgirl."

"Listen, sweetheart... "

"I'm not your sweetheart or your depicter."

"Okay, you're an actress. I'm giving you the opportunity to learn about the business from the ground up, get your face and a couple of other assets in front of the camera. It's called method acting. All the stars in New York are into it, and like a movie star, I'm giving you a stage name. Henceforth, you shall be known as Sunny Shine."

"My mother was right. You are a dirty weirdo. You promised her you wouldn't make a fool out of me. If she sees me on TV in a flimsy get-up, she'll brain me." Margo pushed past Mac. "Too-Da-Loo."

"I wouldn't do that, Miss Shine. We have a contract."

"That contract isn't valid. I'm only eighteen."

"Your mother's not, and I have her John Hancock right here," Mac said, fanning himself with the contract.

"My mother was intoxicated. Give me that." Mac held the contract over her head, laughing as she jumped like a dog for a biscuit.

"I can't stop you from walking out of here; however, if you do choose to leave, you'll be breaking the terms of our contract, and I'll be forced to take legal action."

"What's that mean?"

"It means I'll be seeing you and Mom in court. Get a good lawyer if you can afford one. Sorry, Sunny, I own you."

***

The scent of Tim's simmering cigarette in the car's ashtray tingled Margo's nostrils; she had never craved a cigarette more. "Hey!" Tim scolded with one eye off the road. "Put that cigarette down. You know you ain't allowed to smoke till you're twenty-one."

"I won't live that long."

"I've never seen you act nervous," Tim said, taking the butt from Margo's trembling hand.

"It's not an act! This is the big time, Poppy. I don't want to let everyone down."

"Your mother wouldn't let you go on TV if she thought you'd embarrass her. Why, she told everyone at church to tune in. Mae said all her co-workers at City Hall will be watching."

"I'm going to be sick." The car swerved to the curb.

"It'll get easier," Tim assured with a back rub. "They're called opening night jitters. I don't care what your mother thinks; I like that Mac character. He's no dummy; he's in show business. It's an act."

"You think that's an act!"

"Margo, I've seen a lot of the world before I married your mother, and I've known stranger people than Mac. I can sort the wheat from the chaff."

"After tonight, Ma's going to give him the shaft."

"You're mother's a good woman."

"Are you drunk?"

"No. And it's because of her I'm sober. She's tough on you because she doesn't want anyone takin' advantage of you. Macs got your best interest at heart. That doesn't mean your good looks don't interest him," he said with a wink.

Tim pulled up to the Arcadia Building. "Honey, if you don't wanna do this, we'll go home. But don't miss out on the chance of a lifetime. Rosaria should be a teacher, you, a movie star." He nodded at the building's entrance. "You got an adventure waitin' for you, my cowardly lioness. You don't get to Oz without takin' the first step."

"You really think I can do this?"

"You're beautiful, talented, and I'm your biggest fan. I only wish I were your real..."

"Got to go." Margo parted with a peck on Tim's cheek.

"Father."

"The six o'clock news with Skip Radcliff and Zip DeWolf starts now," came the announcement over the black and white console.

"Can't you stop the TV from flipping?"

"I'm trying, Ma." Colleen cautiously walked backwards to her seat, fearing that if she were to turn her back on the screen, the set would use the opportunity to resume the televised treadmill. "I wish Poppy would hurry home. I don't want him to miss this."

Mae hastily removed her raincoat. "I didn't miss her, did I? The bus was stuck in traffic, so I got off and walked."

"She got there in one piece," Tim hollered as he came through the front door.

"What did I tell you about slamming that door? Now we have the piano playing and the TV dancing." Berta pounded her fist on her chair's armrest, inadvertently halting the rotating horizontal hold.

"Margo had some second thoughts, but I told her..."

Berta shushed her husband. "Here's the weather."

"Over to you, Zip." Rail thin and mousey, his shirtsleeves rolled up and a loose necktie, Zip didn't report the weather; he sold it.

"Spring has arrived," Zip heralded. "But you'd never know it by these cool temperatures. It's like the adage, "March comes in like a lion, and goes out like a lamb."

"So help me," Berta vowed. "If that man dressed her as a lion, I'll feed him to one."

"We have rain in the forecast." The prediction was accompanied by a clap of thunder and a flash of manufactured lightning. Berta felt lightheaded. Her intestines, tied tight, her brain, poised to burst. Tonight, will be the debut of the city's newest star, the brightest in the solar system. Zip waved his hand to the stage wing; the camera followed. "Look, folks, it's Sunny Shine!"

Margo stood stiff behind a piece of white plywood crudely carved into a lightning bolt. Without cloud cover, the audience was treated to Margo's bare limbs. Zip continued with his forecast. "We won't be seeing the sun tomorrow, will we, Miss Shine? Margo's arms flail as a wet mist surrounds her. "We ought to call you Sunny Shy," Zip joked.

Tim put his hand out. "Berta, stop, take a breath."

"Take a breath! I'm going to take a life!" Berta paced the room. "I'll have to take communion at another parish. Mae! The phone, take it off the hook. Colleen, draw the curtains," Berta hollered as if directing a bucket brigade. "Tim!"

"I'm on my way."

"She'll kill me, Poppy. Drive me to the train station. I'm going to New York. I'll find lodgings at The Barbizon, then send for my belongings."

"You're not to blame. That man exploited you, and worst of all, he lied to your mother."

"You're supposed to read people. You said Mac was a good guy, he'd look out for me."

"I've got his number. He's doing what's called pushing the envelope."

"His envelope cost me my job and a beating."

"You'll go back."

"Not after he served me up like a piece of meat."

"Listen, Miss Top of the Round, this is your first rodeo. Your Mac is using the oldest trick in the book. You'll learn this when you join the actors' union. See, what ya do is go into negotiations askin' for somethin' outrageous, somethin' you know management ain't gonna go for. That's what Mac is doin' by puttin' ya in that costume. He knows he went too far, and your mother's gonna blow a gasket. The next move is to negotiate down to the number you originally had in mind, knowin' if you asked for that amount to begin with, they woulda said no, and where can you go from there?"

"Poppy, I have no idea what you're talking about."

"Ya know what Mac's next move will be?"

"Out of the country?"

"He's gonna hear from your mother, that goes without sayin'. He'll promise to dress you in something that don't show so much skin. He'll say, 'Mrs. Ronan, sorry, Berta.' Don't that piss her off? Then he'll say, 'In the future, I'll have you sign off on what Nuala wears.' Your mother will fall for it hook, line, and sinker. Mac will still put you in a skimpy number, your mother will go on the warpath, but think, at least you ain't a lightning bolt. Does this make any sense to you?"

"It won't get me out of a beating, will it?"

"Fraid not."

"Poppy, if you can read people, why did you marry Ma? You were drunk, huh?"

"No. I knew there was more to your mother than the whip, but there are times when we all need a good flogging, and who better to dole it out? I got a strong woman and three of the best girls a man could ask for. Now get in that house and take your licks."

"Ma, I know you're behind that door." To Margo's amazement, her mother was not at her post. "I swear, I'll quit," Margo called out to an empty hallway. "Mac said if we break the contract, we'll have to get a lawyer, and it will cost oodles of money."

"We won't break the contract, he will." Margo spun around to face the voice. Berta stood at the kitchen door, snapping a pair of shears.

"No, Ma, please, not the hair. Beat me, stab me, but don't cut my hair off."

"He won't want a depicter who looks like a Nazi collaborator on VE Day."

Rosaria made her way down to the first floor. "Mom, don't. It's not Margo's fault. If you don't want her on that program, she needn't return, but don't punish her because he pulled the wool over your eyes. Margo is already humiliated."

Berta threw the shears across the room. "I've got plans for those shears."

***

Mac folded his newspaper and came out from behind his desk. "Berta! To what do I owe the pleasure?"

The matriarch removed the shears from her handbag. "You, highland lowlife. You're headed for prison, so am I."

Eyes fixed on her target, Berta kicked the office door shut.

"Let's be fair, Berta, you signed the contract."

"I'll get a lawyer, pay whatever it costs to see you behind bars."

Mac pointed to a canvas bag stamped US Mail. "The audience loves her. The phone's been ringing off the hook. I picked up three new sponsors." Keeping watch over Mac, Berta reached into the mailbag and pulled out an envelope. "This one is from the Catholic Decency League."

"They love her too!"

"You're going from con artist to convict or corpse, the choice is yours."

Faking a yawn, Mac tipped lazily back in his chair. "Go ahead, Berta, kill me. If last night's broadcast embarrassed you, wait till you see your picture splashed across the front page of every newspaper in this town. You, handcuffed, covered in blood, next to a photo of your daughter, Sparkie the lightning bolt. Carve me up, but I'm not releasing Sunny; she's my cash cow."

"Then the cow deserves more moolah."

"You're a shrewd one, I'll give you that, but I'm already paying her a king's ransom." Mac scratched his throat like a farmer setting a price on his prize cow. "You drive a hard bargain. I'll give you the final say on Sunny's wardrobe." Mac slapped his knees and stood.

"Then it's settled. I look forward to seeing you on the set."

"You don't expect me to come to the station? Isn't there a catalogue I can look through?"

Mac sucked in a hiss. "Can't make any promises. I'll see if Iola can dig one up and send it home with Sunny."

***

"I'm home!" Margo called out. "It's payday!"

"Where is it?" Berta asked.

"The money?"

"The catalog."

"Ma, Mac was putting you on."

"He's turned you into a glorified fan dancer."

Margo reached into her handbag and drew out an envelope containing a stack of bills. "Fan yourself with these."

***

The red convertible purred up to the cab stand. Behind the wheel sat Enzo, star of "Cooking with Enzo." The young, handsome, continental chef with a thick accent and the body of a flamingo dancer made women swoon. Margo was no exception, but knew the mild-mannered Enzo was a devout family man. "Miss Shine, come, come, I give you ride, no wait for cab."

"That's very kind of you, Enzo, but I'd be taking you out of your way."

"Where you live?"

"Dorchester."

"Eh!" he said with the sweep of his arm. "Very close, I drive." Enzo leapt from the car to open its door for his pretty passenger, who looked as though she belonged in an ad for the flashy convertible. Margo put her hand to her chest. "This car is amazing! What's the make?"

"She a Corvette C1. I see one, I buy one. Joke, you get?"

Enzo snapped open a silver cigarette case. "You smoke, no?"

"I smoke, yes."

"I love the cigarette," Enzo lamented. "Good for image, bad for taste buds." Taking the first drag, Enzo kissed the cigarette goodbye before sliding it between Margo's painted lips.

"Are all the men from your village so gallant?"

"Always for the pretty lady."

"What village are you from?" The accent evaporated into a coarse local dialect.

"Providence, that's my village. I'm from Rhodie, Federal Hill. Hang on, blondie. This rocket is taking off."

Margo gulped from the speed and revelation. "You're not Italian?"

"I'm Italian all right, just not off the boat like I make out."

"Why the act?"

"You think that knuckle-dragging degenerate would hire a wop from the hill?"

"But he must know your true identity; you're on the payroll."

"I'm an immigrant, no bank account in this country. He pays me in cash, which saves him on payroll tax and insurance. What he don't know is that my wife is a teacher, and her union insures us. My real name is Gideon. My dad said any guy who has a Bible named for him must be okay. He'd already named my brother James. Cooking with Gideon doesn't have the same ring to it. My mother likes that singer Enzo Suaite, so I figured I'd call myself Enzo."

"Mac didn't choose your name?"

"He said, Enzo sounds like asshole, so I could keep my name. Check it out, I say, 'Mr. Mac, what this asshole mean?' He goes, 'Look in a mirror, asshole.' The guy cracks me up."

"It's the next left at the top of the hill." Margo directed. "Your secret's safe with me," she promised.

"Arrivederci," she said with a giggle.

"See you around, doll face."

***

Mac held the dead phone tightly to his ear and placed his hand over the receiver. "Be right with you, Sunny," he whispered, nodding to a chair. Margo patiently waited to learn why she'd been summoned to his office. Mac returned to his phantom caller.

"Let me get this straight. You want me to waste what little time the FCC allows me to cover some teenage heartthrob? I never heard of this Troy Donahue character. Ninety percent of my viewers are males or lesbos. They don't care about some rich, handsome movie star. If he wants free publicity, let him murder some kid... What? You think he's a fag?"

Margo virulently shook her head. "He's not!"

Mac put his finger to his lips and returned to the deadline. "You might be on to something, Willis. Yeah, the tabs would eat it up. There's only one way to put that rumor to bed, if you get my drift. You bring the camera. I'll get the girl. Let me think, what girl... she can't be a hooker."

Margo bounced on her toes. "Me! Me!"

"Are you nuts, Willis? The kid's a minor. Troy will feel guilty and want to marry her, and who knows? He may even fall in love with her.

"Yeah, yeah, I know, but believe me, she's got more brains than he does and she's a mor... Don't you see what I'm sayin'? He takes her to Hollywood; next thing you know, she's a big star, another Monroe, and where does that leave me? Looking for another depicter is where. Then there's that mother of hers. She'll come barging

143

in here quoting the Bible or the Mann Act. You wanna make it look like an accident? Good luck with that. She's not gonna go for the old 'step back.' I want to get the falls in the picture. Willis, I've been in this business a long time, I know how chicks operate. They always choose their mommy over the movies." Margo grew frantic.

"I won't! I swear I won't. Stab her, choke her. I don't care. I want to meet Troy."

"Sorry, Willis, can't help ya." Looking down at Margo on her knees, clutching his leg, Mac smirked.

"Give me a few and I'll get back to ya." Mac hung up the phone with a sigh and looked down at Margo. "You lose an earring?"

"Troy Donahue!"

"You heard of him?"

"Heard of him? I'm in love with him!"

"I went to school with a kid named Troy," Mac reminisced. "Leroy Troy. I wasn't in love with him, per se. I haven't thought of old Troy boy in years. He married a girl named Helena." His pun met a blank stare. "I don't know why I waste them on you."

"Mac! "

"Oh yeah, the Donahue thing. His publicist wants us to set him up with a local girl while he's in town to squash rumors that he's a homo. Wait a minute." Mac wheeled himself to the door. "Iris! Get in here."

"You're sending Iris?"

"Why not? If she catches his eye, she can keep it."

"You want to see me, Mr. Mac?"

"Not with my glasses on. Listen, I've got a proposition for you. Better take it, you'll never be propositioned again."

Margo came to her coworker's defense. "Don't you treat her so harshly."

Iris shook her head. "I'm not upset, Sunny. Mac and I, we have a thing between us, but someday I'll turn the tables on him," she said with a flirtatious smile.

Mac curled his lip. "If that thing is what I think it is, I'll turn a gun on myself. All joking aside. Have you ever heard of a movie star named Troy Donahue?"

"Isn't he the star of that TV show, Hawaiian Eye?"

"Iris, you make it too easy for me. Beat it, the both of you."

"What about Troy?" Margo whined.

"Troy? He flew back to L.A. this morning. I just wanted to see the look on your face when you learned there was a chance you could have met him, and who knows? Oh well, fame, fortune, gone in the blink of an eye. Ain't that right, Iris?"

Margo stomped her foot. "I hate you. You're the meanest man that ever lived."

Mac returned to his magazine and shrugged. "Another satisfied customer."

$\smile\!\!\!\circ$

Chapter Eleven

The taxi pulled up to 13 Mount Nottingham. Rosaria snapped open her embroidered change purse and counted out $2 in change for $1.30 fare. Knowing the driver was uncomfortable taking the tip only added to her humiliation. Now she'd have to face her mother.

"Where in God's name have you been?! Why didn't Blanche drive you home?"

"She left work without me," Rosaria tearfully answered. Berta put the kettle on to brew tea, the panacea for all that ails mankind. Returning to the table, she took a seat next to her downcast daughter. "What happened, sweetheart?"

"A new girl started today. I'll be training her for the next week." Rosaria looked down at her hands, twisting the hem of her skirt. "Her name is Thelma, she's my age and very nice. We talk about dances, fashion, boys, subjects that don't interest the older women."

"Then what's the problem?"

Rosaria reached into her pocket and handed her mother a tightly folded piece of paper. "When I returned from lunch, I found that on my desk."

Berta slowly unfolded the creased notepaper. Nigger Lover. The words hit Berta like a punch to the throat.

"When I left work, Blanche's car wasn't in the lot. I think she's one of the women who doesn't want Thelma working with us."

Berta covered her upper lip with her lower and rocked her head. "Wait till I get my hands on that blue-haired ..."

"Please, Mom, don't. I need this job. It will blow over once they get to know Thelma."

Berta looked into her daughter's tear-filled eyes, knowing this was Rosaria's first experience with workplace cruelty. "Don't they hand me a laugh. I know those people. They'll never forget. They develop ethnic amnesia when it's not one of their own."

"It's not only Blanche, Bridget and Kathleen also share her views."

"You know what I'm going to do?"

"Kill someone?"

"I'll do one better. I'll have Suzie Sunshine tell those reporters at the TV station about this incident. Let the public know how MA Bell treats Negroes and the handicapped."

"Please don't. I know they'll come to like her. Until then, I'll take a taxi."

***

Moving the living room curtain, Berta looked out to the street. The idling engine wasn't from a taxi but Blanche's Pontiac. "Well, I'll be."

"I'm sorry, Rosaria, but we don't want Negroes working with us."

"I liked Thelma; you would have too if you hadn't made her quit."

"You're young; you don't know how it plays out. Say we did like Thelma; that would be fine if it ended there, but it wouldn't. Next thing you know, she's got a friend who needs a job. Thema worked out well. Why not hire her friend? Say that friend is a good worker, and she's got a brother or boyfriend in need of work; he's hired, and on and on.

"The next thing you know, the place is crawling with them, and somewhere down the line, a bad apple slips in. Wallets are stolen, cars are broken into. Rosaria, look at this neighborhood. You're too young to remember what it was like before the war. Before they moved here, back then, you could walk the streets at night without fear of being mugged. We left our doors unlocked. There was an unspoken rule between the Jews and Irish: You keep to yourselves, and we keep to ours. It worked out well for the most part and still would, but just like Thelma, the good Negroes, the educated ones moved in first. Then, along came the bad apples. They took our neighborhood; now they're coming for our jobs. Integration is being rammed down our throats."

"Unsavory people couldn't move in if you didn't move out."

"Why stay? The kosher markets, synagogues, and Hebrew schools have all left. A couple of your Catholic churches have shut down. That's what holds the Irish here. Will your mother stay once Saint Regina's closes its doors?

Saul Levant, you must have heard."

"Yes, it was awful."

"Taking a baseball bat to a 90-year-old man. Those boys were colored. I worry about you, Rosaria; you're a prime target."

"That didn't concern you last week when I didn't have a ride."

"I apologize for my behavior, not my beliefs. You're a sweet girl. No one wants you to get caught up in this. You're an optimist. All of you young people are. Take my son Georgie. I bust my tuchus to pay for his law school, and what does he do? He works as a civil rights lawyer down South. Don't breathe a word of this to the gals at work. They think he's in the Peace Corps. I warned him. 'Georgie,' I said, 'if you're not killed by the coloreds up here, you'll be lynched by the Klan down there.'"

"That's my point," Rosaria argued. "You, of all people, know what it's like to be persecuted, treated like vermin. Why would you treat Negroes in that fashion?"

"No one's talking extermination, just that they stay in their place. I had family in Poland who didn't leave in time. They're all dead. I know what happens to people who don't read the writing on the wall. I'm too old to change; I've seen too much in my lifetime. Your generation will be the one to welcome the Thelmas of the world into your neighborhoods, jobs, and families. But not now. It's too soon."

Blanche squeezed Rosaria's hand. "I'm proud of you and Georgie for standing up to the likes of me. If you're the future, I can rest in peace knowing the world is in good hands." Blanche went around and opened the car door for Rosaria. They hugged.

"Beliefs can change," Rosaria said.

"If mine do, it will be because of you."

Taking a deep breath, Rosaria entered the house.

"What just went on out here?" Berta railed.

"She's sorry."

"Now it's okay to work alongside Thelma?"

"Thelma quit. She couldn't take it anymore. She didn't want the others picking on me. She's accustomed to it."

"Those Jews and lace-panty Irish all scurry away like rats on a sinking ship at the first sight of a black face. We're not like them. We're Celts. We never kiss the ass you should kick."

Rosaria gently smiled. "Is that the motto on the Rourke coat of arms?"

Berta clasped her daughter's hands. "Honey, my purpose in life is to love and protect you girls. I've tried to teach you how to do for yourselves. Your sisters learned that lesson; I beat it into them, they'll make out okay. I tell ya, when the Russians drop the bomb, those two will come crawling out of the mushroom cloud with the cockroaches. Colleen will eat them, and Nuala will make them into jewelry; they're survivors. Rosaria, I never had to raise my hand or voice to you. It's a tough world out there. I won't be around forever..."

"Please, Mom, don't say that."

Berta put her palm up. "You've got to look out for yourself or find someone who will."

"I have."

***

"Gosh, Iola," Margo fretted. "My mother will kill me if I go on the air in this sweater."

The seamstress removed a pre-threaded needle from a stuffed tomato pincushion secured to her wrist. "Mac's orders."

"I know what he's doing. It's called pushing the envelope. I'm putting an end to it." Margo thrust open the door to her boss's inner sanctum. "Mac, I refuse to wear this sweater."

"What are these?" Mac asked, shaking a package of Fruit of the Loom underpants.

"I knew you wouldn't recognize them. They're underwear. New, clean underwear."

"I rinsed mine out this morning, they'll be good to go by noon."

"You're the kind of pig pigs call a pig. Please try them... they're soft."

"The day I get something soft in my pants is the day I wear a diaper, and that day ain't coming soon." Mac held up a film tin. "This came in the mail. It's from an affiliate in Akron. There's a letter enclosed." Mac cleared his throat.

"Mr. Mac Godfrey. I'm forwarding a film of our weather depicter, Miss Nora Easter. We are aware you have a young lady in your employment, a Miss Sunny Shine, who works in the same capacity. Judging by her performance, we feel Miss Shine could use a few pointers from Miss Easter. Enclosed you'll find ... blah, blah, blah.

"That's the gist of it. What he's saying is their depicter has got it all over you. So, you better step up your game. Go the extra mile, put more expression into your interpretation. You've got some stiff competition out there, as you'll see."

"No one depicts better than I do."

"Think so?" Mac pulled down a bracketed film screen on the wall opposite his desk and threaded the film through a projector.

"Hit the lights." It took a few seconds for Margo's eyes to adjust to the rapid flickering of the black-and-white images cavorting in front of her eyes. "They're doing it!"

"Gee, Sunny, someone's playing a trick on us." Hysterical with laughter, Mac rested his head on his desk. "They call her Nora Easter because she blows." Margo wasn't laughing or crying. She sat in silence, eyes riveted to the action taking place on the screen like a child at a puppet show, wondering how the dolls could be brought to life by the perverted puppeteer.

"Sunny, you okay? You're supposed to run out of here, screaming, crying, and carrying on. You're actually watching this stuff." Mac abruptly shut the projector off, causing the sixteen-millimeter film to pop off the reel, sending it twirling around on the floor, unwinding to a stop.

Margo jumped to her feet. "What happened? Why did you shut it off?"

"Because it was turning you on." A sly smile snaked across Mac's narrow lips. "You've never seen porn, have you?"

"No, Mister Mac, I haven't. And I'd appreciate you keeping this form of entertainment to yourself." Her manner softened. "What I mean is, don't get me wrong, I know about sex, the basics, what goes where, or so I thought. We never discuss sex in our household." Margo wound a strand of hair around her index finger. "What I'm getting at is, it would be nice to have someone I could come to with questions, someone I can trust not to laugh at me. Someone with plenty of experience."

Mac backed away. "Is this some kinda setup? I'm wise to you, Sunny. You want me to open your umbrella, then you cry rape and end up owning the station. I may be morally bankrupt, sister, but I'll beat you at that game."

Margo started for the door. "Fine, I'll get my information on the street."

"Hang on. I can't have my depicter pinched for solicitation."

Margo bounced on the balls of her feet and silently clapped. "Goodie. Put the movie back on."

"It will take a few minutes to untangle this mess."

While Mac sat on the floor with his back to her, Margo circled his desk like a shark in search of blood. She found an artery: a wallet parked in his jacket, abandoned next to a pile of boxes. With a magician's sleight of hand, she slipped the wallet from its filthy home. Her aim wasn't to steal money but to gain insight into his cloaked personal life. It held $1.14 and a driver's license. "THIRTY! YOU'RE ONLY THIRTY? I thought you were my father's age, and he's fifty-two, almost sixty."

Mac scrambled to his feet and snatched the incriminating evidence from her hand. "You little thief!" Returning the license to its compartment, he took a monetary inventory. "You don't have to count it. I didn't take your crummy buck fourteen."

"You tried to swipe my wallet."

"It fell on the floor, probably from the weight of all that cash."

"Do you want to watch this smut, or do I send you back to work?"

Wiggling into her seat, Margo mumbled, "Thirty."

"Can we get back to the film? At my age, I may not live to see the ending."

Margo rolled her eyes. "Thirty. Stop! Stop the movie!" she shouted, pointing to the frozen screen. "See? See?"

"See what?"

"His thing."

"What about it?"

Margo walked up to the screen. "He's got his thing here. So how can it be over there at the same time?" she asked, pointing to the far end of the screen. Mac came out from behind the projector with an arthritic groan. "Because this thing belongs to the other guy."

"What other guy?"

"If you allow me to advance the film, you'll see him."

"Two men, one woman?"

"Yes, Sunny, it's called Devil's Delight. You are sexually stupid."

"Maybe so, but I think it's important to know about such practices even if one doesn't partake in them."

Mac stood. "Show's over."

Margo hesitated on her way out to slide the package of underwear across the desk. "Please?"

***

Rosaria sat in contemplation, looking around her bedroom in the house she'd call home for half her life. The house Grandma had loved and left at the same age, but Grandma came back. Rosaria knew *she* never would. Tim tapped the bedroom door frame.

"Can I come in, or is it bad luck for a father to see his daughter in her wedding gown?"

"Oh, Poppy." Rosaria cried, wrapping her arms around her father's waist and pressing her face to his chest.

"Careful, don't wanna get face powder on this jacket; it's a rental. Don't I feel silly in this suit?"

"You look debonair." Father and daughter sat at the edge of the bed, her head resting on his shoulder.

"They say...," Tim cleared his throat. "They say, a parent ain't supposed to have a favorite child. I broke that rule the day I set eyes on you. Patsy's a good man. If he weren't, you wouldn't be wearin' that dress. I made a vow to your mother; now I'm making it to you. I vow not to ruin your wedding day. Your memories shouldn't be of your old man stumbling around drunk. I can't promise I won't cry, but if I do, it won't be from the drink. You may be leaving our house, but never our hearts, and our hearts are open to Patsy." Tim playfully poked his finger into Rosaria's arm. "He's one of us now."

"I love you, Poppy."

"I love you, too, darlin'."

Standing on the staircase landing with the sun shining through the stained glass, Rosaria looked a part of the window in her gown of Kenmare lace and a veil worn as the Virgin Mary had worn hers. She was more than beautiful: she was sacred. Tim led the bride to a waiting limousine, followed by her bridesmaids dressed in rose-colored satin gowns. Entering Saint Regina's Church, Tim wiped cold sweat from his upper lip. Rosaria was serene, regal, and eager to reach the altar where her groom awaited. Neither father nor daughter had difficulty keeping time to the wedding march. Step. Stop. Step. Stop. This was the nightmare Tim played out in his head, and the dream Rosaria surrendered to each night.

The Alpine Club, formerly The Melville Mansion, once served as a gathering place for Dorchester's smart set. The smart set moved away after the war. The club's once-grand ballroom was leased out for wedding receptions to meet property tax obligations.

As a child, Rosaria would watch society ladies in furs and veiled hats being driven to the mansion's door. She wondered if Mrs. Lindsey had been a member. Patsy and Rosaria would be the last couple to waltz across its floor to their wedding song, "Let it Be Me." The mansion was scheduled for demolition.

The ballroom hushed as father and daughter clung to one another as the band played "My Wild Irish Rose."

"I may be losing my Rose, but the scent will never leave me, darlin'."

Watching Margo commanding the dance floor, Rosaria's heart sank; she longed to join her, have Patsy seen her dance as she once had. She promised herself there wouldn't be tears today, no looking back. A new life lay ahead.

Salina nudged Margo. "Who's the dreamboat that just sailed in?. He's not from my side of the family."

"It's Doctor Hirsh!" Margo shuffled across the dance floor. "I can't believe you're here! Rosaria's going to flip."

"I can't stay. I wanted to see my special patient on her special day."

Margo led him to the bride. No longer a frightened teenager, helpless, hopeless. She stood tall, glowing, with open arms.

"You're no longer my patient, so I'm at liberty to kiss you."

"I'm afraid not. She's a married woman," Patsy said with an extended hand. "I'm Patsy Travella."

"Aaron Hirsh." The groom appeared immature in Aaron's eyes. He hoped Rosaria hadn't settled, for fear she'd never attract her equal. "I must confess, Mr. Travella, I was enamored with your wife," Aaron stated, assuming Patsy wasn't familiar with the term.

"The day she walked out of the hospital was the happiest day of my life. I wanted to be here for hers. You promised me a dance, Mrs. Travella, and I'm holding you to it."

Salina's eyes fixed on the bride and doctor swaying in one another's arms. "Wouldn't I love to have him give me a physical."

"You're a married woman," Margo reminded her fellow bridesmaid. The dance ended with a kiss lasting longer than a traditional goodbye.

Salina jerked her head toward the departing doctor. "There he goes, make your move."

Margo winked. "Watch and learn."

Swooping in Aaron's path, Margo asked, "Do you remember when we first met?" Aaron looked past Margo.

A concerned expression flashed across his face. "That man over there."

Margo turned. "That's my dad. Would you like an introduction?"

"Yes. If I'm not mistaken, he's the only Ronan I've yet to meet."

155

"Look at him," Berta whispered to Mae. "Tim's not steady on his feet. He's been drinking. He swore he wouldn't. After the "I do's," he did."

"Berta, I've kept my eye on him all day. The only drink he's had has been water."

"Firewater. Oh, isn't this just dandy? Nuala has that doctor examining Tim."

Aaron shook Tim's hand; it was cold, yet beads of sweat laced his brow. "Call an ambulance," Aaron ordered.

"Why?" a bewildered Margo asked.

"He's having a heart attack. Now go!" Margo froze in fear of her father dying and her mother killing her for drawing attention to the fact. "You, stupid girl! Your father is dying. Do as I say!" the order came with a shove.

Margo threaded her way through the dancing guests who were unaware of the tragedy unfolding. A group of mulling young men followed Aaron's instructions to lower Tim's ridged body to the floor. Without turning, Aaron sensed Berta's presence.

"What do you think you're doing? There's nothing wrong with him that a strong cup of coffee will cure. Play doctor somewhere else, not at my daughter's wedding." Berta jockeyed herself between her husband and the doctor.

Aaron picked the slender Berta up by her waist, moving her out of his way. "I don't have time for you."

"What happened?" Patsy asked, watching Aaron massage Tim's silent heart. Margo answered between gulps.

"Poppy had a heart attack. The ambulance is on its way."

"POPPY! POPPY!" Patsy helped his wife to her father's side. Aaron didn't have the heart to keep her from her dying father, who lay slack-jawed, his glossy eyes fixed on the ceiling. "You'll be fine, Poppy," she said to pacify herself more than him. The wail of an ambulance siren in the distance broke Rosaria's vow not to cry. "We're going to the hospital, Poppy. I love you. Don't die, please, Poppy, don't die!" Rosaria clawed Aaron's chest. "I Need My Father! Don't Let Him Die, don't let him die!"

***

"I'm Dr. Wolcott," said the bow-tied cardiologist, offering his hand and sympathy to Berta, who refused to accept both. "Were you aware of your husband's underlying heart condition?" the doctor asked in a grim voice.

"No. We... that is, my husband and I don't place stock in the medical profession."

"That's unfortunate. Your husband is a chronic alcoholic."

"Doctor, up until a few hours ago, my husband had abstained from alcohol on my insistence. Stopped cold turkey."

"Mrs. Ronan, a man with your husband's medical history should never have been detoxed cold turkey. A total cessation taxed his already weak heart. That's what led to this cardiac episode."

Mae gripped her sister's arm, preventing Berta from lunging at the doctor, who was oblivious to the fuse he'd lit. "My husband is a drunk. He'd been drinking. That's what brought on this episode."

"There doesn't appear to be alcohol in his system." Dr. Wolcott's name came over the intercom, summoning him to intensive care. Without exchanging words, the sisters knew it was Tim.

***

Her arms outstretched, Rosaria stood in her pint-size apartment, reminiscent of her grandmother on her return to Mount Nottingham.

"Oh, Mom, don't you love it? It's not the Mount, but it's ideal for now. We won't raise our family here. We're saving for a home of our own. Look. I can enter directly from the street. The front entrance hasn't steps or a threshold to stumble over."

"Safety first, aesthetics last," Berta said through clenched teeth.

"It's a comfort knowing Mama and Papa are one flight up if we should need them." Berta felt a knife jab into her chest. No longer Carla and Louie, they were Mama and Papa. She wasn't her Rosaria but their Rosie. Chatting about closet space, curtains, and the building's southern exposure, Rosaria hadn't noticed her mother's forlorn expression. "Patsy thinks we can install a dishwasher. I find it an extravagance.... You don't like the apartment, do you?"

"What I love is seeing you happy."

"Oh, Mom, I truly am. "

Berta held her daughter tightly to her chest. "I love this house," she whispered.

"Mom, you're crying."

"Paint fumes. Promise you won't panel the place."

Rosaria held up her hand, her thumb over her baby finger. "Scout's honor."

"I'll go upstairs and get Mae, or she'll spend all day gossiping with Carla."

Mae's voice followed her footsteps. "I'm on my way down."

"Once we settle in, I'm going to have the family over for dinner. Mama is teaching me to make a gravy."

"Tomato sauce," Berta flatly stated. "That's one of those translation mix-ups from Ellis Island."

The substandard front door closed behind Berta, who tapped her knuckles on its frame. "Tin. My daughter lives in a tin shanty like a hobo."

"The building is brick," Mae assured her sister.

"They live on the street. A passerby can look into their front room. There are only two windows, one in the front and one in the back.. There isn't enough room in that house to swing a cat, and she's going to hold a dinner party."

"Come along, Berta. There's a cab stand across the street."

"Where to, ladies?"

"Dorchester," Mae informed the overweight driver as he straightened his cap and turned the meter's handle down.

"You got it."

Staring out the cab's window, Berta huffed. "Look at this town. The streets are narrow, the houses attached; were there a fire, they'd all go up. The thought of Rosaria trapped..."

"Sorry to interrupt, ladies, I can't help but overhear. I've lived in East Boston all my life. It's a safe place unless you're lookin' for trouble, then all bets are off."

Berta leaned forward into the driver's ear. "This town is a tinderbox."

"Nah, we ain't had many fires, cept for the big one. The Luongo Restaurant fire. Six firemen died puttin' that one out. A week later, doesn't The Coconut Grove go up? Now, that was a doozy. Killed something like 400 people."

"Four hundred and ninety-two," Berta corrected.

"Yeah, right, 492. I remember that night real well."

"As do I. You're being paid to drive us home, not take us on a stroll down memory lane."

Mae closed her eyes and whispered, "Berta, please. Not now."

"Take the bridge," Berta ordered the driver. "If it collapses, we fall into the river. If the tunnel collapses, the ocean falls in on us."

Chapter Twelve

"Enzo!" Mac hollered from across the set. "Get your tight ass over here."

Enzo winked at Margo. "Watch this." Humbly answering his master's call, Enzo groveled. "Yes, Mister Mac? I do something wrong for you?"

"You're fired," Mac stated without looking up from his clipboard.

"What you mean, fired?"

"You heard me. Beat it, hit the road, bon voyage, or whatever you Italians say."

"But why?"

"I just got word from Immigration: you overstayed your visa, so pack up your pots and pans."

"I am a citizen now."

"You born here?"

Enzo paused before lying. "No."

"Then screw. I got work to do."

Enzo followed Mac to his office. The door met his face. "What I do? I have a small child to feed."

"Cook her, eat her. If you're still hungry, go to Providence, round up your other bastards and eat them too."

"What this Providence?"

Mac whipped his office door open. "I'll tell you, 'What this Providence' is. It's where you have other women, other children." Mac waved a picture in Enzo's face. "Some broad sent this to me. Tell me this rugrat ain't the picture of you."

"Yes, that picture of my head stapled to the body of the infant Jesus."

"Great. Now I've got the Virgin Mary writing me. I don't need this kinda trouble."

Enzo pushed past Mac and dug into his office wastebasket. "Look! Look! Christmas card, baby Jesus cut from crib."

"I don't know where the kid took off to. Smart money's on Egypt. Besides, it doesn't matter who wrote it."

"Yes, it does!"

"No, it don't," the door closed on Enzo's reply.

Margo rushed to her comrade's aide. "You know, Mac, it's a joke."

"Some joke. Immigration, baby Jesus, the guy's insane."

"You mentioned you wanted to leave Boston and move to a warmer climate. I think Mac has a station down South."

"Sunny, his stations aren't in Atlanta or Miami. They're in places like Kick Ass Creek."

"Allow me to speak with him."

"Knock yourself out."

"Mac."

"Don't you ever knock?"

"No. Why are you letting Enzo go?"

"It ain't up to me. It's the Feds." Mac propped his feet up on his desk. "Some immigration irregularity."

Margo leaned across the desk. "You're a liar. Enzo didn't want you to know, but since he's no longer employed here, I'll tell you: Enzo is not from Italy."

Mac dropped Miss December to the floor. "No! I'm sooo shocked."

"You knew?"

"Sure, I knew."

"Why did you let him go on pretending?"

"Because I'd piss my pants whenever he'd put on that phony accent."

"If it's not Immigration, why are you letting him go?"

"Not that I owe you an explanation, but seeing how much you care about the greaseball, I'll tell ya. He's got ties."

"It wouldn't kill you to put one on."

"Do I have to spell it out for you? He's connected. Ya know, the Mob, Mafia, the Underworld, comprende?"

"How do you know he's in the Comprende?"

Mac threw his arms in the air and raised his eyes to the ceiling. "Say goodnight, Gracie!"

Margo looked up at the drop ceiling's fluorescent light that silhouetted a dead rat. "I don't think Gracie is sleeping. I think she's dead."

"I'll tell ya how I know he's in the Comprende: because I make it my business to know about my employees' personal lives. After hours, Old Skip and Zip become

Snatch and Scratch. Fat Joey, the cameraman, was arrested for makin' off with dough from his last employer, Pizza World." Mac circled the desk like a vulture. "I even know when Sunny is expecting her monthly tropical depression."

"How dare you! How, how, could you?"

"Iola tips me off when the puffy clouds roll in."

"Why that no good..."

"Don't blame her. I make her tell me. She's got a son locked up in McLean's, a real nutcase. She doesn't want anyone to know about him... oops. 'Sides, I need to know so I can make myself scarce that week. I don't want to listen to ya whinin' and cryin' about how mean I am to ya."

"Can we get back to Enzo?"

"Ya mean Gideon? Ain't that a hoot? A guinea named Gideon. You can tell Gideon to find his thrill on Federal Hill or the Federal Pen."

Margo pointed her finger in the air. "I have an idea."

"Let's hear it, Einstein. You do know who Einstein is?"

"I won't dignify that with an answer."

"Just as I thought."

"Assign him to another station. You must have something down South."

"Last time I checked down there, I still had Chickamauga."

"Ick."

"It's a town, not a venereal disease. Trust me, Sunny: Gideon will never outrun the Comprende. They're a ruthless pack of savages. I crossed paths with them some years back. I was driving down to New York on business when I developed a stiff... neck. I figured I better have it tended to by a professional before it got out of hand. A couple of hours later, I come out of the massage parlor..."

"Did you feel better?"

"Much. I go to get my car and find it's been stolen. Long story short: I get a call from Comprende tellin' me I can find my car at the airport. I grab a cab to LaGuardia and find the shitbox in the airport garage. I pop open the trunk and whaddya think is in there?"

"Luggage?"

"A body, Sunny. A dead, human body. When I tell ya, this poor bastard was sliced open from his throat down to his missing dick. Naturally, my curiosity had been piqued. I rifle through his wallet for some ID. That's when I came across one of those organ donor contracts. Well, now it all makes sense. Our hacked-up friend musta overstayed his welcome here on planet Earth. The hospital hired Comprende to hunt the bastard down and strip him for parts. Why, those animals even yanked out his teeth. The dental school musta wanted them. Let that be a lesson to ya: Never sign one of them contracts without reading the fine print."

"Admit it, you never liked Enzo. I don't understand why."

"Sit. I don't have anyone to unburden my soul to. Ya see, I look at a guy like Gideon, young, talented, good-lookin', with a wife and great kid. You ever see her?"

"No."

"Cute as a button. Every year around this time, I'm reminded of what I once had and lost. A wife and twin girls, identical." Mac gazed out the window at a brick wall. "Just a few short years ago, the Missus and I spent Christmas Eve sitting by the fire, admiring the twins. You shoulda seen how excited the girls would get when they knew their daddy was coming. They would bounce and squeal, 'Daddy! Daddy!' I'd kiss them on their loveable little heads. I cherish those moments. Looking back, I wonder what I could have done differently. Where is she now? To be honest, I don't know. All I know is wherever she is, the twins are with her. I tried for custody, but I couldn't take them from her. They were too close to her heart. It would've killed her. Gideon opened that old wound."

Margo silently crept up behind him and whispered in his ear. "I met the old wound, the lovely Wanda Lust. The twins? They're wearing pasties on their lovable little heads."

Mac spun around. "Where did you find her?"

"She found me. She'd seen me on air and wanted to know about our relationship. I told her if she'd come to tell me to get myself checked, she was wasting her time."

"What did she tell you?"

"Not much. Seems I know more about you than she does."

Mac fidgeted. "It was a joke. No harm done."

"No harm done? Iola feels terrible about your failed marriage. That your mother will never get to see the twins."

"She can see them. She just has to pay the cover charge."

"What were you thinking, marrying that woman?"

"As you know, I don't drink."

"You're an alcoholic. It's common knowledge."

"I hate to disappoint you, but I'm not a drunk. What I am is cheap. The night I met the engaging Miss Lust, she slipped me a Mickey. Three days and three grand later, I've got myself a wife and one hell of a hangover. I put an abrupt end to our blessed union."

Mac chuckled, "Iola still asks if I've seen the twins. I told her, 'The next time I see them, they'll be in a bra.'"

"Enzo is going wherever he wants, or the twins will pay Daddy a visit at the station."

"Chickamauga it is."

***

Colleen raced down from the attic. "It's Rosaria and Patsy!" she called down to her mother. Berta looked out the window to see Patsy helping his wife out of their car. "Hold on," said Berta, stepping into Colleen's path. "Take money from my purse and bike down to the bakery for pastries."

"But it's just Rosaria and Patsy."

"They're Mr. and Mrs. Travella. Their company. Now go!" The order came with a shove out the back door. Berta greeted Rosaria on the front porch with a hug. "What brings you to Dorchester?"

"I had an appointment at City Hospital."

"We'd be crazy not to stop in to see you," Patsy added with an awkward grin. Berta assisted her daughter into the house, ignoring Patsy, who lagged behind. Margo ended her phone conversation. She gave Rosaria a kiss, and one to Patsy, who rolled his eyes.

"Wow! I've been kissed by Sunny Shine!"

"Dear Lord, don't start with that."

"She's a star, Mrs. Ronan. Come six o'clock, the bar is packed; we can't wait to see what Sunny is or isn't wearing. When she comes on the screen: Va-va-va-voom."

"Are you old enough to drink?" Berta asked, knowing the answer.

"Well, um, not really," Patsy stammered.

"You either are or you're not."

"I have a soft drink." Patsy resumed paying homage to Margo. "Sunny, I mean, Margo, do you remember when that earthquake hit Alaska? Ma, you see that one?" Patsy eagerly asked.

"No," Berta answered. "Ma doesn't watch the program."

"Rosaria!"

"Colleen, you're out of breath."

"I went to the bakery and got a cake. It's your favorite, strawberry cream."

"That's so sweet of you."

Patsy picked up his story where he left off, much to Berta's dismay. She hoped Colleen's entrance would steer the conversation in another direction. It didn't. "So, anyway, all the guys at the bar went nuts when you came out in a white fur bikini. Fur! Who came up with that?"

"You have to ask?" Berta said in disgust.

Patsy slapped his knee. "That man's a genius. He's got you in a fur bikini with one of those exercise belts, shakin' you around. You're tryin' to hold on to your bikini top when you get a bucket of water thrown at you, and out of nowhere, comes a salmon smackin' you in the face." Patsy banged his palm on the table. "Talk about an aftershock!"

Berta grew impatient. "It's a disgrace the way that man makes light of a national tragedy. There are people living on nettles, and that man throws around a good piece of fish."

"I tell everybody you're Rosaria's sister, but they ain't buying it, cause you're so different lookin'. We oughta get a picture of the three of us. You still have that bikini?"

"Sorry, it was destroyed in the quake, but I do have the scorched shorts from the fire out west."

Berta reached her limit. "The man is sick. He couldn't care less if you burnt to death. He'd just get another pretty girl to incinerate."

"Ma, it was dry ice."

Colleen pouted. "Rosaria, you haven't touched your cake."

Rosaria looked over at Patsy. "I've been nauseated lately."

Margo sprang to her feet. "You're not!"

"I am!" The old house rang out with a toast, cheers, and congratulations.

"I told Rosie, with her being Swedish and me Italian, the baby will be a Swedish meatball."

"Her name is Ronan. She's Irish," Berta insisted.

"Oh, yeah, right, Irish."

"What do you think it will be?" Colleen asked Patsy.

"A girl. Wouldn't that be nice? A beautiful girl, just like her mother. I wanna see the look on the faces of the old Nonie's at the park when they catch sight of my wife and daughter. Then again, a son. Wouldn't that be somethin'? Having a little guy at my side. I was never good at sports, but he will be."

"Twins!" Colleen laughed.

"Could be, twins run in my family."

"Not in ours," Berta said in a sharp tone bordering on anger.

Patsy pulled out his wife's chair. "We gotta go. I can't wait to tell my folks. They'll go nuts when they hear the news!" Kisses and goodbyes were exchanged.

Berta and Margo stood at the window watching the two excited kids walk down the drive. "She'll never carry that child to term."

***

Patsy tidied the tangled bedsheets and fluffed his wife's pillow as if tucking a child into bed. "One of the good things about being pregnant," he said, wearing a boyish grin and nothing else, "Ya don't have to worry about gettin' pregnant. I promise you, Rosie, one day you'll feel my lips on your leg, and we'll celebrate by makin' love standin' up." Patsy put his ear on Rosaria's belly. "I don't hear anything."

"It's too early, silly."

"Are you happy?"

"Of course, I am. Why would you think otherwise?"

"This isn't how we planned it."

"I was overly optimistic."

"And I was a pig who couldn't wait five minutes, never mind five years."

Rosaria stroked Patsy's head. "The baby is coming into the world on God's timetable, not ours. For reasons we don't understand. They'll be revealed to us in time. You're nervous."

"You bet I am. I worry you're not physically able, and I'm not emotionally or financially prepared."

"We're not destitute."

"Not while my folks are living upstairs. But I want to be the breadwinner, the head of the household. Having a wife and child doesn't make me a man."

"We have love. All else will fall into place. You'll get your degree, and we'll purchase a home of our own. But it will take more than five minutes to achieve."

"Bobby's brother can get me a job at the airport. The money's good."

"What will you be doing?"

"Does it matter? I'll be getting my foot in the door. I'm not too proud to mop a floor."

"That would be fine if that's what you want to do with your life... but it isn't."

"What I want is to support my family and make an honest living."

"What were your plans before we met?"

"To grow up."

"I'm serious."

"You won't like the answer."

"I'll be the judge of that."

"Become a priest."

"You're putting me on."

"I'm not. I always wanted to be like the priests. Respected, educated, be there for people when they need God most. When they're experiencing grief or love, help the kids and old folks. Not just administer the sacraments but make a difference in people's lives. Stupid idea. Besides, Mama was against it. She held a knife to my crotch and said, 'I'll prepare you for the priesthood.' I got good grades. Planned on going to Saint John's Seminary after graduation. Then, on the eve of his birth, Jesus sent me an angel, with a broken wing."

Rosaria sat up in bed. "Patsy, wake up."

"Oh God. What's wrong?"

"I have an idea."

Patsy fell back on his pillow. "You scared the crap out of me."

"Get into community service. Volunteer at church, The Knights of Columbus, and the CYO. You love hockey, coach."

"Will they pass the hat for me?"

"The money will come. What's important is to lay the foundation for a rewarding career. When people get to know you, they'll come to love you. When a good position opens, they'll recommend you."

"What about school?"

"You needn't forestall your education. You'll graduate. If you're going to pursue a career in public service, you must focus on your image. How you present yourself is paramount. It sounds daunting, but I can help you."

"You would have made a great teacher."

"I pushed that dream aside. Don't you. Listen to your heart. Working at the airport isn't going to help you achieve your dreams. Spend time with the priests, not the broom pushers."

"Rosie, you're so wise. "

"I listen to those who have the wisdom to share. Seek them out."

"If we have a girl, she'll be smart, pretty, and wait on you hand and foot. If we have a son, he'll be smart, handsome, and you'll wait on him hand and foot."

Rosaria kissed her husband. "You may not be a priest, but you'll make a great father."

***

Colleen raced down the walk as Margo pulled the car to the curb. "Let me hold him," she begged, bouncing on the balls of her feet.

"Mom gets to hold him first," Rosaria said, balancing her son in her arms. Margo placed a firm hand on the new mother's back, not wanting Rosaria to feel she wasn't capable of caring for her son, but why jeopardize the newborn's safety to make a point?

Berta barreled out of the house with the look of a charging bull. "What the hell are you doing? That's a baby, not a loaf of bread!" Scowling, she snatched the infant from its mother's arms. "You could have tripped and killed both of you." Berta's eyes burned into Margo's. "And where's your head? You know better than to allow her to carry an infant! Afraid he'll pee on your dress?"

"I wouldn't allow her to take him from me. No one is going to dictate how I should care for my son."

"Does Patsy know while he's in school, you're roaming the streets with a newborn?"

"I'm not roaming the streets. I practiced carrying him before he was born."

"Practiced on what?"

"A babydoll."

"Where's that doll now? Is it breathing?"

"There's the little man!" Mae sang out. "Get in the house before he catches pneumonia."

"I'm not going to kill my son!"

"It's the hormones," Mae whispered. The gaggle of women filed into the house. The next generation had arrived on the Mount.

"I've chosen Margo to be his godmother. Sorry, Colleen, next time." There was a short silence; all eyes turned to Berta.

"The name?" she asked as if checking a passport at a border crossing.

"He's being named after his grandfather."

"Good, the names blend well. Timothy Travella."

"Fredrik."

Mae gulped, Margo froze, Colleen squeezed her eyes shut.

"Timothy isn't a good name? "

"Mom, you know how dear Poppy was to me. He'd understand. My son won't be a Fred or Freddy. He's Fredrik. If one were to ask the name's origin, he'll tell them he was named for his grandfather, a war hero."

"The Travellas, they agree the boy should be named for the war hero?"

"They're fine with the name."

"Why should they care? They'll call him by some gangster name like Freddy the Fleabag or Three-Fingered Fred."

"My son is not flea-infested and is in possession of all his digits!"

"I know these people."

"You don't know these people, I do! You make snap judgments about people based on their surnames. You're cruel and closed-minded." Rosaria took her son from Mae's arms. "I'm leaving!"

"All I ask is that you consider another name."

"You really don't want him to be named Fredrik, do you?"

"No, Rosaria, I don't."

"Fredrik, it is."

***

The vibration from the slamming door set off a playful rag from the haunted piano, escalating Berta's rage. "That's the last time I go over to that church!"

Colleen followed her mother into the house. "It was a beautiful ceremony."

"The church was stuffy, and they wanted us to go to a function hall to continue the mayhem."

"Mayhem! What are you talking about?"

"I know those people. A fight is bound to break out."

"It was a christening, not West Side Story."

"I'll bet dollars to donuts, half of them haven't been in a church since Easter. Mae and Nuala can go with them, not me. We're lucky Mr. Iguana drove us home."

"Lizard. He called himself The Lizard."

"God bless him. Your great-grand-aunt Rowena had eczema, not as bad as the Lizard, mind you, but bad enough to keep her indoors for the remainder of her life. That sister of yours is a disgrace. Trolling for a man in, of all places, a church. I saw her making eyes at Patsy's cousin. A blond Italian, that's a first. Some Celtic cock snuck into that Sicilian henhouse."

"Margo is the godmother. He's the godfather. At some point, they were going to make eye contact."

"Mae went to the party to spend time with Carla, while Nuala went to make time with Blondie. And that Elba Raskind, Mother of God, that woman could talk a dog off a meat wagon. You know, the next time we'll end up back in that church?"

"When hell freezes over?"

"Mr. Travella's funeral is when. The man looks like death warmed over. Rosaria should have invited her friend, Dr. Hirsh. He would have put Papa out of his misery. Let's be grateful he didn't die before the baby was born, or they would have named him Luigi, as if Fredrik wasn't bad enough. Whatever possessed her to name that boy Fredrik, I'll never know. He's the image of Patsy. You know what they'll do? They'll call him Little Patsy, Patsy Junior, young Patsy. Why didn't they just name him Patsy? No. She wants him to be named after a war hero. It's their baby, let them do as they please. I have no say in the matter. You know me, I keep my opinions to myself."

***

Since Enzo's departure, Margo had taxied to and from the station. In another two weeks, she'd be pulling up to the Mount in a white T-Bird. It was during a promotional appearance at the annual auto show that Sunny met her white knight on four wheels. He'd seduced her with the promise of surrounding her in soft leather, smooth handling, and a high-octane high she'd never come down from.

Boston had been invaded by conventioning Shriners. With the fraternal free-for-all came a shortage of cabs. Even Margo's traffic-stopping legs couldn't lure a cab to the curb. Why not take the train? she thought. Her past shadowed her into the subway.

Stepping off the train, she waited for a bus that would stop at the foot of Mount Nottingham. The sun had set. An autumn fog descended on the city. A misty breeze at her back, Margo turned up the collar of her Burberry raincoat and buried her hands in the coat's deep pockets. Wet leaves resembling soggy cornflakes brought a smile, remembering how she and Rosaria would attempt to outrun the crackling foliage as the two raced home from Saint Regina's.

Having a change of heart, she decided to walk the remainder of the way home. Strolling down the street, she recalled how early sunsets, Halloween, and the scent of an asbestos-covered behemoth in the basement changed the atmosphere of the old house from sultry to spooky. Autumn was a romantic time of year, nature's finale. Burning leaves served as the season's incense, setting Margo's imagination aflame.

Once again, she was a fairytale princess dressed in a gown of golden leaves, living in a castle deep in the Black Forrest. Nostalgia took hold, resurrecting memories of a time when a 5-cent Popsicle brought a fleeting moment of pleasure that now took a sports car to satisfy.

Sagamore Park crowned a steep hill. Dimly lit cement steps formed a crumbling spine leading down to a tranquil tree-lined one-way street seldom visited by cars or pedestrians, which was fortunate for the neighborhood children in their sweaty snowsuits and runny noses, whose sleds and cardboard coasters would come crashing to a halt at the park's foot. No matter the season, everyone knew never to venture into the park after sunset. Margo hadn't been in the park since childhood, when she used it as a shortcut home. This wasn't the 1940s but 1964. She entered, unaware.

A plaque of slick moss clung to the stairway's gap-toothed grin. Unsteady in heels, Margo recognized her folly, wishing she'd stayed on the main road. Already halfway down the steps, there was no point in turning back. The rustle of dead leaves followed her footsteps. Eyes on her feet, she took care not to stumble. A thundering blow to her head brought her to her knees. In an instant, her disoriented brain flashed the image of a fallen tree limb landing on her head. An arm with a cobra grip tightened around her throat, robbing her of precious seconds to cry for help. Her feet left the ground; her arms flailed in a blind panic.

"Is that all you got?" spat a whiskey-drenched whisper as he wound a fistful of her hair around his knuckles, dragging her into the park's wet underbrush. "You owe me. I know this isn't the way you want it, but you do want it." Margo bit the hand covering her mouth, it cost her a tooth. A rag was forced into the back of her throat. Passersby would assume the rustling of bushes was the rummaging of rodents. In a guttural voice, he panted with each thrust. "Every time you do this, you'll think of me."

The long-forgotten scent of damp soil delivered her to the backyard of a three-decker on Half Moon Street, where she sat Indian style with her then-best friend, Evelyn. The two armed, with tablespoons, were determined to dig their way to China. Breaking through to the Forbidden City, the two would be hailed as Goddesses, lavished with treasures of silk and jade. Evelyn raised her head, interrupting the excavation. "Do you think there are Chinese kids digging to America with chopsticks?"

"Yeah, we can beat them." The furious foraging of spoons and chopsticks raced toward the Promontory Point of the Earth's core. Only one person could sour a girlhood fantasy into a Holy Book horror. "Keep digging!" Berta shouted down from the second-floor window. "And you'll find yourself in Hell."

The rape ended with the expression of a man popping open a sealed pickle jar and a moan of pleasure. "Did you enjoy that?" Her mind had left her body. The question wasn't heard. Grabbing Margo's bangs, he pounded her head against a rock.

"Was that a 'yes'?" A powerful kick to her ribs punted her bruised body down to the foot of the hill. Black chinos and a dark leather jacket served as camouflage as he dodged traffic with a feminine skip, escaping into a stream of apathetic pedestrians.

Concealed behind the park's low wall, Margo lay motionless. The silent fog lifted for a light freezing rain that tapped on her pillow of weeping leaves. The silhouette of knobbed and twisted bare tree branches clawed at the full moon like a witch's gnarled and knotted talons. The mud didn't taste like soy sauce but Satan's soup. *Mother was right.* She'd dug her way to hell. Crawling on her elbows, Margo retrieved her pocketbook and crinkled raincoat. Opening the purse with cold, scraped knuckles, she removed folded bills and her license. Tucking them into her salvia-soaked bra, she tossed the handbag into the bushes and slid over the park's wall to a deserted backstreet. Her leg swelled with each step, making the climb up the Mount feel like marching through thick butterscotch. Metallic-tasting blood dripped from her gum, robbed of a tooth. Marty's car occupied the driveway. "God no," she mumbled through swollen lips. The doors' lead glass distorted their faces, its dense wood muffling voices in another heated argument between brother and sister, one that was about to abruptly end. The door creaked open.

"MARGO!" Mae shrieked, rushing to aid her niece, who collapsed into a waiting chair like a puppet with severed strings.

"My God! What happened?" Marty handed Margo a handkerchief, allowing her to spit out blood and half-sentences.

"I...I.. he beat me."

"I'm calling the police."

"No. Please, Uncle Marty, don't. People know me from television. I can't have this come out. I'll lose my job."

"You can't let that Black bastard get away with this."

"It was a White guy."

"How do you know?"

"Because I was there!" Margo cried. "He came up from behind me, put his white hand over my mouth, twisted my arm behind my back, then punched me in the face, and dragged me into the park."

"Sagamore Park?" Berta asked in a rising voice.

"I was walking by the park, not through it," Margo lied.

"Why were you walking? The bus would have let you out at the foot of the Mount. Why didn't you take it?"

"Because I wanted to get mugged. Okay!" Margo screamed from behind an ice-packed facecloth. "I couldn't get a cab. There's a convention in town."

Berta picked up the mud-covered raincoat. "This is in a sorry shape. If it were torn on the seam, I could mend it. You've got yourself a $60 rag. Sixty dollars! Who in their right mind pays $60 for a raincoat? Rosaria paid $50 for her wedding veil, and I wanted to choke her with it."

"If you won't let me take you to the police, at least let me drive you to the hospital," Marty offered.

"No, thank you. I just need an aspirin and a bath."

Mae took Margo by the arm. "Let's get you upstairs."

Berta called after them. "Take a few days off. The sun will shine without you. We'll get the tooth fixed tomorrow. As for Mac, leave him to me."

Sitting on the edge of the cast iron clawfoot bathtub, Margo whimpered. "I'm sorry, Mae."

"Whatever for?"

"For getting everyone upset."

"Oh dearie, they're not upset with you: they're angry at that man. It's a strange way of showing their concern, but that's Berta and Marty for you."

"Will you get the pink robe I like? It's behind my bedroom door."

"I'll be right back." With Mae out of the room, Margo ripped off her bra, kicking it and the money under the tub.

***

"Mrs. Ronan!" said Ronny, holding out a bouquet of red roses. "I won't keep you. I just stopped by with a special delivery."

"They're beautiful, but you know what she'll do with them."

"Tell her they're from a fan. You won't be lying."

Berta waved Ronny into the house. "She won't be home for a few hours. I'll put the kettle on."

Ronny watched as Berta walked to the china cabinet. "There's no need for the good china, Mrs. Ronan. I'm family." Ronny lowered his head. "Or was... look, I didn't come here to win her back. On the contrary, I'm engaged."

Berta made a half-hearted attempt to hide her disappointment. "I'm happy for you."

"I wish it could have played out differently," Ronny said with a mournful sigh.

"I came to the conclusion that I was wasting my time. Being made a fool of."

"She's the one being a fool on that TV program, wearing outlandish costumes."

"It's none of my business, but why would she degrade herself that way? She's better than that."

"Money, attention."

Ronny pressed his lips tightly together and slowly shook his head. "Shame, I could have given her both. So, Rosaria is a married woman! Who would have thought she'd beat Margo to the altar?"

"Patsy's a good boy. Italian, but very nice. I'm a grandmother."

"I heard!" Ronny reached into his jacket pocket with his wounded hand.

"Jesus, Mary, and Joseph! What happened to your hand?"

"I brought my girl a puppy, the mutt bit me. If it happens again, I'll have the animal destroyed. They carry diseases." Ronny took hold of Berta's hand with both of his and folded her fingers over a roll of bills. "I'm doing well. I enjoy sharing my good fortune. Give it to Rosaria. For the baby."

"Oh, Ronald, I feel terrible."

"Save your pity for those who truly need it. I'll never understand why she fell out of love with me, but God does. His ways are not our ways. I trust his infinite wisdom. I hate to sour the conversation, and I assure you it's not why I came here... It's the neighborhood. I worry. A day doesn't pass that I don't think of the Ronan family on the Mount. You're surrounded, and the cavalry isn't on its way."

"They're not savages."

"Some are. I know about Margo being attacked. I'd kill any man who lays a hand on her."

Berta eyed him coldly. "How did you hear of it?"

"Ida, Dr. Thane's nurse. I still come back here for check-ups. He's a great dentist. Did you hear he's moving to Quincy? They keep narcotics in the office. Ida no longer feels safe in this neighborhood."

"Nuala didn't go to Dr. Thane. She purposely went to a dentist in Stoughton, so there wouldn't be any talk."

Ronny nervously rocked on his heels. "All these nurses know one another. With Margo being a TV personality and all, I'm sure the grapevine is buzzing. Did she report it to the police?"

"No, as you say, she's a celebrity."

"Big mistake. With any luck, they could have gotten the monster off the street, but there will always be another to take his place. Mrs. Ronan, I'm begging you, get out before someone gets killed. We have some fine homes on the market. If it's the money..."

"It's not the money," Berta firmly stated. "This is my house. When I leave, it will be feet up."

"The Jews are smart people. They sold and made a profit, the ones who left early. These criminal types don't care if you're White or Jewish. They even kill their own."

"If the others want to run, good riddance."

"Very well. If you change your mind, give me a jingle. Margo needn't know."

"This is not Nuala's house. It's mine."

"What I mean is, she doesn't need to know I've been here. The poor kid's been through enough. Was she beaten?"

"She said it looked worse than it was."

"Then she wasn't... You know."

"God, no!"

"I'm ashamed to say, I tried to get her to go all the way with me, but I planned to marry her. She wouldn't hear of it. No, Margo's a good girl. Too good for me. I hope she finds a man worthy of her. I'd best be on my way. Give my love to Rosaria and Mae."

"It was good to see you, Ronald. I'll be looking for your wedding picture in the society pages. I'm sure she's a lovely girl."

"She's in college. Once she graduates, we'll set the date."

"A college girl? You've done well."

"She's as beautiful as she is smart. I will say this for myself. I have great taste in women."

Margo shook the roses in her mother's face. "Where did these come from?"

"A fan," Berta answered.

Margo studied the small card attached to the red bow.

"The note is in Ronny's handwriting. He wants me to know he sent them."

"Can't you be gracious?"

"No, Ma, I can't. I thought he gave up harassing me."

"He asked you to marry him."

"He was hungover when he proposed. You don't need a crystal ball to see where that marriage would have ended up."

"You'll be pleased to learn he's engaged."

"Lucky girl...wait a minute," Margo said, tapping the card on the vase. "How did you know he was getting married? He delivered these himself. I can't believe you let him in this house!"

"It's my house. I'll let in whomever I please."

"If he's in love with another woman, why the flowers?"

"He heard you were assaulted."

"Who told him?"

"He gave some cock and bull story of how Dr. Thane's nurse knows Dr. Trescott's nurse. In any case, he knows."

"I wouldn't put it past him to have hired someone to attack me."

"Nuala!"

"Ma, Ronny hates me. He hates this town despite the fact he and Daddy-o own most of it. They're the ones who sold to people who couldn't afford the mortgage payments or upkeep. He's the one putting fear into the minds of good, decent people. He doesn't want me. He wants this house, another feather in his cap."

"He has good intentions."

"Ma! The man's a racist, antisemite, and corrupt drunk."

181

"He's none of those things. You let a good man get away."

Margo tasted venom seeping into her saliva. She wanted to spit the poison at her mother to generate the same impact the rape had on her. "Ronny called Rosaria a pitiful cripple."

The words shot from Margo's mouth like a bullet to her mother's heart. Berta crinkled her eyes and hunched her shoulders as she leaned over the roses, as red as her face. "He called her a what?"

"We discussed marriage. Ronny said he and his family would appreciate it if I didn't have Rosaria in the wedding party. He said, 'How's it going to look: Your alkie father hanging off your arm and Rosaria hobbling behind you. She'll look pitiful and make people uncomfortable." I said, 'I know your mother is behind this, and you're a cripple for not standing up to her.'"

"I don't believe you."

"You think I'd make up such a sick, cruel story?"

"I'm calling him."

Margo raced to the phone. "Please, don't. I can't have Rosaria know. She thinks the world of Ronny." Without a word, Berta picked up the vase of flowers, shouldering Margo out of her path as a way of saying, "This goes for you, too."

Margo heard the crash of the metal trash can lid followed by, "Garbage!"

Chapter Thirteen

"Patsy, open up!" Normally, Patsy would welcome a diversion from the *FOUNDATIONS of LOGIC,* but preferred Nietzsche to Nicky.

"Come on, Patsy, I know you're in there." Slamming the textbook shut, he answered his brother's call.

"Patsy, you gotta help me," Nicky said, pushing past his brother and into the cramped first-floor apartment.

"What is it now? Stash a gun? Lie to a girlfriend?"

"It's money."

"Then you've come to the wrong place. You need money, go see Papa."

"I'd rather they kill me."

"Let them."

"I need a couple of grand pronto, or the next time you see me, they'll be pulling me out of the Mystic River. You got dough salted away for the house."

"Exactly, for the house. Not for you to put on a horse. My family comes first."

"They'll kill me, send pictures to Mama of me with my guts hanging out. I'm thinking of her, not me."

"You know what she'll do? She'll look at the pictures, tear them up, and go back to her soap opera."

"What are you gonna tell little Fredrik when you take him to visit his grandparents' graves? Ya gonna say 'Uncle Nicky ain't with them. He died pleading for his life in a Chelsea basement. Uncle Nicky was involved with bad men who wanted money, money I coulda lent him, but I wanted to buy a house with the dough and wouldn't wait a couple of weeks to get the money back.'" Nicky's voice squeaked. 'Why didn't we get the new house, Daddy?'

"Because the bad men took Grandpa away. When he didn't return, Grandma had a heart attack. Don't cry, Freddy; look on the bright side. We inherited their house and got to keep the money that coulda saved everyone's life."

"Cut the dramatics. The money is for Rosie's house, and when Fredrik asks about his uncle, I'll tell him that's what happens when you deal with thugs."

Nicky paced and puffed. "Ask Rosie. She's got a big heart. She'll understand."

"Look, I'll give you enough to skip town."

"They'll find me, kill me, and you'll never get your money back."

"I'll give you a grand. That should hold them off until you can scrape up the rest."

"I owe them three, plus the vig."

"Jesus, Nicky!"

"Last time, Patsy, I swear. I'll get the money back to you with interest."

***

Rosaria had gone to church for a cry and counseling. When she returned home, it was after dark. Patsy sat at the kitchen table with his head in his hands. "Look, I've been thinking it over."

184

"Did you tell Fredrik he'd have to wait a few more years before he can have a puppy and a backyard?"

"Please, Rosie, I feel bad enough."

"Not yet. You still have to inform your parents."

"They needn't know. We can tell them the deal fell through, or the steps were too steep for you."

"You are not to use my disability to cover for your stupidity." "All we need is a little more time. When Nicky gets back..." "It's been six weeks; Nicky is not coming back."

"We'll see the money again."

"Over my dead body."

***

"Mama, Papa," Patsy coughed into his fist. "We... I mean, I have something to tell you. It's about the house. We're not able to swing the down payment."

Carla waved her hand at her son. "Forget about that house. Remember the two-family you looked at? Well, Papa thought if we sell this building, with the money from the sale, plus what you have saved up, we could buy that house together."

"Mama, the money's gone."

Carla limped toward her son, who knew her intent. "You gave that money to your brother." Rosaria gasped and stepped back. Carla's slap sent Patsy into a bookcase, ripping a large gash into his forehead. "How could you put your brother ahead of your wife and child? Years, you scrimped and saved, missing holidays, birthdays, and the birth of your son so as not to miss school or work. You did it all for Nicky to hand it over to mobsters. By now, I thought you had the good sense not to give in to him. You'll never learn."

"He said they'd kill him."

"Good. Save the state on the electric bill. Two boys, one a thief, the other an idiot! I want you out of this house! You won't provide a home for your family; I wouldn't provide one for you. Rosie and the baby can stay." Rosaria stepped between mother and son.

"He's not your boy, Carla. He's my husband, Fredrik's father. We go wherever he goes."

"Can't you see what he's done? He promised you a house."

"What Patsy promised was to love me in sickness and in health, for richer or poorer. He's kept those vows. I don't recall any mention of a house. I'll tell you what he provided: unconditional love. That's something I'm grappling with. He gave me a son. Patsy's done more for me than any doctor or therapist could. He gave me a reason to walk.

"I went from a self-pitying cripple to a wife, mother, and independent woman. It's a house. There will be another. I can wait. I waited twenty years for your son. He's not perfect, nor are we. I may be hurt, but I'm also loved." Rosaria made her way downstairs. Patsy ran after her.

"Rosie," he said in a soft voice. "Thank you."

"Leave me alone," she ordered with a shove.

"Please, hear me out. I'm sorry, not just about the house, but for rushing into marriage. I was a teenager who thought he was a big man. I had a beautiful, classy, educated wife, the kind of woman other men wonder what she sees in him. Some man I turned out to be. Your sister paid for our wedding."

"It was a gift. She wanted to do it for us."

"I promised you a ring, a honeymoon."

"I don't want either."

"But you did want that house. I failed you. I'm not a husband. I'm a stupid kid pretending to be a man. My mother had every right to smack me; she always will. She's my mother, I deserved it. Nicky's been stealing from me since I was a kid. 'Can I borrow this? Will you lend me that?' He even stole my tricycle. Not a bicycle, *tricycle*. I was four years old. He sold it to a kid down the street. Mama would say, 'He's a criminal, don't cave to him!' It's taken all these years, but tonight, I finally learned that lesson—not because my mother slapped my face, but because I broke your heart. Any other woman would walk out on me, go downtown, and find a real man."

"I don't want a man who hangs downtown. I want a man who comes out in a snowstorm to bring home his mother and the woman who will always love him, and that's the kind of man I want my son to grow up to become."

***

Mac's feet swung off the desk as he stashed his photojournalism in the wastebasket. "Jumpin' Jesus, Sunny! How long have you been standing there?"

"May I have a word with you?"

"Only if it's a word." Margo slithered into the chair across from his desk and put her head down over her folded arms.

"Sunny baby, what's with the precipitation? If this has to do with the tornado that hit the Midwest, Iola is making changes. I swear this time you won't lose your funnel cloud."

"I'm pregnant."

Mac's palm slammed down on the desk like a Baptist minister's on a Bible. "JEEZUS! I never should have let you watch those movies."

"I was raped."

"When did this all go down?"

"A few weeks ago. I know it was foolhardy, but I walked part of the way home. The air was charged with dark omens. Crisp autumn leaves painted the pavement, beckoning me to follow."

Mac clutched the back of his neck and rotated his head. "May I interrupt this ode to autumn? I don't need to know where it was done or how it was done. I've done it. Not on a bed of crisp autumn leaves, but I've done it. Follow? Now, who knocked you up? I know people. I'll have the animal castrated."

"You can't."

187

"Whatddya mean, I can't?"

"Have you heard the name Conrad R. Kilday?"

"What about him?"

"I was raped by Conrad R. Kilday Jr."

A wily smile crept across Mac's lips. "Sunny baby, you hit the jackpot! He'll be paying for that baby and your lavish lifestyle for the rest of his life. Screw the castration; his life is over. Marry the bastard."

"I can't. It's my mother."

"Never thought I'd say it. Sunny, you're a genius. Once your mother moves in, he'll never get it up again."

"She warned me this would happen. I don't want to give her the satisfaction of saying I told you so. There was a different set of standards for me, ones she knew I couldn't adhere to." Mac rolled his eyes. "Sure, all kids get into trouble, but she set the bar too high. To make matters worse, she thinks Ronny is the answer to every maiden's prayer."

"I was a young man when this story began."

"You were never young."

"Then listen to the voice of experience. Let's say you took a job out West, someplace like... Pasadena."

"Can't you make it, L.A.?"

"Okay, Sunny, LAAAA. Now, you're in L.A., making good money, your life is peachy, then this happens. I'll even sweeten the deal. You found yourself a great guy, not the answer to every maiden's prayer, but he loves you, wants to raise the kid as his own. Would you keep it?"

Margo lowered her head and whispered. "No. I'm selfish. I was seven when my sister was born."

Mac checked his watch.

"My mother asked Rosaria and me to help with the baby. Rosaria loved caring for our new sister. Not me, no I ..."

"Sunny, save it for Freud. What do you want to do about this kid?" Margo dabbed her eyes with a tissue, smudging her heavy makeup, revealing a crescent-shaped bruise. "Looks like someone gave you a shiner."

"Compliments of Mr. Kilday. I didn't want Estell to know, so I've been applying my own makeup."

"Damn. I just fired Estell for making a mess of your face."

"Apologize. She'll forgive you."

"For the makeup, but not for calling her a washed-up has-been. She had better not pull her suicide routine."

"Suicide!"

"I never told you 'bout that? A couple of years back, the batty broad goes into the bathroom and slices her wrist, like I'm the worst thing she's ever woke up next to. That's bullshit. Ya wanna know what her experience with makeup is? She's got this thing where she has guys smear makeup over their face, then she licks it off. It's some kind of sick turn-on for her. I only hired her out of pity, cause she was going through a messy breakup with a rodeo clown. She must be over him. I hear she's shackin' up with a mime."

"Mac! What about me?"

"You had better decide what you're going to do and fast. In a few months, that weather system will show up on the radar."

Mac returned to his desk, tucked the telephone receiver under his chin. Using both hands, he flipped through a Rolodex.

"Who are you calling?"

"Willis. He takes care of these delicate matters."

"An abortionist? You're sending me to a back-alley abortionist?!"

"You think I'd send you to a back alley?"

"Why not? You live in one."

"Willis ain't no abortionist. He's my go-to guy. He'll drive you to New York, where it's legal."

***

A breeze swept in from the front room. "Nuala, is that you?"

"Yes, Ma." Margo took a deep breath as she swung open the kitchen door. "I'm going upstairs to pack. Mac is sending me to New York on Sunday to audition a couple of depicters for the Denver station."

Berta detected an urgency in her daughter to leave the room, the hallmark of a poorly crafted lie. "Why doesn't he fly them here?"

"Mac didn't want to spend the money to fly them to Boston, so I'm meeting them halfway in New York City."

"Nuala, the man knows his geography. You don't. New York is not halfway between Boston and Colorado. Now, tell me the truth."

"Why would I lie? That's what he told me."

"That story has more holes in it than Carter has liver pills. I know his kind. He's running a White slavery ring."

"It's just a couple of days. I leave on Sunday and return on Tuesday. I'm twenty-one. I don't need your permission." Margo turned on her heels and exited the kitchen.

Berta shook her head. "I don't know what's gotten into that girl. She'll deny it like Saint Peter, but that man is sending her to New York to pose for a nudie calendar."

Mae patted her sister's hand. "Don't let your imagination run wild. I'll have a word with her."

Margo walked into her room. "I have to go. If I don't leave Sunday, it will be too late." A gentle tap and a soft voice broke Margo's mantra. Positioning herself at her mirrored vanity, Margo snatched a tissue and wiped her eyes. "Come in. I'm taking off my eye makeup." A process she took care to point out, fearing her aunt would notice her puffy eyes.

Mae sat on the pink chenille bedspread. "Is this trip necessary?"

"I don't know why she hates Mac. The guy's a pig, but he looks out for me. My job's a joke, but I love that people look forward to seeing me depict. This could be my ticket to the big time. She thinks I'll audition for a Broadway play while I'm in New York and never come home."

"You're pregnant."

Margo looked as if a hypnotist had snapped his fingers in her face. "I...I don't know."

"If I know, you know. And soon, your mother will know."

"I can't tell her."

"You'll have to."

"Here's my plan. I'm going to call home from New York and tell her I'm going to try my hand at acting. I'll put the baby up for adoption, then come home and tell her I failed. She'll like that."

"How will you support yourself?"

"Mac will send me money."

"The child is his?"

Margo squeezed her face. "Yuk, no."

"What you plan on doing is akin to murder. That's why you're going to New York."

"No matter what I do, my life is over. I'll lose my job, my freedom, my looks, and when Ma finds out, my life. I can't keep this baby. She'll poison its mind, turn it against me. And nobody will ever marry me."

"Ronny will. Your mother will forgive you if this baby brings you two back together."

"It brought us together all right. Ronny is a sick, vicious drunk. This baby was conceived after I was raped, beaten, and left for dead in Sagamore Park. I wasn't mugged. Do you want details?"

"People change."

"Change! What planet do you live on? That's so last century. Would you ask Rosaria to marry a man who had beaten and raped her?

Of course not! Then why me? I'll tell you why because I'm a cheap, worthless flirt. Girls like me ask for it. We get pregnant, have abortions."

"Have you ever wondered why I never married, had children?"

"No."

"Yes, you have, everyone has. I can't have children because I made a selfish decision."

"You had an abortion?"

"Back then, there was no going to New York. As you say, only cheap girls get pregnant. The fella would go to the redlight district, ask around, and pay a hefty sum to put you up in a rundown room where you hoped whoever performs the abortion has some medical training. This was the height of the Depression; you could get anyone to do anything for a buck. I was butchered. I'm lucky to be alive. One way or another, God gets his pound of flesh. I was taken to a hospital. Grandma was told my appendix burst. I took the coward's way out to spare myself from the shame it would bring to both families. I was truly sorry for killing an innocent child of God, yet He allowed me to live. I now know why. It's to keep you from repeating my mistake."

"Your history won't change mine."

"Go through with this, and you won't have a history, only a past. Please, Margo. Don't destroy two lives to spare the feelings of one. She'll forgive you. There's a side to your mother that emerges whenever there's a crisis, when someone she loves is hurting, in peril, in need of her strength. Give her the opportunity to show you that side."

"This guy, the father, did you love him?"

"I thought I did. I only saw the good in him, Berta only the bad."

"You're going to tell her."

"No, you are."

"If I don't?"

"Don't make me do it, Margo. You have until Sunday. Think long and hard. You have until Sunday."

***

Since September, Colleen's days were spent in a school uniform, compliments of Sunny, who paid for her to be enrolled in a Catholic girls' high school. Having grown another two inches in both height and girth, Mae suggested they head downtown for a few wardrobe essentials. Soon, there wouldn't be shopping excursions with her aunt; this may be their last.

"I'm taking Colleen shopping; she hasn't anything that fits," Mae informed Berta.

"Did Omar the Tentmaker open a shop downtown?"

Mae reprimanded her sister with her eyes.

"Sorry, Mae, but all that girl does is eat and study; she needs to get on a diet and off the chuck wagon."

The subway train rumbled into South Station, Colleen's favorite destination, dating back to the day she and Poppy met Sister Virginia's train. It wasn't just the rails she found exciting, but the station's platform packed with sailors, an ocean of navy-blue uniforms in the winter months, and waves of white foam in the summer.

As Mae had promised, they lunched at a white tablecloth restaurant with leather-bound menus and black jacketed waiters. Colleen was having a wonderful Saturday afternoon; she only wished Mae shared in the joy.

Having just missed their returning train, the two shoppers adjusted their bundles on the empty platform. Smoking a cigarette, Mae looked off into the distance. Colleen studied her aunt's face. She looked old. Colleen had never noticed the droopy folds of Mae's cheeks or marionette lines previously hidden by her smile.

A tramp tapped Mae's shoulder. "Got a smoke?"

Mae slid a Raleigh out of the pack. She only smoked the brand for its coupons. Poppy said they tasted like camel shit, only Poppy would recognize the flavor. The grateful panhandler tipped his cap and moved on.

Colleen sensed it was time to share a funny story. "I was remembering the time Poppy drove us down to Baltimore for Sister Virginia's funeral. You know how Margo is when it comes to geography. Well, she looks out the car window and asks, 'What ocean is this?' Ma goes mental because Margo's so stupid. Ma turned around and yelled, 'I'll give you a hint: we're in Atlantic City!'

"Then Margo says, 'I didn't ask the name of the city. I asked the name of the ocean. If you don't know, just say, I don't know.' I took a worse beating than she did for laughing." Colleen chuckled over her story.

Her aunt didn't render a smile or a "That's nice, dear." She continued to smoke and stare. The tramp returned.

"Got any spare change?" he asked, holding out his palm as if he knew the answer. Mae snapped open her change purse and handed the man a quarter. He called her an angel and walked on. Wearing a curious expression, Colleen cocked her head. "Why did you give him money? He's only going to spend it on booze."

Mae answered without breaking her distant stare. "Once upon a time, that man was a tiny baby and the most important person in the world to someone." Mae looked into her niece's questioning eyes. "I think his mother is glad I gave him that quarter."

Colleen raced into the kitchen. "Ma, Ma! Look at the dress Mae bought me." Mae labored behind, placing twine-handled boxes on the counter. Berta put down a can opener and gave her sister an exasperated look. "Are you off your rocker? Why buy her a dress she'll outgrow by Christmas?"

Her mother's back to her. Colleen clacked her fingers like a quacking duck. "I'm going upstairs to show Margo the dress. She'll say I shouldn't wear yellow, but it's more orange than yellow."

"Don't bother, Nuala left with one of Mac's weirdo friends."

Mae's face dropped with her bundles. "She's gone?"

"She's gone all right. I don't know why she was in such a hurry to get out of here."

"She left?"

"Yes, Mae, are you well? Mae?"

"I'm fine, just tired."

"A day with Colleen will wear anyone out."

***

Behind the wheel sat Willis. Short, bald, and barrel-chested, he was the Jeff to Mac's Mutt. His face looked like a crumpled piece of yellowed paper. The only hint he had eyes or a nose was a pair of thick black framed eyeglasses worn tight to his face like driving goggles. "Whaddaya lookin' at?"

"Your jacket. This is November. Nylon isn't a year-round fabric, and it's washable. You're repugnant."

"No, I'm Willis. The rules are, no gum snappin', no rockin' roll music, or any of your chin music. It distracts me 'cuz I don't see too good."

"Great, I've got Mister Magoo at the wheel." Margo defiantly slid a stick of chewing gum in her mouth and snapped on the car radio, only to hear the third race from Suffolk Downs. Willis flashed a sideways smile. "Follow the ponies, do ya?" Margo wrestled with the dial.

"Don't bother. I got it rigged."

195

"Is the car heater rigged?"

"If you're cold, there's a blanket in the backseat."

"Is there a body rolled up in it?"

"This ain't The Ritz, and I ain't no chauffeur. You're a kid in a jam. Mac wants to help you. I want to help Mac."

"Why? What's he got on you?"

Willis swerved the car into the breakdown lane. "Let me set you wise, girlie. I know you're all pregnant and emotional, but you gotta understand somethin': Mac don't spend money—but he's spendin' it on you. He wouldn't bankroll this trip if he didn't care about ya. If he scrambled some other dame's eggs, he'd send her into the woods to give birth and sell the kid into slavery."

"I was raped by an ex-boyfriend. This child is not Mac's. I find the mere suggestion abhorrent."

"Abhorrent. Now that's a fancy word."

"Unlike you and your cohort, I have a high school education and a diploma to prove it." Margo accentuated her statement with a head bob.

"Don't get your panties in a twist. Between you, me, and the gatepost, I think our friend had his cables cut, so he don't

have to pay for no kids. Look, you're a nice girl, a talented girl, with a future in depicting. So, let's settle down, relax, and enjoy the ride."

Willis pulled back onto the highway.

"Tell me about Mac."

"What do ya wanna know?"

"Where did you meet?"

"Prep school."

"Prep school!" Margo gave Willis a limp slap on his arm. "You, kidder!"

"Truth be told, Mac and me shared accommodations back in Toledo. That's where I'm from. Mac's old man sent him there to learn the ropes. Mac didn't take to the place, but the old man told him if he screwed up, he'd send him to Altoona."

Margo's eyes widened. "Is Al Tuna some kind of leg breaker?"

"Mac's right. You *are* a dippy dame."

"What do you do for a living?"

"Ya mean, a day job?"

"Yes, a day job."

"I don't work on days."

Margo flung her hair off her shoulders. "Fine, don't tell me."

"I'm a talent scout. I'll let you in on a little secret. Ya wanna hear it?"

"Oh, yes!"

"I thought ya might. I'm the guy who discovered ya. I told Mac about ya, and he sent a good-looking guy out to fetch ya. See, Mac had the idea for a depicter when he saw one in a blue movie. He put the project on the back burner 'cuz he couldn't find the right girl. He auditioned a bunch of them, but none of them wuz any good."

"Does he have a casting couch in that flophouse he lives in?"

"That's just it. He didn't want some dirtbag. He wanted a nice girl, a good girl." Willis snapped his fingers. "What was the word he used? Clean. Yeah, that's the word. He wanted a girl who was clean. The kinda girl the folks at home would look at like she was their daughter, but you knew, given the right circumstances, you could get her to give out."

"Was that the job description?"

Willis curled his lip. "Ya know what you wuz doin' when I first saw ya?"

"Washing my hands?"

"You wuz putting on lipstick."

"That's why you chose me?"

"It was pink lipstick. See, pink says, "I want to wear red, but I'm not experienced, teach me.""

"I can wear red now. I've done it."

"Don't cry, I'm warnin' ya."

"Cheer me up. Tell me about Mac. I can't figure the guy out. He never talks about his personal life. He doesn't sleep, bathe, or change his clothes. He doesn't drink, does he?"

"Nope."

"He's an alcoholic. He says he's not, but he is, huh?"

"Mac, don't waste money on somethin' that's gonna turn to piss or a lawsuit."

"If someone were to buy him a drink, would he drink it?"

"If someone wuz to buy him undershorts, would he wear them?"

Margo's face fell. "He told you about that?"

"He thought it was cute."

"Mac said cute?"

"Those weren't his exact words, but that's what he meant."

"Does he eat? I've never seen him eat. I can't imagine him seated at a table using silverware. I envision him crouching on the floor, eating from a dog bowl."

"I've seen him do that, but not 'cuz he's hungry. He eats at a place down the Combat Zone that serves women." Willis wore a look of amusement, knowing his passenger didn't pick up on the joke.

"Does he have a girlfriend?"

"We shared a couple of hookers, Goldie Fish and Chickee Fox. "

"Do you still see them?"

"Nah, one flew the coop, and the other swam ashore."

"He spends lots of time with hookers, huh?"

"Sunny, I don't keep tabs on the guy. He eats, sleeps, works, and fucks. That's all he does. Mac and me are like cavemen put in the modern world, and that world is changing fast. That don't go over too good with us. We like to come and go as we please, not answer to nobody. We don't have any problem a T-bone steak and a 38D can't cure."

Downcast, Margo lowered her head. "I'm a member of that club now. Only I'm clean."

Willis reached out to stroke her hair. He pulled his hand back. "You ain't like us, never will be. You're goin' places 'cuz people love you. You've got good things in your future."

"You're wrong, Willis. I know why I was raped."

"Ya, do?"

"Yes. It's because I watched those dirty movies with Mac. God punished me by having me raped."

"God ain't like that."

Margo buried her face in her hands and sobbed. "I'm sorry, God, I'm sorry!"

"I know what will cheer you up. Have you ever heard Mac sing and play piano?"

Margo wiped her eyes with her wrist. "Mac sings?"

"You didn't know he was a musician? No joke, he plays piano real good—and what a voice! Like opera."

"Why haven't I heard him sing?"

"Cuz he only sings when he's drunk or in love. And he don't drink."

"Then how did you witness a performance?"

"Like I told ya, we used ta room together. Every morning or thereabouts, he'd look in the mirror and sing to himself when he shaved."

"Mac shaves?"

"Sure, he does. I bought him one of those electric shavers after there was..." Willis paused, searching for the right word from his limited vocabulary. "An incident with a straight razor. Besides, he likes that you don't need soap or water with an electric."

"Let's hear a tune from the Mangus Mac Godfrey songbook."

Willis concentrated on driving. The road was slick, and a light drizzle and fog clouded the windshield. "What songs does he sing?"

"He likes the one that goes, '*When my life is through, and the angels ask me to recall.*'"

Margo joined in. "*The thrill of them all, I shall tell them I remember you.* Oh my God, that's my favorite song... favorite old people's song. What else does he sing?"

"I'm not tell'n ya cuz you'll go back to the studio whistling the song, and I'll end up with a toilet brush rammed up my ass."

"I don't whistle. The nuns told us, whenever a girl whistles, the Virgin Mary cries."

"That's why you don't whistle?"

"Yes."

"If that's the case... "

"What?"

Willis shook his head. "Neva mind. I don't want you going loopy on me."

"Willis!"

"Not for nothin, but if Mary cries when you whistle, and Jesus has you raped for watchin' smut, what are they gonna do to ya for havin' an abortion?" The rain turned torrential. The wipers couldn't keep pace with the fat slush slapping the windshield.

"I ain't nevah seen it rain this bad. I'm pullin' over. This car is surfin'."

"Turn around," Margo ordered.

"Are you nuts!"

"You heard me. Turn this car around. God wants me to have this baby. I don't know why, it's not my place to ask."

"It's mine! I knew I shoulda kept my yap shut."

"God got me pregnant because I'm selfish, jealous, and prideful. I always put myself first. Now I'll have to change my ways. My time and money will be spent on the baby. I'll be robbed of my looks, wear a housecoat, and get Jean Nate for Christmas."

"Listen, girlie, we're thirty minutes from the city; I ain't goin' back to Boston for no housecoat."

"Then let me out of the car."

"And have you drowned in Mary's tears? Not in your life. Speakin' of which, when Mac sees us pull up, he'll go apeshit. You won't need any abortion; he'll rip that kid out of ya and strangle ya with the cord, and then want his money back... I got an idea. We go to New York, tell him you had the abortion, then next week you tell him you were raped again, only this time you're gonna keep it."

"Turn this car around."

"Okay, but I'm a dead man."

***

201

Berta looked out of the front window at the street. "Maybe Marty's right about this neighborhood. I don't think a week goes by that I don't see a police car on the street."

Mae joined Berta at the window. "Those aren't Boston Police, they're State Troopers."

**

Doctor Merrill was old, with a no-nonsense attitude. Margo feared he'd reprimand her for taking up a bed and his time.

"How do you feel?" he asked while taking her vitals.

"Is there anything you can give me for the pain?" Margo whimpered.

"You're receiving pain medication through that glass bottle hanging over your bed. A higher dose isn't necessary."

Margo spit up clear liquid. "I'm not a whiner," she whined.

The doctor took a seat next to her bed. "The X-ray shows you suffered a concussion. There's nerve damage in your neck and spine, but it was internal bleeding that brought you to surgery. The car crash caused a uterine rupture. I'm sorry, Miss Ronan, you lost the baby. Normally, in these cases, I'd perform a hysterectomy. You were unconscious when you arrived at the hospital. I asked your mother to sign the consent form so I could perform the hysterectomy while I had you in the O.R. Your mother was... for lack of a better word, hostile toward any surgery other than what was medically necessary to save your life."

Margo's head dropped back down on the pillow. "Then she knows."

"She knows you had a ruptured uterus, not that you were pregnant. As it stands, you can't carry another child. With a hysterectomy, you'll still have your ovaries and avoid gynecological complications in the future."

" Will I develop a hunch back and grow a beard like my mother?"

"Miss Ronan, do you understand what I've just told you?"

"Yes. I lost the baby, can't have another, and my mother knows it."

"Miss Ronan, you're over twenty-one, an adult. I'm not at liberty to disclose any information regarding your hospitalization without your written consent."

Margo rubbed her temples. "My head hurts, my neck is stiff, and my leg tingles."

"My guess is a swollen muscle is putting pressure on a nerve; it's temporary, but I'll have a neurologist stop in on you."

"Does Dr. Hirsh still work here?"

"Yes, but he's a surgeon, not a clinician."

"Aaron is a dear family friend. He'd be very upset were he to learn I've been admitted and he wasn't informed."

"Miss Ronan, Dr. Hirsh is a very busy man."

Margo rubbed her leg. "Please?"

"He'll be informed. Your mother and aunt are waiting outside. Shall I send them in?"

"I guess so."

Both women appeared more annoyed than relieved. Margo expected a sour attitude from her mother, but not from Mae, whose kiss was cold and mechanical. Margo ran her fingers through her hair. "How do I look?"

Berta took the question. "Your face is in one piece if that's what concerns you."

"Doctor Merrill said I can go home on Wednesday."

"You'll heal better at home," Berta commented as she looked around the room. "God only knows what you'll come down with in a hospital."

"Where are Colleen and Rosaria?"

"It's a school day for Colleen. As for Rosaria, 'Papa' died last night. She's with them. We'll stop by after we leave here."

Margo breathed a sympathetic sigh. "Poor Carla."

"Poor Carla, my eye. Don't tell me she didn't see it coming. I did. Let's see if her son, the thief, turns up at his father's funeral. He's probably riddled with bullets in a shallow grave he was forced to dig for himself. That's how they dispose of his kind."

A beaming candy striper in a red-and-white striped pinafore stood at the door holding a bouquet of pink roses. "Someone has an admirer." The teenage girl gushed as if the flowers were hers.

Margo hastily tore open the envelope. "It's from the gang at the station."

Berta huffed. "That penny pincher probably got a two-for-one deal: a bouquet for your bedside, and a wreath for his friend's casket."

"Willis is dead?"

"I was surprised myself. It's usually the innocent passenger who's killed." Berta stood. "We're leaving. I don't think we're helping your morale."

Margo rubbed her neck. "I wish they'd give me something for this pain."

"Offer it up," Berta recommended as she departed.

Margo gripped Mae's hand. "You go ahead, Berta. I'll meet you at the elevator."

Margo dropped her voice. "I didn't go through with it."

"It no longer matters," Mae replied in a stern tone. "The baby is dead. You needn't worry about having another."

"Please, Mae, you've got to believe me. The car was northbound. I was pregnant when I arrived. I'll let you see my medical record."

"We'll leave it for another time. Your mother is waiting for me." About to step into the corridor, Mae paused. "Who was Willis?"

"A friend of Mac's."

"I didn't think he had friends."

"Now, he doesn't."

***

"Another Ronan to examine."

"Dr. Hirsh!" Margo cried, pushing her breakfast tray aside. "I've lost feeling in my leg. I need you to get it back for me."

Aaron looked into her chart for a name. "Nuala."

"Margo."

Aaron closed her chart and folded his arms. "Okay, Margo. Tell me what concerns you."

"My leg is numbish."

"Have you tried walking?"

"Not really. I'm afraid I'll fall," she lied, hoping he'd assist her with the same affection he'd shown Rosaria.

"Dr. Merrill plans to discharge you tomorrow. You can't return home until you're ambulatory."

"Ambulatory?"

"Walking."

"Oh, well. Um, maybe I can try."

"I'll get Nurse Hoyt in here..."

"We don't need her." Margo tugged on the doctor's jacket, bringing herself to her feet and face-to-face with her latest crush. "I need a second to steady myself."

Aaron held out his arm as if escorting her onto a dance floor, not with the tight embrace she'd witnessed when helping Rosaria to her feet. Margo took a few cautious steps, grabbing onto anything available to steady herself. "That's fine for now."

She returned to her bed as if walking a tightrope. Aaron removed a retractable metal rod from his jacket pocket.

"I'm going to run this down your leg. Tell me where the numbness begins and ends."

Margo slid her pink nightie that could qualify as a negligee up her leg as far as decency allowed. "Isn't there a pulse up here you're supposed to feel?"

Aaron arched his brow. "Not necessary. I think I know what ails you, and going home to your mother is the best remedy. By the way, how's my girl Rosaria coming along?"

"Your 'girl' is a mother."

"A baby! That's great news! Boy or girl?"

"Boy. She had him last year."

"I don't get over to my mother's often, so I'm not up to speed on the neighborhood news. Say hello to Rosaria for me. She's always on my mind."

"I'm sure she is." As he turned to leave, Margo stuck her tongue out at his back.

***

The plan was to casually walk into the studio unnoticed until she could gauge Mac's mood. When the sun appears after a stretch of cloudy weather, people can't help but look up. Any other time, Margo would welcome attention. But not today.

"Yes, I'm fine. How kind of you. I missed you all. The flowers were beautiful."

Margo stood facing the General Manager's closed door. "I dread going in there."

Zip offered words of encouragement. "He'll never admit it, but he was just as worried about you as the rest of us."

Standing tall, she tapped the door's frosted glass with her fingernails, not her knuckles.

"WHAT?" cracked a voice sounding like a lion tamer's whip.

Contrite and teary-eyed, Margo slithered into the office. "Mac?" Seated at his desk, hunched over paperwork, Mac neither answered nor raised his eyes.

"The doctor said I'm well enough to return to work... that's if you want me to."

"It's up to you," he replied into the stack of papers.

"My contract's not up. I wouldn't want to break it."

"We'll survive. You're free to leave. There won't be a penalty imposed." Mac raised his head to steal a peek at her expression.

Margo had never been the object of his ire; it was the smoldering, degrading brand. She stood rooted to the floor, wishing he'd just yell at her. This, from a man she'd regarded as a friend and mentor, even if he didn't view their relationship in the same light.

"I'm sorry, Mac."

"Yeah, yeah."

"Will you look at me? Yell at me. Tell me how Willis would be alive if it hadn't been for me."

Mac slammed down his pen. "Would he? I wasn't there."

"I WAS!"

"It doesn't matter what was going on when the car hit the guardrail. It won't bring him back."

"I wasn't crying, talking his ear off, or grabbing his crotch if that's what your imagination is conjuring up. I dozed off. I awoke when the car veered off the road. For Christ's sake, the man was legally blind!"

"I don't have time to rehash it. There's a storm coming. Why don't you find a raincloud to hide behind?"

Still in pain, Margo backed out of the office. "Thank you for the flowers." As she walked off, she heard him say, "What flowers?"

Chapter Fourteen

Using her vacuum, Freida pushed the hassock out from under her son's feet. "Hey! I was using that." Lee reprimanded his mother.

Freida flipped the canister switch off with her toe. "This is what you do all summer? Read the funny papers?"

"They're comic books. Why shouldn't I goof off? I graduate in a few weeks, passed my finals, and got into Columbia. I don't have to bury my head in a textbook. I hated every day spent in that school. I deserve to sit back and do as I please."

Freida took a seat on the hassock to console her son. "Your classmates didn't know the real Leon."

"If they had, they would have kicked my ass."

"Leon, the mouth."

"I was Leon, The Egghead."

"You could make them eat those eggs," Freida said with a grin and a plan already set in motion.

"How?"

"Go to the prom dance."

"The prom? You need a date to go to the prom, and I don't have an ugly cousin to take."

"She should be one of those head turners."

"If she is the she, I think you have in mind, she's not a head turner, she's a stomach turner."

"Don't be fresh."

"I haven't seen Colleen since grade school. For all I know, she's still there."

"She's a beauty," Freida sang.

Lee's eyes narrowed. "How would you know?"

"Her aunt Mae and Elba Raskind were here last week. You remember Elba."

"Yeah, so?"

"I have them over for lunch from time to time; they worked together at Bloomfield's. The factory closed some time ago. I don't know what was done with the building."

"Mom, Colleen?"

"Colleen came for her aunt. They were to go shopping." Freida pinched Lee's cheeks. "She's not a kid anymore. Maybe you should call and ask her to the dance."

"I can't call her; it's too easy to turn a guy down over the phone."

"Better you go to her house."

"And have her mother come to the door? Not me."

"You could have an accidental meeting."

Lee slapped his forehead with his palm. "Why didn't I think of that? I'll just happen to be at Saint Regina's on Sunday morning."

"Always the comedian." Freida held out the phone. "Call."

"Hello, is Colleen at home?"

"Sure thing, I'll get her." Lee put his hand over the receiver and whispered to his eavesdropping mother. "It's Margo."

The call was answered with an unenthusiastic "Hello."

"Hiya! This is Lee."

There was a painful pause. "Lee. Lee Hirsch?"

"You know some other Lee?" he asked, not pausing for an answer. "Say, I was just thinking, we haven't seen each other in a couple of years."

"Four blissful years."

"For you, maybe. Anyway, I was wondering if we might, you know, go out, catch up on things."

"You need a date for your prom."

"Gee, I hadn't planned on going, but if it means that much to you, I'd be willing to take you so you can feel pretty or something."

"You're still an asshole."

"I'll take that as a yes. I'll pick you up two weeks from Friday at six. Oh, one more thing, no eating with your hands."

Margo reentered the room. "Who was that?"

"Lee."

"What did he want?"

"A date for his prom."

"Talk about hard up."

"Go ahead, Margo, laugh. I'm going to a prom. Psycho Ronny got you thrown out of your prom by showing up drunk." Colleen expressed a phony sense of frustration. "I guess I'm stuck going with him."

"And I'm stuck finding you a dress. It won't be easy: pink, peach, and red draw attention to your blotchy, freckled, dry skin."

"What about yellow? I like yellow."

"Nobody, I mean nobody, wears yellow to a prom," Margo called down to her mother, sorting laundry in the basement.

"Ma, I'm taking Colleen to find a dress. She's going to Lee's prom."

"He must be desperate."

***

Lee stroked the doorbell. Needing a minute to bolster the courage to press, he took a seat on the porch's wicker chair; it crackled like footsteps on gravel. In a black tux with a pink bow box on his lap, he was certain Norman Rockwell had put this adolescent milestone on canvas.

Her arms held open like a magician's assistant having survived being sawed in half, Margo sang out a triumphant, "TA-daaaaah!"

Not accustomed to high heels, Colleen cautiously descended the stately staircase to a round of applause from her mother and aunt.

"I can't wait to see the look on his face," Margo said with pride. "You're almost a thing of beauty."

After a few twirls around the room in her long lavender gown, the doorbell chimed. Margo took hold of Cinderella's shoulders and marched her into the kitchen. "Stand back," Margo instructed her mother and aunt as she held out her arm like a crossing guard. "Don't answer on the first ring." Leaning forward, her hand cupped to her ear, Margo waited... and waited.

"We should have answered it on the first ring. He probably ran off," Berta needled.

"There it is!" Margo flung open the door. "Good evening, Mr. Hirsch."

"WOW! Colleen! You're a sight for sore eyes!" Lee said to everyone's amusement. Colleen entered through the kitchen's swinging door. Dropping to one knee, he spread out his arms in an Al Jolson pose. "Where have you been all my life? Now, I remember the third grade." Colleen swatted his head with her clutch. The audience laughed at the comical couple. "I almost forgot." Lee returned to the porch, retrieving the bowed box. "For you. It's a corsage."

"Why did you leave it outside?"

"In case I chickened out. I didn't, so here," he said, thrusting the box in his date's face. "The florist asked what color dress you'd be wearing. I said ultra-maroon."

Colleen rolled her eyes. "This is shaping up to be a fun evening."

"Pin the corsage on her chest," Margo directed. Lee grinned.

"Don't say it," Colleen warned.

Margo looked down into her Brownie camera. "Stand side by side and pretend you're in love."

"Be snappy with the snaps," Colleen cracked. Lee put his arm around Colleen's waist. She wore a forced smile, not wanting to let on that this was the happiest day of her life. Today, she was the star.

"We must be on our way, Mrs. Ronan. It was a pleasure to see all of you again."

Margo placed a motherly arm around Lee's shoulder. Remember, she's only sixteen, so no monkey business."

"Don't worry, the tux is a rental; I wouldn't want to throw up on it." The insult won him another whack on the head.

Ceremoniously opening the car door, Lee quoted Colleen. "Get in." Being uncomfortable behind the wheel of his father's Lincoln trumped his anxiety at being in close quarters with the powdered and perfumed Colleen. Looking in the rearview mirror, Lee straightened his bowtie and fiddled with the keys. Colleen twisted her face. "If you've got something to say, say it now. I don't want to ruin this dress by jumping out of a moving car."

"My mother was right. You are beautiful when you're disinfected. I'd stack you up against any of those girls at the prom. I can't wait for them to see me walk in with you on my arm."

"These guys, they've been giving you grief?"

"The usual."

Colleen rubbed her hands the way a fly rubs its front legs together. "This is going to be fun."

"Please, Colleen, no jokes or insults at my expense. All I ask is that you pretend to be my girl."

"I thought I was," she said in a low voice while looking out the car window as if she hadn't said it aloud.

***

The music hadn't begun, but the ballroom was buzzing with conversation. The chatter dissolved into dead silence as Lee and his stunning date made their entrance. "Will you look who's here? It's the Hershey bar, and he brought eye candy."

Colleen approached the spokesman of the group, extending her gloved hand à la Margo. "And you are?"

"Spencer Hutchings, class president."

"Is that a step up from class clown, or can you hold both titles?" Colleen had drawn first blood. Spencer gave her a visual once-over.

"Are you sizing me up for a casket?"

"Are you going to need one?"

"If we're stuck sitting at the same table, I'll kill myself."

Lee stepped in. "Spence, this is Colleen Ronan." Until that moment, Lee had never possessed the courage or felt privileged to address Spencer by his nickname.

"As luck would have it, you and Hershey are at our table." Spencer motioned to a group of crooked-smiling Neanderthal ballplayers surrounded by fawning girls in French curls and blue eye shadow. If the seating arrangement's intent was to humiliate Lee in front of his date, the tables were about to turn. Pulling out a chair for Colleen won him an air kiss.

"Have you and Hershey been dating long?" asked the gum-chomping football captain.

"If you're referring to Lee, please address him by his proper name. You're not in kindergarten and take that gum out of your mouth." The quarterback shrank in his seat. "All childishness aside, I had a mad crush on Lee since grade school. He didn't know I was alive until the hormones kicked in. Then, lo and behold, my phone number made it into his infamous black book. I can't tell you what I had to do to get my name at the top of the list."

"Then don't," Lee grumbled.

"As you know, Lee is a gifted intellectual. I, on the other hand, am a scatterbrain," she relayed in an "aw, shucks" manner. "Isn't that right, pumpkin?"

"Keep it up, snookums, and I'll scatter your brains all over the table."

"He's such a brute."

Lee looked up at the massive chandelier suspended overhead, wishing it would come crashing down, putting an end to the evening and the football team. Colleen gave him a nudge. "Sweetiekins, tell them about the first time... we dated, I mean." His eyes and jaw tightened, signaling that an answer wouldn't be forthcoming. "Lee's the strong, silent type. I'll tell them, buttercup."

"You'll tell them nothing. Come on, dream girl, let's dance." Yanking Colleen from her chair, he hustled her onto the dance floor.

The music muffled his rant from curious ears. "What did I say about making fun of me?" he hissed, "and none of that honeybunny shit."

Colleen blinked at his use of a four-letter word. "I'm, you know how I get when I'm nervous, I'm..."

"You're what? Spiteful? Vindictive?"

She was on the verge of saying sorry but reverted to humor. "I don't know how people in love address one another. I was raised in a home devoid of love. Pet names were never spoken; love was a concept, not an emotion. I wouldn't know love if I'd been showered with it."

"That's the same excuse you gave for flunking your geometry exam." Lee pointed his finger up at her face. "I know you, Colleen. I know how your mind works, what you feel or don't feel, believe, and don't believe. I even know when you're lying."

"I don't lie."

"You always lie; that's how you get by in life," he said, breaking free from her arms. "This isn't a joke, a game. I didn't invite you on a bet. You could have said 'No, thank you,' but you couldn't pass up one more opportunity to make a fool of me. Come on, we're leaving. I'll say you forgot to take your medication and wouldn't want them to witness you foaming at the mouth."

He assumed she was following him, but she wasn't. Looking back at her, his anger melted into pity. She stood alone, a solitary soul marooned on the dance floor, wearing the look of a frightened child, lost in an ocean of strangers. No longer oafish, she was statuesque, a goddess in a long lavender gown. The orchestra made her plea for his ears only. What his heart heard was "Come to me, my beloved. I am a wild spirit only your whip can tame." Obeying the siren's song, Lee returned to arms, craving his protective embrace. "YOU CREEP! What's the big idea walking off on me? Now shut up and dance."

"I can dream, can't I?"

"What?"

"Nothing."

The two swayed to "Moments to Remember." Colleen's feet came to an abrupt stop.

"What's the matter?" Lee asked.

"Look." His eyes followed hers. "The girl in the yellow dress," she whispered. "I can't believe she wore yellow to a prom. We're going to dance over to her."

"Don't tell me you've got a score to settle."

"Not yet. I want to see if she's stuffed."

"But they haven't served dinner yet?"

"The boobs, you dope. She can't weigh ninety pounds soaking wet and have a rack like that."

Lee pressed his cheek to Colleen's chest. "It's not her rack that interests me."

"Nice try, chucklehead. By the way, where did you learn to dance? I bet the broom was relieved when the mop cut in."

Lee lay his head on her bare shoulder, laughing at a comment that only warranted a grin.

"Get up. Everyone thinks you're crying over this song."

"My mother enrolled me in a dance class when I was a kid. She thought it essential for a young man to know his way around the dance floor."

"You're not only a great dancer but a good sport. You didn't have to ask me to be your date. I'm glad you did. I don't have to pretend to like you; I do, honest." Any other guy would have kissed her, but this was Colleen. Why spoil the moment? Her apology was enough; the night was young. The song ended to polite applause. "I'm famished. When do we eat?"

"Funny you should ask. We were given a choice between chicken and fish. I took the liberty of ordering you the fish."

"Did it ever occur to you I may not want fish?"

"It's Friday, and they're serving your favorite. Gefilte."

As the evening wore on, Colleen worked the crowd. She'd inherited her father's ability to spin a story, sending the table into waves of laughter. Lee removed the tuxedo's jacket and untied his bowtie. Leaning back in his seat, he basked in his newfound popularity. Colleen massaged his neck and shoulders, bringing a smug smile to his face. For the first time, he felt cool, not because he was cool but because Colleen made him cool, if only for a fleeting moment.

The dinner plates were cleared, and the orchestra played its final song. Headmaster Welles took the stage. "Nobody leave, the votes are in. I'm about to name the king and queen of the prom." Lee looked to the heavens.

"Please don't let it be us." His prayer was unanswered.

"Leon Hirsch and Colleen Ronan."

The queen's face lit up. "Come on, Lee. They want us up there!" He was led by his sleeve to the ballroom's stage as the crowd chanted,

"Hirsch, Hirsch, Hirsch!"

"Boy," Colleen gleamed. "If the kids back at The Talbot School could see us now!"

Holding the tiara in his sweating hands, Lee looked up at the mound of red curls piled high on a head jacked up on heels. He gulped, fearing he couldn't make the stretch. Aware of his dilemma, Colleen bent at the knees. "Thank you," he whispered.

Colleen propped her stocking feet on the car's dashboard. "Is that necessary?" Lee asked, pretending not to notice her silky gown sliding up her legs.

"You," she said, pointing her foot at her driver, "are taking my piggies wee, wee, wee, all the way home."

Lee slapped her foot as she attempted to steer the car with her toes. "Cut it out!"

Colleen cocked her head as if deep in thought. "Do you think it's true the Chinese bind women's feet?"

"Colleen, if the Chinese ever invade, it's your mouth they'll bind. Which reminds me: You speak Latin, do you?"

"Those cretins asked if I did. What was I supposed to tell them?"

"The truth?"

"The Mass is in Latin. I go to Mass."

"Klaatu barada nikto. What's that from? The Day the Church Stood Still?"

"Sounds Latin to me."

"Then it's Latin."

"Don't pretend to scold me. I saw you laughing."

"So, you did notice me."

"I'm your date. I had to make sure you didn't dance with other girls."

"Me? Other girls?"

"I danced with another boy."

"He wasn't a boy. He's a 57-year-old chemistry teacher who, thanks to you, will forever be known as "Old Twinkle Toes."

"We all get called names. When you're an adult, you suck it up."

"Tell that to 'Stuffy.' You brought her to tears."

"She can dry her eyes with all that tissue she shoved in her bra." Colleen ended her statement by sticking out her tongue.

"That's mature."

"My brain has the night off; my body is in charge," she informed with a swift glance, hoping he caught the innuendo. He had.

"Do you think this crown is real?" she asked, waving the tiara in Lee's face as he drove.

"Knock it off, Colleen!"

"Come on, let's see how it looks on you." He wasn't laughing; she backed off. His mood softened with her silence.

"You earned that crown. You were the best-looking, best dancer, and best actress. Thanks for pretending to be my girl."

Colleen stifled the urge to tell him she'd be his girl if only he would ask. "I can't wait to needle Margo. I was Prom Queen... but you're not a king."

"Court jester?"

"A wizard! That's what you are."

"Were I a wizard, I would have turned those guys into donkeys four years ago."

"Why bother? They made asses of themselves. You want to know the best part about being a queen? I can order the wizard's head cut off if he displeases me. But only a king can have the queen beheaded, and I don't want you to have that power." Colleen said, bopping the tiara off his head.

"The king wouldn't cut the queen's head off if he were madly in love with her." Colleen ignored the amorous remark. Wanting the night to linger, Lee drove below the speed limit.

"Are we going to a funeral? Step on it."

"Yes, Your Majesty." Wide-eyed and animated, Colleen sat up, spreading her arms out, blocking Lee's view of the road.

"Cut it out, Colleen! I mean it."

"I've got it! The king cuts the queen's feet off to save her from the horde of Mongol foot binders penetrating the kingdom's borders."

"She'd escape with her feet if she let the wizard take her to a place where she'd be safe, loved, and never again be in danger."

Colleen fell back into a slouch. "It's just a silly crown." The Royal Coach circled the summit of Mount Nottingham.

Opening the passenger door, Lee bent at the waist. "Your castle, my lady." Colleen wrapped her arms around her wizard's neck.

"You have to hold me up; my feet hurt." Lee assisted his fairytale queen to the palace door. "Thank you, Lee. I had fun."

"We always do. You made me feel like one of the guys tonight. I like that feeling."

"Do you like this feeling?" she asked, brushing her finger across his lips. "I'd kiss you," she cooed, "but I don't want you to throw up." With a giggle, she ran into the house, slamming the door and snapping off the porch light. Leaning against his dad's car, Lee looked up at Colleen's bedroom window. It was she who was the wizard, making those four ugly years disappear in one magical night.

***

"Oscar, wake up. He's home." Freida stood at the door like a dog eagerly awaiting her master's return. "You're wearing a smile," she rejoiced with her boy's face between her palms.

Oscar pushed his glasses up to his balding crown. "It was a good time?"

"Dad, it was the best time of my life."

"Good. I'm going to bed."

"Oscar!"

"All right already. I'm listening."

"What did I tell you? Is she a beauty or is she a beauty?"

"Mom, not only is she gorgeous, but you should have seen how she handled those guys. She put them in their place without using her fists or foul mouth. She had them hanging on to her every word, and every word was an insult they were too stupid to realize it."

"What was she wearing?" Freida eagerly asked.

"I don't remember, but boy, did she look swell. I've got to thank you, Mom."

"I told you to take her."

"Not for that, for making me take dance lessons. You should have seen us on the dance floor; every girl was jealous of her, and every guy wished he were me." Lee pulled up a chair. "Now get this, Colleen's down the other end of the table telling jokes and crazy stories, there's a crowd around her, and I'm thinking she's giving me the brush."

"What brush?" his mother asked, confused by the slang.

"The brush, you know, making like I'm not there. You'll never guess what she did. She came up behind me and rubbed my neck, whispering insults about those guys I hate."

"Hate is a strong word," said his father.

"Like I said, hate. Everyone's thinking she's nibbling on my ear."

"She bit you!"

"No, Mom. But if she had, I wouldn't care. Now they all think I'm some kind of playboy outside of school."

"All I want to know is if she kissed you." His weary father asked.

"I'm getting to that. When I brought her home, she thanked me and wrapped her arms around my neck. Our lips were this close," Lee described, holding his thumb and index finger a hair strand apart. "She looked deep into my eyes and murmured, 'I'd kiss you, but I don't want you to throw up.' Isn't she swell?"

"Romantic," said his father.

Lee stood. "I'm all in," he said with an exaggerated yawn. Freida smiled, watching her son walk down the hallway to his bedroom.

Oscar came up behind his wife. "You realize what you've done."

"Not to worry, he's off to college in September, and he'll find a girl who will kiss him. Colleen will be remembered as a childhood playmate."

Oscar motioned to his son's room with his thumb. "She wants to play. He wants to mate. He's getting more than a goodnight kiss in that room."

"All that matters is he's happy."

"Oh, he's happy."

Chapter Fifteen

Since Louie's death, Carla's health had been in rapid decline. Diabetes claimed a foot and was robbing her of her sight. Scaling the steps to her second-floor apartment was impossible. Although treacherous at times, Rosaria found the upper floor's second bedroom well worth the climb. Long overdue, summer finally came to the city. This August morning. Mother Nature exhaled the warmth she'd sucked out of June and July. The temperature topped 100°F.

Rosaria played with memories of her and her sisters riding out a heatwave in their Mount Nottingham basement, which resembled a dank medieval dungeon with its weeping stone walls and archaic furnace enclosed in an asbestos straitjacket. The cellar not only served as a cooler but also as a distillery. During the summer months, Berta would brew a root beer draught, a skill she'd developed during Prohibition when brewing beer was a cottage industry. Tim would say, "Berta, darlin, you can't cook to save your life, but you can brew a beer to save mine." Rosaria sighed, indulging in the memory of a time when money was scarce but love overflowed like the head of her mother's homemade brew.

Fredrik pounded the tepid bathwater like a tom-tom, rousing Rosaria back to the present. Patsy stood in the bathroom doorway, watching mother and son splash one another. Four years earlier, he was a kid himself hanging out on a street corner, playing tough guy, fooling no one. Then, Rosaria stepped into his life. He was blind to her brace now, as he was on the night he asked her to dance.

"Tubby time over," Patsy said, holding out a bath towel for his son. Rosaria lifted Fredrik out of a pool of floating toys. The baby squealed as his father imitated the toddler's attempt to speak. "Ba-ba-ba." Rosaria laughed, watching Fredrik shove his soapy fist into Patsy's mouth to capture his father's tongue. The safety bar next to the tub acted as a crutch, aiding Rosaria in getting to her feet. She wiped her brow with her arm. "You had better get going. Mama's growing impatient."

"The two of you are going down to Mama's apartment. It's cooler down there."

"I'll take Fredrik downstairs once the pie comes out of the oven."

"Who bakes a pie during a heatwave?"

"It's cherrieee pie," Rosaria sang.

"It's crazzeee," Patsy echoed.

"The cherries weren't being eaten. I didn't want them to turn, and the scent is heavenly."

"It may smell heavenly, but this place is as hot as hell. When I return, we'll go to the park. The city turned on the fountain for the kids."

"We don't want to keep Mama's doctor waiting," Rosaria said, playfully pushing her husband out the door. Patsy kissed his wife and son.

"I love you. Stay safe."

"You heard Daddy; we're going down to Nonie's." At twenty months, Fredrik had already begun to walk on his own, yet when alone with his mother, Rosaria placed him in a walker.

"Let's get your toys downstairs. Who's coming with us?" Rosaria picked up a long-legged stuffed egg.

"Humpty Dumpty sat on a wall,

Humpty Dumpty had a great fall.

All the king's horses and all the king's men,

Couldn't put Humpty together again."

Fredrik bounced to the rhythm of the rhyme as his mother tossed the stuffed egg down the stairs.

Fredrik frowned. "Dumpty broken, dada fix."

"That's right, your Daddy can fix anything. Is that pie I smell?" Rosaria turned to look in the kitchen.

Prepared to follow his Dumpty, Fredrik wheeled to the edge of the stairs. Rosaria grabbed the walker before it went airborne.

"You almost gave Mommy a heart attack," she gulped, closing the apartment door. Not wanting her son to sense her fear, Rosaria broke into song while removing the pie from the oven.

"Sing a song of sixpence,

A pocket full of rye.

Four and twenty blackbirds,

Baked in a ..."

Her voice trailed off. The aroma of cherries mingled with burning wood. Smoke billowed from beneath the apartment door. Teary-eyed from smoke, Fredrik wailed. Rosaria wheeled her son to the back window's fire escape, their only way out. Struggling to lift the window screen that had run off its track, a desperate Rosaria landed a knockout punch, sending the screen flying into a neighbor's yard. "HELP! HELP US! FIRE!" The baby's cries grew louder than his mother's plea for help.

"Hush, we're going for a ride." Unable to lift both her son and her leg over the windowsill, Rosaria recited An Act of Contrition. "Oh my God, I am heartily sorry for having offended thee." A plea came from below.

"Throw the baby down. I'll catch him!"

As flames consumed the kitchen, she continued to pray. "I detest all my sins. I dread the loss of heaven and the pains of hell." She was in hell. Flames licking her back like stinging bees, she threw her son over the windowsill and tumbled onto the fire escape after him.

"FOR GOD'S SAKE, ROSIE! DROP THE KID!"

Smoke and panic gripped her throat as she stood on the fire escape, desperately squeezing her son to her chest. A burning ember blew into her eye, searing its lens. Instinctively, her hand shot to the stinging cornea. One-handed, she lost her grip. Fredrik flew into his savior's arms. "I got him, Rosie!"

Fredrik's cry was the same one she'd heard at the moment of his birth. He was alive, reborn. She had to live for her son, for Patsy. Burnt and blinded, she climbed over the railing of the rusted-out century-old fire escape. Its heated metal scorched her hands and branded her inner thighs as she lifted her functioning leg over the rail. With strength she never knew she possessed, Rosaria hoisted the jailed leg over the iron-hot railing. Professor Fuller's words rang in her head. *"Can you run, climb, jump?"* She had run to the window, climbed over the railing, and now she must jump. She sailed forward.

A jutting rod from the rusted structure snatched the brace strap and her only chance for survival. The leg swung. Her head slammed against the brick building with a fatal crack. Mort's prediction had come to pass. The strap held till the end of her life. The weight of her limp, dead body tore the frayed strap, sending her plummeting to the pavement. Rosaria's lifeless body lay cracked and broken on the frying-hot pavement. All the king's horses, and all the king's men...

***

Red-eyed, Salina answered the pounding on the door.

"Where is he?" Berta demanded, not bothering to acknowledge the grieving Salina, whose trembling finger pointed to the locked door at the end of the hall.

"The bathroom."

Berta marched toward the closed door like a barroom bouncer who lost patience with a belligerent patron. Salina stepped in Berta's path. "He's got a gun."

"We'll see about that." The heel of Berta's palm slammed on the locked door. "Patsy, open this door!" Silence.

"So, help me, Patsy, if I'm forced to climb through the transom, that gun had better be locked and loaded." She rattled the door. "Are you listening to me?" Her question hung heavy in the sweltering heat. Her threats grew louder. "Pull that trigger, and you'll spend eternity in the fires of hell, never to be reunited with Rosaria. Is that what you want? She didn't save her son to be raised as an orphan. What am I to tell him? His father took the coward's way out? He wasn't man enough to raise you alone? You lost the right to take your life the moment that boy took his first breath. For Christ's sake, Patsy, if you can't be a man, be a father. That boy is going to need one."

The latch slowly slid aside. His olive skin was wet with sweat. A pistol dangled from his thumb. Berta snatched the weapon and slapped it into Salina's hand. "There's a time to grieve; this isn't it," she lectured. "Wash your face and put on a clean shirt. Nuala is waiting in the car. We have arrangements to make." Berta headed out with the same determination she'd shown on entering. Stopping at the door, she eyed the gun in Salina's hand. "Get rid of that thing."

***

Freida looked over at the mantelpiece clock flanked by her boy's high school graduation photos. "I can't hold dinner any longer. Aaron promised he'd be here by five."

Oscar took his seat at the head of the table. "You want a doctor for a son, you eat late."

Lee knew he'd have to get it out before Aaron arrived to stoke the flames. He coughed into his fist.

Oscar lifted his head. "You have something to add?"

"I was thinking over this New York thing."

"Thing?"

"What I mean is, with Aaron not being around, I'd be willing to take a semester off, then enroll at B.U. in January."

Freida patted his hand. "That's thoughtful, but why not give the New York school a try?"

Oscar slammed down his fork. "For us! No. You want to stay with her. Did she ask you not to go?"

"Colleen's been down the Cape all summer."

"And you've been pining for her since she left. You're not homesick; you're girl crazy." Oscar turned on his wife. "You knew he liked that girl. You planned this because you don't want him to leave home."

"Keep Mom out of it. It's my decision."

"Your decision!" Freida covered her ears not to hear the father and son's first argument.

"You have a full scholarship. You're going." Slow, heavy footsteps crossed the threshold. Freida got up from the table.

"That's Aaron."

"Dad, you don't understand. There's no rush. I'm only seventeen."

"You're too young to know what you want."

"Hey, Aaron," Lee called out. "You're just in time for a fight you didn't start."

Dazed, Aaron wandered into the dining room; his eyes roamed the walls, dodging tears. He steadied himself on the back of a sturdy chair that had been awaiting his arrival. He tried to speak, but saying the words would confirm it was true.

"That fire across town, the mother, the baby." His body fell into the chair, his face into his hands. "She's dead. Rosaria's dead."

Freida covered her mouth. Lee threw a fork at Aaron. "I can handle it. I'm not a baby. I don't want to be around any of you!" He grabbed his jacket off the coat rack. "I can't wait to go to New York. I hate all of you!"

Realizing it was the middle of a heatwave, Lee threw his windbreaker into the hedges that lined the cement steps leading to the street. His thoughts weren't of Rosaria but of Colleen. He wanted to console her. He wondered if the death of her sister had caused a crack in the hard shell protecting her emotions. *"If only I had found the courage to kiss her, ask her to be my girl, I'd be with her now. She'd expect me to comfort her. Now, I haven't the right to intrude on her grief.* "He didn't know where to take his tears; his feet led him to the schoolyard swing.

***

Colleen looked down at her Snow White sister, so deep in sleep; no amount of kisses her Prince could garner would awaken his Princess, frozen in time. Margo embraced Patsy. He'd gone from schoolboy to widower in the span of four years. He looked more like a widower than a boy. "I'm sorry, Margo," Patsy whimpered. "I promised I'd protect her. Like every other promise I made, I broke it. When she needed me most, I wasn't there."

"You couldn't have known."

"Your mother warned me that building was a firetrap, yet I allowed my wife and son to live here. I promised Rosie a house, then handed our money over to my brother. My stupidity killed her." Patsy wiped his nose. "Your mother, is she here?"

"She's coming with Marty and Mae."

"She saved my life after I killed her daughter."

Margo shook Patsy by his shoulders. "Stop it! My mother regards you as a son. She doesn't want you burdened with blame. She was in your shoes. Believe me, she's been through it."

Patsy ran his fingers through his hair. "Rosie was cautious. She'd never leave the stove unattended. She may have been disabled, but she wasn't absent-minded."

"The stove may have been defective. She could have been distracted by the phone or Fredrik taking a tumble. The fire department will sort it out."

A withering voice entered the conversation. "I chose her dress. I hope you approve." Salina whimpered.

Margo complimented her with an embrace, "She looks lovely."

"Patsy wanted her to wear the green dress she wore the night they met. Rosie told him she'd put it away for safekeeping, but we lost everything."

Berta had arrived. Patsy bent forward, steadying himself on his wife's casket. Berta stroked his face and kissed his cheek. She'd never kissed him or the baby. "The last years of my daughter's life were her happiest. It was you who gave her those years." Patsy looked on as his mother-in-law stood over her daughter's eternal bed. He wondered what message she had for Rosie to take with her to heaven. No tears, her daughter's body drained of blood, her blood. A third of her soul lay out before her, yet not a tear was shed, just a pat on Rosaria's hand and a kiss transferred from her fingers to her daughter's forehead.

"Patsy, may I have a word with you in my office?" Carmen Laredo was a childhood friend and manager of his late father's funeral home. Carmen closed the door to his paneled office. "Some shady character came to the back door. The guy gave me this." Carmen handed over an envelope. Realizing his friend was more interested in its contents than he was, Patsy folded the unopened envelope into his jacket's breast pocket.

"Did you recognize the guy?"

"I know what you're thinking. It wasn't Nicky."

Margo leaned into Salina's ear. "I need a smoke. Care to join me?"

"You bet." The two smokers stood under the funeral home's awning at the rear entrance. Salina jerked her head at an Alfa Romero. "Check out the car."

"Shit, it's Doctor Hirsh." Margo blew out her last drag and crushed the cigarette with her heel. Salina slowly shook her head.

"Poor guy, he really loved Rosie. With all the commotion at the wedding, I never did receive a proper introduction."

His eyes hidden behind sunglasses, the otherwise austere physician held out his arms to Margo, who suspected he was the type of man who grew more attractive with age. She wanted to be the woman to put the gray in his temples. "Doctor Hirsh, I'd like to introduce my sister-in-law, Salina Saco. " Aaron offered his hand.

"A pleasure to meet you, Salina. I only wish it were under other circumstances."

The married woman melted. "Same here. Rosie thought highly of you. I had better get back inside. Nice to have made your acquaintance."

231

Aaron turned to Margo. "Leon would have come, but my mother thought otherwise. She refuses to cut the apron strings."

Aaron looked down at his hands. "Rosaria meant a great deal to me."

Margo's heart fluttered to witness a strong man so vulnerable. "We understand."

"Maybe I should just leave the card with you. I don't want to upset your mother."

Margo held out her hand. "Please come in."

Berta received his condolences with a silent nod. Aaron chalked it up to grief. Margo took Aaron by the arm.

"I'll walk you to your car."

"That won't be necessary."

"Perhaps not, but indulge me."

Reading the rage in her sister's eyes, Mae whispered, "She's just being kind."

"Kind, my ass. I know my daughter. She doesn't have a steady, and she's as hot as...Well, well, will you look who just walked in? It's our friend Mr. Kilday."

"I don't think he'll cause a commotion, not here."

"He won't, but I will." After a brief prayer, Ronny got up from the kneeler.

"Mrs. Ronan," he said with open arms and a sympathetic smile. "I'm so sorry. I can't put into words the loss I feel. Rosaria was..."

"A pathetic cripple."

"What?'

"Nuala told me."

"Told you what?"

"Get out." Berta pointed to the exit like a queen ordering, "Off with his head!"

Ronny hesitated but knew arguing with Berta was futile. Kicking a chair over on his way out, Ronny stopped to scrawl "FUCK YOU MARGO" in the condolence book.

"How are things at the hospital?" Margo asked, not knowing what else to say to her idol. A loud crash interrupted Aaron's answer. The couple instinctively ducked behind the sports car. Margo spied Ronny standing at the entrance alongside a smashed potted plant; its soil dusted his shoes and covered the green outdoor carpeted steps. Spotting the platinum ponytail, he charged at the red car. Twisting her hair, Ronny pried Margo's hands from the car door. "A cripple? You bitch!"

"Leave her be," Aaron ordered.

"Keep your hooked nose out of this!" His anger was now directed at a new target; Ronny pushed Margo to the ground. Anticipating a punch, Aaron stepped aside. The air punch threw Ronny off balance; he fell to his knees. Aaron jabbed his fingers into his adversary's neck, leaving Ronny lying on the ground like a rag doll. "Quick, get in the car. He'll be incapacitated for ten seconds. This car will be out of here in three."

Aaron threw the clutch into drive and his foot to the floor, thrusting the vehicle into traffic. He looked down at his petrified passenger, bent over with her hands covering her head. "All clear. You can sit up."

"I'm more afraid of this car than I am of Ronny!" The driver flashed a self-satisfied smile. Margo double blinked. "What did you do to him?"

"The vagus nerve, press on it in just the right spot, leaves a person immobile for about ten seconds. Your friend is up by now. His only wound will be his pride. If you're good with your fists, you use them. If you're good with your brains... well." Out of the corner of his eye, he caught Margo's awestruck expression.

"I'm sorry you witnessed that scene. It seems every time you see my family, we're amid some crisis. You must think we're barbarians."

"No, but my brother does."

Cross-legged, Margo turned her body toward Aaron. "How is Lee?"

"To be honest, I don't know. I took an apartment with a fellow doctor across town. The place is close to the hospital. The mama's boy is off to college in two weeks."

"I haven't cut the cord myself, but I'm determined to move to Hollywood. I thrive on excitement."

"What I just witnessed was more exciting than the emergency ward during a full moon."

"Thanks for keeping me out of that emergency room."

"Glad to be of service. I had better get you back. I won't leave until I'm certain you're safe."

"We should see more of each other, not wait until a family crisis. Don't you agree?"

Given Margo's age and intentions, Aaron didn't want to foster any hope she may have of kindling a romance. "Maybe when Leon graduates, our families could throw a party."

"That's in four years!" Margo placed her fingers on her temples and shook her head. "I'm selfish and self-centered. I apologize."

"Don't. I never do."

"That's what I love about you. You're so compassionate and understanding. I suppose it's part of being a doctor."

"Part of being a doctor is not keeping patients waiting." The car pulled up to the funeral home. "You better get in."

Margo gave him a peck on his cheek. "My hero. We'll see one another soon. I'm holding you to your promise."

Margo resumed her place in the condolence line next to her mother. "Where the hell have you been?"

Margo ignored the question and continued shaking hands. Berta yanked her daughter out of the line and into a secluded side room.

"Ow! You're hurting me! "

How dare you leave your sister's casket to chase down a man!"

"Aaron got me out of a jam. Ronny was going to kill me."

"So am I, and what's with this Aaron business?" Berta poked her finger into Margo's chest. "He's a doctor; address him as one. As for Ronny, I fixed his wagon. A cripple. If he hadn't taken off with his tail between his legs, I would have crippled him."

"I asked you not to bring that up."

"Because it would hurt Rosaria. Well, she's dead."

"What about me? He'll kill me!"

"If he doesn't, Doctor Hirsh will. You saw what he did to your father."

Patsy hesitated to get between Berta and Margo while embroiled in an argument, but it was important. "Mrs. Ronan, someone is asking for you."

"I'll get back to you, Missy."

Patsy led Berta to a dark young lady whose heavy lids fluttered out tears. "Mrs. Ronan, we've never met. My name is Thelma."

***

"You have two more hours tonight. Please eat something." Salina urged her brother. Patsy's jacket slid off the back of the kitchen chair. Salina picked it off the floor. "What's this?" she asked, holding the envelope.

"Some guy told Carmen to see that I got it."

"Open it."

Patsy ran his fingernail under its sealed flap. He lowered his eyes and raised his head. "It's money. Three grand in hundreds."

"Nicky," Salina gasped. Patsy slapped the envelope on his palm and took his jacket from his sister. "I'm going out."

"Please, don't go looking for him. Let the police handle it. Who knows, he may show up at the cemetery."

"If he does, he won't be leaving."

***

Alone with his wife for the last time, Patsy knelt before her. "I told you the night we met that I always keep my promises, but I don't. I promised you a house, a honeymoon, and that I'd always protect you, but I didn't. This is one promise I will keep." Patsy slid a diamond ring on Rosaria's cold, stiff finger. "Someday, Rosie, we'll meet again. When we do, you'll be wearing this ring, and I'll marry you all over again."

***

Colleen kept her head lowered as she followed her sister's casket from the dark, incense-filled church into the light of a burning August sun. Turning from its rays, her eyes met Lee's. He wanted her to see him, to have her know how much Rosaria meant to him. The teenager who shared a park bench with a lonely schoolboy was the only one who could tell him how to console his wounded tiger.

"Lee! Wait up!" He winced at the sound of his name, remembering how Colleen would chase after him on their way home from school. He'd pretend she was a nuisance, all the while wanting her to catch up. Today, there wouldn't be jokes or insults to share. Colleen turned him around to face her and wrapped her arms around his neck. All the hugs and kisses she'd received in the past three days hadn't relieved her pain the way holding Lee had.

"It's okay to cry," she whispered. He should have felt like a baby, but in her arms, he felt man enough to weep. It had taken Rosaria's death to bring about the metamorphosis. Childhood had ended.

"Will I see you before you leave for New York?"

"No. I leave at the end of the week to get acclimated to the school and city."

"You'll keep in touch, I mean I'll hear from you?" she asked, batting back tears not only for the loss of Rosaria but the loss of a friend.

"Colleen, we're leaving." She dismissed her mother with a tsk.

"Yeah, sure, I'll write or something." She kissed his cheek.

"COLLEEN, THE CAR, NOW!"

Berta wagged a black mantilla in Colleen's face. "This was on the ground. It slid off your head while you were chasing down that boy. The damn thing is sacred." Berta stared out the limousine window, drumming her nails on her patent leather handbag. "For the life of me, I can't understand why you girls don't leave the Hirsch brothers to hell alone. The only one of my daughters they cared for is lying in that hearse."

"Lee's my friend!" Colleen cried. "You always hounded me to make friends; I made one, and now he's gone. I hope you're happy."

"Darn right I am, so is he. Boys grow up. I wish I could say the same for girls. And this one," Berta said, swishing her hand at Margo as if shooing a fly. "Every day was Halloween at that TV station, now she's chasing after The Grim Reaper like a seagull behind a garbage truck."

Margo pounded her fist on the handrest. "Dr. Hirsh saved my life. Ronny would have killed me if Aaron, excuse me, Doctor Hirsh, hadn't intervened."

"Ronny may have a temper, but he'd never lay a hand on you."

Margo sat forward. "You think so?"

Mae touched Margo's arm. "Not now. We're all upset. I don't think Rosaria would want us to use her funeral as an excuse to hurt one another. Let's give it a rest."

The four sat in silence as the procession crept across the Mystic River Bridge to Dorchester. Rosaria was coming home.

***

The streetlamps on the Mount still burnt gas. They were one of only a handful of Boston neighborhoods that hadn't converted to electricity. "Witches wearing crowned bonnets, my mother would call those streetlights," Berta recalled as she and Colleen stood on the front porch looking over at the park.

"Let's go in." Colleen urged. It's late; she's at peace."

"Your grandmother claimed the residents on the Mount were up in arms over the city installing those ugly gaslights. They feared explosions, thought they cheapened the look of the park. Now they're considered charming, quaint. Mark my words, the first mugging on the Mount, and they'll be replaced with electric lights like the rest of the civilized world." Removing her eyeglasses, Berta pinched the bridge of her nose. "Go to bed, I'll be up soon. Put your dress on a hanger, not thrown over a chair."

Lying in the dark, still wearing her dress, Colleen watched the shadows dancing on her bedroom ceiling. She reflected on the nights Rosaria would sit at the end of Colleen's bed, reading fairytales. "The Pied Piper of Hamelin" was Colleen's favorite tale.

"Children are rats. They should be run out of town, never to be seen again," deemed the four-year-old.

Colleen's proclamation had brought a frown to Rosaria's face. "Jesus loved the little children. Unless we become as children, we shall not enter the kingdom of heaven."

In a twilight sleep, Colleen mumbled. "Stay on earth with me, Rosaria. Stay with me. Stay... stay."

"Colleen."

Her name came in a whisper that tickled her ear. She felt a cold hand gently brush her cheek. Scanning the darkened bedroom, she was alone. A light radiated up from the staircase, inviting her curiosity to uncover the source. Having spent her entire life in the old house, she was familiar with the location of every arthritic creak the stairs would groan if one were to step heavily on its sensitive spine. Crouching on the landing, looking into the front parlor, Colleen was transported back to a Christmas Eve long past. The three sisters huddled together on the staircase, looking down at the Christmas tree through banister rails and innocent eyes. The sickly balsam glistened in the dark; its branches sagging under the weight of oversized bulbs, handmade ornaments, and clumps of carelessly tossed tinsel. Tomorrow the tree would be ignored, its flaws in full view, but tonight was her night. She was a beautiful tree, a loved tree, their tree.

"Do you think Santa has come?" asked a twinkling voice.

"If there's a doll in that big box, it's mine," whispered another.

"Hush, we don't want to wake Mother," cautioned the third.

The air was sprinkled with magic that night, its spell only lasting till dawn. The Cinderella tree was gone now, replaced by a grieving mother mourning the loss of her daughter. Weeping into a green velvet dress.

Chapter Sixteen

The badge lay on the kitchen table. A promise made to turn it in after putting in his 30 years needn't be kept.

Marie was gone. All that was left to come home to was a squarking parrot whose vocabulary was limited to a wolf whistle and "Stick 'em up." Ross Coleman was a fixture at Station Seven. All the old-timers knew and respected the ruddy-faced Irishman. He'd known the Travellas before Patsy was born and Nicky turned bad. He'd taken a bullet to the ribs, talked a jumper off a roof, and fished more than one body out of the Mystic River. But how do you tell a twenty-four-year-old kid his wife was murdered?

A rap on the door sent the twins racing to be the first to answer. Wide-eyed Lynn dashed into the kitchen.

"Mommy, Mommy! It's a policeman."

Brook invited the officer in. "Are you going to arrest us?" the six-year-old asked.

"No, I've come to have a word with your uncle."

Salina wiped her hands on her apron. "Officer Coleman, come have a seat. Coffee?"

"No, thank you, this isn't a social call," he replied, eyeing the twins. Salina picked up on the cue.

"Girls, why don't you go to the soda fountain for an ice cream?" Salina dug coins from her purse.

Ross wagged his finger at the girls. "Look both ways before you cross the street." The familiar warning carried more weight when delivered by a policeman.

"Patsy around?"

"He's gone to the post office. He should be back any minute."

"I'll come back later."

"Please stay."

Removing his cap, Ross wiped the sweat from his brow with his forearm. "Real scorchah. A couple of boys on Breman Street opened a fire hydrant. We had to send an officer down there. Can't blame the kids, but it's a safety issue."

"Cold drink? Iced tea?" The thump of her brother's footsteps on the stairs brought a sigh of relief to Salina, who was running out of small talk. Patsy's eyes bounced from his sister to the officer, who nervously turned his cap around in his hands, knowing he'd have to choose his words wisely.

"I hate to burden you so soon after Rosie's death... I'll get right to it. The fire department found traces of an accelerant. The fire's been classified as arson." Patsy lunged at Ross, pinning the messenger to the wall. Salina squeezed herself between the two men, freeing the startled officer from Patsy's grip. Ross rolled his shoulders while rubbing his throat.

"Christ, Patsy. No one wants to collar the asshole more than I do."

"My wife was in that house! My son was in that house! If someone wanted me dead, they should have put a gun to my head, not my heart." Patsy sank into the sofa.

Salina rocked her weeping brother in her arms; her pleading eyes met Officer Coleman's. "Why would anyone do this?"

"Insurance." Patsy's head popped up. "Hold on, kid. Nobody's accusing you."

"Then who?" Patsy challenged.

"Your brother's got enemies."

Salina chimed in. "My brother is a lot of things, but he's not a murderer. He knows someone is always home."

"He may, but a stranger sees Patsy and your mother leave the house and thinks the place is empty. All I'm sayin' is Nicky owes lots of people lots of money. Someone figured the house was insured, and Nicky stood to get a cut."

"Nicky's not entitled to a dime. He was cut out of my parents will years ago. He knows that."

"Either one of you heard from your brother?"

Patsy ran his fingers through his hair and avoided eye contact. "Um, no, we haven't seen him."

"I asked if you heard from him." Once again, Patsy jumped the question.

"He didn't even show up for Papa's funeral."

"But he knew the old man was dead?"

"He must have."

"And Rosie?"

"It's been in all the papers. If he doesn't know she's dead, then he is."

Ross put a fatherly arm around Patsy's shoulder. "Listen, kid, you're right. Nicky wouldn't do this, but he's in deep with people who would. It coulda been for money, it coulda been for revenge, but someone wanted that building to go up and I'm gonna get the bastard, even if I have to crawl out of my grave to do it. But I'll need your cooperation." His gut told him the pair were holding out on him; his smoldering anger wasn't helping his ulcer any. Cap back on his head, he shot a suspicious eye at the siblings. "If either one of ya remembers something you're forgetting, come down to the station. I played poker with your old man. He wasn't the only one who could spot a tell. Sorry for your loss."

***

The beef stew was cold, the table silent but for the clinking of Margo's spoon on her bowl. "You're quiet," Berta commented to the once-social butterfly. "The phone no longer rings, you sulk, and haven't bought a new dress in weeks."

"I haven't time for men. I'm in the process of building a new career."

Colleen couldn't pass on the opening. "Ah, yes, where does an unemployed depicter find work when day after day, I see signs in shop windows that read, 'Depicters need not apply.'"

"I didn't know you could read. As I was saying, I've enrolled in The Boston School of Fashion Design," Margo announced while fanning herself with the brochure.

Berta reached for her bifocals. "Let me see that."

Margo handed the brochure to her mother. Berta tapped her finger on the first paragraph.

"Must be able to sew and read a pattern. You're no seamstress."

"No, but Carla is. She'll teach me."

"Carla? Carla, the blind one-footed fat lady, is going to teach you to sew?"

"Just enough to get accepted. I don't want to make dresses. I want to design them."

"You had a good job and a good man, and you lost them both. Now you want to design miniskirts."

Margo rose from the table, kicking the legs out from under her sister's chair, causing a laughing Colleen to lose her balance but not the slice of bread from her mouth.

"I hate both of you!" The slam from Margo's bedroom door signaled the piano to play a familiar rag.

"Hang on, Ma. I'll get to the bottom of this." Colleen sprinted to the second floor, taking two steps at a stride. Margo lay with her face buried in a pillow. Colleen plopped down next to her on the bed.

"Get out!" Margo snapped without raising her head.

"Are you going to tell me what's bothering you. Or do I have to read your diary?"

"I no longer keep a diary."

"You're expecting a call."

"What put that idea in your head?", Colleen leaned over her sister and whispered, "Last night, you picked up the phone on the first ring. That's a Margo no-no. Whoever he is, I like him."

"Have you heard from Lee?" Margo asked out of the blue.

"Funny you should ask. I'm concerned about his safety. Alone in New York City, he's a prime target for thieves and prostitutes. I was thinking of stopping in on his mother, find out how he's doing." Margo bounced off the bed.

"Let me get my coat. I'm coming with you."

"You're checking up on Doctor Hirsh. You are chasing after him. Trust me, he's not your type."

"He thinks so. He suggested we meet for dinner."

"Has it ever crossed your pea brain that he may have a girlfriend?"

"Why? What do you know?"

"That your dura doesn't matta to a brain surgeon who's old enough to be your father's younger brother."

Margo softened her voice, not wanting to appear anxious. "You know what I think? I think he thinks I'm still in mourning."

"Margo, the man is a pompous ass. It will never work out. You're too much alike."

"Laugh, but mark my words, I'm going to get that man. I always get what I want."

***

Yanking a pair of gloves from her jacket pocket, Colleen picked up the old straw rake her grandmother had once employed to perform the same task 50 years earlier. Soon, she'd be seventeen, yet she still enjoyed taking flight on her swing even if she always fell to earth. "God won't take me until I finish raking this yard." Leaves crackled behind her. "Margo, you've never set foot in this yard."

"I called the hospital."

"You what?"

"I had to know. It was driving me crazy."

"And?"

"He's gone to Walter Reed. He's treating returning soldiers with brain and spinal injuries.

"Noble, perhaps I misjudged his character."

"He'll be in Washington for the next six months."

"What's Plan B?"

Margo sighed before answering. "Time for me to get back to work. The Sunny money is dwindling. I never thought I'd have to work for a living. I should have moved to Hollywood right out of high school. What are your plans?"

"I'm going to Emerson when I graduate."

"Sorry, Colleen. I don't think acting is your calling."

"I have no desire to act. I intend to become a playwright. Rosaria said I should put my imagination to good use by pursuing a literary career. I'm getting into that school, not for myself but for Rosaria. Did she give you career advice?"

"Yeah, get married."

***

Margo pulled the plug on Colleen's afternoon entertainment. "Hey! Plug the TV back in."

"Shouldn't you be doing homework?"

"I am."

"Since when have reruns of 'My Favorite Martian' become a homework assignment?"

"Since I decided to join the space program."

Margo fluttered around the room, wearing a faraway look. "He's back. The love of my life has returned."

"Safe to assume the 'him' is the lovable Doctor Hirsh. Why the sudden return?"

Margo sat up from her fainting pose. "Freida had Mae and Elba to lunch."

"Freida?"

"She is my future mother-in-law. Mrs. Hirsch happened to mention Aaron had come back to Boston with a soldier in need of a surgery that can only be performed at The Peter Bent Brigham, where yours truly is applying for a job."

"You've spent the better part of a year studying fashion. You've been hailed as the next Diane Vreeland, and you're giving it up to wear a hairnet and push a food cart because that's all you're qualified to do?"

"I stopped at the personnel office. There's an opening for someone with marketing, fundraising, and public relations experience. Who better to hit people up for money?"

"A loan shark."

"You're looking at one."

"What about references? I don't think Mac will give you one."

"I don't want references from laymen."

"I bet he does."

"Aaron will put in a good word for me. I'm a shoo-in."

"He won't do it. He'll bruise your inflated ego, regard you as some dumb blonde, and humiliate you."

"Humiliate a woman who went on TV with lava running down her leg? I want this job," Margo said, wagging the job posting, "and I always get what I want."

***

Margo thumped through the front door with cement feet. Kicking off her polished pumps, she fell face down on the sofa.

"Is that you, Margo?" Colleen hollered from the kitchen, anxious to learn if Margo had received her prized recommendation. "Did you get it?"

Margo raised her makeup-smudged face off the sofa cushion. "Shut up."

Colleen sat back like a psychiatrist listening to her patient's tale of woe. "Let me guess. He told you're too young, inexperienced, not well spoken, and unfamiliar with medical terminology."

"He didn't raise his head, only an eyebrow. I didn't get dressed up to be dressed down."

"How did you react?"

"I was blindsided. I thanked him for his precious time and left."

Colleen pursed her lips and rocked her head. "I think it's time the doctor got a taste of his own medicine."

Like a crying baby given a pacifier, Margo's tears came to a halt. "You've got a sick, devious plan clamoring around in your twisted brain."

"Oh, yeah."

"What? What?"

"I'm going to dictate a letter. Fetch a pen." Colleen paced the living room's creaking floor as Margo jotted down her sister's words. Cross-legged, she read back the scathing correspondence to its author.

"Dear Doctor Hirsch:

I want to express my gratitude for your keen insight into this young and ambitious girl's thinly veiled flaws. Despite my media and financial expertise, it appears I'm not suited for a career in charitable endowments. I shall swallow the bitter pill you have prescribed. Henceforth, I shall enroll in a course in grammar, public speaking, and the tenets of English.

No one has ever possessed the testicular fortitude to bring my shortcomings to light. If, by chance, we should cross paths again, you'll encounter a savvy, accomplished woman.

A heartfelt thank you,

Miss Nuala M. Ronan."

"Gee, Colleen, I think 'testicular' is out of line. Why not change it to courage? Men like that word."

"We want to showcase the only anatomy you're familiar with. Testicular stays."

"What's with the tenets of English? You make me sound like Tarzan."

"Never mind the English; you'll wow him with Italian. You're going to take lessons from Carla. Here's the clincher: when he calls to apologize, he'll ask you out as a peace offering, knowing you'll offer him a piece, but you're going to turn him down."

"Why would I do that?"

"You're not to see him until you learn Italian, and it will roast his nuts that you spurned his advances."

"Colleen, you're the smartest moron I know!"

***

The pink envelope lay on top of an ever-growing pile of correspondence addressed to Doctor Hirsh. "Are you up for a few rounds of golf?" Short, slim, and muscular, with a closely trimmed dark beard meant to offset his hairless crown, Doctor Stanley Schuyler had known Aaron since their days at Harvard Medical School.

"Get off my desk, Stan. Don't you have anything better to do than hang around my office sorting through my mail?"

"No. Harold Shafter canceled his appointment. Just as well, I had bad news for him," Stan said, passing the scented pink envelope under his nose. "My Sin."

"Tell it to a priest," Aaron sarcastically advised.

"My Sin, it's a perfume. Joanne wears it. I bought my girlfriend the same scent. The wife has the nose of a bloodhound."

"Marriage hasn't slowed you down."

"What can I say? I'm a hopeless womanizer." Stan read the envelope's return address. "Who's Nuala Ronan?"

"From the old neighborhood. I had a thing for her sister."

"Now she wants your thing," Stan said, indulging in another whiff.

"She's a batty blonde looking for a job."

"She wouldn't be the babe I spotted hanging around here last Tuesday? If she is, I've got a position for her; as a matter of fact, I've got four or five positions I'd like to put her in. Open the letter."

"You open it," Aaron said, not looking up from paperwork.

Stan's eyes widened. "Testicular! Swallow! I've got to meet this girl!"

Aaron snatched the steamy note out of his friend's hand. "She's too young for you."

"That's how I like them. Send her flowers and apologize. Just one date, then pass her on to me."

Aaron handed Stan a pen. "You want her? You write her."

Meandering up the Mount with an armful of textbooks, Colleen caught sight of her sister flagging her toward the house. "Hurry up! You've got to see this before Ma gets home."

On entering the house, Colleen dropped her books and gasped. "A dozen red roses!"

"Check out the vase! It must have cost him a bundle."

"Ma's going to break that vase over your head when she learns it's from The Butcher of Boston." Margo caressed the vase as if it were a newborn. "Come upstairs. I want you to read the card." Closing her bedroom door, Margo held the card to her chest.

"He loves me."

"He wrote that?"

"Not in so many words."

"Three are so many?"

Margo cleared her throat as if she were standing at the head of a classroom about to read a book report. "Dear Nuala,"

Colleen shook her head. "If that ain't love, I don't know what is."

"You never will. Now listen up. "Dear Nuala, I must apologize for my faux pas."

Colleen rolled her eyes. "Give me a break."

"What's it mean?"

"For being a jerk."

Margo continued. "My blistering comments were unforgivable. I would never want to discourage you from following your dreams." Margo moaned. "If he only knew those dreams were of him."

"The letter?"

"I applaud your effort to further your education. Please do not judge me by my shameful behavior. There's another side to Aaron Hirsh, one you haven't had the privilege to meet."

Colleen gasped. "Talk about testicular fortitude!"

"I hope these flowers take the sting out of my harsh criticism. Sad to say, our only encounters have been under unfortunate circumstances. I'd like to change that by arranging to meet you for dinner. I will call at the end of the week. Sincerely, Aaron Hirsh, M.D."

Colleen rejoiced. "We're right on schedule. When he calls, tell him you can't see him... yet."

***

"Salina, it's Margo."

"Margo!" Salina exclaimed on the other end of the phone line. "How are you?"

"Better than the last time we spoke. I'm calling to ask your mother for Italian lessons."

"A local boy?"

"Dr. Hirsh, you met him at the wake."

"Sure, I remember that car."

"I applied for a job at his hospital, and he wouldn't put in a good word for me."

"Nobody says no to you!"

"Well, he did. He thinks I'm a scatterbrain, but I'll show him by luring him into my seductive web, promising sexual delights in Italian. Once he reaches that sweet moment of surrender, I'll tell him in English he misinterpreted my intentions, I was merely thanking him for a pleasant evening."

"Say, are you working?"

"No, that's why I need this job."

"Why, I ask, is Mama plans on returning to Italy. It will be her last opportunity to see the relations. I can't go along. I've got Bobby and the kids to look after, and Patsy has school. I don't want Mama to travel alone. The diabetes is bad enough; now she's got heart trouble. If you could accompany her, it would be a blessing. She plans to stay six weeks. All her time will be spent with family, leaving you to experience Italian culture and Italian men. I guarantee you'll be speaking, cooking, and making love like a native."

"Italy? You're going to Italy?"

"Yes, mother, Italy."

"Don't come back with a contagious disease, and you know which one I mean. I know those people. All they want is sex and a green card, and you'll see they get both."

"Margo!" Mae called from the living room. "You have a phone call." Mae held the receiver tight to her chest and whispered, "It's a man."

"Hello, Margo?"

"Speaking."

"This is Aaron."

"Mike! So good to hear from you. The flowers were breathtaking. I only wish I could have kept them from dying."

"Borax. It preserves flowers as well as laundry. My mother is a member of the Twenty Mule Team."

"I'm sorry, Dr. Hirsh, my mother was in the room."

"We wouldn't want her to know Dr. Death sent breathtaking flowers."

"The card was touching."

"I think we got off on the wrong foot. I'd like the opportunity to apologize in person, but I believe your mother has taken out a restraining order. Seriously, I had no idea you were so well-rounded."

"Well-rounded?"

"I'm not referring to your figure; what I mean is you hadn't made it clear you were experienced."

"Experienced?"

"I'm digging myself into a hole."

"You are Dr. Death."

"What I'm getting at is, I'd be willing to give you a recommendation. As you know, marketing is outside my purview, but I've attended enough benefits and fundraisers to appreciate the hard work involved with putting on such affairs, and I think you'd be terrific at it."

"Why, thank you, Dr. Hirsh, but I've put my job search on hold. I'm accompanying Rosaria's mother-in-law, Mrs. Travella, to Italy. She has family there; the poor dear is in failing health. Since I speak Italian, I volunteered for the assignment. Have you ever been to Italy, Doctor?"

"No, and please dispense with the title; it's Aaron." There was an awkward silence; they broke it simultaneously.

"You first."

"No, you." Aaron insisted.

"My first stop will be Milano."

"The car capital!"

"My interest is in fashion, not Ferraris. Then it's on to Florence for the art, Naples for the cuisine, and no trip to Italy would be complete without a visit to Saint Peter's. Shall I pick up a souvenir from the Vatican gift shop?"

"Very funny. Tell you what, let me know when you return to Boston. We'll have dinner, and you can tell me all about your trip to the Eternal City."

Margo hung up the phone. "I've got him."

***

Berta looked over the fold of her morning newspaper. "Who's calling at this hour?" she asked, nodding at Colleen to answer both the phone and her question.

"I bet it's Margo."

"Since when does Margo get up before noon?"

"It's Italy. They're six hours ahead of us. Margo? Margo, are you there?"

"Buongiorno!"

"Ma, it's Margo!" Her head buried in the obituary section, Berta waved Colleen off.

"Ma says hi."

"Screw her, which is why I'm calling. Carla has a sexy nephew, Carlo."

Colleen cupped her hand over the receiver. "You were sent to Italy to learn the language and take in the culture."

"Oh, I'm taking it in. Carlo taught me some Italian. Cazzo mi means fuck me. Cazzo te, means fuck you, and facciamo cazzo means we fuck."

Coleen's voice tightened. "You've been in Italy for three weeks, and all you've done is play hide the salami with Patsy's dirty, hairy cousin."

"That's so derogatory."

"That's what Patsy calls them. His dirty, hairy cousins."

"Carlo is none of those things."

"Patsy's cousins are girls, and you're screwing one of them."

"You're just jealous because I'm in the sunny Caribbean while you're stuck at home with Battle Axe Berta."

"It's the Mediterranean, you dope."

"Caribbean is Italian for Mediterranean. I just know some Italian director is going to put me in one of those Spaghetti Westerns."

"Not before Ma puts you in a shallow grave when she finds out what you've been doing."

"How's she going to know?"

"It doesn't sound like you've been keeping Carla company."

"As a matter of fact, Carlo and I are taking Carla to an opera tonight."

"You? An opera?"

"We'll sneak out on her during the intermission."

"Cazzo te Margo."

***

"Is, is, that you, Dr. Hirsh?"

"Yes," came a concerned voice on the other end of the phone line. "My secretary said you called. I thought you weren't due back for another two weeks."

"My trip was tragically cut short. You're not the only harbinger of death. Mrs. Travella died. She was in my care, and I...I was supposed to... It's all my fault."

"Was it an accident?"

"A heart attack. She was obese, diabetic, and in her seventies."

255

"Given her condition, it was bound to happen. Unfortunately, it was on your watch."

"That's just it. I wasn't watching. You see, I've always had a passion for opera; it's my second love. I've yet to find my first. Carla was disheartened that her time in Italy was ending. Knowing she needed a good laugh, I took her to that funny opera, the one with the clown."

"Pagliacci?"

"You've seen it?"

"Not that version."

"During the second act, she fell asleep, or so I thought. Her nephew Carlo came along. I hoped to arouse the same passion in him that I felt for the performance. I took little Carlo to the restroom. When we returned, there were people crowded around Carla. If I had been at her side, I could have resuscitated the poor woman. Ironically, I'd just taught Carlo how to properly administer mouth-to-mouth. Poor Patsy, I left Boston with his mother and returned with a crudely constructed coffin."

"Please don't cry. If you'd like to postpone our date, I'd understand."

"No, I need to see you more than ever; the prospect of our coming together was the silver lining to my untimely return."

"Very well, I'll come by for you on Saturday evening. I'll need directions to your house," Aaron joked.

"Don't try to make me laugh. I'm not ready to stop wallowing in self-pity.... There's just one thing, could you, I mean, it's my mother."

"I understand perfectly. I'll wait for you at the bottom of the hill. Shall we say, 7:30?"

"Seven. I'll be waiting." Margo slowly hung up, noting Colleen's doubtful expression. "You don't think I can pull this off."

"You didn't learn Italian."

"Enough. I can order from soup to nuts."

Chapter Seventeen

Her evening dress tucked into capri pants, an oversized sweater covering a plunging neckline, Margo attempted to slither into her raincoat and under Berta's radar.

"Going somewhere?" Her mother's monotone voice made Margo's gut cramp.

"Dinner and a movie with friends."

"You're all dolled up for an evening of burgers and gossip with the girls."

Margo held her hand up to halt her mother's rant. Berta cuffed Margo's wrist. "Not taking your car?"

"I'm twenty-two, I don't have to answer to you."

"You're twenty-three and living in my house."

Margo shook her hand loose. "Don't wait up."

Not waiting for Aaron to open the door to his British-engineered Jaguar, Margo leapt into the marshmallow-soft passenger seat like a child embarking on a roller coaster ride. She slammed the car door. It didn't make a sound. Eyes on the road, not the driver, she gave the order. "Drive." "Did you just rob a bank?"

"No, I escaped from prison. You'll be witnessing a murder if my mother catches sight of this car. Don't mind me." Margo added as she shimmied out of her tight pants. Aaron's eyes focused on her liberated limbs. "Watch where you're going, Doc."

"I'm a conscientious driver, but I'm also a man."

"This peepshow isn't for your benefit. I told my mother I was meeting friends for dinner."

"I appreciate your scheming to keep our date."

Margo folded her arms across her chest and pouted. "I'm a grown woman sneaking around like an irresponsible teenager."

"Were you?"

"Were I what?'

"An irresponsible teenager."

"You thought so. When my dad had his heart attack, you yelled at me, called me a silly girl."

"You panicked; that's understandable. I flew off the handle; that's unprofessional. I have a short fuse when I only have minutes to act and have a howling banshee pounding on my back as I'm pounding on her husband's chest."

"You're good at pounding." Aaron looked sideways, raising a brow, an unconscious mannerism he'd developed that women found sexy. Margo was no exception. "What I mean is, I've seen it done on TV, but never in real life. Perhaps you could teach me so I can use it on my mother's face."

"Your mother may employ draconian measures to keep you in line but hats off to Berta: she's raised three of the most charming, enchanting, and witty girls I have ever had the pleasure of knowing."

"In that order?"

"Yes, in that order."

258

"Then I'm the enchanting one."

"You may also be charming and witty, but the enchantment overshadows your other assets."

"That's my raincoat."

"See, you are witty."

"Do you know what that wicked witch calls you? The Grim Reaper. And that's one of the nicer names. It's not you she dislikes; it's the circumstances leading up to my father's death. She's the one who dried him out. She thinks she killed him."

"That's crazy."

"Tell that to a lunatic. Your involvement gave her someone to transfer the blame onto. But let me tell you, when Rosaria was hospitalized, she thought you were the greatest thing since sliced bread. I once made a flippant remark about you that earned me one hell of a beating."

"Your mother beats you?"

"Did."

"So what did you say?" "It was so long ago I've forgotten," Margo said while reapplying red lipstick in the visor mirror. "It will come back to me in time."

The short walk from the parking garage onto the cobblestone streets of Boston's Italian North End proved to be a challenge for the high-heeled Margo. "These streets and my heels are a recipe for a broken ankle." Aaron held out his arm, Margo wrapped it around her waist and rested her head on his shoulder. "I find this part of town so romantic. Don't you agree?"

"I'll agree to anything on an empty stomach." Aaron pulled open the restaurant's elaborately carved wooden door. "I thought this restaurant would take you back to your time spent in Italy." Removing his date's coat, Aaron drank in the vision of her cream-colored cocktail dress that blended so well with her skin tone, it gave the appearance that the dress had caramelized over the contours of her voluptuous form. Her hair was swept up in a mound of curls, a few loose strands hung down, licking her neck as if they had carelessly fallen free, yet he suspected it had taken time to manage the effect.

"Aaron, you made an excellent choice. This restaurant is so old-world."

A young waiter, his face hosting a horseshoe mustache giving him the look of a much older man, introduced himself as Lorenzo.

"Welcome to Montello's," he greeted in a thick Italian accent. With a sweep of the arm and a bend at his waist, the couple were led to a cozy corner table. Margo returned her tall leatherbound menu to the baffled waiter. "We'll share a menu."

"Something from the bar?"

Suspecting his date would answer in the affirmative, Aaron politely declined, fearing Margo's thirst for attention might amplify with alcohol. The waiter clasped his hands. "I'll give you a moment."

"Mi scusi, Lorenzo."

"Signora?"

Margo proceeded to inquire in Italian as to the ingredients and preparation of each entrée. "Thank you, Lorenzo. You've been very helpful." Margo turned her attention to Aaron. "Have you decided, or do you require my assistance in deciphering the menu?"

Aaron wore an intense expression. "How do you say spaghetti and meatballs in Italian?"

Margo tapped his hand with a breadstick. "You don't dine at a five-star restaurant and order the Franco-American special." Elbow-to-elbow, Margo flirted with Aaron and the menu. He never cared for perfumed women. Margo didn't reek of flowers, but a sweet, soothing scent that conjured up memories of some delectable pastry from his childhood. He couldn't recall the bakery treat's name. All he knew was he wanted to taste her. Margo ordered for them both.

"Do you speak Italian?" she asked.

"I regret I never had time to master the Romance languages, and German is not romantic."

"German men can be."

Aaron mimicked her flirtatious expression. "I'm not German. Oscar is German; Oscar is not my father. My father was an officer in the Red Army. He was sent to Stalingrad, never to be heard from again."

"How awful! Do you remember him?"

"Vividly."

"You don't resemble your mother."

"I favor my father. He was very handsome."

"We have something in common. I look like my handsome father. Tim was not my dad. Our father, Rosaria's and mine, died in the war, not in Stalingrad, or Russia, but in a hail of gunfire over the Pacific. That's an ocean in Japan. My real father was Swedish."

"We have the United Nations at this table."

Lorenzo presented Margo's Fettuccine Florentine and Aaron's spaghetti and meatballs. Closing her eyes, Margo wrapped a forkful of pasta around her tongue. "Eccellente, deliziosa, prelibato." One adjective would have sufficed, but her aim was to utilize as many Italian words and phrases as possible. The waiter beamed as he left the diners to their meals. Margo mumbled a mishmash of Italian words strung together. "Forgive me, Aaron. For a moment, I forgot I was back in the States. What I asked was if you noticed me before."

"Before?"

"We first met at your parents' apartment. I had come to retrieve Colleen."

"I noticed, but I make it a policy of staying clear of teenage girls."

"Rosaria was nineteen."

"You've made my point. Heartache gets in the way of hard work. After my experience with your sister, I vowed never to turn a patient into a love interest." Aaron unfurled his silverware from a white starched napkin. "Colleen must be in high school by now."

"She's no longer the maladjusted youth you once knew. She blossomed into a scholar. She'll be heading off to college once she graduates. I never thought I'd utter those words."

"Something tells me the thank-you note was Colleen's handywork."

"You're so perceptive. Colleen's embarking on a career as a playwright."

"And you?"

Margo teased the pasta with her fork. "Like every young ingénue, I flirted with the prospect of one day gracing the stage."

"You never know, Colleen may put you in one of her productions," Aaron suggested, eating more with his eyes than his mouth.

"Goodness, no. I got the showbiz bug out of my system at my last job as a weather depicter on WHBN."

"You were on television! This I've got to hear." In a breathy Monroe voice, Margo proceeded with a sexually charged job description. "Unless you're familiar with the entertainment industry, you may find it difficult to wrap your head around the concept of depiction. In only a few short weeks, management recognized my talent for bringing the weather to life. Be it crashing waves pounding the rocky coast, or a mere salty drizzle that runs down one's cheek as the waves retreat in the silence of a once-turbulent night."

"You do have a talent for description!"

"Depiction," Margo corrected, holding up her palm. "Please don't apologize for your faux pas; it's a common misnomer. The difference is that a union, a bonding, takes place when one is locked in a weather system. Young and starry-eyed, I longed for bigger, harder assignments. I'm not above using my hands and grabbing hold of any opportunity to bring pleasure to my audience. Thus, my talent won me a full-blown job. Difficult? Yes. Most women lack the stamina needed to maintain that position, but not I. How? You may ask. My experience has taught me, it's the slow-growing weather system that thrusts you into a pattern of hot, sticky, wet...

"I'm boring you."

Aaron choked on a gulp of water.

"Do you need help?"

Aaron shook his lowered head. "I'm fine," he answered in a raspy voice. "Went down the wrong way... the water."

"Having spent my life under the same roof as Colleen, I've mastered my gag reflex."

"I find that hard to swallow."

"Touché. There's much more to tell. I haven't scratched the surface."

"I'm itching to hear," Aaron said, wearing a devilish grin.

Margo ran a breadstick across her lips. "Another time."

Assuming Margo was fluent in Italian, Lorenzo asked her in their shared language if they had parked in a nearby garage. If so, the restaurant would validate its receipt. Terror paralyzed her face. Her ego crumbled like the Colosseum. Aaron and the waiter stared at one another, then at Margo. It's said, *"All roads lead to Rome."* Margo had hit a fork in that road. Should she embarrass herself in front of Aaron by exposing her limited Italian vocabulary? Or humiliate herself and the anxious waiter by employing the only Italian phrase left in her repertoire? She chose the latter. Giving Lorenzo a come-hither stare, she coolly smiled and asked, "Cazzo mi?"

Suddenly, the location of the car was of little importance to the stunned waiter, who furrowed his thick brows.

"Cazzo te?" he asked in a voice barely above a whisper.

"Si, facciamo cazzo." Knowing Aaron was unaware of the subject of their exchange, a shaken Lorenzo replied he was flattered, but a happily married man and wished to remain so. Margo hoped his reply was "No, thank you." The shocked waiter backed away from the table.

"What did he say?" a mystified Aaron asked.

"He regretted that the sausage was dry."

Strolling toward Aaron's car, a voice came up from behind. "Aaron!"

"Stan! What a surprise." Aaron snuck a wink at his snickering friend. "Margo, may I introduce Stanley Schuyler. We share a practice. Stan, this lovely young lady is Margo Ronan."

Stan kissed her hand. "A lovely name for a lovely woman." He handed Margo his card.

"When you jilt this guy, give me a call."

Aaron gave Stan a stern look. "Have you been drinking?"

"I may find Margo intoxicating, but no, I haven't been drinking. Joanne and the kids are in Jersey visiting her family, while I'm holed up at The Madison with the woman I should have married. Aaron, you're a sex god. I bid you adieu. "

As he walked off, Margo looked back at the exiting Stan. "I wouldn't want him cutting into my brain."

"Stan's a good guy. Hmm, 'sex god.' That's a title I've yet to earn."

"I'll be the judge of that," Margo purred.

***

With feline precision, Margo slipped in the front door and stashed her crumpled gown into the hall closet. "Just getting in?" came a flat voice. Margo confidently entered the kitchen. "The show got out late. We went back to Lorna's apartment. I slept there." Berta eyed Margo's wrinkled pants and smudged makeup. "And you couldn't call to inform me? If this has something to do with the man that called last week, so help me..."

"I'm an adult, I can go out with whomever I please."

"Not under my roof."

"A roof I paid to repair," Margo hollered back as she stormed up to her bedroom, where Colleen waited.

"Long night?" Margo confirmed with a grin. "Did he take you for breakfast? Or were you it?"

"You'll be surprised to learn he's a very nice man, for a doctor. I'm more impressed by his prowess than his title."

"You slept with him!"

"You knew I would."

"Ma's right, you are a tramp. Where did you do it?"

"He shares a flat with a fellow doctor."

"What did you get for sleeping with that dud?"

"He may be inexperienced, but I taught him a thing or two."

"Did he wear a rubber?" Margo didn't volunteer an answer. "He did! He knows you're a skank."

"All doctors wear one. It's like washing your hands."

"I bet he's doing that now, about a hundred times in scalding water."

"Do you want to hear about my date or not?"

"This had better be good."

"Oh, it is." Colleen shimmied next to Margo on the bed. "Aaron gets turned on when people see us together. He knows they're thinking he must be great in bed to have a girl like me. He could have brought me home earlier, but he knew his roommate was due back and wanted Barry, that's his roommate, Barry, to know he finally has a girl in his bedroom. I heard Barry come in, so I crawled on top of Aaron, and while we were doing it, I cried out, 'I'm a bad girl! A dirty girl! I can't stop. Oh, God, Oh, God!' I knew Barry could hear me, Aaron knew Barry could hear me, and

Barry didn't care who knew he could hear me; he just wanted to see who Virgin Boy had in his room. I won't let up. I'm throwing my head back begging for forgiveness, and Aaron says, 'There's nothing dirty about a man and a woman enjoying one another's body.' I mean, this guy doesn't have a clue." Colleen muffled her laugh into a pillow as Margo continued. "Aaron wanted to go back to doing it, but I wanted to go home, so I said, 'Is that the time? My mother is going to break my neck. God knows what she'll do to you.' The last thing he wants is for Ma to come after him with bolt cutters."

"Margo, you're going to burn in hell for this, but I've got to hand it to you: you set it up perfectly. Now everyone knows he has a hot girlfriend, so when you dump him, he'll be crushed, embarrassed, destroyed."

"I'm not dumping him."

"Once Ma finds out you succumbed to the semitic serpent, she'll kill both of you. Is that what you want?"

"What I want is to attend the hospital's Golden Jubilee Banquet. Boston's crème de la crème will be there, and so will I. After the banquet, it's Splitsville."

***

Aaron removed the cigarette from Margo's lips and dropped it into a coffee cup next to the bed.

"Hey! That's my post-colloidal cigarette. Which means I only have one per week."

"If it were up to me, you'd be smoking a pack a day, but I don't want you to develop cancer and have another Ronan death on my hands. You're the one who will kill me."

"I am that good, aren't I?"

Aaron gave a weak smile. "I know you have your heart set on going to The Jubilee Banquet, but..."

Margo scowled. "But what?"

"Stan has a surgery scheduled for next Friday, he can't... won't operate on this patient. It's an intricate surgery, only performed successfully twice, both by me. The surgery will take ten hours, barring any complications. There's an intern on staff, Doctor Lucerne, who would love to escort the most beautiful woman in Boston to the banquet. He's French; you'll like him. And since I'm the chief surgeon, he can't steal you from me."

"He won't have to!" Margo got out of bed and into her clothes as quickly as she had taken them off.

"I'll make it up to you. We'll have dinner at The Ritz some other time, get a room, champagne, the whole nine yards. I've got you a birthday present that will knock your socks off."

"My socks are going back on," Margo raged while rolling her silk stockings up her legs. "This fucking garter snapped off," she blurted, throwing the clip in Aaron's face.

"Calm down. That language isn't necessary."

"I'll tell you what's not necessary. YOU!"

"I wouldn't break our date, but this is important."

"And I'm not? You can get another doctor to take me, but you can't get one to do that crummy operation?"

"No, Margo. I can't. I'm the best. This patient needs the best, deserves the best."

"And I don't? You know what I think? I think it's all about sex. You won't take me because you're ashamed of me. You think you're too good for me. Pawn me off to some...some, trainee. You promised to take me places and buy me things, and you don't deliver."

"Get used to it, Margo. I'm a doctor, and a darn good one. My patients come first. Always will."

"You may be a good doctor, but you're a lousy lover." Margo snatched her purse off the dresser before bolting out the door.

A naked Aaron leaned over the stairwell railing. "I'll call you in a few days when you cool off."

"I've cooled off, Romeo. I'm ice. You want to be my knight in a shining lab coat? Come to Mount Nottingham and slay the dragon. Then we'll see what kind of man you are."

***

A pouting Margo flopped onto the living room sofa across from her mother, who was knitting a scarf for the church clothing drive.

"Colleen around?" Margo asked.

"She's taking her SATs today."

"That's right, I forgot... Mae?"

"At the church, setting up for the bazaar. Half the dresses donated were from you. They'll fetch a pretty penny. It was very thoughtful of you."

"Anything for Mae... and the church."

"That only leaves me to tell your troubles to, and I know you don't want to do that," Berta said, raising an eye. Margo looked up at the medallion on the ceiling to mask her tears.

"You've been seeing Dr. Hirsh."

"I don't know what you're talking about."

"Denying it doesn't help."

"Colleen told you that blabber mouth."

"She didn't tell me; you did. I can read you."

"It appears my life is an open book."

Berta put down her knitting and took a seat next to her brooding daughter. "I'm sorry, not that you're no longer seeing Dr. Hirsh, but because he broke your heart." To Berta's amazement, Margo didn't retreat. Could the tender approach be all that was needed to end the mutual animosity? "I know you think I don't care; if I didn't, I wouldn't quarrel with you. I have your best interests at heart. You've got to believe me, but you continue to resist taking my advice, do the opposite at your own peril, just to spite me. I'll never be Mae, nor should I. She has the luxury of turning a blind eye when you misbehave."

"Misbehave! Christ, I'm not ten. I'm twenty-four, and now you're sorry. You weren't sorry when I was in a car accident, when I was mugged, lost my job, didn't get into college. Now you're sorry? I don't want your shoulder to cry on. Keep your phony sympathy."

"He promised to take you to some fancy party and had second thoughts. Do you know why? Because you'd be in the company of people who are well-spoken, educated, have careers that make a difference in people's lives. After 'what a lovely dress,' they'll have nothing more to say to you."

"I'm not cheap!"

"Not by a long shot. You're expensive, the good china that's displayed, never put on the table. Nuala, the man is over 40. Do you seriously think he's been saving himself for you? He's not taking you to that ball for the same reason Ronny didn't take you to the country club; you're a pretty trinket, flashy, but lack substance. You have no one to blame but yourself."

Margo came to her feet. "I'm not good enough for Ronny? He's a vicious drunk."

"Doctor Hirsh is a Jew. He's not good enough for you."

***

Colleen popped her head into Margo's bedroom. "Who were you chewing out on the phone?"

"That was lover boy. He's sorry. Wants to make it up to me. Take me out for my birthday, two weeks too late. He said he has a birthday present for me. Well, he can take his crummy flowers and shove them. If I see him again, I swear..."

"Your wait is over," Colleen said, waving Margo to the window. "He just pulled up."

A terror-stricken Margo hopped on one foot, yanking on her shoe. "Get the door before Ma does!"

"Shouldn't I wait for the second ring?"

Stepping out the front door and into the late autumn chill, Margo rubbed her bare arms. "What are you doing here? You've got some nerve, I'll grant you that."

Aaron raised an old straw broom left neglected on the porch floor. "I bring you the witch's broomstick."

"If she sees you, she'll set that broom on fire and ram it up your ass."

Aaron took a seat on the porch swing. "Let her try. I'm not leaving without you."

"Then you'll be leaving without your balls; that's her main target."

"Like mother, like daughter," he said with a wink. "Get your coat, we'll go for a ride."

"I'm not getting in that car with you."

"Fine. We'll walk over to the zoo."

"The zoo? In the rain?"

"It's just a sprinkle."

"Do you have any idea what elephant dung smells like in the rain?"

"No. Let's find out. If you don't come along peaceably, I'll sit in the car with my hand on the horn." Frustrated and scared, Margo reached behind the door, taking the first raincoat she put her hand on. It was big, it was ugly, and it was Colleen's. Aaron took her arm. She shook him off.

Like the animals in the wild that share the watering hole with their natural enemies, only to turn on each other after quenching their thirst, the Franklin Park Zoo, the jeweled clasp in Olmsted's Emerald Necklace Park system, served as the city's watering hole. Its visitors may not share customs, beliefs, or skin pigment, but they all shared the fun of watching the mimicking monkeys, the awe of a peacock spreading its plumage, and the fear of the raging lions in their dilapidated confines. Everyone loved the zoo except the animals and Margo.

The couple sat on a damp, shingled-roofed bench. Slouching with her legs stretched out in front of her, Margo groused. "I can't believe I'm at the zoo, in the rain with you."

"Sit up."

She complied.

"The silent treatment." Aaron teased.

"You think this is funny?"

"No. I think it's juvenile."

"Do you have any idea how you made me look?"

"How could you look anything but beautiful?"

"Is this the lighter side of Aaron Hirsh? The one your evil twin described in the letter after your last faux pas?"

"I make an effort to keep my professional self out of my personal life, but you're drawing him out."

"I'm not interested in Dr. Jekyll or Mr. Hyde. You're a heartless monster. I was a fool to have gone all the way with you on our first date. Now you think that's all I do, all I'm good at."

"That's unfortunate. I apologize if I gave you that impression." Aaron reached into his coat pocket and handed Margo an envelope.

"What's this?"

"A recommendation. I neglected to mention you're good in bed; that's all you do, all you're good at. If you like, I can amend it."

271

Snatching the reference from his hand, Margo shot a sideways glance. "You know I can't work in the same hospital as you."

"Don't trust yourself?"

"Don't get smug with me. You wouldn't treat me this way were I one of your own, a doctor, an intellectual, a Jew. I'm no more than a pretty placeholder who never went further than high school, held a real job, or lived on my own. And I'm not a virgin."

"You're speaking in your mother's tongue."

"Are you insinuating I can't speak my own mind? I'm leaving." Margo took off running.

"You're being childish," Aaron called after her. The flapping raincoat disappeared into the mist.

***

"Will someone get that phone?" Colleen rushed to pick up the receiver before her mother greeted the caller with her 'This had better be important voice.

"Colleen?"

"Speaking."

"It's Aaron."

"Hey, Aaron, sorry, but you just missed Margo. She's lost three pounds, which calls for a new wardrobe. It must be nice to be so shallow."

"Ouch! It wasn't Margo I wanted to speak with, and I'm certain the feeling is mutual. Margo mentioned you have your sights set on becoming a playwright. You're entering college next year, so I thought..."

"I'm only a junior."

"That's all?"

"I'm a late bloomer."

"They're the best kind. Where do you plan on applying?"

"Emerson is my first choice, but when you come down to it, it's your work that brings success, not the diploma on your wall."

"You do realize you're speaking to a Harvard man. When the time comes, I'll gladly write you a recommendation, not out of fear of receiving a scathing letter, but because I believe in you."

"About that letter, Margo was drunk, angry, I couldn't reason with her."

"Oh no, I recognized your sarcasm. I saved the letter. When you're famous, it will be worth a fortune."

"Sorry to burst your bubble, I only dictated the letter, Margo penned it, and like her, it's worthless."

"That's no way to talk about the woman I love. So, Miss Playwright, who's your favorite?"

"Tough call. I have to go with Faulkner. I'm guessing you're an Ibsen fan."

"Oscar calls me Dr. Faustus, your mother calls me Dr. Death, and Margo won't call me at all. I have a favor to ask of you."

"If it involves some medical experiment, find yourself another chimp."

"What I need is a date. I was given two tickets to the Huntington Theater's production of *Uncle Vanya* starring none other than Maximilian Schell. I treated a dear friend of his. The man only spoke German, which I speak, and he wanted the best, which I am. Now, I have two front row seat tickets and an invitation to dine with its star, but no date. So, what do you say?"

"For real?!"

"Would I kid a kidder?"

"No, you wouldn't, and yes, I'll go."

"What about your mother?"

"She won't mind as long as you bring me home alive."

"Then it's a date. Sunday, I'll come to your door, ring the bell, and say hello to your mother."

"Wear a smile and a cup."

***

"I must say, the Ronan dowager treated me rather well," Aaron said as he opened the car door for his date.

"She's just thankful anyone of the opposite sex would want to be seen in my company. Colleen placed her hand across her forehead as if checking for a fever. "I'm destined to roam the earth a fat, friendless failure."

"You will with that attitude. I now know why my brother finds you so captivating."

"You sure know how to talk to a woman."

"The woman I want to talk to doesn't want to talk to me. She thinks I'm only interested in her body."

"That's all there is, Aaron." Colleen bounced in her seat. "I have an idea for a play I want to pitch to Max. It's entitled '*Midnight for Margo.*' The scene opens in a cheap hotel. The room is illuminated by a neon sign from the barroom below flashing '*COCKTAILS.*' We see a boozed-up blond, the kind of dame with too much time on her hands and too much liquor in her system. She sways to 'Harlem Nocturne' from the mouth of a slow, sultry, alto sax. Her sleeveless cocktail dress hugs a body that served more men than Charlie the bartender the day Prohibition was repealed. Off stage, we hear the gruff voice of a man fed up with the drunken burlesque show." Colleen twisted her mouth and deepened her voice. "*Knock off the Salome routine.*"

Margo holds her arms out. '*Dance with me, Joey.*'

Don't make me rough you up.

'*You and what army?*'

The 42nd. Most of them were boys when you had them; some never made it home.

An enraged Margo hurls an empty whiskey bottle at Joey's head. He grabs her peroxide mane and pushes her bloated face against a mirror freckled with rust and nicotine. *'Take a good look, Margo, a real good look. That's the face I wake up to in the morning. The toilet bowl doesn't like looking up at it, neither.'*

Stop, Joey, you're hurting me!

Slap, slap, Margo falls to the floor."

Aaron cringed. "Better end it there. I don't have the stomach for blood and guts."

"That's not what I've heard. You spent time patching up GIs coming back from Vietnam."

"I figured it was time to step up and repay the country that took me in. Every night, I remind myself that someone died for me today."

"Lee's wrong. You're not a man who can't see beyond his own nose or reflection in the mirror."

"He said that!"

"I added the nose part."

"With friends like you, I don't need enemies. "

"Without friends like me, you wouldn't have friends."

***

The familiar roar of a Ferrari brought Margo to her bedroom window. Her pulse raced along with the car engine as she looked down at Aaron walking Colleen toward the house. It wasn't fair; when she saw Aaron, they had to meet in secret. She hated them both. She loved them both. The two swung hands as they approached the front door.

"It's not every day a budding young playwright receives a glowing review from an Academy Award winner and a promise to write a letter of recommendation to Emerson on her behalf." Aaron recounted with pride.

"Max may have an Oscar, but he's no Dr. Hirsh."

"I am a ladies' man, aren't I?"

"What you are is the kindest, most considerate man I've ever had the pleasure of knowing. Not that I've known any men." Colleen studied Aaron's face. "You remind me of Poppy. You remember him? The man you murdered."

"I've killed so many."

"Thank you for giving me the most exciting day of my life."

"As of today, I've fallen in love with all three Ronan sisters."

Colleen tiptoed past Margo's open bedroom door. "How was your date?" Margo asked.

"You broke his heart."

"Listen, kiddo, *you're* the one who concocted this scheme. You're the one who said to put him in his place and seek revenge. You told me to send that letter, improve my image, and learn Italian. You told me to date him, and you told me to dump him."

"I didn't tell you to fuck him! "

"You knew I would; you thought it was funny. He's buttering you up to score points with me. Why else would he spend his precious time with you?"

"For once, I agree with Ma. You are a shameless slut."

***

Mae walked across the leaf-covered yard. "No rake?" she asked a brooding Colleen sitting on her swing. Its twisted ropes spun the long-legged teen at a dizzying speed.

"I didn't come out here to rake," she answered, coming to a halt. "I came to fly off the swing, never to return."

"School?

"No."

"A boy?"

"The boy isn't mine."

"There's a difference between a man being kind to you and being in love."

"Oh, Mae, I'm not infatuated with Dr. Hirsh. It's Margo. She used him. Now he's in love with her. He calls her 'his girl' all the while she's seeing other men. Dr. Hirsh is over 40, a big-time surgeon. He knows famous people, yet when he talks about Margo, you'd think he was sixteen and the most popular girl in school gave him her number. I was embarrassed for him. She only went out with him to get a job and revenge."

"You're romanticizing their relationship. He's a grown man. He can handle rejection."

"I learned a valuable lesson watching Margo operate. I don't ever want to hurt or be hurt that way. I'll wait until I'm married to someone who loves me as much as I love him—that's if that someday and someone ever comes along."

"You can't waste a lifetime searching for someday and lose today. When Mr. Right comes along, you'll know it."

Chapter Eighteen

Arms folded across her chest, Berta stood back and nodded her head. "You're back where you started, standing behind a cash register."

Poising with one hand on her hip, the other held out wrist down, Margo quoted her haughty-voiced boss, Miss Millet. "We are not a department store, darling. We are Draper and Dracut. There is no need for a cash register when one is in the Social Register."

Mae fawned over her niece. "I don't know anyone who shops there. I can't afford to window-shop in that part of town."

Margo's face lit up. "I'm glad you mentioned the windows. I'll be window dressing and modeling for customers. Miss Millet said she might take me on as her protégé. Me! An assistant buyer for Draper and Dracut. Think of it: I could meet a rich, handsome businessman."

Berta tempered Margo's enthusiasm. "You had one."

"Can't you be happy for me?"

"When are you going to smarten up? Colleen has."

"Colleen had help!"

"You didn't think you needed it. You were going places on your looks; well, looks don't last, and you're not equipped for the workforce. A salesgirl, well, congratulations."

"I hate you!" Margo screamed, running from the kitchen.

"Go on, Mae. Chase after her. Tell her how talented she is."

"I've never interfered with the way you raise the girls, but she's been through a hell of a lot in her young life."

"When I was her age, I was a widow raising two children, but she's too selfish for that. It's time she left the sandbox."

Margo sat in the carriage house on a dusty pile of National Geographics tied up in twine. A sliver of light sliced across the dark carriage house floor. "Honey."

"Forget it, Mae. No more pep talks. There's no pleasing her."

Mae knelt before her red-eyed niece. "Margo, listen to me. Life is too short. You're wasting time. Once she's gone, you can't say 'I forgive.'"

"I'm not mending fences because I don't love her. And I'll *never* forgive her. You make it sound like I'm to blame."

"She bears the brunt of it. You're both grown women, reconcile."

"Reconcile! It takes two to tango, and my dance card is full. I'm going to prove that I can be successful. I'll be a buyer with my own office and staff."

"When you do, I'll give Mort a call. He knows everyone in the business; he'll help you get started."

"You miss him, don't you?"

"I miss them all."

"But he was special, huh?"

"I was his secretary; we were close."

"You loved one another, didn't you?"

"The man was married; there's a line you never cross."

"Was he the one?"

"God, no! There will be no more talk of it. Let's get inside; it's cold out here."

"It's colder in there."

***

The white dress box with a blue bow lay on Mae's bed. The gift-giver hid behind the closet door like a cat poised to pounce on a baited mouse. Margo wrapped her arms around her waist, rocking as if her bladder were about to burst. "Come on, come on." Mae's slow, steady steps came to an abrupt halt at her bedroom threshold. Margo flung the closet door open. "Surprise!"

Mae slid the ribbon off the dress box that bore the Draper and Dracut trademark silver signature.

Margo congratulated herself. "I chose the perfect gift for the perfect aunt."

Parting the silver tissue paper, Mae gently lifted the blue Oleg Cassini dress out of its box like a newborn from its crib. "My word, it's so extravagant. It must have cost you two months' salary."

"You always say life's too short, live for today. That's just what I intend to do. I want to pamper you now. When I saw this dress come in, I snapped it up. I figured I had better buy it before Jackie Kennedy does. Please say you like it. You never wear blue, it's your color." Mae ran her hand over the dress's soft embossed brocade. A melancholy look veiled her face as if looking at a picture of a long-departed friend. Margo wondered if Mae had worn a similar dress when she was young.

"Are you okay?" Margo asked, cocking her head.

"Yes, I was just imagining how lovely I'll look in it."

"Try it on. If it's a poor fit, I can have it altered free of charge."

Mae stood at her dresser mirror, holding the gifted garment against her shoulders. "I have a padded hanger for it."

Margo's face fell. "You're putting it away?"

"I'm saving it for a special occasion where all eyes will be on me, and everyone will comment on how beautiful I look. I'll be wearing this dress and thinking of you."

***

Set back from the street, Draper and Dracut's entrance was lined by apple blossom trees and a canopy-covered door. It was more of a salon than a department store with floor-to-ceiling windows looking out at the Boston Public Gardens.

"There's no reason why this dress can't be worn by both the mature woman and one of the younger set," Margo instructed the seasoned sales staff. Adding a belt and scarf to a mannequin as stiff as a Draper and Dracut client, Margo ended her demonstration with a jubilant "Voila! It's now fresh, youthful, and dare I say, hip. Not only do we make a sale on the dress, but also on accessories. Always remember, a seamstress can sew a dress, but it's the accessories that make the dress and pump up the price."

"Miss Ronan," sounded a voice schooled in proper diction. "I'd like a word with you in my office."

"Yes, Miss Millet." Blood leaked from Margo's veins into her stomach. Riding an emotional high since being awarded the position of Senior Sales Associate, she feared she was about to be reprimanded for two returns. The gray-haired Miss Millet's face was pancaked and taut, her demeanor prig and toney. Yet Margo suspected that at the end of the workday, old Eunice returned to her Beacon Hill digs to sip sherry and mourn the loss of her youth and any opportunity for marriage.

Margo marveled at the grandeur of Miss Millet's sanctuary. An oversized Baroque mirror hung behind a Chippendale desk. A blue Japanese vase equal to Margo in height stood in the shadow, refusing to be ignored, reminding her of a similar vase in the Singer Sargent painting, Portraits de 'Infante, that had seared into her memory when she came across the image in a coffee table book on Boston artists. She vowed a replica of the vase would one day grace her home. Following Miss

Millet's direction, Margo closed the door, fearing she might be closing the door to her career.

"I can explain. Mr. Townsend came across the invoice for the handbag his wife purchased last week. As for Mrs. Ames, she discovered a slinky nightie more suited for her husband's secretary's figure than her own."

Miss Millet toyed with a single strand of pearls worn over a dowdy brown suit, Margo thought a poor match. "Out of curiosity, how did you resolve their complaints?"

Margo scooted to the edge of her seat, eager to impress Miss Millet with her sales savvy. "Mr. Townsend complimented me on my earrings. I suggested he purchase a similar pair for his wife from our jewelry counter as a peace offering. My suggestion resulted in a sale and a new Draper and Dracut devotee. As for Mrs. Ames, let's just say some matters are best left to a marriage counselor."

Miss Millet gestured to a teacart dressed in English china and a silver tray of pastries, possibly from the Titanic's dessert menu. "Tea?"

Margo's brain told her to oblige; her stomach warned there would be consequences, calories being the least of them. Her nervous system seconded the motion. "No, thank you."

"This conversation isn't about a disgruntled customer. Miss Ronan, you know the difference between a fad and a timeless fashion staple, can judge the durability of a fabric, and possesses a keen eye for the quality of the stitch."

"I spent time in a garment factory as a child."

"It served you well. I've also noted your respect for currency. "

"You mean I'm good with a buck."

Miss Millet's face cracked into a smile. "Yes, good with a buck. I'm promoting you to District Buyer. Fair warning: expect senior staff to resent your rapid rise."

"Criticism is mother's milk to me. I promise I won't disappoint you."

Margo crept into a fitting room. "Psst... Connie." Looking in both directions as if dodging traffic, Connie dashed into the lavish fitting room with more square footage than her Back Bay apartment. "I've been promoted!" Margo blurted. The two friends silently hopped and hugged. "I'll tell you all about it over lunch."

Connie Crawford, the former Constance Hamilton, was not "to the manor born." Her charm and physical attributes propelled her into Boston's cash class and the bed of jetsetter Ogden "Ham" Hamilton, now Inmate 62740 at Lewisburg, Virginia. He was in for embezzlement of government funds. The scandal was fodder for Page Six tabloid readers. Emerging from the messy divorce penniless and friendless, she'd been reduced to selling dresses to women she had once rubbed elbows with just months earlier.

Margo tapped her index finger over her lip. "Hmm, where haven't the two hardest-working women in retail lunched? The Public Gardens! Grab your brown bag, Connie. We're going to watch the swan boats."

***

Margo brushed leaves off a lagoon side bench while Connie stood at the water's edge tossing bread crust to squawking ducks.

"Keep feeding those ducks, and there won't be anything left of your ham sandwich," Margo called over to her friend.

"How do you think I keep my girlish figure at 40?" Connie said, returning to the bench. "Speaking of ham, Ham has a brother, Woodrow Hamilton."

"Woodrow?"

"We call him Woody. His work requires him to travel. I'm not sure what he does, only that he writes and lectures on medical ethics. He has an apartment here in Boston. I think you'd make a great couple."

"A doctor? Ethical? Not my type."

"He thinks you are."

"Say, have you been talking me up to him?"

"He's seen you and likes what he saw."

"As always, it's all about my looks."

"Just keep him in mind."

"Sorry Connie. I've been seeing a banker."

"Is it love?"

"Hell, no. But I'll keep your brother-in-law as a backup. In the meantime, Banker Boy will be making deposits and withdrawals."

***

Connie stood at Margo's office door, her head lowered, and her eyes raised, looking like a frightened schoolgirl, not a middle-aged woman. "Miss Ronan?"

"Connie, I'm your friend, not the school principal. Come in, close the door."

"I have a favor to ask. Miss Charlotte Van Neste will be arriving this afternoon to choose a wedding gown. Her mother's a loyal customer of our New York store. She insists her daughter's gown carries the Draper and Dracut label. Charlotte attends Vassar, and she's dissatisfied with the selection in New York."

"Who can blame her? We don't cater to young brides."

"That's why I'm coming to you. You're young. You know what girls her age like, and I fear I'll be recognized: there's bad blood between the Hamiltons and the groom's family."

Margo stood. "I understand and look forward to meeting Miss Charlotte Van Neste."

***

"My mother is making me buy my dress here. I wish she'd butt out: It's my wedding," the plump brunette said with a pout.

"I promise you won't leave without a dress you'll both be pleased with," Margo assured the disgruntled bride-to-be. Charlotte unfolded a creased page torn from

Vogue. "I want this dress. It's the one Kim Novak wore to the Academy Awards." Margo found the figure-hugging white satin gown more suited for a wedding night than a wedding day. "It's beautiful, but you're having an autumn wedding in Boston, not Southern California. I have just the dress." Margo disappeared behind a curtain, returning with a cream-colored gown slung across her arms like a limp corpse.

"I don't like it," stated the defiant Charlotte.

"Allow me to take it out of the garment bag; it looks different hung."

Charlotte shook her head. "It's smothered in pearls and lace. Only old ladies wear pearls. What's with this thing?" she grumbled, tugging on the dress's satin sash that ran from the right side of its waist, attaching to the opposite hem. "I want to look like a bride, not the wedding cake."

"Please try it on."

Charlotte shrugged. "You're the expert."

Margo detected a bump arising from the future bride's belly. If correct, the child would arrive six months after the honeymoon conception date. Charlotte stepped out of the fitting room looking like a child stuffed into a snowsuit. Margo flashed an optimistic smile. "Love it?"

"No. Maybe if this apron were removed."

"It adds an extra layer of elegance. Trust me, your mother will be very pleased."

***

Margo fell back on her bed, exhausted as she readied for her business trip. "I think I have everything."

Colleen looked over the six-piece set of luggage. "Everything but the kitchen sink. You'll only be in New York for three days."

"And three nights. My days will be spent at corporate, being indoctrinated in the Draper and Dracut philosophy. Make the sale and look good doing it," Margo joked as she sat at her vanity, brushing her hair. Colleen sat on the bed, studying her sister. Margo lowered her hairbrush and looked at Colleen's reflection in her mirror. "Something bothering you?"

"Until now, I never saw you the way others do. You're beautiful, generous, and honest... kinda."

Margo scooted next to Colleen on the bed. "Are you okay?"

Colleen answered with an unconvincing "Yeah."

"It's not like you to give a one-word answer."

"There are times I wish I were more like you. This is one of them."

"Oh, I get it. You've got a crush on a boy and want me to school you in the art of seduction."

Colleen cracked a sideways smile. "You did promise me lessons the summer we spent on the Vineyard."

"And look what that got me: Ronny. Has this boy asked you on a date?"

"A date? He doesn't know I'm alive!"

"Then stop playing dead. You're not the wallflower type."

"If I looked like you, he'd notice me."

"You don't want to be me. I've already won the roll and don't need an understudy. Who's the leading man?"

"Fran's brother Alexander."

"Fran. Fran the dyke Fran? You surround yourself with lesbians, then wonder why boys don't ask you out."

"Alex knows I'm straight."

"Then act the part. When I get back, I'll give you that lesson. Strange, when I'm at work, I'm no longer a dumb blonde. I'm knowledgeable, respected, and people seek my advice. I'm finally doing what I was put on earth to do, and I did it on my own. Someday, I'll have my own fashion line, and you'll have a guy who loves you for you, warts and all."

"Hey!"

"I'm no role model; looks don't last, neither does love, but don't pass up the chance to experience it."

Mae had him under surveillance since joining the city payroll, She feared one day they would collide in a hallway or share an elevator. This morning, she'd see that they would. The door revolved in sync with her stomach. She'd been waiting since 6 a.m., the past hour spent keeping her courage up and her breakfast down. Mae snuffed out her cigarette with a shaking hand while struggling to bolster the nerve to approach a man who three decades earlier had fallen to his knees begging her not to leave him.

In her sight, he stepped into an empty elevator. Mae hopped in like a schoolgirl onto a swinging jump rope. "Good morning, Councilor Bullard." Eyes fixed on the closing doors, he mumbled, "Morning."

The scent of his aftershave raced to her brain, unlocking hidden memories. Did he still whip up his Barbasol in the soap dish she'd bought him for Christmas back in 1932? She noted his telltale mannerisms. Tapping foot, impatience, tightened jaw, anger, clearing throat, nerves. The only button pressed was for the third floor. He knew he wouldn't be exiting alone.

"Might I have a word with you, Councilor?"

"Pardon if I appear rude, but I arrived early to catch up on paperwork. Give my secretary a buzz. See if she can fit you in." He headed for his office at a quickening pace, fast but not fast enough to look as though he were fleeing.

"Eugene... Gene, it's not about us."

"Come in, take a seat." The request sounded more like an order than an invitation.

"I have a favor to ask of you." Leaning back in his chair with fingers laced behind his head, a slow smile crossed his lips.

"I wondered how long it would take you."

"It was you who sought me out for this job."

"They needed someone with your expertise in the property tax department; you got me my first job in that Jewish sweatshop; it was the Depression, I'm grateful. I read that Bloomfield's was closing its doors. I had a hunch you were still slaving for the old man. Twenty years, did he ever give you a raise?"

"Mort took over for his father."

"Oh, yes, Morton," Eugene said with steepled hands to his lips. "Let me guess, he made you his personal secretary, or was it his private secretary?"

"It wasn't like that."

"I bet he wished it were. A Protestant was out of the question, but a Jew, wouldn't your mother love that?" Putting his hand on his hip, he mimicked a Jewish hausfrau. 'My daughter, Mrs. Bloomfield.' How is the old... your mother?"

"She died ten years ago."

"I'm sorry."

"You're not but thank you for being polite."

"And her heir apparent?"

"Berta is well. She's the reason I've come to see you."

"OH NO! Whatever it is, the answer is no. My balls don't want to make a new home in my throat."

"It's Berta's son-in-law: he needs a job. Patsy goes to college at night. I thought something part-time."

"Mae, the jobs are posted. Have him apply, and I'll put in a good word for the kid." Eugene walked to the door and held it open for Mae, who remained seated.

"Rumor has it you're going to seek higher office."

The door slammed. "You'd actually blackmail me?"

Mae turned in her seat to face him. "I swear I never breathed a word of what happened. I never will."

"Then what are you suggesting?"

"Patsy's from East Boston. You don't have support in that district."

"And I never will. Potosi has that town sewn up. To be honest, I don't give a lick about East Boston. I can win without them. There are more Os than ginzos in this city. As for the Negros, we give them the vote and they don't use it."

"You may not take the district, but you could make a dent in Potosi's support, make him sweat."

"How? By giving your in-law a job?"

"Patsy is the widower of Rosaria Travella."

"The crippled woman who burnt to death?"

"She fell to her death. Rosaria was my niece, Berta's daughter."

"Why didn't you say something? I would have sent flowers, set up a college fund for the baby."

"It's not too late. Patsy is well-known and well-liked, and everyone loved Rosaria. The tragedy is still raw in the community and will be for some time. Please, Gene, hear me out: Let Patsy run your campaign in East Boston. What do you have to lose? He'll get them to the polls, and it doesn't hurt that he's a young, good-looking widower. You've got the female vote right there. Have your photo taken standing in front of the burnt-out building, handing an oversized check to the Red Cross or March of Dimes, with Patsy standing next to you. That's when you announce your candidacy for mayor and introduce Patsy Travella as your man in Ward One. The Italians are tight-knit, like the South Boston Irish. They stay, not run off to the suburbs like the ones in Roxbury and Dorchester. Get the East Boston vote, and you'll have them for your political career."

"You've really thought this through."

"He's the father of Berta's grandson. I never married. Berta's children are mine."

The councilman came around his desk, standing behind the seated Mae, he kissed the top of her head. "I'm sorry I deprived you of a family of your own."

"Don't be. It was my decision. The blame rests with me."

"I'm still in love with you."

Mae thought, *Ten minutes ago, you didn't want to share an elevator, now you want to get in my pants*. She clasped his hands to keep them from wandering. "Please, Gene, give him a chance to prove himself."

Returning to his desk, Eugene scribbled on a sheet of stationery and handed it to Mae. "Give him this. If he comes through for me, and I'm elected, I'll see he goes places."

Mae sprang to her feet in the hope of making an exit without having to thank him physically, although she would if it guaranteed Patsy a job. "This will put you in good standing with Berta."

"Fuck Berta."

Mae wore an involuntary smile, pretending to find the insult amusing. Pressing the elevator button, Mae mumbled. "She's the only woman you haven't."

Chapter Nineteen

Time spent in New York had been invigorating; Margo was a star. Rumors were circulating that Miss Millet was on the verge of retiring. Margo was the only qualified candidate. The blue vase would be hers.

A wide-eyed salesclerk halted Margo and Connie at the store's entrance. "Miss Ronan, Miss Millet wants to see you in her office. She's not pleased."

Margo rolled her eyes. "My first day back, and I'm called on the carpet."

"Good luck," Connie whispered with a nudge.

An open newspaper covered Miss Millet's desk. "Close the door."

Margo didn't wait for accusations to fly. "I have nothing to do with advertising."

"And you have no business on the sales floor."

"I don't understand?"

"Allow me to refresh your memory. The Charlotte Van Neste wedding gown. To be more precise, Charlotte Van Neste-Kilday's wedding gown."

"Kilday?"

"You sold the bride her wedding gown. If you had read the society page, you'd know the scandal you generated." Miss Millet jabbed her finger into the incriminating photograph of the bride's bulging belly. The caption read. "The bride's grown from Draper and Dracut, Boston." With one fell swoop, Miss Millet scattered the pages onto the pale blue carpet.

Margo jumped back. "I swear, the gown I sold her hid her condition."

"So, you knew she was pregnant, yet you put her in a revealing gown. The only reason we avoided a lawsuit is that the bride's mother didn't want publicity. However, the Kildays are not as forgiving. The Kilday Corporation owns this property along with most of the real estate at the end of Boylston Street. Our lawyer received notice, either the perpetrator of this cruel joke will be terminated, or we'll be evicted. Draper and Dracut have occupied this corner for generations. If we move, we'll lose half our clientele."

"Please, Miss Millet, hear me out."

"Your only out is the door."

"The gown I sold Charlotte had a sash; you must have seen the gown when it came in, the cream with pearls. She removed the sash. How can I be blamed for the alteration?"

"The Kildays want someone's head. You signed the receipt; you're the sacrificial lamb."

"The New York store needs help. I'll start as a salesgirl, a stock clerk."

"I can't authorize a transfer or grant you references."

"Oh, please, Miss Millet."

"I'm truly sorry, Margo, but your career in retail is over."

Once again, Margo found herself covering for Ronny's sins. Because of him, she'd lost a child, a career, and nearly her life. He'd pay dearly.

***

"Move out!" Colleen fell face down on her bed, pounding her fist into the mattress.

"It's temporary. Ma thinks I'm filling in at the New York store. Once I find work, I'll move back."

"No, you won't. Why would you?"

"I can't stay with Connie indefinitely. Her lease is up in six months."

"What about your car?"

"I entrusted Ma with the keys. There will be no joyriding."

The sisters sat in silence, looking out at the fallen foliage that covered the park like a pawl. Colleen's words rode on an exhale.

"This house was so alive when we were growing up; it's dying like those leaves. It even smells old."

"That's your feet."

Resting her head on Margo's shoulder, Colleen forced a smile. "This isn't how our lives were supposed to have turned out."

Margo kissed Colleen's head. "I miss her too."

***

The knock on the apartment door came before the first coat of polish had dried on her toes. Margo hobbled on her heels to let her friend in. "You're lucky I moved in with you, Connie. The next time you lock yourself out, you'll have to call a locksmith." Margo opened the door to a wide grin and a stock of red hair. *Howdy Doody in Valentino.*

"The first lesson in city living is, never open your door to a stranger," he warned. "Unless he's a handsome stranger."

Margo slammed the door in his face. The doorknob rattled. "It's Woody, I'm both handsome and strange."

Margo cringed, knowing he was only the latter. "Dr. Hamilton," Margo greeted, opening the door with an insincere smile.

"Please, it's Woody, like the woodpecker. Heh-heh-heh-HEHHHH-heh."

Her head lowered; Margo offered a silent prayer to her feet. *Help me, Jesus.* "Gosh, you just missed Connie. I'd invite you in for coffee, but it's instant and I don't cook. Perhaps you could come back later, on Halloween." It was clear the man was impervious to insults.

"Nonsense. Are you hungry for Hungarian?"

"Am I what for what?"

"Hungarian food. The Café Budapest is around the corner." Woody consulted his watch. "They start serving dinner at six."

Margo's cold reception warmed as she eyed his timepiece. "Your watch is exquisite."

"Vacheron Constantin, a gift from my kid sister. She's attending boarding school in Geneva. I'm told it's very expensive."

"The school or the watch?"

"Both. Now powder your nose and slip into a pair of open-toe shoes, while I book a table."

***

The lobby was dark, the ceiling draped in a canopy of silk. The cry of a gypsy violin floated in the aromatic air.

The maître d' in Dinaric dress and Lika cap, hypnotized Margo with his dark Dracula eyes, burrowed beneath knitted brows.

"Your first visit to The Pest?"

"Oh, yes!" Margo exclaimed. "I've never been anywhere so mysterious and romantic."

Woody delighted in her childlike wonderment. Once seated in the cavernous dining room, they were greeted by a swarthy waiter in tight, high-waisted black pants and a vest. Embroidery ran from the collar of his white shirt down to his belt. In a thick Eastern European accent, he introduced himself as Vadic. His flowing sleeve swept across their table like a bed sheet drying in the wind.

"A drink from the bar?" he asked.

Woody snapped the menu closed. "Palinka and a TOST for the lady." Woody turned to Margo. "You're too young to drink."

"And you're too ignorant to ask," Margo mumbled.

"If you're adventurous, and I think you are, I suggest the paprikash."

"If a goat's head is delivered to this table, I'll have your head."

"You don't like goat's head?" Woody teased.

"I had it twice this week."

Over laughing, he turned to the other diners for validation. "She's had goat's head twice this week."

"What is paprikash?"

"It's chicken."

Valdic placed their drinks down. "Have you come to a decision?"

"Nokedli and chicken paprikash," Woody answered.

"And for the lady?"

"Same," Woody answered without looking at his date.

"Very good, sir," Valdic backed away with a slight bow.

Woody shook out his napkin. "You asked about my family." She hadn't and knew he wouldn't ask about hers. "I have two sisters, June and Augusta. Care to guess their birth months?"

"June and August?"

"March and December!" he blurted. "You're not the first to fall for that one. I call June, June bug. She's at school in Switzerland, and Augusta lives in New York at The Dakota with her husband, David. They're expecting twins."

"Twins!" Margo painfully exclaimed.

"They have two sons, ages two and four. We're all excited about the big event. God, do I love being an uncle. The boys are named Michael David and Philip David. I call them M.D. and PhD- get it?"

Margo wasn't a drinker, but the kiddie talk was unbearable. "May I taste your drink?"

"I don't advise drinking on an empty stomach."

Ignoring the warning, Margo knocked the drink back in one gulp. "That's got a kick to it. I'm sorry I drank it all. Order another one and one for yourself."

As expected, the conversation returned to babies. "With the twins due in a month, I'm on a mission to come up with cute names. It's tough when you don't know their sex."

Margo leaned across the candle-lit table and slurred, "If they're boys, why don't ya name 'em Vincent David and Stephen David. Ya know, VD and STD, get it? Sorry, it's the Palinka talkin'. Excuse me, I gotta hit the John David. I'll be back in a jiff." In three-inch heels, Margo solo line-danced to the ladies' room. The ceramic tile floor echoed the clack of her heels as she paced. "I can't take any more baby talk." Bracing her hands on the sink, she looked in the mirror with fixed eyes, "I've got to get out of here. If I only knew how to say fuck me in Hungarian, I know Vlad would take me up on the offer. What am I thinking? I'll tell him I can't have children, a botched abortion. Yeah, twins. That'll work."

Margo returned to the table where her dinner awaited, looking as if it had already been consumed and found its way back to the plate. Woody looked intently at his drunken date. "Do you feel better?"

"I'm not used to alcohol. It hit me hard."

"No more Palinka for you, little lady. Doctor's orders."

"I apologize, it's just all this talk of children upset me. You see, I can't have..."

Woody cut into her explanation. "Let's get the violinist over here." With the wave of a hand, the wandering Roma was at their table.

"Please, a love song for the lady." His eyes closed; Woody swayed to the melody the gypsy sawed out. The serenade over, Woody vigorously applauded and rose to his feet, motioning Margo to do the same.

She remained seated. "Your chicken thing is getting cold."

"I love the violin," he said, returning to his meal.

"Woody, I have a confession to make. Children aren't in the cards for me."

"Say, have you ever had your cards read? There's a room upstairs where they read cards, palms, tea leaves, the whole crystal ball thing. Let's head up there after dinner." Woody gave an impromptu impression of a fortune teller.

"I see a mysterious redhead who will sweep you off your feet, shower you with gifts, take you to distant lands, the Bahamas, the Riviera, the Greek Islands."

"Wouldn't that be nice?"

"What do you say? I have friends living in the South of France, Antoine and Frederika. I met Antoine in college. His father is the French Minister of Health. Antoine founded a medical supply company; he's done quite well. I haven't been over there since Alicia was born. She must be four by now. They're so cute at that age. I'm always welcome but feel like a third wheel. I'm overdue for a visit. Why don't you come with me?"

"That sounds exciting!"

"What's exciting is seeing Alicia. You're going to love her."

Margo looked deep into Woody's eyes and gently stroked his cheek. "Would we be able to spend time alone? I'm sure your friends are fine people, but I have an overpowering sensation that there's a chemistry developing between us that I'd like to explore."

"I have a solution. After we visit with Antoine, we'll take his yacht and crew for a summer sail on the Mediterranean."

"When do we leave?"

"Not until the twins are born."

"Of course, we wouldn't want to miss the blessed event."

"Does July sound good?"

"There's just one glitch: I'm in the process of job hunting. If I find one, I may not be able to take the time off," Margo said, expecting him to say, "Job? Nonsense, I'll support you." He didn't.

"What field interests you?"

"I applied for a position in public relations at The Peter Bent Brigham but was beaten out by a more qualified candidate."

"You don't want to work for them. I can get you a job at the Mass General Hospital. Have you heard of the Maxwell Hamilton Cardiac Center? My grandfather received excellent care in the cardio unit. When he died, he bequeathed half his fortune to the hospital. You find a job you're qualified for, and I'll put in a good word in my 'or else' voice."

Margo toasted with her TOST. "The Mass General may be in the cards."

The couple strolled hand in hand along the brownstone-lined Commonwealth Ave toward the Back Bay flat. "Constance described you as a daring risk-taker. I'll add gutsy strategist as well."

"Am I?" Margo asked.

"I heard about the wedding dress. Well played."

"It wasn't a stunt. The Kildays think it was an act of revenge. Now, there's a bounty on my head. I dated their son, Ronny, when I was in high school. Ronny had a sweet side, but once alcohol hit his bloodstream, look out. I suspect his father beat him. There was always a football injury, though I never attended a game, or a fender bender that left him bruised, but the car without a scratch. I didn't need a crystal ball to see what lay ahead. That's one family you don't want to tangle with."

"Don't I know it. Their daughter, Abigale, and I were married."

"You and Abby? I had no idea she had been married. Don't leave me hanging. What happened?"

"We were kids, seventeen and eighteen, when we eloped. The marriage was annulled. I won't lie: I'm still in love with her. Always will be. The long and short of it... she was pregnant. Her parents shipped her off to have the baby and put it up for adoption. Somewhere out there, I've got a son or a daughter."

Margo's heart melted. "If it's any consolation, Abby married a great guy."

"He'd have to be. Abigail wouldn't settle for less...children?"

"Three. Bruce owns a lumber company in New Hampshire." Margo strived to lighten the mood. "Bruce's last name is Dick. Mrs. Kilday didn't want people to know her daughter married a Dick, so she tells everyone Abby's married name is Richard."

"You better get inside; Constance will be worried," he said with his head hung. Their date ended where it had begun, at the apartment door. His kiss was smooth, soft, arousing.

"I could get used to this," Margo moaned.

"Let me know what you want to do for work."

"And you let me know when we sail for France."

***

The front door slammed. "Here we go again!" Berta stormed out of her kitchen, landing a knockout blow to the piano's abdomen. Most times, the assault would silence the rambling rag; this was not one of them.

Margo banged on the keys with her fists. "I'm going to quit that miserable job! All the girls in the office are jealous of me. They laugh at me behind my back. When

I returned from lunch, I found a sheet of carbon paper on my chair waiting to kiss my white skirt."

Berta shook her head. "You never worked in an office. Catty coworkers come with the territory."

Margo liberated her swollen feet from slingbacks. "Catty? These girls use letter openers as shivs."

"Dating doctors doesn't qualify you for a management position. You start in the typing pool."

"I don't need a doctor to get me a job. I found one on my own. I was sitting in the hospital cafeteria, alone, when a well-dressed man approached me. He works for a pharmaceutical company. He said they're always on the lookout for attractive women as sales representatives. He said doctors will buy anything from a pretty girl."

"You're going back to sales? This time as a drug pusher?"

"Ma, a drug rep, is not a drug pusher. I give out samples to doctors; if they prescribe them, I earn a commission."

"Once word gets out that you're peddling drugs, we'll have every junkie on Blue Hill Ave beating a path to our door."

"These are prescription drugs, not street drugs."

"Junkies don't care. I know the type; they'll swallow anything in a brown bottle. Honey Haggerty's grandson, Crazy Burt, a full-blown addict. What does he do? He gets his hands on Honey's stool softeners- prescription stool softeners, I might add. He downs the entire bottle. He's in a coma now. If he lives, and there's no guarantee he will, he'll be wearing a bag. God forgive him, 19, and wearing a bag. And you want to be a part of that 'scene.' How can you sleep at night knowing what your drugs did to that boy? If your generation spent more time on your knees than on the junk, we could keep our doors unlocked."

"What in God's name do you want me to do?! "Margo cried. "You pick the job. You pick the man. You choose how I should live and die. Would that make you happy? I'm a grown woman. I live at home, go to church, pay board, and clean the house. Once I finish training, if there's an opening out of town, I'm taking it."

***

Ferrying a shopping cartful of file folders from one department to another was demeaning. Nonetheless, Margo volunteered for the assignment to escape the petty cliché that festered in the office. The sound of his familiar laugh weakened her knees. She held tight to the cart's handle and puffed air.

Exiting the auditorium, looking like a foreign correspondent in a dark green belted raincoat and scarf, Aaron exchanged handshakes and back slaps with white-jacketed colleagues. Was he joining the staff? Accolades for a presentation or a promotion? She had to know. His admirers slowly dispersed. Aaron pulled up his coat's collar, adjusted his scarf, and prepared to step into the revolving door leading to the street.

"Aaron."

"Margo?" he replied with squinting eyes and a slow smile. His arms weren't held out to her. He didn't look angry, but not particularly pleased to see her. "Working for the competition?" He cordially asked as he came closer. He didn't offer his hand or share an embrace. He eyed the cart, not her.

"Why yes, Dr. Woodrow Hamilton is an acquaintance of mine, a friend actually." She hoped he recognized the name and prayed the two had never met. "Woody, Dr. Hamilton's glowing recommendation secured me my current position."

"File clerk?"

"Goodness, no. Our file clerk is out sick today. I run my department as a team. I may be upper management, but I pitch in. I find it sets a positive example. What a fortuitous encounter. I'm resigning next week. I've been lured away to join Bentham Pharmaceuticals."

"Sales rep?"

"How perceptive you are. Have you also jumped ship?"

301

"Far from it. I'm conducting a lecture on the future of the CAT scanner."

"What's a CAT scanner?"

"A form of nuclear medicine that's on the horizon. You wouldn't understand, so I won't waste my time explaining it. I've got to get back to the Brigham. Say 'hello' to Colleen for me. Oh, and congratulations on your little job."

No longer enamored by her, he'd morphed into the sinister Mr. Hyde who dismissed her from his office and snapped at her as her father lay dying. It was time the good doctor was thrown off his high horse.

"Get back here."

Stopping short of the exit, Aaron changed direction and turned his ear in half profile as he advanced toward her. With each measured step, the heat generated from his anger and her passion set Margo's skin ablaze. Her heart pounded out of fear and desire.

"What did you say?"

"You heard me."

"Where do you get off using that tone with me?"

Grabbing him by his scarf, she pushed him into a hallway alcove. Nose to nose, Margo grunted, "Fuck me."

Her demand was received as if she'd ordered him to eat a cockroach. "I don't need you. I get more than I can handle."

Margo methodically rubbed her hand over his crotch. Her eyes were still locked on his. Aaron removed her hand. "Cazzo, you, Margo. That's not a question." The insult came with a shove.

"Take me," she ordered. His finger threaded through her looped earring; Aaron painfully pulled her to his lips.

"You want it?"

"I need it."

"How do you want it?"

"Fast. Hard and fast. I hurt you; punish me."

"You don't know what pain is."

"Show me."

Aaron twisted her arm around her back like an escaped convict with a gun to a petrified prison guard's head. His breath on her neck, he whispered, "Keep walking." His willing hostage was led down a stairwell she suspected only the maintenance staff knew existed. At its foot was a bolted metal door. Using both hands, Aaron lifted the bar and maneuvered his captive down a dark corridor illuminated by dim emergency lights strung from the peeling ceiling.

"Where are you taking me?"

"To the old annex."

"They're tearing it down."

"I know a way in. I did a rotation here as an intern. The annex was in use back then."

Sheets of plywood and wires snaked across cracked tile floors. The hallway was cold,, she was sweating. Aaron slammed his palm against the door to a long-neglected bathroom and flung Margo onto its chalky plaster-covered floor.

"Where am I?"

"Where you belong."

"What are you going to do?"

"Give you what you deserve."

Her long-held fantasy had become a reality. Clutching the toilet tank with both hands, she cried. "Stop! You're hurting me!"

"Not fast enough? Hard enough?" he grunted. The thought of who he was, where they were, and what he was doing ignited a spark, giving her brain the order to surrender. Standing over her, Aaron zipped his pants and splashed water on his face as if setting out to work. Bending down, he wiped his wet hands off on her crumpled skirt. "Pull yourself together. I'll be outside. Don't take too long, or you can find your own way out of here."

Margo staggered from the restroom. "My stockings are torn. You ran my stockings!"

"Go back to work limping, tell them you fell."

"They won't believe me."

Aaron landed a sharp kick to her shin. "They'll believe you now."

"Oow! You bastard! Why did you kick me?"

"It's what I wanted to do to you for the last six months. That, and bang you on the floor of a public toilet." Margo put her arm around his waist for support. Aaron wore an exasperated expression. "What a baby."

Hobbling alongside her attacker, Margo whined. "I'm sore and it's your fault."

"You think your leg hurts now, wait till tomorrow."

"It's not my leg."

***

Spring had arrived. Taking advantage of the unseasonably warm weather, Colleen sprawled across the wicker chaise on the front porch with a Tiger Beat Magazine on her lap and a transistor radio buzzing the summer sounds of The Beach Boys. Shielding her eyes from the sun, she spotted Margo limping up the walkway. Colleen ran from the porch, not to assist her sister but to share the latest celebrity gossip.

"You've got to read this," she said, flapping the teen tabloid in Margo's face. "Paul McCartney is dead. You believe it?" Margo swatted the magazine away from her face. Gripping the porch's lattice work, she staggered into a waiting lawn chair. Colleen wore a curious expression. "You look like you've seen a ghost."

Margo adjusted the wrap around her wounded ankle. "I saw a ghost all right, and it wasn't Mrs. Lindsey or Paul McCartney. It was Aaron. I ran into him at the hospital."

"What did you do?"

"Let him screw me in a bathroom."

Colleen stood back and gasped. "Ma's right, you are a nympho."

"What was I supposed to do? I had to get back at him."

"That's how you get back at someone? Oh, I get it. You gave him a venereal disease, brilliant!"

"You want to know the weird part?"

"It gets weirder?"

"He was so mean to me, treated me like a stupid little girl pestering him, looking to be punished." Margo threw her head back. "It gets me so hot."

"How are you going to explain to Woody that you screwed some guy in a toilet?"

"Aaron is not some guy."

"He became one when he followed you into that bathroom."

"Woody needn't know. Aaron and I are having a parting of the ways."

"More like parting of the legs."

"It was a one-time thing. I'm meeting him for lunch tomorrow to break it off."

"You'll sleep with him."

"Wanna bet?"

"Yeah."

"What's the wager?"

"If you don't sleep with him, I won't tell Ma about today. If you sleep with him, I'll cut your hair off. Then we'll see if Prince Charming really loves Rapunzel. If you want to keep your hair, keep your legs closed."

Chapter Twenty

She planned to have lunch at an open-air café on Boston's fashionable Newbury Street, not sitting in a crowded waiting room surrounded by Doctor Schuyler's restless patients. Margo buried her head in a copy of *Look Magazine*, not wanting to stare or be stared at.

A young couple came through the door with a rambunctious three-year-old wearing a homespun dotted Swiss pinafore over pink dancing tights. Jumping from toe to toe, she sang, "When you wish upon a star," breaking the uncomfortable silence choking the waiting room.

"Maggie, come sit down," her mother scolded with a thick Southern twang. The singer looked directly at Margo, who couldn't help but notice the child's frozen eye. "Look!" she exclaimed, pointing at Margo. "It's Tinkerbell!" The mother shushed her daughter.

"What's your name?" Margo asked the little singer.

"Magnolia."

"What a charming name. My name is Margo, but I prefer Tinkerbell."

Magnolia bashfully approached her new friend. "You're pretty."

"Why, thank you. I looked like you when I was your age, but you have a prettier smile. Teeth need water and sunshine. If you don't smile, the sun can't shine on them. I lost my smile, but since meeting you, my smile has returned."

Aaron stepped into the waiting room with open arms. "It's my best girl!" Margo headed for his embrace. "Not you. Magnolia is my best girl." Little Maggie ran to him, flapping her arms like fairy wings. Aaron lifted her up and balanced her on his hip. The child removed Aaron's glasses from his nose and transferred them to hers.

"Magnolia," her father said, wearing a stern expression.

Aaron laughed. "You want to break my glasses, so I won't look at other girls."

Magnolia giggled.

"Forgive me," he apologized to Margo. "These are the Bradshaws, Laurel and Glen, and you already met this cutie."

Magnolia pointed to Margo. "She's Tinkerbell."

Aaron gasped. "If she's Tinkerbell, then I do believe in fairies!" Aaron put the child down.

"How's she doing?" he asked her anxious parents.

"Good," her dad answered. "We're here to see Doctor Schuyler for a follow-up. He used that new machine on her; there's no sign of a tumor."

"That's the best news I've heard all year!" Aaron crouched down to Magnolia's level. "You weren't afraid of that machine, were you?"

"Nope."

Aaron inspected the child's eye. "Has she been to an ophthalmologist?" he asked, looking up at the couple.

"Yes," her father answered. "He thinks it's best to wait till she starts school to fit her for an eye."

"Are you going to get another blue eye?" Aaron asked the child.

"I want a pink one!"

"You are too young!" Aaron placed his arm around Margo's waist. "We're heading out. I'll see that Stan keeps me posted on our patient's progress."

The couple smiled at Margo. "A pleasure to meet you, Mrs. Hirsh."

Caught off guard, Margo replied, "Yes... and you as well." *Mrs. Hirsh* she liked the sound of it, so did Aaron. As they walked toward a bank of elevators, Margo looped her arm through Aaron's. "Did you operate on Magnolia?"

"She's Stan's patient. Maggie is the Bradshaws' only child; they can't have another. Stan has a daughter Maggie's age and wisely declined to perform her surgery. So, the Iceman scrubbed in."

"She's the reason you couldn't take me to the Jubilee Banquet."

"It doesn't matter if the patient is 4 or 94, if I'm called in, all else takes a backseat, even the woman I love." Aaron lowered his head and laughed. "You may be Tinkerbell, but I'm the scary doctor. Magnolia has always been afraid of me, but today, knowing you were there, it wasn't an act. I am a different man around you. I'm actually a nice guy."

"I think it's time the Iceman melted. I've never made love to anyone I loved more than myself. I want to know what that feels like. Let's skip lunch." She was in love with Doctor Jekyll and at the mercy of Mr. Hyde; what more could a girl ask for?

Margo looked out the window of Aaron's Tag Top Porsche. "Isn't your apartment back there?"

"I moved last month. I took the money I had saved for a Trans Am, you would have loved it, and used it to buy a two-family in Brookline, you'll hate it. I intend to put my mother and Oscar on the first floor and rent out the second."

"Good luck with that."

"I'm working on it. The house is for investment only. I have my eye on a house with a four-car garage in Chestnut Hill."

The Porsche took a sharp turn that wouldn't have been sharp had the driver adhered to the speed limit.

***

"Welcome to Casa Hirsh," Aaron announced as he scooped up a pile of envelopes lying beneath the mail slot. "It's not much to look at, but the squirrels inhabiting the chimney like it. May I offer you a drink? I believe the former owner left a can of prune juice behind."

"That doesn't contribute to the mood."

"This will." Aaron passionately kissed her willing lips. Margo pulled him toward the bedroom by his belt. "Steady girl," Aaron cautioned as if he were breaking in a wild filly. "What's the rush? We have all night, unless you're still playing Cinderella and must be home by midnight."

"Rapunzel. Will you still love me in short hair?"

"What?"

"Inside joke."

"You haven't told me what you think of the place."

"It needs a woman's touch."

Aaron lowered his gaze. "So does this."

"Naughty boy. Race you to the bed." Margo blinked. "A twin bed? Who sleeps in a twin bed?"

The answer came with a wink and a tongue click. "Twins."

Stretching out on the narrow bed, Aaron watched Margo perform a striptease, tossing her bra and gartered stockings in his face. "Da, da, da. Da, da, da, da." Aaron tapped the mattress the way one would when granting a dog permission to come up on the bed.

"Shows over Gypsy, time to get down to business." Elevating his body over hers, his intense, dark eyes danced from her breasts to her lips. "I've never wanted a woman

310

the way I want you," he moaned between kisses and thrusts. "You love the way I feel inside you. Every time we do it, you'll think of..."

"STOP! STOP! GET OFF ME!" she screamed, pounding on his chest. Breaking free, Margo crawled from the bed to a corner of the sparsely furnished room, rolling herself into a protective ball. Those words dragged her back to Sagamore Park. She wasn't in the Chinese underworld, but in a pile of cold, wet leaves, fighting for her life. Her arms flailed as if swatting a swarm of bees.

"Get away from me! Kill me! Why don't you kill me? I want to die.. I want to die..." Aaron draped a blanket over her shoulders and joined her on the floor. Holding her tightly to his chest, her hysterical cries continued, mingled with dialogue.

"Take a deep breath," Aaron instructed. "You're safe. No one can hurt you. You'll be all right."

"I'm not all right! I was never all right. I was raped. I was a virgin and I was raped... I was raped... I was raped." Her voice trailed off.

"Shh, shh," Aaron whispered as he reached for a box of tissues on the nightstand. He wiped her nose the way a mother would for her baby. Her eyes looked as if they were following a fly around the room. "Ronny, he... he dragged me into the park, it was night, he knocked me down, pulled me into the bushes. He beat me, he raped me. I'm dirty, broken. I was asking for it. It was supposed to happen." Margo paused to gulp air.

"I thought I'd never enjoy sex, but I do. I've had sex hund... plenty of times, but you said what he said, he said..." Aaron rocked her in his arms. Margo nuzzled under his chin. "I said I was mugged, no big deal. I never cried, never told anybody. I knew one day it would come back to haunt me."

"You're here with me. I'll protect you. I swear, no one will ever hurt you again because I'll always be with you." Aaron's voice lightened. "You are going to take a long, relaxing bath, while I make a pot of tea. Then we'll crawl into bed and do something we've never done before."

"What? What?"

"Sleep." They shared a kiss. Margo looked deep into Aaron's eyes.

"I'll never be afraid again." Helping her to her feet, they walked into the bathroom. Sitting on a hamper, she watched Aaron draw a bath the way Mae had on that awful night. Margo closed her eyes as she slowly sank into the tub's steamy water.

Aaron returned with her handbag. "You'll need this."

"Don't tell me you installed a pay toilet?"

"Wouldn't your mother love that. If I'm not mistaken, this bag contains a pack of cigarettes."

"I stopped but lately..." Aaron covered her lips with his finger, then tapped the side of the pack, removing two sticks of tobacco.

"Take two, and make love to me in the morning. Doctor's orders."

"You'll let me smoke in your house?"

"No. I'm allowing you two. You need them more than anything I can prescribe."

"Matches?"

"No."

"Stove?"

"It's electric."

"That'll do."

Aaron returned to the bathroom holding a lit cigarette like a birthday candle. Margo wiped her hands on a dry washcloth before taking the cigarette from his hand. "No ashtray? I'll use the soap dish."

"Pig."

"You really love me, huh?"

Aaron brushed aside a tear. "It's the smoke," he explained without being asked.

312

"Do you need me to scrub your back?" Aaron called from the bedroom. The bathroom door whipped open. Margo stood wearing a red plaid robe, strands of her wet hair resting on its collar.

"Please say this robe was a gift."

"You like it?"

"Hate it."

"It was a gift." Aaron placed their cups on the bedside table. "Come lie down."

Snuggled together in the narrow bed, Margo found sanctuary under Aaron's chin as she drifted off to sleep, sucking her thumb.

***

"Oscar around?" Aaron asked with a kiss on his mother's cheek. Half closing one eye, Freida backed away. "Why?"

"I want a word with him."

"Please, no arguments."

"This isn't about what you want. Tell me where he is."

"He's tutoring."

"Tutoring where?" Freida remained mum. Aaron's voice rose. "He's at that school in Grove Hall, isn't he? This neighborhood isn't dangerous enough? The man lost his way home from the senior center four blocks away. He'll kill someone with that car."

"He gave up his license. The bus driver knows his stop."

"What are you trying to prove? You don't have to live like this. You're no better off than you were in Russia, always looking over your shoulder, not able to walk the streets at night, beaten, robbed, ridiculed. Only now you're old, he's going blind, not steady on his feet."

"Those children won't graduate without his help; they appreciate what he does for them."

"And I didn't? Is that what you're saying?"

"Yes," Freida admitted in an unguarded moment.

"I got excellent grades. I didn't need to spend eighteen hours a day studying under his watch. Unlike Leon, I had a social life."

Hearing slow, heavy steps, Freida's voice lifted. "Oscar, look who's here. Aaron is joining us for dinner."

With the aid of his wife, the old man removed a jacket only a few years younger than himself.

"I didn't come for dinner."

"Your mother never sees you. Me, I can do without the uproar."

"I'd stay longer if I didn't have to keep watch over my car."

Oscar rubbed his temples. "Next time, take a bus."

"Better I should have my car stolen than be stabbed on a bus."

Oscar waved his stepson off. Aaron threw his arms in the air. "What is it going to take to get you out of here? Abe Gutzman was brought into the emergency department in a coma."

"Brain dead?"

"Yes, Mamushka, brain dead. That's what happens when you have a bullet lodged in your head. It wasn't enough that they robbed the register; they had to shoot the old man."

Oscar pounded his fist on the rickety kitchen table. "WE STAY!"

"Don't you people understand?"

"We are not 'you people.' We're your parents!"

314

"*She* is." Aaron silently counted to ten. "Listen, I bought a house in Brookline with you in mind." Oscar shook his trembling finger in Aaron's face. "You don't dictate to us where we live."

"Brookline is not a shtele!"

"It's not home!"

"Please," Freida pleaded. "No more fighting. We're happy here, we stay."

"Stay? Stay like you did in Russia?"

"No one will come for us. We keep to ourselves. Isn't that what you said? It's that mindset that puts you in a camp and your parents in a pit."

Freida bristled at the mention of her parents' execution. "You weren't there!"

"Darn right I wasn't." The frightened boy that Aaron thought he'd smothered over 30 years ago crawled up into his throat. "You sent me away. I was dead to you. You didn't want me because I reminded you of Dada. You... you sent me halfway around the world alone, yet you wouldn't let Leon cross the street by himself. You didn't stay in Russia to care for your parents; you stayed for him. I hope he was worth it."

Oscar had held his tongue, wanting his wife to experience the side of her son she'd been blind to, but no more. Seizing Aaron by his lapels, Oscar shook his stepson. "You speak that way to me, you always have. But don't you ever speak to her in a threatening tone or question her love for you. You're better than us, a doctor, an American. What would you be had you stayed in Russia?"

"Loved. But I don't need yours," Aaron said, breaking free of Oscar's grip. "I found a woman who loves me. I'm married."

Freida dropped into a chair. "Married? You married? A doctor? A nurse, maybe?"

Oscar bobbed his head. "I'll tell you what she is, a goyim. Was it out of lust? Or to assimilate?"

Freida wiped her eyes with her apron. "You got married without introducing her? Are you so ashamed of us?"

"You've met her. You've met the whole family."

Oscar wore a smirk. "It can only be one girl from one family. How long will she stay out of the limelight and take orders from you?

"She's young, shallow, but find out for yourself. In the meantime, leave us be."

***

Her bedroom door slammed behind her. Colleen lurched forward, snapping a pair of shears. "I'm going to cut that ponytail off and present it to Ma."

"Wait!" Margo said, holding up her left hand. "Look," she said, flashing an opal. Colleen dropped her weapon.

"You're engaged?"

"Look closer. That's a gold band." Hands over her mouth, her eyes on the ring, Colleen slowly shook her head. "She's going to kill you, but not before she smashes your pelvis with a sledgehammer, rips out your spleen, smears it on the wall, and blames you for ruining the wallpaper. What bathroom did you honeymoon in?"

"The Ritz. He took me there for dinner, that's when he proposed. We spent the weekend in the bridal suite, then went to City Hall this morning and got married."

"Shucks. I wish I had known. I would have bought you a wedding gift. Are you still registered at Esso? 'Service with a smile!'"

"Take a good look at this smile. Once she's told, she'll knock my teeth out. Help me pack. Aaron will be here in an hour. I want to make a quick getaway."

"You won't get far, she's in the kitchen. Where will you live?"

"Aaron bought a house in Brookline. There's a second bedroom. You're always welcome."

Colleen opened her mouth, but her throat prevented words from escaping. The sisters embraced. Wiping her eyes, Colleen turned Margo towards the door. "Time for Margo to face Grendel."

She both feared and delighted in breaking the news of her marriage. Berta stood over the kitchen's porcelain sink, scrubbing a basting pan left to soak overnight. Her back was to Margo, but she was aware she was being watched. "Forget your toothbrush?"

"As a matter of fact, I had."

Berta continued scraping off hardened turkey crust with fingers as raw as her emotions. The kitchen table and two decades formed an invisible wall between mother and daughter. "I don't suppose there'll ever be a good time to break the news. I'm married."

Greasy water swirled down the drain as Berta twisted a dishrag like a condemned chicken's neck. "Not a Catholic, I'm guessing."

"Enough guessing. It's Aaron. You knew I was with him."

"I imagine his parents are thrilled their son, the doctor, married Sunny Shine."

"I don't care what they think."

"Where will you live?" Berta asked, staring out the window over the sink.

"Aaron has a house in Brookline."

"Ah, yes, Brookline."

"Don't give me that 'Ah yes, Brookline.' Where do you want us to live? Charlestown? South Boston?" Margo came around the table and turned Berta to face her. "Will you look at me!"

Berta slapped down the damp dishrag as her gauntlet. "What do you want me to do? Wish you all the best? Congratulate you for putting your hormones before the church? When you come to your senses, the church will forgive you and welcome you back to the fold. I can't say I will."

"You were grateful for all Aaron did for Rosaria, and what Lee did to help Colleen with her grades. "

"And I should thank him for bedding my daughter? It's always about you, Nuala. You want what you want, when you want it, and to hell with everyone else."

"I should have married Ronny, a drunk?"

"There are other men out there, good, sober, Christian men, with money in the bank. You married Dr. Hirsh because you hate me, or was it because I wouldn't let you wear lipstick at thirteen, or allow you and Rosaria on that dance program?"

"I could have been discovered!"

"Your ass is what would have been discovered."

"It's my ass that paid for Colleen's education, Rosaria's wedding, and to have the house painted."

"And it's your ass he's in love with. He'll leave you once he meets an intelligent, fertile Jewish woman. You're no more than a pretty place holder."

"I thought you hated Aaron because he loved me, but that's not it, is it?"

"Don't feed me that antisemite malarky. I don't want my daughter to marry outside the faith. That makes me an antisemite? The Hirsches don't want their son to marry a Christian. What does that make them? Is there a name for it? We didn't put them in camps; we got them out. Now the liberators are labeled oppressors. The war is over. When will they put it behind them? We have."

"They're not like us."

"Bingo! They have scars, we all do, but we don't whine and complain about past injustices, dwell on them, or throw them in the faces of people who didn't inflict them. We cover them up. In this world, there are victims and survivors. Survivors move on with their lives. Victims whine and get stuff. It will never be enough for them. We gave them a homeland, now they want us to furnish it and get rid of the neighbors. Being White, a Christian, is our original sin. We kill Jews, keep slaves, steal land from Indians, and nuts from squirrels. We're responsible for all the ills of the world. Our family wasn't living in this country 60 years ago, yet we inherited the sins of strangers long dead whose skin pigment resembles ours. They don't take ownership of their ancestors' sins. But as you say, they're not like us. Put yourself in my shoes, Missy. There was a war going on. We worried about our sons, brothers, and husbands. Your father died in that war. Every country had camps, including ours. Ask our veterans, the Chinese, and Filipinos, how well the Japanese treated them. You don't hear them bellyaching. There will always be war. Genocides are going on as we speak, in Asia, South America, and Africa. But you don't care about those people, and I'll tell you why. Because they're not like you. They don't speak your language, share your customs, or pray to your God. You don't need my shoes, you're wearing them."

"Love supersedes race and religion."

"You were baptized in the Catholic church, educated in a Catholic school, received the sacraments of the Catholic faith, and you cast it all aside for a good-looking doctor with a fat wallet. You're right, it's not about religion, it's about money."

"That's not fair!"

"You wouldn't give him the time of day, much less your body, had he been poor, or was it because he showered attention on Rosaria and didn't give you a second look? He'll divorce you before you get the rice out of your hair."

"I don't need your blessing, and the squirrels can keep their nuts!"

Margo loaded up the T-Bird. "I'll leave the rest of the suitcases for Aaron's car... Colleen? Where are you?"

"I'm around back." Margo entered the backyard where Colleen sat on Poppy's homemade swing. The ropes frayed, its wooden seat bleached by the sun. Colleen kicked up dust beneath her feet. Margo stood behind her sister, holding on to the swing's ropes. "You start college next year. Your time will be spent with new friends. I'm not moving to another planet."

"You may as well be."

"We'll buy you a car."

"You've been married less than 24 hours and you're already spending his money."

Margo lowered her head and kissed the top of Colleen's. "I love you, and I love Mae. You're my only family. I'm not going to lose either one of you. Come on, I'll let you follow us in the T-Bird."

"You'll let me drive your car?!"

"Drive it, not have it." Margo waved her arms. "Here comes the groom!"

Aaron leapt out of his Porsche. "Colleen!" His greeting came with a hug. "You've been crying."

"You bet I have. Thanks to you, I'm related to Lee." A silhouetted figure peered out from behind the sheer lace curtain that shaded the door's window, spying on the laughing trio as they drove off. "Good riddance."

Chapter Twenty-One

The sprawling one-level Lloyd Wright-inspired home was six miles and six decades from Mount Nottingham. Its kitchen was electric; never again would she light a four-legged gas oven hooked up to a copper boiler deemed unsafe and illegal. Nor would she ever share a bathroom with five other women. She had her bathroom, and Aaron had his. The toilet was flushed, chain wasn't pulled. Clothes weren't washed; they were sent out. A landscaper cared for the grounds, not her sister, with a straw rake. No hardwood, her floors were carpeted. The home's entrance wasn't dominated by an imposing mahogany monstrosity with a macabre history. A five-foot-high blue Japanese vase, a replica of the one in Miss Millet's office, graced her foyer. She possessed all she desired. She was lonely, bored, and friendless.

Two rings, then hang up. Colleen knew the code and promptly returned her sister's call. "Colleen, what do you say we go shopping and get our hair done? You've never had a massage or a real manicure, and God knows you could use a new wardrobe since losing the blubber you've been carrying for eighteen years. Trust me, you'll never find a man if you continue to wear patched jeans and T-shirts that look like you've been hit by a balloon filled with bleach."

"It's tie-dye."

"It's ugly. It's been six months since I've been to the Mount. I haven't seen Mae. I've only spoken to her over the phone. I gave you a car so you could visit me."

"It's school. I have to keep up my grades for a scholarship."

"We have a color TV," Margo tempted. "If only I could come over there."

"Believe me, you're not missing anything."

"I'm missing you and Mae."

"I'll bring her by next week."

"Honest?"

"Honest."

Hearing the clanging of a garage door rolling up at the order from a button pressed by a modern-day Alibaba, Margo lost herself in the memory of an apartment on Dahlgren Street. Like sleeping dogs hearing their master's footsteps, she and Rosaria would push their paper dolls aside, racing to be the first to greet Poppy at the end of his workday with slippers and the evening edition, his wife with a kiss. Colleen never shared the warmth radiated by the loving couple left behind in a rundown three-decker. Poppy's ruddy complexion dimpled; her mother's smile soured in a grand house that thrived on anger and resentment, where liquor had always been a prelude to an argument.

The anchor of addiction sank the entire family into the cold, dark waters of Neptune's intoxicating lair. No longer Poppy's little mermaid, her ship had come in. She survived the wreck.

Margo greeted her husband in a burst of excitement. "Aaron, Aaron," she rejoiced, dragging her harried husband to a wallpaper book. "Help me pick out a pattern."

"What, no kiss?" Pulled by his necktie, his eyes widened. Aaron's tongue felt as though it had been sucked into a vacuum cleaner hose. He garbled, "Ew aped my ung."

"I'll eat the rest of you once we've decided on these samples."

"I will after dinner, the one I don't smell."

"I thought you ate at your mother's?"

"No time, unbeknownst to me, she was dressed and waiting to be driven to sit shiva for Elba Raskind."

"I had no idea she'd been ill."

"Heart attack, long overdue."

Margo laughed. "Your mother, in your car, with you at the wheel."

"God, do I miss Leon at a time like this. I'd forgotten how rarely my mother ventures out. Mae was there."

"She and Elba were friends dating back to their days at Bloomfields."

Aaron placed his arm around his wife's shoulder and squeezed. "Sit, we need to talk."

Margo inched toward the sofa. "Why, what's happened?"

"It's Mae, she's not well. She has a persistent cough."

"Mae has allergies. Remember, she coughed during our wedding ceremony? I'm so happy she was there to see us wed. I always dreamt of a big wedding, but running off with you was so romantic."

"She's sick. Mae is very sick."

"You're mistaken. She's aged. Colleen said Mae no longer colors her hair."

"Margo."

"Was Mort there?"

"Who?"

"Morton Bloomfield. He's tall, or he looked tall to me, but I was just a kid when I last saw him. Gosh, it must be fifteen years, maybe longer. If he were there, Mae would be at his side."

"Will you listen to me?"

The pace of Margo's monologue quickened as if to outrun Aaron's prognosis. "Mae was Mort's secretary. We would tease and say he was sweet on her."

"Margo, enough!"

"There's no need to raise your voice."

"You're not listening."

Margo folded her arms across her chest. "Fine. What did you want to say?"

"She's dying."

"That's absurd. Did you examine her?"

"The whites of her eyes are jaundiced, she's lost weight."

"Cigarettes will turn your eyes and teeth yellow."

"So will cancer."

Margo dropped her head into Aaron's lap. "I know she's sick."

"You've got to convince her to see a doctor."

"God, please, take me, not Mae."

"Margo, she has to be told."

"She knows. Colleen was worried and pleaded with Mae to go to the hospital, but she refused. Colleen informed Doctor Abbot. He said Mae had been to see him, but rejected his advice, saying it was God's will. This is why I broke with the church. I kept putting it out of my mind. I was going to tell you, but I didn't want to put you in the crosshairs. Colleen said my mother is in denial and avoids Mae. Mae needs her and that witch..."

"That witch is frightened."

"My mother frightened?"

" Rosaria, Poppy, her mother, and your father all died unexpectedly; she didn't have time to process her grief until they were buried. It's different with Mae. She can't bear to watch her sister die; she's doing her grieving now."

"Ma never thought it would be just her and Colleen."

"Neither did Colleen."

***

The house was still, the lights low, Dr. Abbot's squeaky shoes on the creaking stairs carried a warning to the three waiting women as Jacob Marley had to Scrooge. Tonight, he was Gerard Abbot, a neighbor, doctor, friend who loved Mae enough to disavow an oath taken to a profession for a promise made to a friend.

"Berta, girls, she wants a word with each of you." Not wanting to touch the flesh of the other, Berta and Margo each took one of Colleen's hands as the trio ascended the staircase to Mae's room. The sisters waited outside the bedroom's closed door.

Berta sat at her dying sister's bedside holding Mae's soft, pale hand. "Berta?"

"Yes, Mae, I'm here."

"I have a request. Forgive Tim for what he was, Fredrik, for what he did, and your father for both."

Berta looked away. "It doesn't matter."

"It does. Mother didn't want us to repeat her transgressions. I did. I'll pay for that sin."

"Good God, Mae, you don't owe God."

"Oh, Berta, if only mother had been honest with us, we wouldn't be burdened with her guilt. Break the chain. Don't deprive your girls of true love. Let them follow their hearts, not antiquated beliefs. They won't abandon you."

"Everyone does. It will happen to them if I don't prevent it."

"That's not your job. Your past needn't be their future. The mold has been cast, but the clay has yet to harden. There's still time."

Regaining her composure, Berta stiffened her spine and returned to the hallway where her daughters sat on the top step of the stairs.

"She wants to see you," Berta said, nudging Margo with the toe of her shoe. "Get in there."

The wooden rocker Mae once employed to silence a colicky Colleen waited next to Mae's bedside, where Berta had left it. Margo dragged it across the room, not wanting to sit on a chair warmed by her mother.

"I can't do this, Mae," Margo confessed from the foot of the bed.

"You can," Mae stated with closed eyes.

"You're all I've got, Mae. Rosaria was my only true friend. I'll never have a family of my own, and now I'm losing you. I shouldn't be selfish at a time like this, but that's what I am: selfish."

"You have Aaron, Colleen, and your mother."

"Don't let our last conversation be about her."

"Do you know why the two of you butt heads?"

"Yes, Mae, I do. She wanted me to marry a wealthy, Catholic drunk. Give her grandchildren to manipulate."

"You won't bend for her?"

"Never."

"Have you considered she may envy you?"

"I doubt it."

"She does. Berta was once like you, spoiled, headstrong, and darn good-looking, I might add. She was going places, going to marry, move out west, but your grandmother chained her to this town, this house." Mae's voice was fading. "The war, the fire, and a legacy destroyed it all. Your mother looks at you and sees the woman she always wanted to be."

"The whore of Babylon?"

"A woman who shares her beauty and enthusiasm for life, who provides sunshine wherever she goes. Allow your mother to be a part of the adventure." Mae stroked Margo's hand. "That special occasion has arrived. I want to meet my maker wearing that beautiful blue dress, and I'll be thinking of you."

Colleen curled up on the bed next to her mentor, confidant, and guardian angel.

"I won't be here tomorrow. You have many tomorrows ahead. I want you to know you can still come to me with your troubles, questions, and heartaches. I may not look as I do now, but you'll know it's me. All you need to do is call my name and I'll answer."

"Don't go away, I'm frightened. Don't die. If you die, I'll lose my way."

"God has been trying to show you the way."

"How? By killing my sister, Poppy, you?"

"His reasons will be revealed."

"He's taken away everyone I loved."

"It's time to find others to love. You've been in a tug-of-war with God. In a tug-of-war, you stand your ground; you don't move as long as you're tugging on the rope. Let go of the rope and you'll land where God wants you to be, surrounded by the love you've always deserved. Let go of the rope, and an angel will catch you."

The following day, Mae was gone. On her bed was Mae's favorite bedspread that bore the stain from a glass of grape juice Colleen had carelessly spilled. The robe with a zipper that Colleen had broken hung on the back of the closet door. Grandma's picture in a cracked glass frame stood on the bureau. Colleen had promised to replace it, a promise never kept. Mae used the spread, wore the robe, kept the frame, and forgave her niece. Standing at Mae's bedroom window that looked out on the leaf-covered backyard, itching to be scratched by the old straw rake, Colleen watched her swing swaying in the breeze.

An angel had just taken flight.

***

Colleen leaned back in a kitchen chair, tossing oranges in the air, snapping them up before they could land in her lap. Berta looked over at the citrus circus act. "If you're not going to eat them, put them back in the bowl. Ringling Brothers won't hire you as a juggler; they'll put you in a freak show with Man Mountain Dean. What are you, five-eight or five-nine?"

"Ten."

"You must get your height from your father's side; there weren't any giants on mine... although...,"

Colleen braced for another episode of *Tales from the Celtic Crypt.*

"It's said, Grandma's Aunt Edwina was a Brobdingnagian, but she had an excuse: the woman had a goiter. Ever see one? Hideous. She looked like a pelican."

"Is this the same Aunt Edwina with stage four eczema?"

"That was her twin, Rowena."

"Didn't you tell Patsy twins didn't run in our family?"

"They weren't identical. I doubt anyone had trouble telling those two apart. Martin called. He and Irena will be staying with us for a few weeks. A tree fell on their house during the windstorm last night. The weathermen are calling it a windstorm. If you ask me, it was a tornado."

"Why not ask Sunny Shine?"

"I don't want to discuss your sister."

"You'll let that pervert in this house but not Margo?"

"Marty married in the Catholic faith."

"I thought your creepy brother was afraid of Mrs. Lindsey's ghost?"

"This will put his screwball stories to rest."

"I won't be around to witness the outcome. I'm staying with Fran until he leaves."

"I don't want you in that part of town. I know those people. They won't be happy until they turn you into a homo."

"You sent me to an all-girls high school and wonder why I have lesbian friends."

"What will I tell Martin when he asks where you are?"

"Try the truth, that will be a first."

***

Marty barreled through the front door with a James Cagney swagger. "To think my sister lives like this."

"You can find out what it's like to live in a Howard Johnson's Motel; there's one down the road."

"Marty's not suggesting you move," Irena apologetically explained. "What he means is, you should consider updating the place, paneling the walls, dropping the ceilings, and installing fluorescent lights. Putting down wall-to-wall carpeting was the smartest thing I've ever done."

"I don't doubt it."

Marty ran his hand over the living room's green Damask wallpaper. "Christ, Bertie! This paper is original to the house!"

"I like it," Berta lied, "Mother said it was imported from France."

"They used arsenic in the paper back then. You get this stuff on your hands and in your mouth, you'll get brain damage. I bet that's what drove the Lindsey gimp batty."

"Who told you he was insane?"

"He took a header over the balcony, didn't he?" Marty lit a cigar. "The place is a fire trap, you of all people, living in a matchbox. "Be reasonable, you and that kid can't keep up with the maintenance this house requires."

"If you have such disdain for my house, my family, and my hospitality, best you leave before a ghost, or the wallpaper kills you."

"Get your coat, Berta," Irena said, giving her husband the eye.

"The flower show is in town. We'll leave Mr. Grumpypants to make friends with the house."

Berta reluctantly removed her dark blue coat with a velvet collar and buttons from the hall closet. Its warmth didn't come from its threadbare fabric but from the memory of Tim's face the night he gave it to her, not for her birthday or Christmas but just because.

"It looks better on you, darlin', than on Myra Lloyd. You have the figure for it." She did. Tightening the belt, she remembered how Tim's arms felt around her waist, how they laughed when she came to bed that night wearing only the coat. It was the last time they shared a laugh, the last time they made love.

Marty took the stogie stub from between his teeth. "You still wearing that old rag? Give it to Saint Vincent de Paul's. Let some bag lady get a winter out of it. Or are you afraid someone might mistake her for you?"

Berta whipped a thorny shillelagh out from a nearby umbrella stand. Martin's voice shook. "It's a joke, Bertie!"

"Tell the joke to the doctor who removes the wooden punchline out of your arse."

"Pay him no mind," Irena advised as she held her palm open to her husband. "The keys." Marty dug into his front pants pocket and slapped the keys to his prized Chrysler in his wife's hand. "Don't forget to put the seat back where it belongs."

***

Curled up on her friend's recliner, Colleen stretched and yawned. "I'm finally free to do as I please."

"Not under my roof."

"Oh yeah?"

"Yeah, I call the shots." Stocky and spectacled, Fran Melzian's only resemblance to a woman was attributed to the tiny pigtails tied tightly behind each ear, drawing attention to her long Armenian hairline.

Colleen stuck her tongue out at her friend. "You're not the boss of me."

"You had better knock off the innocent schoolgirl routine because we are going clubbing."

"Something tells me I'll be spending the evening in a gay bar."

"We are going to The Other Side. The place is out of sight. Sylvia Sidney is performing there tonight. It's in the Bay Village."

"Bay Village? Isn't that where The Coconut Grove used to be?"

"So, they say. Did you bring your ID?"

"I didn't think I'd need it."

"You may look twenty-one, but you'll still need an ID even if it's fake. I'll drive you back home."

"I can't go back there. I swore I wouldn't set foot in that house until that pervert left. He tried to mess with me when I was a kid. My mother beat me, called me a liar." Colleen sat up. "Wait a second, I shoved the ID under a loose shingle on the front porch. We'll wait until it's dark, and run up on the porch and grab it. They'll never know I was there."

Looking for evidence that the house was uninhabitable, Marty took the opportunity to do a fire inspection. He headed for the attic.

The top story was once the sleeping quarters for the live-in help. Colleen was the only one to venture up to the attic. The climb taxed Marty's wet lungs and clogged arteries. Crawling through a small door that led under the eaves, Marty puffed, "Just as I suspected, these walls ain't insulated," he said, pulling out yellowed papers cocooned for decades behind thin wooden slats and crumbled horsehair plaster.

"This is how they insulate, with newspapers from the Taft administration?" He could feel the slender spine of a 60-year-old journal. "What do we have here? Looks like a diary, probably Margo's. This ought to make for good reading." Read he did, not the salacious sexual exploits of Nuala Ronan but Nuala Rourke, penned by Annabel the maid. Marty licked his fingers with each turn of the page. "Holy Jesus, why would she put this smut in writing?" He read on. "I'll be damned. The old lady humped Stumpy. Wait till Berta gets a gander at this."

The pornographic prize under his arm, he headed down the steep attic stairs. The soles of his new leather shoes slid on the step's lip, propelling him over the balcony balustrade. The journal flew out of his arms, its loose pages fluttered down, coming to rest over Marty's dead body. The thud from the impact prompted the phantom pianist to play a ragtime tune.

***

A wide-brimmed hat covered her red hair. Sunglasses shaded her green eyes. Colleen slouched down in the front seat of the noisy Volkswagen. Fran swatted the hat off Colleen's head. "What are we? Lucy and Ethel? And get rid of the glasses. "

Seeing the empty driveway, Colleen's anxiety abated. "Good, they're out, I'll make this quick." Dashing from the car to the porch, Colleen peeked through the door's window and gasped. Her arms flapping as if swimming to the car, she breathlessly collapsed in the passenger seat. "Go, go, get out of here!" The Beetle puttered around the park, chugging to the foot of the Mount.

"What happened?"

"It's my uncle. I think he's dead."

"You gotta go back."

"No way. He might still be alive. Let him rot there."

"Did you get the ID?"

Irena took plants and ceramic pots from the car, handing them off to Berta, who arched her stiff back. "I'll get Marty out here to help us." Berta didn't scream; she never screamed out of fear, only anger. Looking down at her lifeless brother, his eyes wide in terror, Berta looked up at the balcony. A split spindle gave it a proud gap-toothed grin. Berta calmly gathered the papers littering the corpse. "Irena! Come quick, it's Marty!"

Chapter Twenty-Two

Colleen draped herself across a sofa Fran had rescued from the curb out front of a Northeastern frat house. Its colonial pattern and Minutemen lamps were a poor match for the apartment's bohemian décor. "My mother will never go for it."

"Tell her you're going to a New Year's Eve party at your sister's; she'll never call over there to check up on you."

"Gee, Fran, I don't think Margo would want me leaving town."

"What better place to spend New Year's Eve than New York City? My brother's having a party at his place in Manhattan. All his friends are actors and artists; you could make professional contacts. You like Alex. He'll get a kick out of seeing you again."

Colleen snapped her fingers at Fran. "The phone."

"Hang on a sec," Margo reached across Aaron's desk to click off the recorder. "Sorry, I couldn't hear you. I'm listening to an educational tape recording entitled, 'Europe, Art, War, and Industry.' I'm broadening my horizons. Are you sitting down? My influential husband has procured a position for me at the hospital. I'll be hosting my first charity event. It's a fashion show at the Copley Plaza. Let Miss Millet put that in her pipe and smoke it."

Colleen interrupted with an "Ahem, as I was saying, I'm going to New York City with Fran tomorrow night. I plan on telling Ma I'm attending a party at your house."

"My goodness, you're a grown woman," Margo huffed. "You don't need her permission. God only knows where I would have ended up if I hadn't broken ranks. As long as you're living under her roof, one I paid for, thank you very much, you'll always be treated as a child. Grow a set or find a set, that's what I say."

"Until my testicles drop, I'll need your help. Fran's brother Alex is hosting a New Year's Eve party; he lives in Manhattan's Garment District."

"Alex? Isn't he the boy you have a crush on?"

Colleen played deaf to the question. "Fran said all his friends are artists and actors; they're part of the New York theatre scene."

"I repeat. Isn't he the boy you have the hots for?"

"He's not a boy," Colleen whispered, not wanting Fran to hear. Margo took a drag off a forbidden cigarette.

"As I recall, Alex was a dead ringer for Wally Cleaver, and you're telling me he's living in Hell's Kitchen with a pack of hippies?"

"It's Manhattan, and you wouldn't know a hippie if you fell on one."

"I pray I never do."

Colleen dropped her voice. "Fran doesn't know I have feelings for her brother; if she did, she'd rag on me. Besides, it's been over a year since he's seen me, I'm a very different girl... woman. I've lost weight. He complimented me on my long red hair, that's why I haven't cut it."

"I'll pick you up, we'll go to the Boston flat and give you a makeover, then drive you to the bus terminal. Agree?"

"Agreed."

Berta returned to her kitchen. "I closed off your bedroom. Since you've set up headquarters in the attic, there's no point in heating the other bedrooms. Now what's this talk of a party?"

"Margo is hosting a New Year's Eve party. I'm taking Fran along."

"Your sister is comfortable having Fran? She wouldn't want her highfalutin friends to think her sister is a homo.... Oh, this is just an excuse to drink."

"Right, like that drink-counting, glass sniffing sister of mine is going to allow me to drink. And Aaron is just as strict."

"Jews don't drink."

***

Colleen pointed to her friend sitting on the stoop of a brick rowhouse. Margo's expression soured. "Blue jeans and a fringe cowboy jacket? She looks like she's going to a rodeo."

"Margo, please. Don't start with her."

"I'll be nice."

Fran hopped into the backseat of the double-parked Porsche. Colleen made the introduction. "Fran, you remember my sister Margo."

"Sure do, good lookin' as ever." Margo accepted the compliment with a curled lip smile.

"Thank you, Fran," Margo said, pushing in the car's cigarette lighter and unclasping her purse to retrieve a pack of Salem's. The dashboard lighter popped. Fran slid the cigarette she harbored behind her ear and wedged her shoulders between the sisters. Margo held the metal lighter's ember to Fran's filtered smoke. Colleen opened the window to suck in the freezing air.

"Where are we headed?" Fran asked between puffs.

"To my flat in the Back Bay. I can't have Colleen going to New York dressed like an uptight provincial."

Fran squeezed her eyes and shook her head. "You have a house and an apartment!"

"It's more of a closet both in size and content. It was a sublet. Aaron took over the lease from a woman I once worked with. I envy you, When I was a teenager, we'd ring in the new year at a sock hop, sipping soda through paper straws under the watchful eyes of adult chaperones." Colleen rolled her eyes for Fran's benefit.

Margo maneuvered her car into a parking space marked NO PARKING ANYTIME. Colleen pointed to the sign. "You can't leave the car here."

"If they don't like it, they can ticket me. If I don't like it, I'll tear it up."

The three entered the one-bedroom apartment. The efficiency kitchen's stove was covered with shoeboxes. Colleen placed them on the floor. "Nice way to start a fire."

"If I'm going to burn anything, it will be your coat. You're not going to New York in a brown wool coat with wooden buttons held by twine."

"It's warm."

"It's ugly." Margo crooked her finger. "Come with me." The girls followed Margo into a plush pink bedroom. "I have just the thing."

"I can't fit into any of your clothes."

"You'll fit into this," said Margo, kicking a box out from under the bed. "Open it."

Colleen lifted a soft burgundy leather jacket from the box.

"Aaron gave it to me for Christmas. He knows better than to buy me a leather jacket; it's not my style or size. He saw the price tag and assumed I'd like it. Try it on."

"It's so soft, "Colleen said as she stood at a full-length mirror inspecting her backside. "It's supposed to come mid-thigh; this jacket barely covers my ass."

"Freezing your ass off is the price you pay to look hot. You have long legs and a big bust, flaunt it. Now take off that tacky turtleneck."

"It keeps me warm. This jacket only closes with a belt." Colleen reluctantly surrendered the sweater, tossing it at Margo, who returned the pitch with a white dress shirt. "Put this on."

"It's Aaron's! Can I keep my own underwear?" Colleen posed like a scarecrow while Margo buttoned the shirt.

"Leave the top button open and tie up your hair."

"If I put up my hair, it won't fit under my hat." Margo snatched the stocking cap out of Colleen's hand.

"Synthetic is pathetic. Word to the wise, you two may think you're street smart, but New York is a horse of a different color. It makes Boston look like Sleepy Hollow."

"And you're sooo worldly."

"I mean it, Colleen," Margo shot back.

"I'll look out for her," Fran promised.

**

The New York Port Authority Bus Terminal had a Dickensian feel. It was host to the poor, addicted, and mentally ill, begging for money or offering services to obtain it. A woman in a tattered coat barely covering her free-range backside studied the offerings behind the candy vending machine. "Come to Mama," she coaxed, a bag of M&Ms. Its thud stirred excitement equal to starving Berliners spotting bags of candy dropped during the airlift. Colleen wiggled as if a bee had flown down her back. "These people are skeevy."

"May I offer you fine ladies a tour of my fair city?" asked a pimped-up Puerto Rican not much older than the pair. Fran placed an affectionate arm around Colleen's shoulder. "No, thank you. We know our way around."

The two scurried down a flight of stairs leading to the subway. This was not the South Station of the 1950s. A graffiti-covered train rumbled into the station. "Five hours on a stinkin' bus and on to a stinkin' train. I hate this town."

"Christ's sake, Colleen, give it a chance. Things are about to get interesting." Muscling off the packed train of merrymakers, the pair slid through the slushy streets to a shabby tenement. "This is Alex's place; there's no bell." Fran put two fingers in her mouth, letting out a piercing whistle. "Alex! Open up!" The hippie Margo prayed never to meet, stuck his head out the third-floor window.

"What are you doing in New York?"

"Let us in before we freeze our asses off," Fran demanded. The clanging from their feet on the metal stairs played the same tune as The Talbot School's stairwell. Fran pounded on the door. "Open up."

Colleen's nostrils tingled with the scent of pot and strawberry incense. "Are you sure this is your brother's place?" The door flew open before Fran could answer. It was Alex. No longer the all-American boy. The crew-cut had grown into a Beatle mop top. His thick-rimmed glasses had been replaced by round wire specs, the necktie with love beads. The siblings exchanged palm slaps as Colleen surveyed the cracked plastered walls covered with Peter Max and Warhol posters.

"Why didn't you tell me you were coming to town?"

"You know how impulsive I am," Fran answered with her back to Colleen, not wanting to come face to face with the expression she knew her friend was wearing. Alex called into the bedroom. "LaRue, come out here. There's someone I want you to meet."

Colleen swallowed the Adam's apple she'd just developed. A tall, flat-chested redhead reeking of Yardley's Eau De London oozed out of the bedroom wearing the turtleneck Margo had confiscated. "LaRue, this is my sister Fran and her friend..." Alex hesitated. Colleen didn't give her name. "Colleen, right?" Her confirmation came with a wobbly smile.

Fran sized up her brother's paramour with one word. "Phony."

Alex apologized for his sister. "Fran is as blunt as your haircut."

"Alex insisted I color my hair red," she informed the duo in an exaggerated British accent.

"We're going to make the scene at a friend's pad. You kids want to tag along?"

Colleen kept her eyes fixed on the wall art, not wanting Alex to sense her disappointment. Fran wrinkled her nose. "Nah, we're going to bail, check out the clubs."

"You got enough bread? New York's not cheap."

Fran patted her back pocket. "I came prepared."

LaRue rested her head on Alex's shoulder. "We don't want to be late, luv."

"You kids listen up. No drinking and no drugging, dig? Call me tomorrow, but not too early." Alex exchanged smiles with LaRue, who wiggled her finger. "Ta Ta."

Colleen's wet, freezing feet stomped on the clanking stairs. "Wait!" Fran called after her. The request was answered by a slamming door. Fran slush surfed down the snow-covered street in pursuit of Colleen, who pushed Fran away. "You're an asshole; so is your brother. He wasn't having a party. You made that up to get me here."

"Don't blame Alex."

"I thought he was a cool guy. Now it's all 'groovy, boss,' gear."

"It's a put-on for La Lu Lu. By Valentine's Day, he'll be wearing an Aloha shirt, hanging ten with a surfer girl. Who cares about him? Men are chameleons."

Colleen turned up the collar of her borrowed jacket. "I don't know why I let Margo talk me into dressing like this, and you talk me into coming here."

"Let's get warm. There's a club down the street, I know we can get in. I have a friend who works the door."

"A woman at the door? It's a dyke dive. I'm going home."

"You're going back to the bus terminal and let that sleezy PR show you his fair city? Come with me and save yourself a blow job."

A reluctant Colleen followed Fran. Each street they passed was seedier than the last.

"Are you sure you know where you're going?"

"That's the place!" Fran pointed to a woman standing guard at the club's entrance. "That's Phyllis!" She was a large woman, much older than Fran. In a biker's jacket and cap, she resembled Marlon Brando in *The Wild One*.

"Franny! You made it!" The greeting came with a motherly embrace.

"This is my friend Colleen."

"That's ex-friend."

"Don't mind her, this is only her second time in a gay bar."

"This isn't an ordinary gay bar," Phyllis explained.

"I never thought of a gay bar as ordinary," Colleen shot back.

"Believe me, Colleen," said the compassionate bouncer, "This place is dynamite. Let's get inside. You'll feel welcomed."

The club was dark, the music loud, it stank of beer and sweat. Brick walls were covered with balloons and streamers. Christmas lights ran along the ceiling. Masquerade faces flashed in front of her, not human faces but those found at Mardi Gras and carnival fun houses. The heat in the packed club gave Colleen an appreciation for Margo's fashion wisdom; the wool-laden coat would have melted to her body and signaled she was a square.

"What will it be?" Phyllis hollered over Sam and Dave's *"Hold on I'm Coming."*

"I'll have a Coke!" Colleen yelled in a hoarse voice.

"Get us a couple of Black Russians." Phyllis gave Fran a thumbs-up.

"Fran! You can't get plastered. We have to be back in Boston by morning."

"I just might stay over."

Colleen stomped her foot. "I'm leaving."

"Relax. If you didn't come to drink, stick around for the floor show."

The recorded music abruptly halted. Like a sideshow hawker, a colorful character in a sequined jacket took the stage. "Ladies and gentlemen, and only you know which you are. Let's celebrate '68 with these New Year babies." A chorus line of men dressed in feathers and fishnets cancanned to cat calls. Frans slapped Colleen's back. "Don't tell me this isn't more fun than any party Alex could put on."

The crowd thickened. Her Coke arrived in a cup smaller than a dentist would ask you to rinse with. An elbow jabbed into her shoulder, causing the drink to spill on Margo's jacket. "Shit."

"Sorry." A deep voice apologized from behind. The offender in a long dark coat ran out a side door that only a regular would know existed. The music was loud, the lights low, but her memory was sharp. "Lee?" Her pulse raced with her feet as she battled with the festive clubgoers to reach the exit. Colleen pushed the door's metal bar with her hip. The splintering cold air flushed the smoke out of her lungs and the steam from her sweating body. Bending over, her hands rested on her knees, she found herself in an alleyway, the only light coming from a neon sign flashing "Girls, Girls, Girls?" A solitary figure stepped out from the shadows. "You never could run."

"Shit, you scared the shit out of me, you shit."

"Did you find what you were looking for?" Lee asked, keeping his distance.

"I...I...had no idea, honest. I came with a friend. We were going to a party and kinda ended up here." Colleen explained, wearing a difficult smile. Lee opened his coat, revealing a black dress complemented by dark stockings, black boots, and a paisley scarf, looking more like an Italian widow than a drag queen. "I don't make a habit of wearing women's clothes, but a group of us figured we'd have some fun, you know, let it all hang out." With his coat open, he made a full circle. "Get a good look for the folks back home."

"God, Lee, I'd never say anything." Colleen fiddled with her frozen fingers as if signing the deaf. "I'm on my way back to the bus terminal. It's too cold for Times Square, and too hot in the club. Take care of yourself, and Happy New Year." Her voice had a tremulous quality new to his ears, one he interpreted as fear. With her back to him, Colleen cautiously stepped around discarded liquid bottles and wooden pallets. Lee turned her in the opposite direction. "The bus station is that way. You'll never get a cab tonight in this weather. It's about half a mile from here. I'll walk with you."

"Good idea."

"You're beautiful."

"The jacket is Margo's. The shirt is Aaron's."

His eyes were fixed on the shirt's open top button. "You wear it well."

"You're fresh," she cracked, looking up for an instant. His eyes locked into hers.

"I'm not blind."

"Yes, you are. Say, what happened to your Coke bottle glasses?"

"Contacts."

"I like them. I always wanted brown eyes, but my mother gave me black ones."

"How is your mother?"

"Older, meaner."

"I hear we're in-laws. I hope Margo knows my brother is a sex maniac."

"My sister's a skank."

"Hmmn, it may work out after all." Lee stared up at the mound of red curls gathered in a clip behind her ears. "You haven't cut your hair. I was afraid you had."

Colleen laughed while tugging on his shaggy locks. "What's with this?"

"Guys wear long hair now." He took her hand from his hair and held it.

"So, um, what are your plans?" she stammered. "I mean, after graduation."

"Not sure. What about you?"

"I've already graduated. I started at Emerson last September."

"And everyone thought you wouldn't make it out of grade school."

"I wouldn't have if not for you." Colleen wiped her nose on her jacket's sleeve. "Jesus, it's cold." Lee handed her his handkerchief. She dabbed her eyes, wiped her nose, and rubbed the arm of the jacket before returning it.

"Keep it. Are you, um, dating anyone?" he timidly asked.

Colleen gave a sideways glance. "No, all the guys at school are..." she hesitated. "Are the theatrical type. Besides, what man would be brave enough to tangle with my mother?"

"I would."

"You're different. You're Lee." But he wasn't Lee, her wizard, Aladdin. His carpet had taken him to a land she didn't want to inhabit. The crunch of rock salt mocked the fragile silence. Colleen stared ahead as if she knew the direction she and the conversation were headed. "Are you seeing someone?" she quickly asked.

"Only in my dreams, and they're all of you. Don't get me wrong, I have friends."

"On what planet?"

"Shut up."

"No, you shut up." Colleen clutched him by his overcoat and screamed. "RAT! Goddammit, I hate this city."

"You don't have rats in Boston?" he chuckled.

"Not since you left town." Her tears of laughter turned to sorrow. "Why Lee? Why?" His reluctance made her fear she wouldn't get an answer.

"My parents prepared me for college, not for life. I was overprotected. I suppose it's that whole second-generation thing, not wanting your child to experience the cruel world they were forced to endure. They did me no favor. I came here at 17, I don't have to describe the kind of kid I was. I'd migrate to anyone who'd befriend me. I'm ashamed of myself, but I'm proud of you."

Lee motioned over her shoulder. "That's the terminal across the street."

"You had better come with me. I was approached by a pimp when I got off the bus. On closer inspection, he concluded I wouldn't be a good earner; he may have lowered his standards and come on to me."

Lee's steps came to a halt. His hand yanked hers. "Don't you ever, ever, put yourself down or allow anyone else to!" Sensing her shocked reaction, he relaxed his expression. "Except for me," he stated with a playful wink.

Colleen was in love. Arm in arm, they entered the harsh light of the terminal. Observing Lee looking over at the departure schedule, her heart spoke to her head. *"It's a costume, beneath the dress, there's a man."* She wanted him. The memory of wrestling with him in the backyard excited her. She wanted to rub his shoulders as she had at the prom. He wanted to kiss her then. She wanted to kiss him now.

Looking up from the schedule, he smiled. "Next bus to Boston leaves in four minutes."

"Why was he smiling?" she wondered. Was he glad to have seen her? Happy to see her go? She had to know. Gleefully, Colleen rubbed up against the yellow tiled wall encrusted in food particles and a variety of bodily fluids. "I can't wait to tell Margo where her jacket's been." Leaning against the wall, she bent at the knees, slowly raising and lowering her body, knowing Lee would find the gesture both amusing and erotic.

He didn't laugh. A look of superiority took control of his face, making her feel foolish, like a silly child. He had grown up. She hadn't. Facing her with his left hand on the wall behind her head, he slid the other under her jacket. His arm felt like a warm towel around her waist in the frigid New York night. His embrace tightened as he lifted her from a squat. Eyes closed, he parted her lips with his tongue. Their bodies responded to what had been buried in their hearts since childhood. As if detecting a magic elixir on one another's lips with only seconds to retrieve its life-saving properties, their kisses grew deeper, faster in a rapid attempt to confiscate ten years of love in three minutes. Colleen's hair escaped its clip, covering Lee's head in a bouquet of auburn curls. Her long leg snaked around his thigh, attaching his lower body to hers.

"You're finally in my arms," he moaned in a voice as low and deep as his kisses. "I want you to..." The hiss from a Boston-bound bus broke the Wizard's spell. "If you had kissed me like that on prom night, I wouldn't be standing here in a dress. You had better go or you'll miss the bus."

"I missed the bus a long time ago."

Now it was she who ran from window to window for one last look at the lover left behind. He was no more than a silhouette; a ghost she could put her hand through. He didn't wave or look back but dissolved into a sea of lost souls. In the dark, she felt free to weep. "I hate this town," she whimpered. "New York is a circus, reducing my wizard to a clown. He hadn't finished his sentence. I want you to what? Go home? Stay? Keep my secret?"

"What was that!"

"Jesus, Fran, where did you come from?"

"I saw you run out of the club. I promised your sister I'd look out for you. I followed you, got on the bus, and watched the show the two of you were putting on. It looked like the farewell scene from Casablanca, only I couldn't figure out which one was Ingrid Bergman. So, who is he... it was a he?"

"Lee's a childhood friend; my only friend when I need one most." Fran came around and took a seat next to a grieving Colleen.

"You're upset," Fran consoled with furrowed brows. "You got it bad for him."

"Since the third grade."

"You do know..."

"Don't say it."

"Someone has to."

"He's not gay."

"Alex isn't a hippie; that's a phase. Your friend is gay, that's a way of life."

"It was just a dress."

"A real man wouldn't be caught dead in a dress. Would Steve McQueen wear a dress? Charles Bronson?"

"I'm not in love with Charles Bronson."

"I am, and I'm a lesbian. Don't torture yourself. As much as you want to turn them, you can't."

"You said men are chameleons."

"He may change his clothes for you, but he'll always prefer a man. You're heading for a heartache."

"I'm already there."

"Be reasonable. He was in a gay bar wearing a dress. What more evidence do you need?"

"I was in a gay bar wearing a man's shirt. Would a gay man kiss a woman the way he kissed me?"

"Yes. Men are dogs, all of them, gay, straight, and in between, and you were kissing a poodle."

Colleen rested her head on Fran's lap. "I get sick at the thought of him being with a man."

"Then think of yourself with one."

***

Unlocking the front door, Aaron stomped snow off his shoes. Margo followed, laughing. "Your friend, Dr. Everton, made a total ass of himself. Wait till tomorrow."

"Shh, shh," Aaron nodded over at Colleen, asleep on the sofa.

"How could she have been in New York at midnight and home before us?" asked a mystified Margo. "She has her own room. Why is she on the sofa? Something must be troubling her, and she was waiting up for me."

Aaron covered Colleen with the Afghan his aunt Nelda made for him. Margo hated the brown and gold knitted nightmare. "Sweet dreams," Aaron whispered.

***

"What would you ladies like for breakfast?" Aaron asked, wearing a ruffled white apron. Colleen answered with a wolf whistle. Aaron came out from behind the kitchen's island countertop stove. "Like it?"

"It's you."

"It must be. My lovely wife has yet to tie this apron around her 24-inch waist, even while watching *The French Chef*."

Margo lowered *The Times'* entertainment section and stuck her tongue out. Colleen's eyes ping-ponged between the couple.

"Am I witnessing your first spat of the new year?"

Margo eased over to her husband's side. The two shared a passionate kiss.

"I just lost my appetite," Colleen groaned.

Aaron waved a spatula in the air. "You'll regain it once you've tasted my world-famous flapjacks."

"Even *I* know how to flip a pancake. It's not brain surgery."

"My first Colleen insult of the new year. Tell us about your adventures in Gotham City."

"Not much to tell. We went to Fran's brother's party. It was a bust. So, a group of us went to Times Square. It was too cold to hang around till midnight, so we came home." She wasn't about to divulge Lee's secret but was curious to learn if Aaron was aware of his brother's transformation.

"I saw Lee in Times Square," she blurted. Aaron and Margo looked at each another.

"Our Lee?" they asked in concert.

347

"Yes, that Lee."

"How is he?" Margo anxiously asked.

"I didn't get the opportunity to speak with him. Too crowded, too cold."

"How did he look?" she pressed.

"You'd never recognize him."

"I'm sorry you didn't stay long enough for the ball to drop."

"So am I."

Chapter Twenty-Three

Fearing she'd miss Lee's call, Colleen found herself a prisoner in her home. It was time to scale the wall. "Where are you off to?" Berta asked Colleen, who sat on the coat tree bench, tugging on her snow boots.

"I have Fran waiting at the foot of the hill. Her car can't make it up the Mount."

Berta looked out at the icy street. "Shame about Dr. Abbot. Light in the loafers, but a darn good doctor. They're tearing down his house to build an apartment building, and the rest of them are covering their houses in tin. I remember a time..."

"I'm sure you do. I'm expecting a call from a boy I've been assigned to do a writing project with. If he calls, get a number."

"I don't understand any of this."

"You don't have to and don't bother with dinner, I'm eating out."

The street was cold, her tears were warm. She'd come prepared with Lee's handkerchief wound around her knuckles like a prizefighter's taped hand. "Where is she?" she grumbled while stomping her frozen feet. "That's either a snowplow or a Beetle." Fran doubled-parked and beeped. Once inside the car, Colleen hugged herself. "Shit, this car is cold."

"It runs, what more do you want?"

"Heat."

"Ladies first," Fran said as she pulled open the heavy red and gold door to the Hong Kong Foo Restaurant. "They call this place the Hong Kong Flu. I chose it because it's dark and I know you'll be crying in your tea." Colleen sat in the booth, looking up at the ceiling. Fran shook her head. "We came here for a Pu Pu, not a Boo Hoo."

"Don't be funny."

"Okay, I'll be serious. What are you going to do after your semester break?"

Colleen shrugged.

"I'll tell you. You'll lose weight, lose sleep, and lose your scholarship, while he goes on with his life, not giving New Year's Eve a second thought. Eat something!" Fran wiggled a limp eggroll under Colleen's nose. "Come on," she teased. "You wanted it back at the bus terminal."

"You're sick."

"He knows your address, he doesn't write. He knows your phone number, but he doesn't call. And he knows you love him, and he doesn't care."

Colleen's eyes glazed over. "I hadn't thought of him in years. He left for college a goofy, callow kid; now he's a grown man."

"The jury's still out on that charge."

"I have a new picture of him in my mind. Closing my eyes is like drawing down a shade with his image etched on the inside of my lids."

"Get real. He's an opportunist. He saw an opportunity to kiss a girl, and he took it. Evidently, he thinks men taste better."

"I thought he'd call to see if I kept his secret."

"Why bother? He knows you wouldn't fink on him... would you?"

"No! Never!"

"Get over this. He's the only man you've known; it was your first kiss, now you've got it in your head he's your adult lover." Fran poked the air with her chopsticks. "Time's a wast'n, and he's not wasting his time on you. There are plenty of fish in the sea; get your feet wet, not your eyes. Once you understand men, you'll never allow another one to take advantage of you again. One day you'll look back on this and laugh."

"Or puke."

"You gonna eat that eggroll?"

***

Aaron held an apron around his waist. "Tie me up," he ordered his wife as if she were a scrub nurse gowning him for surgery.

"Keep that talk for the bedroom," Colleen quipped.

Aaron raised a brow. "What time did you get in, wise guy?"

"I went to the midnight showing of *Casablanca*. I have a paper due on it," she lied. Fran's description of Lee's kiss sparked a sudden interest in the film. "I wanted to sleep in, but the scent of your cooking acts like a snake charmer's flute luring me to Aaron's magic kitchen."

"My wife has never heard the music." Aaron cocked his head. "Isn't that right, hon?"

"I do my cooking in bed."

"Margo!" Aaron said in alarm.

Colleen came to her sister's defense. "Don't act shocked; you knew she was a pig when you married her."

"If you two will excuse me," Margo said, getting up from the breakfast bar with The Boston Globe, "This little piggy is going to the living room with the lifestyle section."

Aaron turned his attention to Colleen's empty plate. "What will it be? French toast? Eggs? Pancakes?"

"I'm not hungry."

"Crepes?" He tempted, passing a warm sample under her nose, and Colleen relented.

"Make mine strawberry, hold the whipped cream."

"Coming right up."

Colleen could always take a punch but never expected the visceral blow Aaron was about to land.

"Honey," Margo called into the kitchen. "Tell Colleen about Lee." Just the mention of his name sent her stomach to her feet.

"He's moving to Chicago. My mother is beside herself. He landed a job with Marlowe and Mayfield, it's a prestigious accounting firm." Colleen lowered her head as if saying grace, praying she wouldn't cry.

Aaron continued the torture. "The kid's crazy. Sure, the money's good, but he'd be better served to stay in school and get an advanced degree. Christ, the kid has more brains than I do, and I'm a renowned surgeon. I wonder if the boy genius realizes that if he leaves school, he'll be called up. Think my mother is upset now? Wait till the draft notice shows up on her doorstep."

Margo weighed in. "I know men and I say, he met a girl from the windy city and he's moving there to be with her."

"Or him."

"Aaron, don't be cruel." Margo scolded.

"This is news? The only girl he ever went on a date with was Colleen, and she was returning a favor; that doesn't count. If the mama's boy doesn't want to pick up a rifle, he better pick up a purse, or he's bought himself a ticket to Da Nang."

Colleen felt the VC bullet rip through her throat. Whether Chicago or Vietnam, he'd been taken from her. There were so many questions she wanted to ask but couldn't let on that her dream of a life with Lee had been stolen. Why bother? Aaron wouldn't have answers. To him, Lee was insignificant; to Colleen, he was her world.

Aaron poured himself a cup of coffee. "His parents plan on heading down to New York to see him graduate. Why bother? Oscar's dementia is to the point where he wouldn't know his son if he fell on him. Which is another thing, he can't walk unassisted. The man belongs in a nursing home."

"Why don't you drive them?" Margo suggested. "It will probably be the last time the four of you will ever be together. After all, they attended your graduation."

"Mine was held in Cambridge. I can still see the smug, self-satisfied look on Oscar's face, as if it were he who received the Medical Degree." Margo walked to the kitchen sink. After washing the newspaper ink from her fingers, she dried them on Aaron's apron.

"You may not have wanted them at your graduation, but Lee wants them at his."

"I'll drive them!" Colleen volunteered.

"That's good of you, but after an hour in a car with my mother, you'll drive off a cliff."

"I'd like to see Lee again."

"You'll get your chance. He promised his parents he'd come home to see them before he moved. Once he sees his father's condition and the neighborhood, he'll hightail it out of town with them in tow. That's the only way they'll leave that slum."

"Do you think he will?"

"Will what?"

"Come home."

"He promised his mother he would. He'd never disappoint his mommy."

"Will you let me know when he arrives? You know, for old time's sake."

Aaron carelessly shrugged his shoulders. "If I know Leon, he'll call you."

But he didn't know Lee. He never would.

***

The fork picked off the fish sticks' crust, soggy from weeping coleslaw. Berta inspected Colleen's dinner plate of food, rearranged, not eaten. "You have the appetite of a bird. That's no way to lose weight. People who yo-yo diet pack the weight back on and then some. I never tipped the scales. Do you know why? I eat properly. You gulp down your food and run out the door. You'll end up like your aunt Virginia. That's why she went into the convent, too fat, too bossy. Men don't like to be bossed around."

"Neither do grown children!"

"What's gotten into you? I don't hear any talk about your internship at the Cape Cod Playhouse. The chance of a lifetime, you called it. An opportunity to rub elbows with celebrities."

"I'm on the fence about it."

"Now you want to stay in the city with your mother. I thought your goal in life was to get as far away from me as possible."

"It is, but a position opened in New York's Playhouse in the Park. If I get it, I'd be even further away."

Berta folded her arms, bobbed her head, and tightened her gaze. "Something is going on here. I haven't figured it out yet, but I will, and so help me God, if you're passing up the opportunity to work in your chosen field for some scheme cooked up by the Queen of Chestnut Hill, I'll make the two of you wish you were never born."

"We already do!"

"Don't get flip with me, Missy. I've supported your dream of becoming a playwright with free room and board, so you needn't work, and have time to study. This may come as a shock to you, but I want you to succeed, not become a secretary like your aunt or a gold digger like your sister. You're taking that internship, or I'll change the locks."

Her mother's tirade bolstered Colleen to put an end to the drama. It was time to call Margo. Phone in hand, she prayed into the receiver. "Pick up. Pick up. Margo! I caught you at home."

"Just got in from a tennis lesson. What's up?"

"Back in January, you mentioned Lee was coming home to see his parents after graduating. I wanted to wish him well. Do you have any idea when he'll arrive?" she asked as if the answer held no emotional consequence.

"Hang on a sec. Aaron!" Margo called into the next room. "Did Lee ever make it home?"

"Come and gone. Why?"

"Colleen was asking."

"Darn, I forgot. I promised I'd let her know when he came back. Hand me the phone."

"Sorry, Colleen, I meant to call you. I've been tied up at the hospital, not that that's any excuse. Leon left a couple of days ago. He could only stay a week. He must have already started his job. Good luck to him."

Colleen agreed in a sleepwalker's mumble. "Yeah, good luck."

"He should have stayed here, gotten his master's degree, the kid's got a head for numbers."

"Not my number."

"I'm sure he was thinking of you, but he has a lot on his plate right now."

Colleen's stomach had become a slinky. "I bet he's changed," she gulped. "I mean, how did he look?"

"Never made it over there. I spoke with him briefly over the phone. He sounds good. One of his co-workers found an apartment for him. Have you ever been out there?"

"No, I've never left home."

"I've only been there once for a conference. Next time I'll have a place to stay," he chuckled. "I'm joking. Leon's a slob, so am I. Aren't I, hon?"

"Yes, he is," Margo called out in the background.

"Unless he found someone to pick up after him, if you know what I mean."

"Yeah, I'm sure he has," Colleen whispered, blinking back tears. "He's a great guy. He deserves to be happy. So, um, I guess I'll have to wait until his next trip home."

"Next time he returns, it will be for his father's funeral. I don't give Oscar much time."

"You were always good at predicting deaths."

"Now you sound like your mother. I'll give you back to Margo."

"We haven't spoken in a while," Margo remarked. "How are you?"

Colleen cleared her throat to answer. "I'm taking an internship at the Cape Cod Playhouse."

"That sounds exciting! When do you start?"

Colleen's emotions hijacked her response. "I, um, can't remember. I wrote it down somewhere."

"Are you okay?"

"I'm sorry I missed my old tutor. I was wondering if he asked about me, if I got out of grade school, or some other smart aleck remark."

"As I said, I didn't know he'd come back."

Colleen collected herself. "You just got in. I won't keep you."

"Call me before you leave for the Cape."

"Gotta go."

She'd never fainted or felt faint; girls who did were showoffs. Clutching the phone to her chest, she slid her back down the bedroom's closed door. "You were just around the corner," she cried out to ears halfway across the country. "I sat in front of your building every night for the past month. All the while you were behind that door, breathing the same air, hearing the same street traffic. You could see my house from yours. You knew I was waiting, but you didn't care."

Disbelief turned to anger as she savagely paced her room. "I want to vomit you out of my system, have a blood transfusion. You took advantage of my stupidity. Big joke. You said you'd knock the chip off my shoulder, that's the only promise you've kept." Colleen's mind raced. *"He was running away from me. Why did I give chase? I know why. I'm a frustrated virgin willing to give myself to any man who shows an interest in me. Most girls my age have married, their desires satisfied. Not me. I'm chasing down a crossdresser and wondering why he doesn't call."*

The cardboard box of mementoes on the closet's top shelf wobbled with age. The first to go were the petals of a dried corsage. "Loves me, loves me not. Loves me not, loves me not," she chanted, violently tearing at the carnation. The cheap rhinestone crown crunched under her heel. "Snap, crackle, pop. A fake like him." At the bottom of the box lay a yellowed envelope. *"Just tear it up,"* she told herself. Her fingers cramped as she slid the gray photo with jagged white edges out of the creased envelope. The young couple, he proudly grinning, his arm around her waist, the same arm he'd placed around the same waist on New Year's Eve. Standing next to him was his date, wearing a snarky expression, pretending the prom was a chore, a favor to be repaid. Only Colleen knew what went through that girl's mind. She recalled the thrill she felt having a boy wanting her next to him, proud to have her pretend to be his girl.

"If only I could go back to that night, be transported into the picture, let him kiss me. Would we be married? A baby on the way? This has got to stop." Squeezing her eyes shut, she tore the 4x4 memory in two. It felt like a bandage being ripped off a raw wound. She watched shreds of fantasy and regret whirling down the toilet.

***

It was Sunday evening, and the car dealership across from The Talbot School had been converted to a food pantry before the '64 model could hit the showroom floor. The children who'd entered the first grade the year Colleen walked out of the schoolyard for the last time were now in high school. There it hung, beckoning her back. Hundreds of children had left the ground on it, yet it would always be her swing.

She covered her ears, blocking the sound of his laughter. Sitting with her knees to her chest, she cast off. The swing's metal chains cranked. Was it from age? Her weight? Or was it mourning with her? "Why can't I fly off the swing, Mae, be with you, Poppy, Rosaria? You're the only ones who truly loved and understood me. If you were here, I know what you would say. Colleen, you're too good for that boy. God has laid out a path for you. You've taken a painful detour." Colleen brought the swing to an abrupt stop. "You promised I could come to you. You would send me a sign." Colleen sighed. "It's time to leave the schoolyard." Giving the swing a forceful push, its chains latched on to each other, twisting into a lover's embrace. She walked off, not stopping to look back.

Chapter Twenty-Four

The army-trained nurse hung up the phone. "That's odd. I'm told he's in the cafeteria. Dr. Hirsh, eating among the common folk?" she questioned aloud. "Go get'em," she said, slapping the young intern's back. Dr. Papadakis wedged his way into the knot of noontime diners. Dr. Hirsh wouldn't rip the head off a first-year intern in public, he assured himself as he tentatively approached the legendary taskmaster sitting alone, a book in one hand, a corned beef on rye in the other.

"Dr. Hirsh?" Aaron closed his book and raised his head. The green doctor spewed a rehearsed monologue. "I'm Dr. Papadakis. I wouldn't interrupt your lunch if it weren't an emergency. I was told you're fluent in Russian."

"My native tongue."

"Great, we, I, there's a patient in the E.R., a fifty-eight-year-old man with a two-week history of pain and tenderness in the right lower quadrant. Leukocyte count is 13.4x10/12. I've no doubt he has an inguinal hernia, but his breathing is labored, he's febrile, and nauseous. I suspect we're dealing with more than a popped gut. Mister..." The intern fumbled to pronounce a difficult name to a difficult doctor. "Vytautas Januskas doesn't speak English. His wife is with him, but she's no help. He's boisterous, disruptive, and refuses to sign the surgery consent form. In short, he's a major pain in the anal sphincter. Now he wants to go home. If he walks out of here, he won't survive."

Aaron wiped a smudge of mustard from his lip with a napkin and removed his bifocals. "Are you finished?"

"Yes."

"Then lead the way."

The two headed down the marble main staircase and through the crowded lobby. "Most of my time is spent lecturing and placating the rich and famous. I miss patient contact. What did you say your name is?"

"Tomas Papadakis."

"You're a twin?" Aaron looked back at the astonished intern who'd stopped in place.

"How did you guess?"

"Tomas means twin. Is it fair to assume your twin's name is Thos?"

"Theodora, we're fraternal."

"I just broke the first rule of medicine, drawing a conclusion without considering all the options."

"May I be honest with you, Dr. Hirsh?"

"Wouldn't have it any other way."

"You're not the ogre they make you out to be."

"You mean a major pain in the anal sphincter? It's your lucky day; I chewed out two residents for breakfast. I'm full. By the way, Januskas is Lithuanian."

"You speak Lithuanian?"

"And German, Polish, Romanian, Hungarian, Latin, and Hebrew, of course."

"Greek?"

"It's Greek to me." Tomas conjured up a smile in response to Aaron's attempt to be humorous.

The emergency ward exhaled with Aaron's entrance as he introduced himself to the patient in Lithuanian, putting the hostile foreigner at ease and allowing Aaron to conduct an examination. Tomas and a young female doctor stood aside, observing a master at his craft. After checking the patient's vitals, Aaron instructed Mrs. Januskas to take hold of her husband's hands.

"You may find this painful." Not wanting to appear weak to a strong man, Mr. Januskas looked up at the ceiling and gritted his teeth. Palpitating the warm, tender abdomen, a slow smile crept across Aaron's lips. With a few short sentences, he gave the grateful patient a pat on the back, assuring him he was in good hands with Dr. Papadakis. Taking the manila folder that held the patient's chart and a signed consent form, Aaron tapped Tomas on the head. "As for you, that hernia is strangulated around his appendix. Get him to surgery stat."

Returning to his opulent office, Aaron reminisced about his time as a green intern, content with spending his career in a surgery suite rather than tangle with the likes of a Vytautas Januskas. That all changed the day he met Rosaria. A light tap on his office door returned him to the present. "Come in."

She had the look of a woman from the last century, a suffragette or anarchist. Her hair was dark, wild, and wiry, gathered into a loose bun. He craved to examine her figure, but her magnetic violet eyes wouldn't release his. "Sorry to disturb, secretary not at her desk."

"Please have a seat." Aaron motioned to a leather chair next to his desk rather than the one across from it. As if submerging into a warm bath, she slowly sank into the chair. "My name is Dr. Magdala Pouzy. I come for further study at the medical school."

"You have an unusual dialect... Hungarian?"

"You have good ear. My mother was Hungarian, my father Basque. I grew up speaking French, Spanish, and Hungarian. I am Israeli now. Have you been to the Holy Land?"

"No, one day perhaps. Now is not the time."

"My country will always be in turmoil. Do not allow fear to keep you from your homeland."

"I was referring to my workload, not safety concerns."

"I come to see you because…" She turned her head and waved her hand across her face. "You are a very important man."

Aaron saw through her attempt to appear timid. "That aside, what can I do for you?"

"Dr. Papadakis mentioned you spoke German. I would appreciate help with translation. I have a research paper, and many of the old texts are in German. I would not ask for much time."

"I'd like nothing better than to assist a visiting doctor."

"Nothing?" The innuendo was ignored but not lost.

"I enjoy translating. It keeps my linguistic skills sharp. When would you like to meet?"

"You are a very busy man. I am only here to study, observe; my time is not structured."

"Well, my dear girl—I'm old enough to call you a girl. If you have your research material on hand, we can meet when I finish up here."

Aaron gestured to a stack of reports. "I have a private office on the fifth floor of The Countway Medical Library. How does four o'clock sound?

"How important you are, I am very fortunate."

Aaron turned up his thumbs from his folded hands. "Then it's settled."

She rose from the seat in the same slow manner she had descended. "I go, now. At four, on five."

Aaron looked on as the sexy centaur exited with a mixture of a strut and a march. He found her attractive in an earthy sense, not his type. Still, he was drawn to her. She was confident, in control, yet longed to be dominated.

He wanted to break her in.

The office was no more than a hole in the wall next to the library's conference room, where Aaron would conduct weekly lectures.

"*Look at me*," Aaron warned himself as he cleared his desk of paper cups that held remnants of week-old coffee floating in a puddle of curdled cream. "*I'm behaving like a schoolboy. I'm a married man. A happily married man. I can't jeopardize my marriage, career, reputation, for a momentary fling. For all I know, she may be married, have children, or just bring a tease. Keep it professional, I don't want her to think I'm a letch.*" Aaron positioned himself behind his desk, bifocals resting low on the bridge of his nose, and he buried his head in a stack of meaningless papers.

"Dr. Hirsh."

Aaron came to his feet. "Dr. Pouzy, please come in if you can fit. What I mean is, this office is tiny. I'm not implying you're large."

"No explanation needed. Sit."

Aaron purposely ignored the order. "I try to maintain a clean office, but as you can see."

"What I see is a man of great knowledge, great power. I think there is more to Dr. Hirsh than a messy desk."

Aaron sat. Dr. Pouzy followed suit. "I have a question for you."

"By all means, ask."

"Why did you translate for Dr. Papodakis? I was in the room. You were very kind to that man."

"Mr. Januskas?"

"Yes, Januskas," she repeated as if expelling a bad taste from her mouth. "He was about to leave the hospital, destined to die a painful death. You stopped him. Why?"

"It has to do with being a doctor. The patient has to trust you, know you care, and feel comfortable answering uncomfortable questions."

"Such as, what did you do during the war?" Aaron leaned back in his chair, stroking his five o'clock shadow that ran on daylight saving time.

"So that's what this meeting is about," Aaron said, noticing she didn't bring books or paper.

"You read his chart. You see, he's from Kaunas. Are you not familiar with the Kaunas massacre? You saw his TDA insignia tattoo."

"What I saw was a man in pain with the possibility of dying, not a Nazi sympathizer with a gun to my head. Another time, in another place, I've no doubt he'd kill me. I took an oath, Dr. Pouzy. I've treated murderers, rapists, and child molesters; now I'll add Nazi to the list. I treat diseases, not social ills."

"I have difficulty understanding the apathy of Jews who should know better than to say, forget."

Aaron came to his feet. "My mother survived the camps, I understand."

"I was unaware, you are so Americanized."

"When I came to this country, I didn't speak English or understand the customs. I worked very hard to become an American, not only to be accepted but also admired. I love this country; it took me in. I don't care who did what to whom. If my mother can forgive, and she has, who am I to pick up the sword? I don't hate Germans. I hate the politics that encouraged the eradication of Jews. Antisemitism still exists; it always will. I don't allow it to consume me."

"It should. You are Jew."

"I hold many titles. Professor, doctor, immigrant, son, husband, the list goes on."

"You did not say, Father."

"I'm not."

"How sad, your wife is not Jewish?"

Aaron had spoken his piece. "Excuse me, Doctor Pouzy, it's late, and as you say, I'm a busy man."

"I offend you, speak of painful past, lecture on your duty to your people."

"I'm a doctor, they're all my people. I heal wounds, I don't open them. Good day, Dr. Pouzy."

***

Stan parked his feet across Aaron's desk. "All work and no play makes Dr. Hirsh a very dull boy." Aaron slammed the file cabinet drawer shut. "I'm not looking for fun, I'm looking for Jerome Kilton's pathology report. I should have received it yesterday. Mr. Kilton is anxious, and I'm..."

"And you're lying. If you're waiting for that Pouzy broad, take my advice and steer clear of her."

"She's harmless,"

"Harmless! She's been hitting on all her landsmen who have money and a medical degree. She's looking for recruits and a husband."

"I'm married, remember?"

"No, *you* remember. You've got a good thing going, the money, the title, the wife. You know what your problem is? You get off on playing the hero, saving the damsel in distress. You rescued Margo and her sister Rosaria, but this dirty waif is a bloodsucker: she wants your body and soul. Come on, Aaron, you know me, I'll hump anything with a hole, but she looks like something you'd scrape off the bottom of your shoe, in Chinatown."

"I feel sorry for her. She's young, at that age you're looking for a cause to latch on to."

"I have a policy: never feel sorry for an ugly woman. You tell her she's beautiful, and she buys the bullshit. She stops trying to look presentable. But tell her she's a dog and she'll set out to prove you wrong. She'll lose weight, shave, and run a comb through her hair.

"As for Pouzy, she looks like The Bride of Frankenstein on a bad hair day. You know what you ought to do? Take Margo on a second honeymoon."

"We never had a first, and our second anniversary is next month."

"And they said it wouldn't last."

"They did!"

"Spice things up: fly down to Miami Beach, buy her a bikini, take a picture of her in it for me. By the time you get back, Mag the Hag will be back in Israel." Stan jerked his head at the door. "Let's get out of here, play some racquetball. Leave her a note."

This very handsome, very important doctor goes to play a very important ball game with a not-so-important doctor.

"Come on, let's get out of here."

***

Berta motioned with her head for Colleen to answer the phone.

"Oh my God." Margo squealed, "You'll never guess where Aaron is taking me... Miami Beach! Why don't you house sit? A change of scenery will do you good. We leave on Friday. Come after school."

Colleen's eyes drifted to her eavesdropping mother, shaking out her newspaper like a sheet on a clothesline. She hesitated, "I'll get back to you."

"That was Margo, they're going on vacation."

Berta spoke into the newspaper. "Miami Beach or the Catskills?"

"I'll be housesitting for them. They leave Friday and arrive home on the 23rd."

Berta raised an eye. "Do as you please."

***

"A week, Margo," Aaron reminded his wife. "This isn't The Grand Tour. There's no need for five suitcases."

"But we'll be going out every night."

366

"And you'll be shopping every day. Only bring the essentials." Aaron playfully swatted Margo's bottom. "Now get packing."

Margo glanced over at Aaron's open carry-on case. "Say, what are all these magazines and newspapers? I thought you no longer subscribed to this stuff?"

"I picked them up at a newsstand, something to read on the flight."

"The Forward, Shaa'num, Lamerhov? Most of this stuff isn't in English."

"It's not 'stuff.' These are troubling times; it's important to be informed in world affairs."

"Don't be such a pessimist."

"I am when it comes to the Middle East. We have a doctor from Israel studying at the medical school who tells of unrest in the region, stories you'll never read about in American publications. That's why I read this stuff. I should do more than send money. That's why I volunteered my services to our returning soldiers. I owed a debt to this country, and I owe as much to my homeland."

"I thought Russia was your homeland. "

"You don't understand, you never will."

"That's what you said when I was reading *Wealth of Nations*. Now I know more about finance than Adam Smith. We Irish have our own troubles, but you won't catch me making a bomb."

"Send money."

"You have. Didn't you see the thank-you note from the IRA?" Margo rubbed Aaron's back. "Honey, we can't cure the world's problems. These countries are going to battle it out, whether we aid them or not. Let them work it out amongst themselves."

"That's the same argument used back in '39, and look what it got us, a world war."

"Once again, my mother was right. She said if there's another world war, it will start in Israel."

The two lay on the bed surrounded by clothes and suitcases. Margo stroked her husband's cheek. "You have such pride of country. You ought to consider a second career in politics. Johnson's not seeking a second term. Why not throw your stethoscope in the ring? You'd make an okay President, and when it comes to First Ladies, I'd make Jackie Kennedy look like Phyllis Diller."

"Have you forgotten? I'm not native born, thus not eligible for the Presidency—but I am qualified to be the Prime Minister of Israel."

"Right now, I'll settle for Mayor of Miami," Margo said, looking at Aaron adoringly. "You know what you are?"

"Horny?"

"A patriot. Patriots are loyal."

***

Spotting the abused Impala pulling up to the Pan Am terminal, Margo stood slack-jawed. Aaron squeezed her hand. "We survived the flight. We'll survive the ride home." Without offering a greeting, Margo wrapped a handkerchief around her hand before opening the driver's side door. "Get out," she ordered her sister with a jerk of her head. "Aaron is driving. Before you get comfortable in the backseat, go help him with the luggage."

"Stay put," Aaron called out. "I've got them."

Margo pointed her polished fingernail at Colleen's face. "So, help me, Colleen, if any grease gets on my luggage from whatever is rotting in that trunk, you'll find yourself locked in it."

"Don't take a nutty, the body has decomposed by now."

Winded, Aaron took the wheel. "Why didn't you take one of my cars?"

"Your cars are all nose, no trunk. Is it true that a car looks like its owner?"

"Judging by the look of this clunker, I'd say that's a fair assessment."

"Your cars burn gas."

"Your tailpipe needs a lift."

Margo whipped off her sunglasses and rubbed her temples. "Aaron, please. Do not encourage her. "

"Did we miss anything?" Aaron asked.

"Not much," Colleen informed with a shrug. "I checked your house every day but couldn't stay there, Ma fell."

"Your mother fell! This is a stupid question, but did she see a doctor?"

"She determined it was a broken foot and prescribed ice and only light housework."

"Did Dr. Abbot look at it?" Aaron asked.

"He died last year."

Margo's blood boiled. "She fell on that staircase, didn't she? I knew this would happen, but nobody listened to me. The house is cursed. I'm getting her out of that crypt. Aaron got his parents out."

"Not without a fight," he added. "Oscar needed professional help. Since the King assassination riot, there's no amount of money you can pay someone to go into that neighborhood carrying medication. I gave it to them straight: move or Oscar goes into a nursing home."

"Any good news?" Margo asked.

"Ma finally found a junk dealer to haul away the Lindsey's old car from the carriage house. I told her she shouldn't have paid him. He's going to make a pretty penny for the scrap metal."

Aaron looked into the rearview mirror at Colleen. "What make?"

"To quote Grandma Rourke, 'Tis a six-cylinder, fifty-horsepower Duryea Model S.'"

The sudden slam on the brakes jolted the Impala's passengers forward. "Christ, Aaron! You almost killed us," a shaken Margo screamed.

"AWWH!" Aaron cried out as if he'd touched a hot iron. "There's been a Duryea sitting in that carriage house all these years, and you never told me!"

"What's the big deal?" Margo huffed.

Aaron's voice rose to a soprano range. "I would have killed for that car."

"Had I known, we would have gotten rid of the car and my mother."

"This isn't funny, Margo."

"You wouldn't want that stupid car, it was really old...but it ran. Are you crying?"

As the battle-scared Chevy neared the manicured enclave, Margo tied her scarf tightly under her chin and shaded her eyes behind oversized sunglasses. "Drop me off at the shopping mall."

"What!" Aaron snapped.

"I can't be seen arriving home in this...this..."

Colleen offered the missing words. "Graduation present."

"Once you drop off the suitcases at the house, swing by the mall in the Porsche."

"This silliness has gone too far. You don't owe the neighbors an explanation."

Margo held up her index finger. "I have an idea. I'll tell them I had a bout of amnesia and was found wandering along the highway dazed and confused, when a girl in a beat-up car drove me home. Naturally, you offered the misanthrope money for my safe return, but she refused the offer, asking only for advice regarding a recurring yeast infection."

"Must you girls always lie your way in and out of unpleasant situations?"

Margo answered with a firm yes. "They're not hurtful lies, they're protective lies used to avoid arguments."

"A lie is a lie. They're all dishonest."

"Pardon me, St. Aaron."

"I'll be the first to admit I'm not perfect."

"The first?"

"As a doctor, I've made it a policy to be truthful with patients. You don't tell them what they want to hear, but what they need to know, no matter how upsetting."

"Colleen, go help Honest Abe with the luggage."

Aaron shook his head. "That won't be necessary. Go in the house, I've got them."

Margo turned the house key. "Wait till you see the dress Aaron bought me. I told him the vacation was enough, but when he saw the look on my face, the dress was mine." Aaron toggled up the walkway, Chaplin-style, gripping a suitcase in each hand.

"That's the last of them," he puffed. Margo snapped open a suitcase in search of her booty. Looking down at a stack of unopened mail, Colleen's stomach cramped. On top was an envelope written in Lee's scrawl. "There's a card from Lee."

"I'll sort through the mail later," Aaron said.

"It looks like a birthday card. Open it. He may have sent you money."

"Ha, ha," Aaron adjusted his eyeglasses. Her birthday had passed two months earlier without notice, yet Lee took the time to choose a card for a brother who didn't consider him blood.

"The kid has the memory of an elephant. I have no idea when he was born."

"Saint Patrick's Day," Colleen said. "I would tease him about it. We joked about everything."

Margo disappeared behind her bedroom door. "The neckline is more suited for pearls, but... AARON! Someone's been here! It's Ronny. He's come to kill me!" Colleen stood plastered to the wall as Aaron roared past like a runaway train.

Colleen held Margo in her arms as Aaron searched the house for evidence of an intruder. Margo shivered as if an icy snake was slithering down her arm. Aaron returned to the living room. "Nothing appears to be missing."

"He didn't come to steal. He came to kill!"

Colleen fumbled her words. "I... I came by every day, honest. I was here this morning. There was nothing out of place."

Margo freed herself from Colleen's grip. "I'm not crazy! Someone has been in our bed!"

Aaron held up his palms and slowly approached his terror-stricken wife. "No one thinks you're crazy. If you're uncomfortable staying here, we'll go to the Boston apartment while the police comb over the place." Colleen's eyes set off a silent alarm as they cut to the kitchen door that led out to the garage. "What? What?" Margo screamed. "What are you looking at?" Aaron examined the splintered door frame. "I'm calling the police."

Colleen rocked her sobbing sister in her arms. Margo gulped. "It's Ronny, he was here, I know it."

"It wasn't him," Aaron said, hanging up the phone.

Wearing a perplexed expression, Margo lifted her head. "How do you know?"

He had his own suspect.

***

"Good morning, ladies." Aaron greeted his adoring receptionist, who responded with tense glances. Aaron's smile faded.

"Who's in my office?"

"I tried to stop her," the office manager answered. "I was about to have you paged. I didn't call security with her being a doctor."

Storming into his office, Aaron stood at the open door. "Get out."

Magdala circled her prey. "Are you angry? Do I offend you? You leave town, not tell me."

Aaron closed the door and tempered his voice. "You were at my house. I've had a security system installed. I suggest you return to Israel ahead of schedule or be incarcerated in an American prison."

"I look like prowler?"

"A stalker."

"You do not frighten me. I am not the one who has reputation to protect." Shaking out her hair that was as unruly as her disposition, Magdala unbuttoned her lab coat, revealing a bosom as ample as her buttocks. "You like?"

"I do not want," he answered in disgust.

"Have closer look, you may change your mind. I feel we have connection, not only in spirit but also in body. You have much to teach me."

"One of which is self-control. Now get out."

"What would secretary think if she found me like this, if your wife should be told?"

"She wouldn't believe it."

"Why does she not believe?"

"You're homely." Aaron reached for the phone. "I'm calling security."

"I go, but I leave my coat."

Aaron blocked her path. "Cover yourself up."

"I return to Israel in two weeks, no one will know, as you say, who would believe?"

His eyes were on the road, but his mind was on his marriage. Magdala was strong, independent; she didn't need a man; Margo always would. He yearned to make an impact on the world beyond the operating room, far from their upscale neighborhood. He longed to go where he was needed. Margo needed him once. She was a different woman from the one he married. No longer a childish flirt, he had schooled her well, molded her into a classy, confident beauty, obsessed with fashion and celebrity, a fixture at the country club, darling of the cocktail party set. Margo was holding him back. Saving lives wasn't enough; he was called to help save a nation, a people, his people. He was a Jew first, one who'd spent his adult life buried under the trappings that success brings. He was six feet under, Margo was his headstone.

***

Most of the attendees had departed the ballroom. Aaron teasingly nibbled on the back of his wife in a red satin gown's neck.

"All eyes are on you, my dear, not the Surgeon's General."

"At three hundred dollars a plate, they deserve a show," Margo purred.

"Let's give them a one."

"Get a room," a voice barked from behind.

"Stan!" Margo exclaimed, "Where's Joanne?"

"I sent her to bring the car around. She doesn't want a drunk at the wheel."

Stan's half-closed eyes drifted across the ballroom. "Well, will you look who's here? Joanne can wait. I'm sticking around for this."

Margo sized her up as a novice in heels with a calico nationality. In a multi-colored shawl and long muslin dress, she looked like she'd come to read palms, not mingle with dignitaries. Aaron braced himself for an awkward introduction.

"Dr. Hirsh, I come to congratulate your lovely wife." Magdala held out her hand to Margo, who picked up on the accent, sparking the memory of Aaron praising a visiting doctor whom Margo was led to believe was a man.

"You have way with people, Mrs. Hirsh, such charm and poise."

"Why, thank you, Doctor... you are a doctor?" Margo needled.

Aaron hastened to get through the introduction, hoping the faster he spoke, the sooner Magdala would leave. "Darling, this is Dr. Pouzy; she came from Israel to study at the medical school." His manner made Margo feel like a senile grandparent being introduced to a familiar family member. "Dr. Pouzy is returning home next week. She'll be missed."

"I spend much time under your husband's tutelage." That was it. That was the word. Both women understood its verbal nuance, a female codeword prompting the release of a pheromone causing backs to hunch, steampipe hisses that would end in air scratches and a climactic spit.

"Are you a neurologist, Dr. Pussy?"

"I am a gastroenterologist. I treat the tummy."

"I know what a gastroenterologist is, Doctor Pussy."

"Sorry, but I find women of great beauty seldom have brain."

"I've seen my wife's scan. She has a brain." Neither woman took note of Aaron's lame joke. Margo retracted her claws.

"So nice to have met you, Dr. Pussy. I like to put a name with a face."

Stan leaned into Margo's ear. "MEEEE YOOW."

Magdala shot Aaron a salacious look. "Pleasure is all mine." She left with a hiss in Aaron's ear. "Shiksa."

It was April, but the ride home was frosty. "My dear, you look ravishing. I've never seen you in that dress."

"Since when did you take an interest in my wardrobe?"

"Fair to say you didn't enjoy yourself?"

"Fair to say you did? As a rule, you hate these affairs, unless you're having one."

Aaron swerved the car off the road. "Look, if this is about Magdala,"

"So, it's Magdala, is it?"

"The girl has a crush on me, follows me around like I'm a matinee idol. I only tolerate it because she'll be leaving next week."

"She's a hag. You could do better. Don't sell yourself short."

"There's no reasoning with you."

"That's because I don't have a brain. I'm too beautiful; you need to do a scan to find it. I'll walk the rest of the way home."

Margo slammed the door to his Grand Prix.

"Get back in this car. You're acting like a child."

Margo walked to the driver's window. "Which am I, a wife or a child?"

"You're not a lady."

"And that Hungarian hump is?" Aaron sprang from the car, twisting Margo's arm. He threw her onto the car's backseat and himself on top of her.

"Let me up!"

"Shut up."

"You're shut off. The next time you need to get your rocks off, she can give you a Balkan blow job."

"You have a dirty little mind."

"And you love my dirty little body," she ended the accusation with a slap to his face. "Who's pussy now?"

They were embroiled in a violent game of pattycake. He'd never raised his hand to a woman; she was an animal to be tamed. Aaron landed a blow to her cheek. She savored the sting. He was shaken more by her response than his own actions. "Is that what you want, Margo? Is that what turns you on?" Gathering a mouthful of saliva, she spat in his eye. Keeping watch on her with his sighted eye, he calmly removed a handkerchief from his suit jacket pocket and wiped his lid. "I detect the stench of nicotine. Someone has been smoking, and it's not my tailor."

"Someone gave me a reason to smoke and for a divorce."

"Spousal abuse?" he asked with a smirk.

"Alienation of affection."

Aaron threw his head back and laughed. "You don't get enough? You want it now?"

Margo backed up against the car's locked door and peddled kicked. "Get away from me." He knew what lay beneath her gown: nothing. It was difficult to distinguish her flesh from the seat's soft leather. "Get off me!" she yelled, yanking his head from side to side by his ears.

"I hate you!"

"But you love this."

Aaron adjusted the rearview mirror that had been kicked out of place. Shifting his car into gear, he looked back at his sexually spent wife lying face down on the backseat.

"So much for shutting me off."

Chapter Twenty-Five

"Breakfast in bed?" Margo questioned with a yawn. "Someone wants a favor."

"An opportunity," Aaron called out from the shower.

"I can't hear you." The water slowed to a trickle.

"I think you'll enjoy this assignment," Aaron said as he dried his scalp with a monogrammed towel. "The hospital is planning to build a health center on Blue Hill Ave. We're in search of benefactors. I'm asking you to have lunch with Mrs. Zeigler. She's a very wealthy widow who grew up on Eire Street and wants to help revitalize her old neighborhood."

Margo lowered her teacup. "I don't think any amount of money can bring the area back to its former glory. So, what's her backstory?"

"Mrs. Zeigler is in the autumn... late autumn of her years, yet she's spry and well preserved. Mildred, emphasis on 'dred,' began working in a sweatshop at the tender age of twelve, her good looks and feminine wiles won the heart of the owner's son, Zigfried."

"Ziggy Zeigler!"

"You've heard of him?"

"As children, Mae would occasionally take us into Bloomfields, Mort would tease us and tell us there was a boogieman named Ziggy Zeigler who kidnaps unruly little girls."

"That's not far from the truth. The boogieman ran off to Paris with his fourteen-year-old bride. Ziggy finagled a job for Mildred with the House of Paquin. When Ziggy died a few years ago, Mildred inherited a bundle. Now she's back in Boston, living at the Copley Plaza, where you are meeting her tomorrow. We desperately need her financial backing, and you're just the man to get it. You'll need a new dress for the occasion. Take my credit card."

"The last time the card was in my custody, you had to use a defibrillator to revive it."

Aaron brought her hand to his lips and kissed it. "Money is no object when it comes to making my wife happy."

"You drive a hard bargain."

"Mrs. Zeigler is toying with us. One minute she's on board, the next minute she's jumping ship. We offered her a position on the finance committee, but that's not enough; she wants a hand with the design. It's a clinic, not a cocktail dress, but try telling her that."

"I will."

***

The Dining room offered a postcard view of Trinity Church and a carpet so plush, Margo had the sensation of walking on a mattress.

A dashing dead ringer for David Niven in a suit worthy of Aaron's closet greeted Margo as she scanned the surroundings for her hostess.

"I'm Mrs. Hirsh. Mrs. Zeigler is expecting me."

A gravelly voice, glazed in a French accent, crackled from a dark corner of a bright dining room. "What I expected was to witness Venus rising, so says your husband."

"My husband is biased."

"I'm not. You're lovely."

Her skin was a tight fit for her frame. Silver bangs hung like tinsel sprouting from a lilac petal hat, hiding any evidence of a plastic surgeon's craftsmanship. Women of wealth seldom divulge their age, but their hands do. Hers were gloved to the elbow. Margo positioned herself in the center of the horseshoe-shaped upholstered booth. "What a privilege to meet you, Mrs. Zeigler."

"Mildred."

"Mildred. My husband is seldom impressed by medical laymen but finds you fascinating." The compliment brought a blush to Mildred's kabuki-powdered face. A slight nod and a young waiter stood tableside like a genie summoned from his lamp.

"Two Gibsons. You do drink?"

"Yes," Margo lied.

"Splendid. Am I correct to assume you were sent to win me over?"

"Win you over?"

"The health center."

"Not my original intent; however, it would be a feather in my cap."

"I applaud your candor. I've been playing hard to get with the board. I love to be courted. I visited the proposed site. It's blighted. I'm much older than you, Mrs. Hirsh."

"Margo," she blurted. It was her intention to use her birth name, but her chosen name reached her lips first, which proved to be a fortunate slip. The gin martini sent Margo's head into a dervish spin.

"I remember a time, Margo, when Mount Nottingham was home to some of Boston's most prominent businessmen. Now, there's not a white face to be found."

"You're mistaken. My mother still lives on the Mount."

"Goodness, why?" "Stubborn, proud. I'm concerned for her safety."

"Where exactly does your mother live?"

"Thirteen Mount Nottingham, I was raised there."

"Number 13, oh dear. We're purchasing the vacant lot behind your mother's house. The city may require additional parking— there's a possibility her house could be taken by eminent domain. You can rest assured the city will compensate her handsomely. Number 13 was the Lindsey house."

"Why, yes. We purchased the property from Mrs. Lindsey's estate."

"Claudia Mishell- Lindsey."

"She was Jewish?"

"They all were m'dear. Back then, the Mount was known as Heeb Hill."

"Mr. Lindsey?" Margo gingerly asked.

"Linksy. He Anglicized his name from Hymen Linksy to Henry Lindsey. He was a diamond merchant. The bulk of the family fortune was hers. Are you familiar with the house's history?"

"Only that it's haunted."

"I don't have an appetite for gossip, but local legends have longevity."

Margo circled the rim of her cocktail glass with her finger. "Legends?"

"When I lived in Paris, I employed a cook named Genevieve, who once worked for the Lindseys. Coming from the area, I was curious about the goings on at Number 13. I never saw the interior, but the staircase was said to be a work of art. Are you aware that it was the center of a lawsuit?

"No."

"Mr. Lindsey purchased a New York mansion from a financier friend who had fallen on hard times. The two brokered a deal: Mr. Lindsey would buy his friend's mansion, then sell it back at a profit once the man regained his financial footing. It was a gentleman's agreement. Unfortunately, Mr. Lindsey wasn't a gentleman. The property was returned sans the staircase. Alas, Mr. Lindsey met his fate at the foot of the stairs. His son Robert also fell to his death from the balcony. Thus, the tale of the vindictive staircase became lore. It's said Mr. Lindsey's friend had a curse put on the staircase, that all the Lindseys and their descendants would lose their lives on the staircase."

Margo felt as Pandora had on opening the forbidden box. "How did a young man like Robert fall off a balcony?"

"He didn't fall, he jumped, or so they say. According to Genevieve, Robert lost his leg fighting in the Philippines. His face was also marred. Once home, he had a tryst with an Irish housemaid named Nuala. A femme fatale name if ever there was one."

The narration was interrupted as Mildred eyed their empty glasses. "Jonathan."

"Yes, Madam."

Margo cringed at the prospect of downing another shot of gin, but a snoot may loosen Mildred's tongue and jog her memory.

"Smoke?"

"I do, but I can't."

"Ah, yes, a doctor's wife."

Their iced martinis arrived on a silver tray. Jonathan lit Madame's Gitanes Blonde cigarette that slid snugly into a four-inch onyx holder that she waved like a baton as she spoke. Fearing the conversation would drift to another subject, Margo's wet brain scrambled for a question. "This Nuala, was she a willing participant?"

"Back in the day, the well-to-do cast a blind eye to dalliances with the help. Genevieve claimed the two were devoted to one another. Alas, a scullery maid, found the couple in flagrante delicto. While making a hasty retreat, Robert pushed Nuala aside, breaking a railing spindle and Nuala's heart."

"Was Nuala dismissed?"

"The scullery maid claimed to have letters Nuala had written detailing the affair and threatened to expose the couple. She was unaware that Nuala was illiterate. A photograph of Robert in a silver frame was stolen from Mrs. Lindsey's nightstand. It has never recovered. Each maid blamed each other. Both were dismissed. Weeks later, voila! Nuala's pregnant." Margo felt queasy knowing she was about to enter a door her grandmother had nailed shut. "What happened to the baby?"

"Since all parties involved are dead, I have the license to repeat the story. Mrs. Lindsey sent Genevieve to France under the guise that she had given birth to the boy."

"Boy?"

"There was a twin, a girl. She remained with her mother in King Solomon's bargain. Nuala was compensated for sacrificing her son with a diamond ring."

"She sold her son for a diamond! Why didn't she throw the girl in for matching earrings?"

"Mrs. Lindsey had no knowledge of the girl. She wanted the family name carried on, so she was only told there was a boy. Mrs. Lindsey was French by birth and had family in Paris. She was grand in her ways, claimed she descended from the Rothschilds, if you can believe that."

"I'd like to," Margo said in a soft whisper.

"Robere was raised in the lap of luxury. The couple continued their clandestine affair long after the twins were born. The two carried on in Robert's Tin Lizzy. As I mentioned, Robert lost his leg, so Nuala served as a chauffeur as well as his paramour. A delicious tale, someone should put it to pen and paper." Like a gunslinger prepared to exit a saloon, Margo knocked back her drink.

"What makes you think all parties are dead? The twins would be entering their sixties."

"Robere was an army officer, killed in the war. He left a wife and children. When Mrs. Lindsey died, her lawyers set out to find her heirs, but none were found. Transported seems to be the likely scenario."

"A death camp?"

"C'est la vie. Fate is fickle. The pauper daughter was the fortunate one after all. There are things money can't buy. Pity Robert never revealed her existence; she'd be a very wealthy woman today."

Margo gulped. "Just how much money are we talking about?"

"Not Rothchild rich, but enough that any descendants wouldn't have to work a day in their lives."

Margo released a sigh like that of a small, dying bird. Red lights splintered the lens of her eyes. Stinging bees raced through her veins. Her mother's life had been layered with lies and myths. Twenty years ago, she bought a house that she rightfully owned. It still carried a mortgage. Mrs. Zeigler signaled the waiter. Margo made her apologies. "I'm a bit woozy, I must be going."

Mildred waved her gloved hand. "Nonsense, sit, there's more to tell. They say Robert plunged to his death on hearing the news that Nuala had returned to Ireland with the girl. Having a wooden leg, he probably lost his balance on a scatter rug, but everyone loves a love story, so the romantic version became neighborhood lore. Wealth makes fertile soil for rumors. I can attest to that."

"No trace of Nuala?"

"None. More than likely, she was swallowed up with the other Irish immigrant girls raising children in drunken... sorry, I didn't mean to offend you."

"No offence taken. It appears I'm only one-quarter Irish. I'm Swedish and ...ish, ish."

Mildred sucked a long drag off her long cigarette. "Time marches on. The neighborhood needs a health center. Number 13 is a sad reminder of a bygone era. Will you be accompanying your husband on his humanitarian mission to Israel?"

"No, I'd just be in the way."

"When does he leave?"

"He'll be packing his bags as soon as I get home."

"Did you drive here?"

"No, I arrived by taxi."

"The doorman will have one waiting for you. I so enjoyed myself," Mrs. Zeigler said with an extended hand. "I'm going to suggest you replace me on the finance committee. I'm a figurehead. You're ahead with a figure." The two women laughed and kissed one another's cheeks. "Au revoir."

"Au Revoir," Margo echoed.

Flopping into the backseat of a waiting taxi, her ears stung from the truth, her head spun from the alcohol. "Some lunch, no food but a feast of information. My husband is leaving me, and my mother is a Jewlic."

***

Pacing the library's carpeted floor, Margo consulted her jeweled wristwatch. Shrugging her shoulders, she poured herself another whiskey. Alerted by the purr of Aaron's car engine, she resumed her rehearsed pose, perched cross-legged on Aaron's beloved desk that now held a nasty water ring. She counted out his footsteps as she drummed her nails on the iced crystal tumbler.

Aaron carelessly tossed his raincoat onto the loveseat and deeply exhaled as he stood before his wife like a soldier in the presence of a senior officer. "Go ahead, Margo; hit me with it," he said, slapping both hands on the side of his thighs.

Drink in hand, Margo slid off the desk. "One word. Israel."

"I don't know what you're talking about."

"It's a country in the Middle East. One you plan on running off to."

"There's talk of war, I'm flirting with the idea of volunteering my services."

"That's not all you're flirting with and volunteering your services to. Your Zionist zeal surfaced when you met that pussy person."

"When I treated wounded soldiers at Reed, you called me noble. I do the same for Israelis, and you accuse me of desertion. You're a mean drunk with a dirty mind."

Freon hissed through her veins. "I may only have a twelfth-grade education, buddy boy, but I've gotta PhD in men. When does the caravan leave? I want to pack your fiddle. You will be fiddling?"

"You'll never understand. I'm the son of a survivor; Israel is my ancestral home. I know the risk I'm taking. I'm doing this for my parents, not me."

"Don't you dare use your parents to justify an extramarital affair! You're the one who forced them out of the neighborhood they called home since coming to this country. They knew the risk they were taking. They weren't fearful. Sound familiar? I'm divorcing you."

Aaron bobbed his head. "Again, with the divorce. What will your saintly mother think of having a divorced daughter?"

Margo leaned into his ear. "She'll be thrilled."

"She'll take you back?"

"I'm going nowhere. You're the one dodging bullets in a war zone to get laid."

"You stink of tobacco and booze."

Margo fluttered her empty glass. "Time to refresh my drinkie."

"You disgust me." The insult was met by a slap of whisky in his face.

"Wipe it off," Aaron calmly ordered. Margo tossed his raincoat on the floor and draped herself across the loveseat. "Fuck you."

Aaron pulled her up by her chin and to his face. "I said, wipe it off."

"I'll do one better." Margo dragged her tongue across his rough beard and licked her lips. "That's how I wipe up a drink."

Returning from the sideboard with a drink in hand, Aaron slowly poured it down his pants. "Wipe it up."

***

The house was sweltering. Berta sat on the back porch cooling herself with a homemade cardboard fan. She'd spent the past few nights sleeping on a recliner in the TV room. The second-floor bedrooms were too hot. Colleen had an internship at the Cape Cod Playhouse, escaping the city heat, and wouldn't be back until after Labor Day. Alone in the house these past months, Berta found she'd begun to talk to herself aloud. "Perhaps I should cave to Colleen's plea to adopt a dog. Why bother? I'd grow fond of the animal, and it would die or run off like all the others. Patsy no longer brings the boy around. Just as well, he's a reminder of Rosaria. This is a jealous house. It wants me to itself."

Berta looked across the yard at the backyard swing. Tim was so proud of that swing. "Oh, Timmy, what have I done? You were the only person I ever shared a laugh with. Yours was the only shoulder I cried on, and I killed you. I should have let you drink. It was the only pleasure in life left to you. I should have had Rosaria vaccinated; had I, she wouldn't have been paralyzed, escaped the fire, and found a more suitable mate. I chased Nuala off, with good reason. You would have accepted Aaron. I can't... I refuse to. It's my fault this family was cursed. If I had never been born... I'm afraid I'll be the only one this house keeps alive."

***

The sun crawled through the bedroom's drawn shades as Margo curled up to her husband's chest. "Six am, time to get up, Dr. Hirsh. You have an eight o'clock meeting."

Aaron kissed Margo's inner thighs. "I'll tell you what I want."

"What you want is illegal in this state."

"So, we move to Alabama."

Margo kicked Aaron off the bed. "Time to hit the shower."

"Care to join me?"

Margo held the bathroom door open. "After you."

"How do I look?" Aaron asked, indulging in a final homage to his reflection in the bedroom mirror.

"Satisfied."

"I will be once I make my announcement to the board this morning."

"What announcement?"

"I was going to give you the good news tonight, but it's only fair you be the first to know. I'm resigning from the hospital."

"But... but you can't! You're the top doc; you've worked tirelessly to get where you are. It's been your dream to become the Chief Surgeon. People fly in from around the world for a consult."

"My point exactly. I've reached the summit; there are no more mountains to climb. I want a life outside of the hospital." Aaron held Margo in his arms and kissed her forehead. "We've been through a rough patch in our marriage due to my blind ambition. I want to change that."

"Seeing a marriage counselor helped. We haven't fought in months." Margo's face suddenly turned dark as she backed away. "You're going to Israel. You promised you would never leave me. You promised I'd never be afraid again. You promised!"

"I'm not going anywhere. I'll have more time for us."

"What will you do?"

"Take some time off, teach. I wouldn't do this if we weren't financially secure."

"Will Stan take over your practice?"

"Stan is taking a position at Mount Sinai in New York. He was never happy in Boston."

The couple walked to the front door, where they shared a kiss. "Now I can spend time being a husband and father."

Her brain refused to absorb the words. Her skin shrank as the phrase seeped into her pores. "Father?"

"We can discuss it tonight. I'll be home early, we'll celebrate." Margo stood frozen, watching Aaron drive off. *"He must know. It's a joke. Aaron doesn't joke."*

Margo rummaged through her closet for a hidden stash of cigarettes. Her hand was unsteady for a match; she flicked a lighter and continued the conversation with herself. *"We never discussed children, not before or after we married. He forgot. Nobody forgets something like that."* She smoked and paced. *"Maybe he found a doctor who can fix me or wants to adopt. Why did Colleen take that internship? I need to talk to her."*

Margo fell face down on the sofa and wept. "I should have listened to you, Mae. I'm sorry, I'm sorry."

Aaron arrived home early as promised. "The worst is over," he announced with a kiss, not noticing Margo's swollen eyes. "In two weeks, I'm a free man. Let's go out for dinner, somewhere romantic." Margo gripped the fireplace's mantel; her shoulders sagged. Aaron rubbed her back.

"You're upset."

Her voice shook. "You mentioned children."

"Not right away, but eventually. Don't tell me you're afraid of losing your figure?"

"No, my husband."

"I'm not going anywhere. I plan on being a hands-on father, not when it comes to diaper duty."

"Aaron, please, stop. I can't have children. I thought you knew." The admission landed her face down on the sofa with her husband standing over her.

"You tricked me."

"No! I swear. You knew. You must have known."

"What am I, clairvoyant?"

"You were my doctor, you knew!"

"I was never your doctor."

"You were!" Tears accompanied her plea. "When I was in that car accident, you examined my leg, you saw my chart, knew my uterus had ruptured, knew I lost a baby."

Aaron lowered his voice to a snarl. "No, Margo, I didn't know. Had I known, I never would have married you."

"That's a lie. You know, you've always known."

"I wasn't your doctor. I just stopped in to examine your leg. A leg is not a uterus, I thought even you knew the difference."

"My chart, you opened it to find my name, you read it."

"Even if I had, which I didn't, I'm supposed to remember some patient's complication years later?"

"I wasn't some patient! I was the woman you loved. The woman you promised to always love."

"You were no more than a whiny teenager. You meant nothing to me. I only stopped in on you because you were Rosaria's sister. Did it ever cross your pea brain to refresh my memory?"

"You never brought the subject up, never mentioned birth control. When we went to Miami, you said how lucky we were not to have children, be able to travel."

"There's a lot of assuming going on in this marriage," Aaron lectured with a finger in her face.

Margo stood up. "I assumed you married me because you loved me, not to bear your children."

"And you assumed I'd be so taken with your physical appeal that once your infertility came to light, it wouldn't matter to me. Well, it does."

"You married me for sex, someone to parade around, make men wonder what you had in your pants to have a woman like me. Where does love enter the equation? I loved you from the moment I set eyes on you. I want to continue loving you even if you don't love me. There must be a doctor who can fix me, a treatment, or some procedure they can do. I still have all my parts."

"You're missing the most important part, your brain."

"And you lack a heart!"

Aaron stormed into the bedroom. Margo followed. "What are you doing?"

"What does it look like? I'm packing." Margo grabbed his arm. He wrenched it free. "I gave up my position for you."

"I never asked you to. You didn't feel the need to consult me." Aaron pushed her to the floor and stepped over her.

"Where are you going?"

Aaron picked up his crumpled raincoat. "Find a doctor who can fix you. I'm not him.

***

Margo snapped up the phone on the first ring. "Aaron? Aaron, is that you?"

"It's me! I'm back!" Colleen joyfully announced. "I can't wait to tell you about the theatre company. You'll never guess who I got to work with. Are you sitting down? Robert Goulet! What a cool guy and what a voice." Colleen sang into the phone. "*If ever I would leave you...*"

"HE LEFT ME!" Margo wailed.

"Simmer down. Aaron would never leave you. He loves you, fears you. What good would he be to another woman when his manhood has been hacked off?"

"This is serious, Colleen. She's ugly."

"I'll be right over."

Margo met her sister at the front door. "I hate him. He promised he'd never leave me, and he left." She said, taking her anger out on a sofa pillow. "I hate him. I hate him." Her voice trailed off. "I love him. I love him."

391

Colleen walked her sister into the kitchen. "I'll make coffee." Margo rested her head on the table as Colleen consoled her grieving sister. "Did he admit to the affair?"

"No. They never do. He left me because I can't give him children."

"He must have known."

"Of course, he knew. It was a convenient excuse to run off with that Hungarian sea hag."

"Hungary is landlocked."

"I don't need a geography lesson."

"You do but now is not the time. Where did he meet the hag?"

Margo put on a Zsa Zsa Gabor accent. "She is very intelligent Dr. Pussy who comes to very big hospital to be under tutelage of very famous, very important man who teaches her much." Margo broke out of character. "You know what really pisses me off? He confirmed Ma's prediction. She said he'd leave me for one of his own. She was right. She's always right. I hate her for it. He'll be sorry. Prior to meeting me, he didn't have much experience with the fairer sex. He doesn't know how our minds work, what evil we're capable of."

"You don't seriously believe Aaron never dated?"

"He may have, but they were nice girls like Rosaria. I was his first, and he hit one out of the ballpark. Now he thinks he's God's gift to women." Margo pounded her fist on the table. "I'm hiring a lawyer. A handsome lawyer. I'll claim desertion."

"Keep your chin up," Colleen encouraged. "You'll find another sexual deviant."

"NOT LIKE HIM!"

Chapter Twenty-Six

Invitations lay scattered over Aaron's desk. Colleen eyed an ivory letter opener. "Am I allowed to carve my initials?"

"No," Margo reprimanded. "I'll tell you what you can do."

"If it's licking stamps, count me out."

"Save your saliva. I want you to come with me to the fundraiser."

"You don't need me there."

"I do. I do. This will be my first public appearance since Aaron's departure."

"You'll be hobnobbing while I'm out back playing cards with the kitchen help."

"You need to get out. You spend too much time in your own company. I won't let you spend the best years of your life sitting around studying. I'll dress you up, it will be like prom night."

Colleen stared out the window. "No, it won't."

"Grab your bag, we're going shopping."

***

"That wasn't so bad, was it?" Margo asked as she piled garment bags and shoe boxes on the bed.

"I never knew how lovely Neiman Marcus was in summer. I may vacation there."

"I do. Now get dressed, I'm running the show, so we must arrive early."

Built in 1902, the exclusive Chamberlain Towers Hotel retained a turn-of-the-century elegance. Its exterior archways, turrets, and watchful gargoyles had grown a decades-old beard of English ivy. A brass-buttoned doorman ushered the sisters into the Gilded Age. Colleen marveled at the multi-tiered staircase in the heavily cushioned and curtained lobby.

A crystal chandelier hung from the 40-foot-high ceiling above a plush circular banquette settee flanked by potted palm plants. The dim lighting shone a flattering glow on the mirrored wall panels of the palatial ballroom inhabited by the ghosts of flappers in fringed dresses and spats-wearing gents foxtrotting on the parquet dance floor.

The room was old when the hotel was new. Colleen's head spun. "How did you snag this place?"

Margo's eyes swept the ballroom for a familiar face. "It's owned by The Melbourne Corporation, an Australian company, I'm guessing. They're kind enough to donate the space whenever we need it."

"Don't let me keep you from mingling. I'll just sit here looking at you adoringly like everyone else."

"I didn't bring you here to be a wallflower. I'll introduce you to the staff."

"I don't want to tag alongside you like a puppy dog." Colleen spotted a guest attempting to catch Margo's eye. "You're wanted."

"She can wait."

"Go."

"Okay, but I'll be back in a jiff."

Colleen studied her sister crossing the room as if she were walking on air. Since the death of Rosaria, Margo lost her zeal for dancing. Perhaps tonight she would shine. Alone, listening to the pianist play "Moonlight Becomes You," Colleen felt like Daisy Buchanan at an Astor soiree awaiting the arrival of Jay Gatsby; she needn't wait long. A deep, robust laugh rose above the music and chatter. Colleen turned her head under the guise of adjusting a loose earring, a tactic that had served her well in the past.

He was tall, very tall, fair-haired, with a face that hadn't matured with his body, the way she imagined Santa Claus looked in his youth. Listening attentively to a colleague's joke, the young Chris Cringle slapped the narrator's back with a "Ho-ho-ho." His broad smile signaled that her ruse hadn't fooled him.

Colleen wished she'd checked for the location of the ladies' room on her arrival rather than taking note of the fire exits. Given the room's age and elegance, she suspected the facilities were concealed behind a false bookcase. In desperation, she made her way to the bar. The gentle giant blocked her path. Wagging his finger and squinting his cocktail eyes, he gave her the old, haven't we met? Look. "Cardio?" he asked in a thick drawl.

"Wino. Now shove off, I'm responding to an emergency at the bar."

"Aren't you too young to drink?"

"Aren't you too old to be hitting on a girl who's too young to drink?"

Hands over his heart, he wore a sad clown expression. "You wounded my pride."

"I'll wound your groin if you don't step aside."

"And wake me from this dream?"

"Just who are you?"

"Doctor Clayton Vaughan at your service."

"What is your service?"

"Gynecology."

"Are you drunk?"

"Yes, ma'am."

"Spoken by an honest man."

"First compliment of the evening."

"You expect more to come?"

"If I play my cards right."

"You're playing solitaire, Doc."

"Please join me, I'm seated up front."

"How did you score a table up front? I happen to know that table set you back three large."

"My daddy is... was, loaded."

"My daddy is... was loaded. All that bought me was a reputation." Taking a seat, Clay leaned back in his chair.

"Waiter, a bourbon rocks and a Shirley Temple for Captain January."

"The name's Colleen Ronan."

Their drinks arrived. Clay raised his glass. "To Colleen Ronan, down the hatch."

"Cin cin."

"Here's mud in your eye."

"Slainte."

"Salute."

"Bottoms up, gynie."

"In full disclosure, I'm a gynecological oncologist. I'm more intrigued by cancer than female anatomy, except for that woman." Clay raised his glass to Margo as if toasting a bride.

"Her? If you think her mason will meet your dick son, you're delusional."

"Think she's too good for me?"

"I think she's too old for you."

"I don't mind warming up leftovers."

"Leftovers"! You're more insulting than I am, and that's saying something!"

"Allow me to explain. She was left behind by Dr. Aaron Hirsh, The Dr. Aaron Hirsh."

"Is he dead?"

"Probably wishes he were. He left that exquisite specimen of womanhood for the Crazy Israeli. That's what we called her."

"Who's we?"

"Everyone at the hospital. Her name is Magdala Pouzy, rhymes with choosy, which she isn't. She's the kind of ugly that makes your eyes sting. She came to Boston to study, but her pursuits were not academic in nature. She was in search of a wealthy doctor to take back with her."

"If she wasn't choosy, why didn't she hit on you? You're loaded?"

"I'm not one of the Chosen People. She didn't get a bite until she bit Dr. Hirsh."

"She sounds like a vampire."

"It's no joke. This Pouzy character is dangerous; she stalked more than one doctor who spurred her advances." Clay's hand embraced his amber elixir as he pointed to Margo with his pinkie finger.

"Look how she holds sway over the crowd; it's truly an art."

"Are you going to pick up where her husband left off?"

"Me? No. She's a prize for Cary Grant, not Ernest Borgnine."

Colleen crinkled her nose as if detecting a sour odor. "She's attractive in a coarse sort of way. I know her type, she's a grifter, a money-grubbing grifter."

"I hate to face the jury you're on!"

"Don't believe me? Open your wallet."

"What?"

"Your wallet, open it, flash the cash, and she'll come running like a filly at Belmont."

"Are you crazy?"

"Wanna bet?"

"I'm not a betting man, but what do I have to lose?"

"The contents of your wallet. If she comes over, the money is mine."

"If I win, what's the prize?"

"Whatever your little 'ole heart desires."

"You're on."

Clay kept a cautious eye on Colleen as he removed the wallet from his jacket pocket. Five drinks had left his fingers numb. The wallet belly flopped to the floor. "Second time tonight it tried to run away."

While he focused on the floor, Colleen waved Margo over. Clay grasped the carpet. "I know it's down here. Wait...wait, I got it."

Margo tapped her toe on the fugitive wallet. Clay's eyes crawled up Margo's leg. "Ma'am?" he said with a gulp.

Colleen stepped in. "Mrs. Hirsh, this is Dr. Clayton Vaughan."

"A pleasure to make your acquaintance, Doctor. I must warn you: my sister is a prankster."

Looking like the cat who caught the canary, Colleen batted her eyelids.

"I've discovered her talent firsthand."

Margo offered hers. "Forgive me, I can't stay and chat, but I do hope we meet again." Clay fell back into his chair, watching Margo wiggle across the room as Colleen counted out her winnings. "Two hundred and seven dollars!"

"My children will starve, but take it, you outfoxed me."

"Your children eat at expensive restaurants."

"I apologize for my rude comments; I was out of line, but there's no denying your sister is divine."

Colleen's heart sank. Margo always received compliments on her appearance and style, while Colleen only provided a laugh track.

Clay jerked his head toward the dance floor. "Care to trip the light fantastic?"

He danced like a circus bear lumbering from side to side. His chest felt warm against her cheek, his damp dress shirt smelled like Poppy. Closing her eyes, she was dancing with her dad at Rosaria's wedding. They were all together that day, Rosaria, Poppy, and Mae. She wept into Clay's shirt, hoping he didn't notice. He hadn't. "My makeup is running. I better go to the ladies' room and powder my nose."

With Margo schmoozing and Clay nodding off at the table, Colleen inched her way to the bar. Partially veiling her face, she ordered a bourbon. The bartender raised a brow. She answered his expression. "For him."

"You're too young, and he's too drunk, but I happen to know he won't be driving."

"No?"

"He lives upstairs." Cloaking the drink with her wrap, Colleen ducked into a bathroom stall and gulped the drink down.

As the evening wore on, the couple's laughter grew louder, competing with the orchestra. Margo hawked the ballroom, no sign of Colleen. She desperately maneuvered her way through the exiting crowd. Questioning her vision, she squinted her eyes to watch her sister on the veranda in the arms of a man. Margo knew the day would arrive, but him? Dumfounded, she held her breath and her hand to her abdomen. *"They're kissing! She's kissing him the way I would!"* She knew she shouldn't look, but like a car wreck, she couldn't take her eyes off the oral collision.

Clay clung to Colleen's arm as Margo tugged on the other. "We are leaving," Margo ordered.

"When will I see you again?" Clay slurred, "So I can win my money back... where's my wallet? I've been pinched."

"And pickled," Colleen chuckled. "Check your jacket."

"Whaddya know!" he exclaimed, waving the wallet as he rocked on unsteady feet. Colleen slapped her drunken dance partner's back. "Gotta go, Doc."

Clay pawed her arm. "Wait, wait, let me get my number. I mean, your number, I wanna see you again."

Colleen scribbled her phone number on a cocktail napkin. "Just so you know, we're sisters, not roommates."

"The thought never entered my mind."

"Then you're gay."

Clay waved the numbered napkin. "We'll see, won't we?"

Margo took her anger out on the car's clutch. "Are you satisfied? You made a total ass of yourself."

Slouching with her eyes closed, and head resting against the car's passenger window, waving her arms as though conducting an orchestra, Colleen sang out. "Is everybody a hippie?"

Margo closed her eyes as she spoke. "You- are- intoxicated."

"I'm feeling groooovy."

"That man got you drunk. He knew you were a minor, yet he plied you with liquor."

"He's not a man, he's a doctor, undress him as one."

"He's a churlish predator who should lose his medical license. By God, if Aaron were still at the hospital..."

"But he ain't."

"I pray you haven't inherited your father's insatiable thirst for alcohol."

"Ya know what you are? A prude. Now that you're alone, you're even prudier."

"I'll tell you what you are. You're the pathetic product of a soulless alcoholic couple who forged an alliance with the devil for a drink, resulting in the birth of a satanically conceived lower form of life."

One eye dead closed, Colleen twirled her finger in Margo's face. "Ya know what your problem is? Ya don't know how to have a good time. You're an old stick in the mud."

"Your name will be mud when Ma gets a load of you."

"Ya know what she's gonna say? She's gonna say. 'That sister of yours wuz too preoccupied lookin' to replace that daddy killin' Jew bastard doctor that she didn't notice you wuz drinkin.'" The accusation was punctuated with a hiccup.

"So, help me, Colleen, if you puke in this car, I'll throw you out and back over you." Colleen stuck her finger down her throat.

"You won't think it's funny tomorrow when you're making love to the toilet bowl."

"Does a toilet flush when it comes?"

"Get out. You can stagger home."

"Okie dokie, but I'm not going home. I'm going to the Towers." Colleen waved a set of keys dangling from a peace symbol key chain.

"He lives there."

"Those are your keys, you horse's ass. He couldn't afford a night at The Towers; it cost a fortune to stay there."

"He thinks I'm worth it." Colleen tugged at the door handle. "Let me out."

Margo automatically unlocked the car door, sending Colleen tumbling to the pavement. "Oopsie daisy."

Margo pounded her head on the steering wheel. "How did I get myself into this mess?" She packed the legless Colleen into the car's backseat. Her eyes closed, Colleen sat in silence for the remainder of the ride home. Chin to chest, her head bounced to the rhythm of the road.

Her rude awakening came with repetitive slaps to her face. "Okay! Okay!" Stumbling from the car, she placed her hands on its hood to steady herself.

"Get off my car and into the house," Margo ordered. Watching her sister zigzag up the walkway in a drunken game of pin the tail on the donkey, Margo reluctantly came to Colleen's aid. With her arms slung over Margo's shoulder, Colleen broke into song.

"Strangers in the night."

"God, not the singing."

"Exchanging glances LOOOOVERS at first sight, what were the chances?"

"Let's get you inside. Where are your keys?"

"I know, I know, don't tell me... I give up. Where did ja put them?" Margo pushed Colleen into the wicker chair next to the front door. Rapidly ringing the doorbell, she scurried to her car, leaving her mother to listen to the song's last line. "It turned out so right for strangers in the night. Scooby, dooby, do."

She heard cracking from an aluminum ice tray, one after another, four trays. The cubes dropped into a bucket of water. Having witnessed her mother administer an Irish baptism on Poppy, Colleen knew if she didn't lock her bedroom door, she'd become the olive in a mattress martini, shaken and stirred. The phone rang, Colleen rejoiced.. Execution postponed.

With a huff, Berta put down her bucket to answer the phone. "Hello."

"Colleen?" the male caller asked.

"This is her mother speaking."

"Forgive me, Mrs. Ronan, your daughter shares your voice."

"She'll appreciate you saying so."

"I'm Dr. Clayton Vaughan. I had the pleasure of meeting Colleen last night at the fundraiser Margo hosted—she's a tireless worker. You must be proud of her."

"One would think. Colleen! The phone, now!"

Her brain had grown a coat of fur that ran down her throat. Her stomach felt as if it had been put through a blender.

Colleen cleared her morning voice and reached for her bedside phone. "Dr. Vaughan, how good of you to call."

"I feared you might hang up on me."

"You got past my mother. I owe you a few minutes of my time."

"Your mother, how shall I phrase it?"

"Oozes with warmth and wit."

"Now I know where you get yours."

"Seems like we're picking up where we left off."

Clay gulped. "Yes, um, about last night. You wouldn't know it from my performance, but I'm rather shy. I noticed you when you arrived. I needed liquid courage to approach you. I'm not on service Friday, I'd like to spend the day with you."

Colleen fought to contain her excitement. "My body is paying the price, but I enjoyed myself last night for the first time in a long time. I'd love to see you again."

"Shall I come by your home?"

"No, you'll never find it. I'll meet you in the hospital lobby. If that's okay?"

"Of course, the lobby at noon, on Friday. I look forward to seeing you again."

Colleen held the receiver to her chest before slowly returning it to the cradle. Twenty years old, this will be her first date. As Aaron pointed out, the prom didn't count.

Chapter Twenty-Seven

"Brigham Circle," the trolley conductor announced. A line formed at the accordion door opening out to a rotary across from the Peter Bent Brigham Hospital, for whom the circle was named. The rotary monument post was trimmed with a broad cement rim, which served as seating for intoxicated panhandlers, interfering with the flow of traffic.

Colleen felt a pang in her stomach. Had it not been for her mother, surely Poppy would have been among the men in tattered coats sitting on the rotary's trampled grass. *"What about Clay? Could Margo be right?"* Was a stethoscope all that stood between him and the squadron of squatters? Did she want to take the mantle of strong savior? Why else would Clay be drawn to her?

"Colleen!" a voice called out, breaking into her internal dialogue. "I spotted you getting off the trolley. I'm all yours, beautiful."

"Don't call me beautiful. I may find myself believing you." Clay rubbed her chilly fingers the way Rosaria had during their winter walks to school. "Clay, are we on a date?"

"Why do you ask?"

"I want to know who's paying."

Clay slid her pocketbook off her shoulder and shook it. "I'm paying. Why don't we walk over to The Towers for lunch? It offers a magnificent view of the Emerald Necklace. I'm always rushing to the hospital, never taking the time to stop and admire this glorious park. What better time than autumn?" The couple strolled through crackling leaves that sounded like rustling dress paper.

"Do you like Boston or just the views?" Colleen asked, leaning over one of the park's stone bridges to watch the slow-flowing stream. Clay rocked his hand from side to side. "The change of seasons is a feast for the eyes, but surviving the winters? Not for me. I suppose New England is in your blood."

"It's all I've ever known."

"That's a big world out there."

"I'm only twenty, still in school; the world can wait."

Clay inhaled deeply. "I've never felt so alive since coming to Boston. I've learned so much at The Brigham. The cases are interesting, the research is cutting edge, I've met and mingled with some of the best minds in medicine, which includes your brother-in-law."

Colleen looked into Clay's eyes. "Someday you'll be the best-known doctor in Savannah."

"I don't want to be the best known. I want to be the best."

"You'll be the best loved. There's something to be said for one's bedside manner."

"Southern charm doesn't impress Southerners." Clay ended the statement with a deep kiss.

Colleen's lips formed a slow smile. "I'm impressed." As they walked toward the Towers, Colleen stopped. "Look!" she exclaimed, pointing up at a flock of Canada geese.

Clay rolled his head back to watch the birds take flight. "Reminds me of the Rachel Fields poem.

"Something told the wild geese,

It was time to go.

Though the fields lay golden,

Something whispered, Snow."

The screech of tires followed by the slam of a car door infuriated Berta, who'd just hung up on a carpenter who knew less about shingles than she did. "Replace wooden gutters with aluminum? Over my dead body."

Margo's voice echoed from the foyer. "Where is she?"

"I don't object to your coming here, but must you use your car to alert the neighbors of your arrival? Now what's this all about?"

"Your darling daughter has snagged one of the wealthiest bachelors in the country."

"You're back on the prowl?"

"Not me! Colleen. Where is she?"

"I haven't seen Scarlett since she met Rhet."

Margo hollered up to the attic. "Colleen! Get down here!"

Tying the belt to her flannel robe, Colleen stomped down the staircase like a pouting child. "What's worth waking me up at nine on a Saturday morning?"

"Do you have any idea who you've been dating?"

"Are you referring to the fat, balding, liquored-up Southerner who is the man of my dreams? Dreams I'd like to get back to." Colleen turned. "I'm going back to bed."

"Oh, no, you don't." Margo led her sister to the sofa. "Dr. Clayton Melbourne Vaughan is the only child of the late Dr. Duncan Vaughan and Roslin Melbourne Vaughan."

"Thanks for the genealogy lesson. May I go now?"

"No. Sit." Rolling her eyes, Colleen returned for further interrogation. Margo continued. "The world-renowned Melbourne-Vaughan Cancer Center in Savannah was named for his late mother, who succumbed to ovarian cancer. I've been doing some digging."

Berta looked up from her morning paper. "That will be the day you pick up a shovel, unless you're holding a map with an X on it."

Colleen shrugged her shoulders. "I know he's wealthy, so what?"

Margo's eyes lit up. "Tell me all about your date. Where did you go? What did you do? How much did he spend?"

"We had lunch at The Towers."

"I bet you didn't have to wait for a table. He owns the place! God only knows what else is in his portfolio. You're going to find out."

Colleen stood. "I'll do nothing of the sort."

"When are you seeing him again?"

"Next Sunday, he wants to meet the family."

"We don't have family... oh, no. He is not coming here."

"Ma's cooking dinner for the four of us, won't that be fun?"

"She's a lousy cook," Margo whispered.

"Then the company will have to be appetizing."

***

Colleen opened the door before Clay had the opportunity to ring the bell. Margo breezed into the room as the couple exchanged kisses. "Dr. Vaughan," Margo greeted with an extended hand. Clay kissed it. She placed her other hand over her heart. "I do declare."

Colleen led Clay to her mother. "Mom, this is Dr. Clayton Vaughan. Clay, I'd like you to meet my mother, Roberta."

"A pleasure," Clay said with a smile on his face and an eye on the staircase. "What a splendid home you have. Is it a Gould house?"

"There's a ghoul all right," Margo cracked.

Clay elaborated. "Augustus Warren Gould was the architect of many homes in the Boston area. I'm a great admirer of old homes and young ladies." Colleen found it embarrassing to be wooed in her mother's presence. Clay ran his hand over the staircase baluster. "I must say, I've never come across a staircase as regal as this; it rivals any I've seen on Beacon Hill or Nob Hill. I suspect it's not original to the house."

"You don't?" Margo probed.

"The front door and interior woodwork are oak. The staircase is mahogany. When these homes were built, it was desirable to have the woodwork uniform. I'd be interested in its history."

"It has a history of killing people."

Colleen took Clay's gifted bottle of wine. "I'll put this on ice."

"It's a Cabernet, it's served at room temperature," Clay informed with a smile. "I'll need a corkscrew; this vintage needs time to breathe." Clay followed Colleen into the pantry.

Margo nudged her mother. "He didn't waste time getting to the booze."

The dining room looked as it had a century earlier. The table and sideboard were orphaned by Mrs. Lindsey, The china,, a wedding gift to Berta and Fredrik. The heavy drapes shielded the peacock wallpaper from the sun.

"This roast is exceptional," Clay complimented his hostess. "Colleen led me to believe you lacked cooking skills."

"I'm surprised Colleen didn't lead you to believe I was dead."

"Speaking of dead –"

409

Colleen cut Margo off. "My mother and Margo have an ongoing feud. Margo thinks we should sell and move to the suburbs."

"Not only do I hate this house, but I also hate the neighborhood."

Clay took a sip of wine. "Hate a house this grand? Unthinkable."

Margo leaned forward. "That staircase killed four family members, possibly more."

"Four?"

"Yes, mother, four. Not only Grandma and Uncle Marty, but Mr. Lindsey and his son."

"Who told you that?"

"Grandma," Margo lied.

"She said no such thing."

Clay poured himself another glass of wine. "I find this intriguing."

Margo covered the rim of her wine glass, preventing Clay from replacing the few sips she'd taken.

"It's not intriguing, it's downright spooky, and I don't want my mother and sister killed. They're the only family I have."

"Have you considered consulting a medium?"

Berta directed a steely eye at Margo. "There's no hocus pocus here."

Clay turned to Colleen. "Where do you stand?"

"Margo is right, many have met their end on those stairs, but I love this house. Living here is worth the risk. Margo and my mother romanticize a dark fact."

"Me, romanticize? That's a first," Berta huffed.

Margo turned to Clay, with her back to her mother. "The hospital plans to build a health center a few blocks from here. The project is being partially funded by Mrs. Zeigler, who hails from the area and backs up my ghost theory."

Clay's eyes rotated around the room. "Haunted or not, I admire how you've painstakingly managed to keep it true to the period."

"It's called neglect," Colleen joked.

"Must you always poke fun? Dr. Vaughan was extending a compliment."

"No apology necessary, Mrs. Ronan, that's one of the qualities I love about your daughter."

The three women shot a "Did you hear that?" look at one another.

"My, my, where did you find that piano?"

"Where it stands," Berta answered. "It was here when we moved in."

Clay excused himself to investigate. "What a wonderful gift. They stopped making this model in the late 1800s."

Berta followed Clay to the musical monster. "We know very little about it."

"May I?" The doctor wiggled his fingers over the keys. "What will it be? Chopin, Gershwin, The Beatles?"

"Ragtime!" Colleen requested.

Margo tsked. "Doctor Vaughan is classically trained. He doesn't play such rubbish."

"I play whatever my audience requests. Ragtime it is." The silky strokes from the warm fingers of a skilled pianist relaxed the instrument's stiff spine that had spent years ignored, save for a passing pounding. The piano's chest muscles exhaled its theme song.

"That's the song it plays on its own!" Margo cried.

Clay abruptly halted his performance. "It's a player piano. I'm guessing a scroll is stuck inside. May I?"

Berta shrugged. "Be my guest." Clay clenched his teeth as he wrestled with the embedded scroll. A turn of the crank, the piano squealed as though she were about to give birth. "Success!" Clay read the musical brail with the same intensity he would a patient's test results. "Sure nuf, 'The Weeping Willow Rag.'" Colleen looked on in awe; her hero had drawn the sword from the stone.

Clay slapped both hands on his thighs and rose from the piano bench. "I must be on my way, rounds being at 6 am, and I need my beauty sleep." Catching sight of his reflection in the coat tree mirror, he paused. "I take it back, what I need is a beauty coma. What better way to have spent a Sunday afternoon than in the company of three lovely ladies?"

Colleen took hold of Clay's arm. "I'll walk you to the car."

The sisters crossed paths on the porch steps. Margo closed her eyes and deeply inhaled. "It's coming on Christmas, and I smell diamonds."

"He returns to Georgia next month."

"You'll have to work fast. Why not give him a going-away present, seal the deal, have the wedding before you show?"

Berta opened the front door. "I thought you left."

"Apparently, I'm no longer needed to amuse our guest."

"You're always the spoiler, Nuala."

"If you're insinuating I'm competing with Colleen, you're wrong."

"Mom! Margo! Stop! We had a wonderful day. We were laughing, there was music, I was proud of you both. For one fleeting moment, I thought maybe, just maybe, we could project some semblance of a normal family. Clayton never experienced this family's dark side; he never will. I'm going to Savannah, there's nothing for me here," Colleen cried as she ran to the carriage house.

Margo gave chase, calling back to her mother. "See what you've done!" Winded, Margo crept through a cobweb-covered side door into the hollow carriage house. "Sorry, I spoiled your day. It's not just Ma, it's my fault too."

Seated on an overturned bucket, Colleen looked up at her sister. "What are you, ten years old? You turn into a defiant child whenever you're around her. Why can't you just walk away? You play right into her hands. I'm seeing Clay on Tuesday; he wants to discuss our future."

Margo lit a cigarette. "Sounds serious. When did this come about?"

"Just now."

"He'll retract his promise when he sobers up."

"You can't find anything wrong with him, so you label him an alcoholic. Wise up: everyone who drinks isn't a drunk."

"I don't want you to end up like Ma, saddled with an alkie. No one, not even she, deserves that." Margo held up her palm.

"I know, all my choices have been foolish and selfish, but no one has been hurt by them except for me."

Colleen sniffled. "Why did you dislike Poppy? He never hurt you."

Margo nervously puffed on her cigarette, knowing she should keep her resentment to herself, but the thread had been pulled.

"He ruined our childhood because he wanted to drink. That came first, not his family, job, or reputation. For Christ's sake, he turned Rosaria's wedding day into the day her daddy died."

"It wasn't a choice."

"He may not have chosen to be a drunk, but he chose to remain one."

"It's a disease."

"That's bullshit. We pity the cancer patient, but if there were a cure and they wouldn't take it, would they still have our sympathy? Some people like being sick.

413

They crave attention, the control it gives them over others. He held all the cards. Ma's a bitch, but she'd take a bullet for us. Not good 'ole Tim, he's a sweetheart, a gentle soul who had a tough life. He pulled on heartstrings while Ma wheeled a whip. Given the choice, I'll sacrifice my hide, not my heart." Margo snuffed out her lipstick-rimmed cigarette and knelt before her sobbing sister. "Please, Colleen, don't do this. You put your time in. Don't allow alcohol to bleed into your adult life."

Colleen yanked her hand out of Margo's and stood. "Clay is not an alcoholic."

"His hands were shaking, you saw them."

"He was nervous."

"I know men. You've never had one break your heart, experienced the pain they can inflict once they know you love them. You love Clay because he reminds you of Poppy. Any man you fall in love with will."

"If he is an alcoholic, he'll need me all the more."

"You're a better man than I am, Gunga Din."

***

The glittering green stones looked up at him from the white satin-lined box, the way Colleen's adoring emerald eyes had last night. Promises weren't made, but lying in his arms, she believed he was waiting for their wedding night to consummate their love. He knew he was leading her on; they could never marry, he'd be condemning her to a life of childless servitude. Even if she were willing, he wouldn't allow it. She was young; her heart would heal. Whether his would was a moot point. He had to return home.

Margo kissed her bed partner's neck as he slid the cigarette from her fingers. "This is a non-smoking hotel room."

"Why do I sleep with doctors?" Margo asked, waving smoke from her eyes. "This cigarette is my reward for a stellar performance."

"An orgasm wasn't enough?"

"Never in my wildest dreams, and they are wild, did I think I'd be traveling to New York to have one, because my husband left me for that, that, creature."

"The man's an arrogant ass. Get over him."

"I wish it were that simple. I find myself comparing every man to Aaron."

"How do I stack up?"

"Find yourself a gypsy."

Stan rested his head on his elbow. "How's Colleen and Dr. Vaughan getting on?"

"She's headed for a heartache."

"It's part of growing up, they love ya, and they leave ya."

"What makes you think he'll leave her? Are you holding out on me?"

"Me, listen to gossip? Never. He's returning to Georgia, end of story."

"He has a girl back home, huh?"

"What makes you say that?"

"Because they haven't gone all the way."

"He's a gentleman."

"He's a gynie."

"Meaning?"

"Aaron was a neurologist. It didn't take him long to get on my nerves. I smell something fishy."

"You're acting like a mother hen."

"Who's taking advice from a cock."

"Stay out of it, Margo."

"He's an alcoholic, isn't he? You doctors know one another's business."

"No. Case in point: the two of us sneaking around."

"I'm not asking you to divulge his medical history. Just his drinking habits."

"That's medical; alcoholism is a disease."

"A drunk is a drunk."

"Colleen's young; she'll bounce back. You did."

"Colleen's not like me. She's a good girl. She wants to be loved, not laid. He gave her an emerald necklace. You could buy a house with what he paid for that trinket. Not a house like mine, but a two-bedroom ranch in a mixed neighborhood."

"Can't a man give a woman a gift without a motive?"

"I've never known one."

***

The corridor was cold and sterile. At its end, a nurse's station. A gaggle of white capped well-wishers gathered around Dr. Vaughan. They had worked with him for the past four years; Colleen had only known him for two months. He had never introduced her to anyone at the hospital. If he had, it would have been as Dr. Hirsh's sister-in-law, not as his girlfriend. Had he dated any of them? Given them necklaces? They were women who had adult relationships. She was just a goofy college kid, a clinger. He was just being kind, nothing more. *Why did I come here? We said our goodbyes last night. You look foolish; don't make the same mistake you made with Lee. When a man runs, don't chase him.*

Clay spotted her as she headed for the stairwell. "Colleen." She turned, knowing it was a mistake.

"What are you doing here? I promised I'd call as soon as I landed."

"Then what? You go your way, I go mine?"

"You have school, don't pass up the opportunity to get your degree."

Colleen whispered a scream, "That's in two years."

"I'll send you a plane ticket. You can visit during your semester break. Now go home."

Colleen could no longer control her tone. "Go home? What am I? A stray dog?"

Clay put his finger to her lips. "Shush."

Colleen slapped his finger away. "Don't you shush me."

A surly Southern voice welcomed itself into the argument. "The man's right, keep your voice down. I'm tryin' to die in hereya."

Clay smiled and waved Colleen over to a partially closed door. "There's someone I'd like you to meet."

"You come out from behind that doowah, Dr. Vaughan, you too, darlin'. Don't be afraid, I won't bite. I lost my teeth years ago."

The door opened to a room adorned with flowers. "This," Clay introduced with fanfare. "Is the salty Miss Pepperton."

Her complexion had a gray pallor, her bloated face was crowned with a stock of white hair that gave her the look of a troll doll.

A white-coated colleague followed Clay into the room. "Morning, Miss Pepperton. May I borrow Dr. Vaughan? I'll return him shortly."

"Scoot," she answered with the wave of her IV-bruised hand. "I'll make my own introductions."

Clay kissed Colleen's cheek and whispered, "You've met your match."

Colleen's eyes wandered the room to avoid the old woman's belly that appeared to be on the verge of giving birth. "What lovely flowers."

"You would think I'd won the Derby. Uterine cancer, in case you're wondering. My name is Myrtle Pepperton, one of the Remington Parish Peppertons. My grandmama survived the warwah by eatin' crickets and crabgrass. Damn them Yankees."

417

Colleen offered her hand. "My name is Colleen Ronan, one of the County Cavan Ronans. My great-grandmother survived the famine by cannibalizing great-grandpappy. He died not knowing what was eating him. Damn those potatoes."

"You're all right, kid. Help me into that chair." The soft, crepey skin on Miss Pepperton's arms made Colleen fear it would slough off. The old woman melted into the vinyl recliner. "That's betta. Top drawer next to the bed, you'll find a pack of cigarettes. Fire one up for me." Colleen did as she was told. "I've been smokin' this godawful brand for the coupons. Some good they'll do me now. You smoke?"

"No."

"Good, you won't end up in this place... cards?"

"It's been a while, but I can clean your clock."

Miss Pepperton raised her sparse brows. "Aren't you the confident one? The cards are next to my smokes. You shuffle, and I'll deal. I see you've been keep'n company with my favorite doctor. You two involved in a personal way? It's none of my business, that's why I'm askin."

Colleen shook her head, "Yes."

"You love him?"

"Very much."

"And he you?"

"Yes."

"How long have you been keeping company?"

"Two months."

"That's all?"

"Long enough to know we're in love."

Miss Pepperton parked her cigarette in an ashtray and dealt the cards along with advice. "What we have hereya, is what's called a whirlwind romance. A whirlwind

418

won't kill ya, it knocks you around, spins you in all directions so you don't know which way is up. That's so the next time one passes through, you'll know to take cover." Miss Pepperton fanned her cards. "You fixin' to follow the doctor?" she asked, making a point not to look up at Colleen.

"That option is still on the table."

"Wipe it off," she said, lifting one eye off her losing hand.

"You're jealous," Colleen teased.

"Am I?"

Colleen's hands shook. The old woman took note. "You ever seen that Wizard of Oz picture?"

"Hasn't everyone?"

"Never cared much for it. They wanted Shirley Temple for the Dorothy role, but by then, she was a big star, didn't need the work. You remind me of her. Anyone ever tell you that?" Colleen felt faint. Myrtle didn't look like Mae, but those were Mae's words, her phrases, her brand of cigarettes.

"You look a might peeked, honey. You not feelin' well?"

"My Aunt would call me Curly Top."

"Did she?"

"I miss her."

"I'll be dead myself if I don't finish this story. Like you, Dorothy was swept up in a whirlwind of sorts. Being young, she didn't want to waste her life on the farm. Can't say I blame her. I don't care if the good Lord offered me ten more years, if I had to live them out in Kansas, Lord Jesus, take me now. Well, don't Dorothy get her wish? That twister lands her in Oz, sure, it was fun for a spell till she discovers the man behind the curtain with all the promises wasn't a Wizard after all. Ya see, Oz was in her own backyard. Any of this makin' sense to ya?"

Batting back tears, Colleen choked out a "Yes." On the other side of the door, Clay listened.

"I had a sister, Rosaria. She could size you up in an instant, look into your very soul. She called me the Tiger, a wild cat, who, when offered a warm, loving home, turns her back on it, not wanting to be confined; knowing she'd always be looking for a way out, a chance to return to a miserable existence, but it's all she knows. On those frigid winter nights when she's hungry, cold, and afraid, she looks into the window of a warm, loving home and wonders if she should have gone inside."

"And then?"

"Spring returns."

Clay made his presence known with an "Ah, hmm. Are you ladies going to make a night of it?" Colleen stood and shook Miss Pepperton's cold hand. "A pleasure to have made your acquaintance, Miss Myrtle Pepperton of Remington Parish."

"And you, Miss Colleen Ronan of Mount Nottingham."

"I'll come by again," Colleen promised.

"Don't worry your pretty little head, darlin', by tomorrow, I'll be an angel."

Colleen tossed her cards on the bed. "I won."

"Yes, Curly Top, you have."

Clay gave Colleen a curious stare as they walked to the elevator. "You look like you've seen a ghost. Coming to a cancer ward wasn't a good idea."

"You're wrong. I was meant to meet Miss Pepperton, it's just..."

"Just what?"

"How did she know I was from Mount Nottingham?"

Chapter Twenty-Eight

The air was crackling cold, too cold for Margo's short red wool coat and tall black leather boots. In her black mink hat, she resembled one of the Queen's guards. City Hall was a block away. Knowing she'd find Patsy in the newly constructed eyesore, Margo determined it was time to wish her brother-in-law a Merry Christmas. If by chance the city's involvement in the health center project should crop up, perhaps he could assist in expediting the process. The clacking from her high-heeled boots echoed throughout City Hall's brick floor lobby. Margo tsked, a disgrace, bricks are for streets. It's only a matter of time before a vagrant spits or urinates al fresco on the floor of "The People's City Hall."

A young man in a dark blue blazer bashfully approached her. "Ma'am... Miss, may I assist you?"

"Would you be so kind as to direct me to Councilor Travella's office?"

"This building is a maze; I had better take you there." Her pimpled escort held open the elevator door. Patsy's office was located on the second floor, a simple finger point and a short escalator ride would have sufficed, but why not have Christmas come early for the lad? Margo stepped into the empty elevator. "Anyone ever tell you, you look like Grace Kelly?"

She ran her gloved hand down his blushed cheek. "Only you and Prince Rainier."

The doors opened to cement walls and floors. "His office is at the end of the hall. I can walk you down there, so you don't lose your way."

"I lost my way with my first kiss," Margo said with a wink.

She stroked the door's nameplate. COUNCILOR PASQUALE L. TRAVELLA. The scent of Rosaria's favorite dusting powder filled Margo's nostrils. A burning warmth passed through her body as she placed both hands over her diaphragm. *Take a deep breath. This isn't Sister Mary Cyprian's office; no need to be nervous. Hold it together.*

Hearing a gentle tap on his door, Patsy adjusted the eyeglasses he should have been wearing since sixth grade. "Yes?"

The door swung open. "I haven't asked but yes is always the correct answer."

Patsy stepped out from behind his desk with open arms. "Margo! What brings you here aside from those endless legs?"

"Oh, they end." Margo looked up from Patsy's embrace. "Quite the office, more befitting a bank president than a first-term city councilor."

"Give it time. The building is new; things tend to get very old very quickly in this place."

"Not you. You'll always remain a young man with an old soul."

Patsy pulled out a chair for his guest, who removed her gloves finger by finger. "I was lunching at The Parker House when it hit me, I hadn't seen Patsy since the election. I hope I'm not taking you away from city business."

He wheeled a chair next to her. "How's your husband?"

"Aaron is no longer with us."

"He's dead?"

"No, silly. He moved to Israel to help his people."

"You didn't want to accompany him?"

"And get sand in my nails?"

"I like Aaron. Rosie did too."

"Don't cry for me; there will be others," Margo said, reaching into her pocketbook for a cigarette.

Patsy flicked a lighter he used as a paperweight. Remembering Rosaria had broken him of the habit before it became one, Margo returned the pack to her handbag.

"How's life on the Mount?"

"Colleen is at Emerson. They're producing one of her plays."

"Dare I ask?"

"My mother? Nothing has changed on that front. She's living in a big house in a bad neighborhood. Which reminds me, I'm on a committee raising funds to build a health center on Blue Hill Ave. They're interested in purchasing a vacant lot abutting my mother's property. There's a chance her house will be sacrificed."

"Shame, it's such a beautiful home."

"It's not a done deal. We're at the mercy of the bank and the city."

"I understand why you want to save your mother's house."

"No, Patsy, I want it destroyed, ripped from its foundation, reduced to a pile of rubble."

"I don't get it."

"All I need is a name, someone at the top who can help me. My mother won't leave on her own, but if the city takes her house, she'll have no choice but to move."

"Something tells me if Margo wants Berta out, Berta is going." Patsy walked over to his desk and opened its top drawer. "My only suggestion is that you speak with someone in Community Development. They handle these matters. I'll write

423

down their number. They may ask." The drawer slammed shut. "Christ, Margo! You almost took my fingers off!"

"The mayor."

Patsy shook his head, "Oh, no. Don't go there with the mayor."

"I hear he's a ladies' man."

"Please, Margo, I beg you, this is a matter for Community Development." Crossing her silk-stockinged legs, Margo looked down at her meticulously manicured nails. Patsy slouched in defeat.

"You won't take no for an answer."

"Never do."

Patsy straightened his necktie. "I can't decide which makes me more uncomfortable, you, or this foolish tie."

"I like it, and the suit; very well made."

"Bobby's family is in the business. Check out the shoes. My son shines them. I told him, 'If you want to follow in your father's footsteps, start by shining his shoes.'"

"Slave labor."

"Labor of love."

"The mayor?"

Patsy removed his glasses and sat next to Margo. "Look, I may have read too much into it, but the only time I had a conversation with Bullard was when I worked on his campaign. He gave the impression that he and Mae were romantically involved at one time, and Berta was instrumental in breaking them up. He described your mother as a cold, calculating, and I won't repeat the other c word. I pretended to find the remark amusing. I would have done anything to keep that job."

"He sounds like a man after my own heart."

"It's not your heart he'll go after."

"Just give me his number and I'll take it up with him."

"You'll take it up all right."

"Saucy boy."

Patsy shook his head. "Why do I give in to you?"

"You're only human. When do I receive an introduction?"

"You can introduce yourself. He's holding a private reception for himself at the Monadnock Club. He'll be meeting with a group of businessmen, emphasis on men. If you're the only woman in the room, you'll have his undivided attention."

"And how does a woman get in the room?"

"By accident. You apologize and head for the door. I guarantee he won't let you leave. Share your frustration over your mother's refusal to leave the home she loves. Let it slip you're Mae's niece. When he realizes Berta is your mother, he'll have her forcibly removed. Don't get me wrong, I honestly like… respect, your mother, but I agree it's just a matter of time before something unfortunate happens. The city will see she's generously compensated."

"When does the meeting take place?"

"January 10th, but please try Community Development before you resort to Plan B, and no Plan C. I'm serious, Margo."

She kissed Patsy's cheek. "Thank you."

"I feel like Judas."

Margo ran her finger around the edge of Patsy's tidy desk. "The buzz is you're on the fast track to the corner office."

"Just talk. I'm still wet behind the ears."

"Everyone knows and loves you; even the Irish are Patsy Travella fans. Of course, having the name Patsy helps."

"Having a sister-in-law named Sunny Shine helped." Patsy parted the air with his hands.

"'Patsy Travella will put a Shine on Boston.' I wish you had run that by me before you mailed out those flyers."

"Be honest, that was a great picture of us."

"The fur bikini would have made a fetching photo."

"It got you elected," Margo noted with a wink and hip-chuck.

"And in hot water with my wife."

"How are Angie and the girls? Sorry, we didn't attend the wedding. Too soon, you understand."

"Of course, I do. I didn't expect to marry right away, but..."

"But what? You never told me how you met."

"I feel uncomfortable talking to your family about my new wife and kids. Berta must think I'm a 'scoundrel' as Rosie would say."

"My mother thinks you're a terrific guy. Being a war widow, she understands. Our father, Rosaria, and mine, was a fighter pilot."

"Rosie mentioned he was some kind of war hero."

"He was shot down over the Pacific. My mother never speaks of him. It's too painful. By the way, Angie is a widow. My mother wouldn't approve of her grandson's mommy being a divorcée."

"Angie is Mom, Rosie is Mommy."

"So, fill me in. How did you find her?"

"We found each other. Angie worked as a file clerk in the licensing department. We'd cross paths now and then. I never gave her much notice. So, on this particular day, Salina was unable to pick Ricky up at school."

"Ricky?"

"Sorry, Margo, Fredrik wasn't working for him, and I refuse to call him by his gangster name, 'The Fleabag.'

"So, I'm waiting for Ricky, when I recognize Angie outside of the school. We make small talk. You know, the kids, school, the neighborhood. Come to find out I had been in the same Boy Scout troop as her brother, Sweet Pea."

"Sweet Pea?"

"Diabetic. From then on, any time I'd see her around City Hall, we'd stop and talk. One day, I ran into her at lunch; it was one of those accidental encounters that aren't accidental. It became a regular thing for us. Then lunch turned to dinner, and dinner turned to love.

She's no Rosie in the looks department, but I'm nuts about her. I never thought I'd fall in love so soon. With Rosie, love hit me like a ton of bricks. This time love snuck up on me."

"How does Fred... Ricky, like being the only man in the house?"

"What am I, chopped liver? Ricky stayed with Salina and the twins for those first few years, so living with women is nothing new for him."

"How is Salina?"

"Great. The twins entered high school this year. Can you believe it? I was fresh out of high school when I married Rosie. How time flies."

"She'd be so proud of you."

"God, how I wish she lived to see me receive my degree. If it weren't for Rosie, I'd be pushing a broom at the airport. She coached me, taught me how to dress, speak, and present myself. Did I hate it when she'd correct my English. I'm finally the husband she deserved, but she's not here to share in it."

Margo rubbed Patsy's back. "Rosaria wanted to be a teacher. She didn't marry a polished politician. She married a loveable schoolboy. You're what her heart wanted, a boy to teach, and a man to love."

"Ricky wasn't planned. Rosie had this crazy plan that we'd wait five years to start a family, allowing me to finish school, get a good job, the suit and tie kind of a job, then we'd buy a house, raise a family. There was no such thing as the pill. Even if there were, she wouldn't have taken it. I was barely twenty, sex and self-control don't exist at that age. She told me not to feel guilty; it was God's plan. He wanted the baby to come into the world on His timetable, not ours." Patsy paused to wipe the corner of his eye.

"God knew Rosie wouldn't be with me in five years; he wanted to give me a gift, a part of her to love and care for the rest of my life. She was right, Ricky wasn't an accident."

"Does he remember any of it?"

"For the first few months after the fire, he'd say, "Mommy broken, Daddy fix." I couldn't put his mommy back together again, but I found him a great mom."

"Your brother?"

"No sign of him, he's dead, I'm sure of it. Every wise guy and bedbug came out of the woodwork, offering to track him down. Poor Sergeant Coleman, he swore he wouldn't rest until Nicky was captured. Two weeks before he was due to retire, they found him on his kitchen floor with his service revolver in his mouth. Suicide, my ass. He was murdered."

"We don't know what goes through someone's mind. There are those whose life is their profession; retirement is a death sentence."

"He's going to hammer his parrot's head in before he shoots himself. I ain't buying it. He knew suicide meant never being reunited with his wife in heaven. Would you believe the church wouldn't allow him to be buried in a Catholic cemetery? Consecrated ground, they call it. The man never went a day without going to Mass; he was a lector, a Eucharistic minister, and he can't be buried next to his wife?"

"Where is he buried?"

"Next to his wife... don't ask."

"I know better."

"I made a stupid mistake, and so many lives were destroyed by it. I am a patsy. I promised my mother I'd find Nicky and kill him. Angie and the kids can visit me in Walpole. I gave him that money to keep him from being killed. Now I'd pay that kind of dough to have him murdered."

Margo tucked in her lips and concentrated on the window view of the Custom House. "I offered Rosaria money for the down payment on the house. She refused to accept it."

"Rosie was stubborn; she'd never accept help."

Margo covered her mouth. "I've lived with the guilt all these years."

Patsy dropped his hands on Margo's shoulders and squeezed. "Let it go. If Rosie didn't take your help, it wasn't meant to be."

Margo wiped her eyes and smiled over at a picture on the windowsill. "Is that your baby picture?"

Reaching back, Patsy handed the framed photo to Margo. "Me? Look at those eyes, they're Rosie's eyes."

They weren't; he was the image of his father, but Margo loved that whenever he looked into his son's eyes, Patsy saw Rosaria.

"I was about to pick him up at hockey practice. Why not come along?"

Margo desperately wanted to see her nephew, but not in East Boston, not in an ice rink. "Why not? I'll follow you in my car."

"I take the subway to work. I'm only a couple of stops on the Blue Line."

"You are a man of the people." Margo buttoned her coat and slapped Patsy on the back. "Come on, Charlie, it's time you got off the MTA."

The baby blue knitted scarf looked ridiculous tucked under the collar of Patsy's camelhair coat. Margo swiftly directed her eyes back on the road. Patsy caught her glance. "It's a father statement, not a fashion statement. My daughter has discovered the wonderful world of yarn. Last year, it was macaroni art."

The Jaguar sped through the Callahan Tunnel like a bullet through a shotgun barrel, breaking out to winter's fading sunlight. Patsy directed Margo to a park running along the East Boston waterfront.

"Come, I want to show you something." Patsy threaded his arm into Margo's, leading her to a set of crumbling stone stairs that led to an abandoned immigration station. "They're called The Golden Stairs that led Italian immigrants to America's golden opportunities. My parents climbed those stairs when they arrived here as children. Will you look at that skyline?" Patsy said, turning his attention across the muddy coast to a panoramic view of Boston. "All those wealthy fat cats living across the harbor are paying big bucks to live in a high-rise with a view of an airport and rotting piers, while we look over at a shining city on a hill."

Margo turned up his coat's collar and rested her head on his shoulder.

"I tell you, Margo, they've been short-shifting East Boston for years. What are we? A poor man's Southie? Everyone wants to forget the past, move on, ignore the immigrants whose shoulders this city rests on. It's high time those shoulders shrugged."

"You've come a long way in a short time."

"We all grew up that day." Patsy directed his eyes back to the city. Margo felt as if she were eavesdropping on a private conversation he was having with the object of his affection.

"As a kid, I'd look across this harbor at the city; it looked like Oz, a place where magic happens."

"You know, you'll be The Wizard one day."

"Not me, I know what's behind the curtain. Politics is a dirty business." Patsy held out his leg and wiggled his foot.

"I wouldn't want to soil my freshly polished ruby slippers."

Margo clung to his arm. "Make a decent woman out of a dirty city."

"I promised Rosie I'd take her on a honeymoon once I got some money in my pocket. I spread a map out on the bed and said, "Pick any place in the world and I'll take you there. She put her hand over Boston and said, 'We have the world at our fingertips, let's explore.'

"She'd take me to Chinatown for their New Year. Roslindale for Greek Independence Day, Charlestown on Bunker Hill Day. South Boston for Saint Patrick's Day and Halloween in Dorchester. To see your mother." The two exchanged smiles.

"The first time I walked into the Copley Square Library, I felt like I was in a palace, and some goon would throw me out for trespassing. Rosie pointed to an inscription over the door that read, FREE TO ALL. Ten years later, I'm a trustee of that library. Rosie did that. You should have seen the look on her face when we entered the Gardner Art Museum. She was mesmerized by those paintings. Who needs the Louvre? We were in Paris. All for the price of a subway token. Our honeymoon was a world tour without leaving home. I fell in love with a woman and a city.

"It's our ethnic neighborhoods that bring beauty and texture to this town, not some Beacon Hill brownstone with a gaslight stationed out front. What I love are the places and faces that don't appear on postcards. Charlestown's Irish. West Roxbury's Armenians. The Polish in South Boston, the French and Spanish living in Jamaica Plain. The parade of pastel dresses and hats filing into a Roxbury church on a Sunday morning."

Patsy's voice turned grim. "Now, the powers that be want to mix us up in an ethnic stew where you won't know a Pole from a Puerto Rican, tell us where to live, send our kids to school, what language to speak, food to eat, holidays to celebrate, and books we can read. Where are we? In the goddamned Soviet Union? Rosie and me, we came from different worlds within the same city, brought together by love, not legislation, but love takes time. The government wants too much too soon. There's a storm brewing. This town is headed for dark times." Patsy waved his hand across his face. "Sorry, Margo, I'm off on one of my tangents."

"That wasn't a tangent. That was a nomination speech."

"Come with me, I want to show you where the building stood. "

"Oh, Patsy, I can't."

"It's no longer a burnt-out shell. The city built a Head Start Center on the site. It's a pre-school program for inner city kids. Rosie would have loved that. They're putting up a plaque with her name... Jeez, Margo, I didn't mean to make you cry."

"They're happy tears. Don't we have a hockey game to get to?"

"You're right. We don't want to keep Little Phil Esposito waiting."

"Do I know him?"

"Obviously not."

Patsy clapped his hands and let out an ear-piercing whistle. "Ricky! Over here! Your aunt has come to see you!"

"Auntie Sunny!" the high-pitched voice hollered from across the rink. Margo shot a disapproving look at her brother-in-law.

"Don't blame me. You're the one who came to his third birthday party as cloudy with a chance of rain. I never knew my son had so many friends from the shipyard." Ice blades slammed against the boards. The resemblance to his father was undeniable.

"Do you like hockey, Auntie?"

"I never followed the sport. Hockey doesn't have cheerleaders."

Ricky stood on the tips of his blades to give his aunt a kiss. "Thank you for the birthday present."

"Did it fit?"

"It fit," his father answered. "I didn't know they made smoking jackets that small."

Margo ruffled her nephew's dark curls. "We have another Hugh Hefner in the making."

"Don't listen to your aunt, she's fresh. If you ever bring home a girl like her, I'll send you to your room."

432

"If she's like me, she'll follow you."

"I'm receiving my first communion on May 7th. Will you come? It's at Our Lady of Mount Carmel Church. Do you need directions?"

"I've been to that church. I'm your Godmother, and your Godfather is..." Margo put her index finger to her cheek. "It's on the tip of my tongue."

Patsy smirked. "Don't you wish. It's my cousin Big Ralphie."

"Big Ralphie?"

Patsy gave her a nudge and a wink.

"Damn. He asked me out and I shot him down."

"Big mistake, Margo. Big, big mistake."

Ricky tugged on Margo's sleeve. "Like I was saying," Patsy gave his son a sharp look.

"As you were saying."

"As I was saying, try to come. Mommy will be there."

Margo's throat filled with Novocain; her tears raced to reach her eyes before an answer reached her lips. Her nephew's bewildered face in her hands, she realized Patsy was right, those were Rosaria's eyes looking up at her.

"Your mommy is wherever you are. I'll keep the 7th open."

"Come on, Bud. Mom's holding dinner, and your aunt's legs are turning blue in that miniskirt."

Margo kissed them both. Hastily heading for the exit, her boot heel wedged itself between the rink's floor mat. Wiggling her heel free, she caught sight of Patsy, one hand on his son's shoulder, the other clutching a duffel bag stuffed with hockey equipment.

"I've got to get out of here," she recited under her breath as she bolted from the rink. The cucumber sandwich she'd eaten for lunch wrestled with her throat to once again see the light of day. Driving to the end of the parking lot, she opened the car door, leaned forward, and vomited.

"I can't do this, Rosaria," she sobbed into the steering wheel. "I'm sorry. I'm sorry, I love you, but I can't. This is your town, where you lived, loved, and died. Please forgive me, Rosaria. I can't come back here. I can never come back."

Chapter Twenty-Nine

Margo walked her fingers across Stan's forested chest. "Something's troubling you."

"Has Colleen heard from Clay?"

"He'd been calling a couple of times a week. Then the calls stopped. She plans to see him to return the necklace. I think she's crazy. God knows she earned it, and not the way you think. The poor kid has never been in love, and that cad dumped her. Just as well; he's a drunkard or gay. Is he gay?"

"Clayton wasn't gay or a drunk; he had a disease."

"Had? Wasn't?"

"He's dead."

Margo sat up. "Dead!"

"Huntington's disease. He'd inherited it from his mother."

"Damn you! You knew Colleen was falling in love with him. Why didn't you do something?"

"I can't disclose that information. All I knew about their relationship was what you've told me. And you tend to exaggerate."

"Why did he bother going to medical school? He busted his ass at that hospital."

"He had a 50-50 chance of inheriting the disease. What was he supposed to do? Sit around and wait to see which way the pendulum would swing? Clayton helped a lot of people in his short life. He'd been experiencing symptoms, ticks, tremors, slurred speech. He couldn't risk Colleen getting pregnant or having her witness his slow decline. He killed himself last week while he still had the wherewithal to carry it out."

"He exchanged a handful of years for a handful of pills."

"He used a shotgun. His brain was killing him; he blew it out."

***

The beat-up Impala had met its maker in the great Chevy plant in the sky. Reduced to commuter status, Colleen waited for the return bus home from the supermarket. Snow crunched and squeaked like Styrofoam under her cold, wet feet housed in fashionable, but impractical boots. Alone on the bus stop bench, she transferred her dry wool mittens from her hands to her feet. Shoving the damp socks into her coat pocket, she caught her reflection in a vacant storefront window. The sun was not only setting in the sky but over her dying neighborhood.

What more could time take from her? Today, she was the cold, hungry cat. Did she genuinely love Clay or Lee, or was she looking for someone to carry her off the Mount? "Why wait to be rescued?" she asked herself. *"I should break free, Margo did. I'll start over where no one knows me, erase my past, invent my own history."*

The drone of the bus engine had a calming effect; she would have nodded off if not for the potholes turning the bus into a stagecoach.

A buzz signaled a stop request. Bumping her way to the open exit door, hugging her groceries, Colleen stumbled to the street, landing on the frozen pavement. The jagged edge of a diesel-dusted snowbank left its mark on her cheek and a gash across her soggy shopping bag.

Hands tucked under his armpits, he stomped his feet on crunchie rock salt. A rolling can of creamed corn bumped against his shoe. "Colleen!"

Winter's late afternoon sun reflected off the snow, blurring his features, but she knew it was him. Aiding Colleen to her feet won him a powerful shove. "Get away from me!"

"Just... just... listen."

"Fuck you, Leon. Fuck you!"

"Please, let me explain! You owe me that much."

"I owe you nothing! Apparently, that kiss was for your amusement. Have you come back for more laughs? See if I'll do more than kiss you if you put on a pair of pants? You can wear whatever you please, but underneath it all lay a cunning coward who can't get past his lonely childhood. Grow up. You may come to like it."

Looking around at bystanders enjoying the soap opera unfolding before them, Lee lowered his voice. "Please, Colleen, calm down." His plea only amplified her voice.

"Why Lee? Why did you leave town without seeing me? Why did you come back?"

He pulled her to his chest. His scent was familiar. Looking into his deep, brown eyes, she silently prayed that her anger would outweigh her desire to kiss him. "Let me pass," she demanded. The two dodged from side to side. His eyes on hers, he didn't see the kick to his calf coming. Making a break, she marched toward home.

"Come back."

An airborne box of raw dough hit its target over his eye. Its contents popped through the cardboard casing, seeping a sticky dough that adhered to his face. Shaking a handkerchief from his overcoat pocket, he wiped the blood-speckled goo off his forehead. Yanking her alongside him like a parent pulling a crying child from a toy store window, Lee marched her down the avenue.

"Where are you taking me?"

"Somewhere we can talk in private." His reluctant hostage in tow, he walked at a rapid clip.

Wide-eyed, Colleen looked up at the broken building. "This is your parents' place."

"I'm surprised you recognized it." She would have been mortified were he to discover she'd engaged in a sad ritual of passing the building long after it ceased to be a home. Holding a firm grip on Colleen's arm, Lee fumbled with the house keys.

"You can let go. I won't run, honest." His hand slid off her arm. The cold, ceramic tiled hall floor held the muddy footprints of careless moving men who'd scratched the entryway's dated wallpaper. Having moved most of the Jewish residents out of the old neighborhood, they knew the paper would never be replaced. Lee squinted his eyes to read the thermostat.

"I don't know why my mother insists on keeping the utilities on. Who cares if the pipes freeze, or a rat catches a cold? We'll never sell this dump." With the turn of the dial, the radiator clanked like a hammer on metal. Colleen's throat tightened as she surveyed the lonesome apartment. All that remained were a few sticks of furniture wrapped in padded moving blankets waiting for a van that would never return.

"Don't bother with the heat, I won't be staying." She walked to the door and turned her head. "How did you know I'd be on that bus?"

"Your mother told me."

"My mother told you?"

"When I phoned, she said you had gone grocery shopping and would be back in about an hour. She didn't recognize my voice. I got the impression you were waiting on another man's call."

"I am."

Lee caught her as she opened the door. He slammed it shut. "Wait."

"Get out of my way,"

"You're going to listen to me," he ordered with anger equal to her own. Any sympathy she had for him abated.

"You think I'm so malleable that you can twist my emotions to suit your every whim? You shattered my dreams, made a fool of me as well as yourself."

"I wasn't ready for a relationship. I thought by moving to Chicago you'd forget about me, find yourself a real man, but I couldn't get you out of my head. If there's a chance."

"There isn't. I have a ticket out of this town. I've found a safe place far from the Mount. There'll be no tears or heartache, just love and acceptance." Colleen's voice wobbled; her lips twitched, exposing her vulnerability. "Please," she meekly implored. "Let me go home. I'm cold, tired, and confused." Digging into her coat pocket, she removed a damp sock and blew her nose into it. Lee's mouth twisted in disgust.

"A sock? You'll get athlete's nose."

"So, it's going to be like that, a joke."

"Colleen, it's always been like that with us."

"There is no 'us.' There's you and there's me. And you're going to let me out of here."

He'd never witnessed her breakdown yet; there she stood, a grown woman in tears, pleading with him to let her go home. He knew that desperate feeling; he didn't want to be the man blocking the door.

"Go," he surrendered. Turning his back to her, he crossed the room to a barred window that faced the street. Her forehead pressed to the door, her hand on its knob, Colleen swallowed hard.

"Do you have any idea what you put me through? The night you left town without a hello or goodbye, I walked those streets crying. See that bench at the bus stop? I sat there for over an hour looking up at this building. What I thought I'd see, I don't know. I was like a bloodhound following a scent that led me here, then went cold." Her voice shook. "I wanted to touch the door handle you must have turned on your way out, as if it would relieve the ache in my bones."

Lee turned from the window. "You were on that bench? Christ, Colleen, you could have been robbed, raped, or worse!"

"I didn't care. It took me months to trust people not to take advantage of me, to look forward to a future that wouldn't include you. I have someone waiting for me. Had you come a week later, you wouldn't have found me." Lee held out his hand, directing her to a blanketed wingback chair. Removing her coat and running her fingers through her wet ringlets, Colleen took the seat. "You have my undivided attention."

Lee focused on the floor. "I couldn't face you when I returned home. I was afraid you were angry, repulsed, or had found yourself a real man. It appears I'm correct on all counts. I'm doing well. I was asked to be the district manager. It would mean putting down roots."

"Don't let me stop you."

"You could. Those years we spent at the Talbot School were the best years of my life. You had me believing my future would be a fun-filled adventure. It wasn't. Do you remember that weirdo on Normandy Street?"

"Mister Malformed?"

"You gave him that name."

"Seemed appropriate."

"Mister Malformed stopped me as I walked past his house on my way home from school."

"His house wasn't on your way."

"I know it was stupid, but I heard the kids talking about him. I wanted to see what he looked like. I got a good look. He was sitting on his front porch. He wasn't what I imagined. He was frail, moved like a marionette. I wasn't afraid. He wasn't scary, but pitiful. I felt sorry for him. He called me over, said a portrait of his late mother had fallen off the wall and was wedged behind a heavy Davenport. He needed a strapping young man to assist him in returning his beloved mother's image back to its rightful place. Describing a sofa as a Davenport and me as a strapping young man should have tipped me off to what was to come."

"No Lee. No! No!"

"I knew you were obsessed with the guy. I thought seeing the inside of his house would score points with you."

Colleen choked out an apology. "I'm sorry, I'm sorry," she cried into her hands. "I teased you, bullied you, called you a sissy, dared you to do things even I wouldn't have done. I loved you. I didn't know, I didn't know."

Lee continued, not to punish her or invoke pity but to flush out the past. "He was nice. I kinda liked him. He asked about school, said there was a bike in the basement, and I could have it. I foolishly followed him down. I figured the worst he could do was kill me. I didn't know you could kill someone and not have them die. I was ignorant of sex between a man and a woman, much less that of a young boy at the mercy of a child rapist. The whole time I was thinking, he wouldn't do this to Aaron or the boys who hang outside the corner store. I figured it was understood weaklings like me were fair game for sick men to abuse. That's why Aaron tried to toughen me up so this couldn't happen.

"Now that it had, there was no turning back. I was dirty, someone to be preyed upon, and everyone knew it." Lee's eyes crawled around the room. "He actually shook my hand, said we were buddies. I never went near his house again until the Saturday I heard sirens coming from Normandy Street. I prayed he hadn't killed some other boy. I ran over there." Lee clenched his teeth and balled his fists. "Over and over, the car rammed him into the tree.

"Aaron still reminisces over his glory days at Boston Latin. 'Great school, good times, you'll love it.' I didn't. The guys at school called me The Egghead. I'd never know who or when, but once a week, I'd get an egg cracked over my head. Big joke. One day in the middle of a name-calling session, one of the guys called me a faggot. It was just an ugly name to him, not an observation, but it got me thinking. How do they know? Do you just have to look at someone to know they took part in a homosexual act? Was I giving off vibes?

I thought my mother was insane to suggest I take you to the prom. Then it hit me. Why not? I'll have an ally, and God help the guy who throws the first egg. Once again, you came through for me. You showed them to be the fools they were and me the man I'd always dreamed of becoming.

"Some of the guys at college befriended me. I'd follow anyone who gave me the attention I craved. They were gay, so what? I was liked, made to feel wanted. I never had male friends, been a part of a group. We went to parties, clubs, and the theater. They enjoyed my company, thought I was witty. Everyone knew I didn't share their sexual preference, and it was okay; that wasn't what our friendships were about. Colleen, I never would have survived college if it weren't for those guys. We thought it would be fun to dress me as a woman. It was New Year's Eve, and everyone at the club was in on the joke."

"Not me! Why wasn't I let in on the joke?"

"Would you have believed me?"

"Yes! I would have believed anything you told me that night!"

Lee returned to the window and looked out at the setting sun. "Bumping into you wasn't an accident. I wanted you to see me. You always made me feel like a man, as a child in the library, as a teen at the prom, and that night in the bus station. I may have been in a dress, but I never felt more like a man. Now here I am, all grown up. You can go now. I said my piece. I don't want to interfere with your plans. I didn't come here seeking pity. I just had to know, be certain there was nothing here for me."

Colleen joined him at the window. "The night I sat crying on that bench, no one stopped to ask what was wrong, if there was anything they could do. The only person to approach me was a bum asking for spare change. I gave him a quarter. He called me an angel. I didn't give him money for altruistic reasons, oh no. I wanted something from God, a favor, some sort of miracle for my generosity to one of his lost sheep. My Aunt Mae would tell us, 'The best miracles take the longest to arrive.' Colleen looked into Lee's eyes. "I'm glad I gave that man a quarter."

They kissed as though ten seconds had passed since their lips last met. "I hate you for what you did to me, for making me love you." Colleen moaned.

His kisses reached her feverish earlobe. "I swear I'll never leave you. I love you. I fell in love with you the first time you told me to go to hell. I want to take you, but not here in this cold, dusty room."

Colleen pried her face from his. "I was willing to give myself to you on a urine-soaked terminal floor; I don't mind a little dust."

Like a matador taunting a bull, he stripped the chair of its blanket. The bashful boy was now her prince, transforming the torn gray blanket into the magic carpet of her childhood dream.

Tonight, the carpet would carry them to a land they had never visited, an erotic land where their long-held desires could be shared, never to return to the schoolyard. When did the dark hair surface on his chest? Those weren't the shoulders she massaged at the prom. Hearing the click of his belt buckle, Colleen unbuttoned her sweater.

"May I?" Lee asked. "I've dreamed of this moment for a long time." Colleen removed her hand from the zipper of her soggy corduroy bellbottoms. His kisses accompanied her pants' slow descent to her feet.

"Mittens!"

"Yeah, mittens. You got a problem with that?"

"They're on the wrong feet, you dope. This wasn't in my fantasy," he grumbled.

For a man who never held a woman's naked body, he seemed familiar with the territory. His lips kissed their way back to hers.

"I know you can please me the way you had night after night in that bedroom down the hall. I thought those fantasies would be the only sexual pleasure I'd ever experience, and it was with you, Colleen. It was always with you."

From the schoolyard to this moment, their lives had been spent in a foreplay of shared jokes, insults, and adventures that provided a respite from a world neither felt they belonged. Together they had walked hand in hand down a path they both knew would lead them here, in one another's arms. The lovers didn't grope or fumble; they knew intuitively what pleased the other as if the act had been choreographed. The girl who terrorized and teased him as a boy, tormented and tantalized him as a teen, lay beneath him at his mercy, begging to be satisfied.

"My body has always been yours," she confessed in a soft whisper. "Claim it."

With that phrase, they were virgins no more. Melting in complete surrender, she called out his name. It wasn't followed by 'Wait up,' but 'I love you.' His parents no longer in the next room, he was free to openly rejoice in the arms of his captive.

The room was silent. The only sounds were the voices of school children racing home, hurling snowballs at one another. Lee stroked Colleen's cheek. "Are we a team again?"

"Yes," Colleen resigned. "We're a team.'"

"You went from 'Fuck you, Leon' to 'Fuck me, Lee,' in what? Twenty, thirty minutes?"

Colleen's head shot up. "You're gloating."

"Maybe I am."

"Maybe you should." Lee stroked her long hair that looked like red seaweed against her porcelain skin.

"I feel like the weight of the world has been lifted from my shoulders."

"It has. You released it into me, and I will destroy it. No one will ever hurt you. I'll see to it," she vowed.

"What about you?" he asked, brushing stray strands of hair from her eyes. "What did you let go of?"

"I've had an ongoing beef with God. I hate him. I hate him for taking Poppy and Mae, for giving Rosaria polio, then killing her in such a cruel fashion. What I let go of was my pride, the need to control what I can't and shouldn't. I now know why he took them from me: It was time to move on, make room in my heart for others. What I let go of was the rope. I'm where I belong."

Colleen ran her fingers down Lee's cheek. "Was it really always me?"

"It was always you."

"For real?"

"For real."

"It was prom night, wasn't it?"

"No. However, I did give it to you good that night and you loved every minute of it."

"It probably was a minute."

"My obsession began much earlier. I was walking home from the post office one afternoon. I must have been fourteen or fifteen. I heard a group of girls laughing as they slid on the bank's ice-covered parking lot. One of the girls caught my eye; she was taller than the others. You were wearing a hat, so I couldn't see your hair. You and another girl were holding hands, spinning each other around on the ice. Once up to speed, you let go of your partner's hands, sending her gliding across the ice, slamming into the side of the building.

"I remember thinking, what a mean thing to do to a friend. Then you did it. Bending forward, with your hands between your thighs, throwing your head back, you laughed. That's when your hat fell off, and I realized it was you. I loved to watch you strike that pose even when you were a fat, ugly kid. So, you can imagine the impact it had on me as an adolescent. You came to me that night, naked, in that pose. You laughed at me. I kissed you to make you stop. You can guess the rest. Did you ever think of me that way?"

"Not until we met in New York. I must have repressed any affection I had for you, and it came rushing out with that kiss. Although there was this one time, it wasn't love, more like jealousy."

Lee sat up. "I'll settle for jealousy, let's hear it."

"Poppy read in the paper that the zoo had purchased a man-eating lion. He asked if I wanted to see it. I was so excited thinking I was going to see a lion eat a man."

"Stop, stop. I just shared a sweet story about how I fell in love with you, and you come back with a man-eating lion story?

"Allow me to finish. On our drive to the zoo, we stopped at the traffic light in front of The Beth El. I saw all you boys in black suits and skull caps. You were among them, and I get this weird feeling."

"Why? You knew I was Jewish."

"Yes, but I'd never seen you being Jewish."

"I don't get it."

"Take the Travellas, for example. They eat different food, speak another language, have customs I don't follow, but we have a shared religion that acts like a password, allowing me into their world. Seeing you that day, I realized I didn't have your password -never would."

"If you like, I can give you the password." Lee brushed Colleen's hair from her ear and whispered. "Klaatu barada nikto."

Colleen slapped his arm. "May I continue?"

"But of course."

"From that moment on, I looked at you differently, like Superman. In public, you were Clark Kent, but when you go to the temple, you change into..."

"Superjew!"

"Don't joke. I was Lois Lane. I knew your secret but pretended I didn't. I'd wonder how you'd feel seeing me leaving Saint Regina's holding a missal and wearing a mantilla."

"Wow! You, wearing only a mantilla." Colleen landed a sharp jab to his chest.

"Ow! You broke my rib. I'm not joking."

Colleen rolled her back to him. "You're Superman. Heal your own damn rib."

Lee pulled her to his wounded side. "I'm going to tell you something, and I don't want you to ever forget it. You come first, nothing, I mean nothing, comes between us. Not a yarmulke or a mantilla." A sinister smile crept across his face. "A mantilla... wow!"

"Got to go," Colleen announced.

"It's down the hall, but I don't think there's toilet paper. Better take your socks."

"Home. I have to go home. I set out for the supermarket two hours ago. My mother will wonder where her smoked shoulder is."

"What will you tell her?"

"I'll lie," Colleen answered while struggling to fit her feet into mittens.

"I'm going to give you a lesson in lying." Lee concentrated more on Colleen's figure shimmying into damp pants than on her instructions.

"A lie must always contain a kernel of truth, so you can convince yourself it's not really a lie." Lee buttoned her sweater and nodded his head. "Truth makes a good lie. Got it."

"My explanation will go like this. I slid on a patch of ice as I stepped off the bus. My shopping bag broke, sending the groceries into the gutter. That's the kernel of truth."

"Great story," he complimented while tugging on his pants.

"I'm not done. Here's the lie. The bus driver insisted that I go to the hospital to have my foot X-rayed. Thank God it wasn't broken. I was kept for observation due to a mild concussion. After a few hours, I was allowed to leave. I grabbed a cab and came home."

"That's it? Your mother won't ask any questions?"

"Just one. "How much did the cab cost you?"

Lee stood behind Colleen, kissing the back of her neck. "I love your neck."

"My mother will break it if I don't get home."

"Come on, my car is parked across the street."

"I'd rather walk."

"So, we walk." Hand in hand, they climbed Mount Nottingham as if time had returned them to childhood.

"I'm coming back to Boston."

"You'll be leaving a good job."

"I'll find another." Looking over at the lit porch, Lee straightened Colleen's scarf and dusted snowflakes off her shoulders.

"You had better go in. My meter is running."

Opening the old oak door, Colleen stared up at the infamous staircase and over at the piano with its phantom pianist.

Kansas wasn't so bad after all. She inched into the kitchen.

"Where in God's name have you been? "Berta squawked. "Don't tell me you never made it to the market."

"I fell."

"What do you mean, you fell?"

"I slipped getting off the bus. The groceries went into the street. The bus driver insisted I be taken to the hospital, my ankle appeared to be broken."

"And you couldn't call me?"

"I was being ferried from one department to another. I couldn't get to a phone. I don't want to talk about it. I just want to soak my foot and go to bed." Colleen clung to the staircase banister and winced with each step as Berta looked on.

"Doctors use mittens on sprained ankles these days?"

"I, um. There's an ace wrap underneath."

Berta studied Colleen's gait. "If you were a horse, they'd shoot you."

"Yes, Mother, I don't doubt they would."

"By the way, how did you make it home?"

"I took a cab."

"What did that cost you?"

"My virginity."

"If it was more than a three-dollar fare, you both got screwed." Berta shook her head, watching her daughter hobble to the top of the stairs. "Liar."

The bathroom still retained the clawfoot tub, box and chain toilet, whitewashed wainscoted walls, and a skirted sink. Charm and taste were of no concern to Berta. The bathroom functioned; there was no need for alterations. Colleen fastened the door's hook and eye latch and removed the robe covering a full-length mirror hanging on the back of the bathroom door. She scrutinized her reflection, wondering what her naked body looked like through Lee's eyes. Her virginity taken, she expected to look different.

The only difference was that the body in the mirror was no longer hers; it belonged to Lee. Sliding her long legs into the short tub, she rehearsed for their next encounter.

***

Headlights illuminated the front window. Freida hated the bay window that didn't open. She hated everything about the house. Once Oscar was deemed mentally incompetent, Aaron wasted no time taking charge of his parents' legal affairs. First on the agenda was removing the couple from their home. Freida yanked open the front door. Lee stood holding his key and wearing a broad smile.

"Where have you been? You could have been dead in a ditch!"

Lee held out his arms. "I'm fine, see!" Freida slumped onto the sofa, dropping her head into her hands.

"Your father is sick, Aaron is gone, and then you disappear. You are all I have." Lee slid next to his weeping mother, giving her a hug.

"No more tears. I'm coming home to stay. Today is the happiest day of my life."

"It will be the shortest day of your life if I don't get an explanation."

Unmoved by his mother's tears, he walked to the kitchen. Freida followed. "Have you heard a word I've said?"

"Anything to eat?"

"Look at your coat! It's covered in mud. You're limping!"

Lee stuck his head in the refrigerator. "You can blame Colleen."

"Colleen?"

"I wanted to see her but didn't want to tangle with her mother. I figured at some point I'd catch her entering or leaving the house. Any potato salad?"

Freida slammed the refrigerator door. Her eyes melted in tears; her tongue slid into Russian. "You are my hope, my love. If you die, I die with you."

"Pickles? Anyway, I'm standing at the foot of her street freezing my ass...ophagus, off, when I see her getting off the bus."

Lee stopped chewing. "Mom, she's gorgeous."

Freida stood over her son with her arms folded across her chest. "She was pleased to see you?"

"No. She slapped me, kicked me, and told me to get out of her life. Check out my eye, she got me with a can."

"You'll get tetanus and die!"

Lee looked off as if under a spell. "I can lose my eye, I have another, as long as I have the memory of her face when I told her I loved her. It was so cold out that her spit froze."

"Good that she should hate you."

"She loves me."

"Loves you? She breaks your leg, cuts your eye, and spits on you. Is this some mating ritual?"

"Must be, because we did."

Freida covered her mouth and backed away. He wasn't boasting to a male buddy about his latest conquest; this was his mother.If only he could push the admission back down his throat. With one sentence, he went from alpha male to a frightened ten-year-old.

"You raped her!"

"I didn't rape her."

Freida collapsed into a chair. "My son, a rapist."

Lee dragged his chair next to his mother's, holding her hand, he professed his love for Colleen. "She's all I've ever wanted, and now she's mine. Please be happy for us."

"If you impregnated her, you'll be forced to marry."

"She's pregnant."

"Please, Leon, no jokes."

"I'm marrying Colleen."

"She's to tell her mother you had your way with her? I should have tickets to such a roller derby. You're young; date other girls."

"Jewish girls?"

"You may come to like them."

"I've got my khaverte." Lee kissed his mother's cheek. "Ouch! She cut my lip. I'll put ice on it."

"Better you put ice down your pants. That's what keeps you chasing her."

***

Colleen twisted her fingers around the coiled telephone cord. "Margo?"

"Colleen, speak up."

"I need to see you."

"Drive over."

"The car's dead. I wish I were."

Margo's stomach turned; she didn't want to be the one to inform Colleen of Clay's demise but couldn't stand by while her sister suffered the pain of being rejected. "Clay?"

"Not a word."

"Please don't go to Savannah. Wait until you hear from him. Stay put. I'm coming to get you."

***

Colleen was waiting in the park when Margo pulled up. "Get in, we'll drive to the beach."

The sisters sat in silence, looking out at the choppy steel-gray surf. The winter wind blew hissing sand against Margo's salt-covered sports car. "This is costing me a paint job," Margo remarked, attempting to lighten the mood.

"This news is going to cost me my life. Why is love so complicated? Why can't I tell Ma I'm in love, be happy for me?"

"This isn't about Clay, is it?"

"She'll kill me, but she has to be told."

"He's Black."

"No."

"A woman. I knew it, I knew it!"

"It's Lee."

"She'll kill you. Lee- Don't that beat all? Where in God's name did you meet up with him?"

"He came back to help his mother settle into the house Aaron owns."

"I own."

"I went food shopping. When I got off the bus, he was there."

"Hang on. Lee just happened to be standing at the bus stop in the old neighborhood?"

"He'd come to check on the apartment building. You own that, too?"

"God no."

"We went over there and then, you know."

"Well, I'll be. You held out for Lee."

"It wasn't like that. My plan was to kill him."

"That's how relationships end, not begin. Regrets?"

"I love him."

Margo reached into her purse and squeezed the keys to her Boston flat into Colleen's hand.

"You love birds will need a love nest while he's in town. Tell Ma you're house-sitting for me. I'm spending New Year's Eve in New York. Please be careful, Ronny is on the prowl. Since Aaron left, I've been receiving hang-up calls. He may know I keep a place in town, so don't answer the door for anyone." Margo flopped her head back on the car's headrest and blew out a puff of smoke.

"So, the Wicked Witch gets the news for New Year's. Promise me you won't tell her until I get back. I want to be there to support you." Margo snuffed out her cigarette. "Screw it. Let's tell her now."

Colleen remained in the car, wringing her hands. "Come on," Margo called out as she headed up the walkway to the house. Realizing Colleen wasn't following the order, she returned to the car.

"I'm afraid," Colleen confessed.

"Is your fear of her stronger than your love for him?" Margo yanked her sister out of the car.

Christmas bells hanging from the front door jingled. "Colleen, is that you? I'm in the living room, come help me take down this God forsaken tree." Berta's slim form was obstructed by the buxom balsam. "I can't reach the lights on the upper branches. You have the height. I don't know why I bother with a tree. The holidays aren't the same without Rosaria. You'd think Patsy would come by with the boy. Busy man, new family, not that he ever felt at home here." The tangled string of lights led Berta around to the front of the half-naked tree and face-to-face with Margo. "Oh, it's you. Where's your sister?"

"Merry Christmas to you, too."

"If you had been here for Christmas, I would have given you a proper greeting, but you were in New York doing God knows what."

The thumping of Colleen's boots as she stomped snow on the welcome mat acted as a boxing bell, putting an end to round one. Colleen led her mother by the elbow over to the couch. "Come sit, I have something to tell you."

"If it's about the house, it's not up for discussion."

"It's not about the house, it's me, I'm..." Colleen hesitated.

Margo shooed her with her hand. "Go on, tell her."

"I'm in love."

"Dear God. I thought you had cancer. Now come help me with the tree."

"Please, Ma, sit. There's more."

"You can talk while we work."

Margo lit a cigarette. "She's stalling Colleen. She does this whenever the conversation is headed in a direction she doesn't want to go."

Berta threw down the delicate miniature lights to the floor. "Put that cigarette out. The floor is covered in dry needles; you'll burn the house down."

"That's the only way to get you out of this haunted house."

"It's Lee," Colleen blurted. "I'm in love with Lee."

Berta backed away. "Where in God's name did you dig him up? We just got rid of one, and you drag home his brother. Tossing Dr. Vaughan over for a... a..."

Margo couldn't contain herself. "A Jew. Is that the term you were searching for?"

Berta gave her daughter a stony stare. "You keep out of this."

"No, I won't."

"Don't start with me, Nuala. I'm trying to prevent Colleen from repeating your mistake."

"She's not me. Lee is not Aaron. If you turn her away, you'll be alone."

"Please stop, both of you." Colleen pleaded. With a jab of her finger, Margo pushed Colleen back onto the couch.

"Butt out! This isn't about you."

Colleen threw her arms in the air. "Here we go again."

"There are only the three of us. Colleen is the glue that holds us together."

Berta turned to a shaken Colleen. "Go on, go. You won't get an argument from me. I'm done."

Margo directed her anger at both her mother and sister. "That's it? That's all you have to say to her? She doesn't get the stealing nuts from squirrels' speech?"

"I always knew Colleen would run off with some weirdo."

"Weirdo!"

Berta turned back to Margo. "You could have had any man you wanted, but you wanted someone I wouldn't approve of. You married Dr. Hirsh to spite me. You saw a handsome face and a fat wallet, and you were gone."

Margo frantically buttoned her coat. "I don't know why I came here. You lost us. All you have is this stinking house, and you're going to lose that too. Come along, Colleen."

"I'm not leaving."

"Fine. Stay."

The slamming of the door knocked its bells to the ground.

"Ma."

Berta put up her hand. "Don't say a word."

"This has to be said. I love you, and I love Lee. I even love this spooky old house."

"Are you married?"

"No."

"Mr. Hirsch is low-hanging fruit; this will kill him."

"If it kills him, it kills him. I have no control over other people's lives. I thought I did, but I let go of that notion. Whatever happens between you and Margo is your business; I'll stay out of it, but I never want to lose your love and approval."

"Have you broken the news to Dr. Vaughan?"

"I'll write, he'll be happy for me."

"Always liked Lee," Berta admitted. "He has your father's good qualities. Never cared for his brother. I imagine few people do."

"You wish it had worked out with Clay."

"He would have gotten fed up with your shenanigans and left you. Lee knows you have a screw loose. I hope he has a good screwdriver."

"I'll stay with you tonight. We'll ring in the new year together."

"No, you spend it with Lee. Tell him... You know."

"Happy New Year?"

"That he's welcome."

"Thanks, Mom."

"Is he still afraid of me?"

"Yes."

"Good ."

Chapter Thirty

Stan sat up in bed. "Sorry. I can't stay for the ball drop, so let's fill our glasses and toast to the new year."

Margo rolled onto her chest and held out her champagne glass. "To the worst year of my life."

Their glass clink was followed by a kiss. "I would have loved to have seen the look on your mother's face when she learned about Leon. You missed a great opportunity to drop the J-bomb on the old girl."

"Me? Tell her Grandma was a fallen woman."

"He was single, she a widow, where's the crime?"

"They weren't married. Don't think I wasn't tempted, but I haven't any hard evidence. If a team of lawyers couldn't locate the twins, then it's only hearsay. I'll bide my time," Margo said, with a smoke-eyed squint. "I can't persuade you to stay?"

"Joanne and the kids come first. I've got a New Year's resolution for you."

"I know: stop smoking. I have a better one. Stop sleeping with married men."

"Technically, my dear, you're still a married woman."

Margo's mood turned downbeat. "You haven't heard from him?"

"Not a word. You miss him?"

"Somewhat," Margo admitted with an unconvincing shrug. "That's not to say I'd take him back."

"Yes, you would. You're still in love with him."

Margo lay back and took a slow drag. "There's a side to Aaron few people saw. If he loved you, cared for you, had something to teach you, he was a kind, patient, generous man. He didn't play God like most doctors. Aaron was a saint. Saints have flaws."

"You, my dear lady, have had too much of the bubbly. Anyone who thinks Aaron is a saint must be drunk."

"It's because of Aaron that I am a lady. Sure, I was always attractive, okay, stunning. What Aaron called a second-string pin-up."

"This from a saint!"

"You can't understand him the way only a wife can. When I introduced Aaron to my father at Rosaria's wedding, he told me to call an ambulance. I hesitated for fear my mother would kill me for causing a scene. When I returned, my mother was standing between Aaron and Poppy. Aaron picked my mother up by her waist, moving her from here to there.

"I'd never witnessed anyone stand up to my mother. I was eighteen, he was an old guy but strong, sexy, masterful. I was determined to marry a man like Dr. Hirsh. To this day, she calls Aaron, 'That daddy-killing Jew doctor.' A grown woman using that language—disgusting."

"You'll take him back."

"Oh, no, I won't. Not after he's been with that gypsy. Would you believe, when we dated, he didn't have a clue how to pleasure a woman?"

"You're kidding, right?"

"Forty years old and as pure as the driven snow."

"Margo! That man has plowed more snow angels than the D.P.W. He lost his virginity in the womb. I don't think a day has gone by that he didn't get laid. Aaron's a legend; men bow to him, women bow before him. He told me he gave up the innocent routine; he was too old, chicks weren't buying it, but you did. This is priceless. Get this, Virgin Boy was seeing two other women while he was dating you. I sent you the roses and note, he couldn't be bothered. Aaron wasn't into you until he got into you."

Margo sprang off the bed. "Why that daddy killing Jew bastard! That's why he wore a rubber."

Stan staggered around the room holding his side. "That night in the North End, I didn't run into you by accident. Aaron called me from the restaurant; he wanted me to check you out. One look at you, and I said to myself, 'That lucky bastard. I bet she's great in the sack.' You are."

Margo held an empty champagne bottle over Stan's head like a club. "What else did he tell you about that night?"

"Just the funny stuff." Stan dropped to his knees, hugging Margo's leg, pleading for forgiveness. "Please, Margo, don't kill me. I'm not like the others, I don't think you're a bad girl, a dirty girl." Stan raised his voice an octave. "I'm so turned on. Spank me, Aaron, spank me."

"I never said 'spank me.' It wasn't funny enough, he added 'spank me!' You know what I'm going to do?"

"Kill me?"

"Later. I'm going to hop a flight to Haifa and track down that dirty boy, snap his head off, hollow it out, and leave it in a playground."

"Come on, babe, it's New Year's, let's let bygones be bygones. I'm sorry, Margo, but you were a young, spoiled, cock tease who wanted to play with the big boys. Well, that's what the big boys do, we love ya and laugh at you for loving us. As for Aaron, a genius."

Wearing a far-off look, Margo dropped down on the bed. Stan snapped his fingers in her face. "Margo... Margo, are you okay? I've never seen that look on your face."

"It's because I'm thinking," she muttered. "He was a genius, a tender, considerate genius."

"Did I miss something? Are we talking about the same Jew bastard?"

"It may have been an act, but I bought into it. He made me feel like I was the master, the instructor. I felt proud, needed, and loved. Why that sly fox. We'd be out with his highbrow friends; you were never there. I'd say something he thought was stupid. He'd berate me in front of everyone. I'd give him a vengeful stare that said, 'Wait till we get home, to bed. I'll show you who's stupid.'

"Any other man who treated their wife as he had would be banished to the sofa, not me. There I was making mad passionate love to him. He'd swear never to humiliate me again, but we both knew he would." Margo teared up. "Now that's what I call a genius. And I let him slip through my fingers. My mother said this would happen. That witch looked into her crystal ball and saw my marriage fail because it was based on sex."

"What's wrong with that?"

"I no longer satisfied him."

"I'm not buying it." Stan sat at the foot of the bed, sipping champagne. "I still don't get it. Why would he leave a hot, sexy woman like you for a wildebeest?"

"I'll tell you why—he wants children, and I can't have them."

Champagne spurted out of Stan's nostrils; his flapping hands reached for the starched white napkin, collaring the bottle's neck. "Aaron's sterile," he choked. "He got a case of the measles as a teenager; the fever boiled his balls." Stan rolled on the bed in a fetal position, laughing. "He's sterile, you're sterile, and he wears a condom. You can't make this stuff up!"

"I was so fucking stupid! And you—"

"Me! What did I do?"

"You could have said something?"

461

"It was none of my business. Matter of fact, you were yank'n his chain, playing hard to get. He'd never been jilted; it drove him nuts. He was hell bent on winning you back." Stan poured himself another drink. "Come on, Margo, you couldn't have been so naive to think a good-looking guy like Aaron had never been with a woman."

"I thought he was a scholar, a bookworm with more important things on his mind than sex."

"Margo. We're men. There is nothing more important on our minds, and his worm wasn't in a book."

"My mother was right. I'm only good for sex."

Stan nuzzled his head on her shoulder. "What you are is every man's fantasy. Plenty of women would trade their PhDs to have what comes naturally to you. Men aren't impressed by how many letters are behind your name, as long as you let us in your behind. Speaking of behind, I'm late."

Margo buttoned up Stan's overcoat the way a mother would sending her son off to school. "You're one of the few men I trust."

"Keep your chin up," Stan advised with a casual kiss. "Almost forgot." He dug into his coat's pocket and tossed the room key to Margo. "Happy New Year."

***

"This is some place your sister has. Commonwealth Ave, nice address. What's next, The Chamberlin Towers?"

Colleen put her nose in the air. "We're too good for The Chamberlin."

Lee sank into a pink velvet chair, flopping his arms over its sides in a ragdoll pose. "Your mother's okay with us spending the night together?"

"She likes you."

"Good. I was afraid she'd cut your face and I'd have to dump you."

"You can thank Margo for keeping me out of the hospital; she was there to support me. As expected, they battled it out like two tomcats over a queen. My mother was so exhausted after going six rounds with Margo, she had nothing left for me. All she said was she hoped you were still afraid of her and a good screw."

"Now I am afraid! All's well in the Hirsch household. She took the news rather well, not at first, but after her 'I'm so disappointed in you' spiel, doesn't she pull up a chair and ask all about you. My mother knew how I felt about you since I was in grade school. She saw how I came to life whenever you were around. I'd come home from the library and tell her all the funny things you'd say and do. I'd go to school with a smile on my face and come home still wearing it. All my parents wanted was for Aaron to be successful, and me to be happy." Lee jerked his head toward the door. "Let's walk over to The Common before the crowd hits town."

After creating a flock of snow angels, a hunchback snowman, and landing a slushy snowball down Lee's back, the exhausted pair took a seat on an icy bench watching the sun set over Boston's changing skyline.

"Do you remember where you were last New Year's Eve?" Lee asked.

Colleen placed her index finger on her cheek. "Hum, let's see, New Year's Eve fell on December 31st that year. I recall going to a strange club, in a strange city, meeting a strange man."

Lee cut in. "Every New Year's Eve, you're going to remember that night, a night I want to forget. Colleen, every day I'm with you is the happiest day of my life, then another one follows. The day we met, I made a list of what I wanted. On the top of that list was to make you my friend, and one day my wife." Lee dropped to one knee in the snow. "This is the New Year's Eve I want you to always remember." Removing the soggy glove from her left hand, he slid a square-cut ruby ring on her chilled ring finger. "Colleen, would you do me the honor of becoming my wife?"

Looking up from the crimson stone, Colleen vowed. "I'll be you your Queen, and you, my Wizard."

"Let's get back to the apartment. I had a couple of other things I want to do to you on that list."

"Like I didn't see this coming." She said, wiggling her left hand in Lee's face.

"Shut up."

"No, you shut up."

***

Fluffing the feather-filled pillows against the bed's tapestried headboard, Colleen snuggled up to Lee's chest. "Something on your mind?"

"May I ask you a personal question?"

Colleen ran her hand down his bare torso. "Can't get more personal than this."

"Is it true you found another guy?"

"It's true."

"Did you love him?"

"Yes."

"Your mother?"

"She liked him, too."

"What was he, an ax murderer?"

"Close, a doctor. We met at one of those galas Margo puts on for the hospital. We dated for a short time. When his residency was up, he returned to Georgia. I planned on joining him."

"What will you tell him?"

"I'll take the coward's way out and write. Do you have a girl in Chicago?"

"When you're a single guy working in an office where women outnumber men three to one, you get plenty of attention. I said I had a girl back in Boston, when I return, I'm going to ask her to marry me."

"Had I said no?"

"I would have told them you died in a horrific car accident."

"What kind of car was I driving?"

464

"You weren't driving. Your drunken sister was at the wheel, claims she doesn't remember any of it. You know, Chicago is a honeymoon Mecca."

"You want me to go back with you?"

"Only for a couple of weeks."

"What will I do there? You'll be at work while I'm alone in a strange city."

"You could sleep in, watch TV talk shows, go through my stuff."

"Tempting, but I plan on finding us a place to live while you're away."

"We could take the apartment above my parents. Margo will gladly evict the hot nurses Aaron rented it to. If Chicago is out, where would you like to honeymoon?"

"Niagara Falls!"

"And risk you throwing me over the Falls?"

"You have a point."

"I think we should head for a tropical destination."

"You hate summer."

Lee tucked in his chin, "I do?"

"Every year when school got out, you'd say how much you hated the summer. I never asked why. Frankly, I didn't care. I do now."

"When school wasn't in session, I had nowhere to go, nothing to do."

Colleen played an invisible violin. "Join the club."

"You had your sisters; there was always something going on at your house."

"Didn't the Hirsch family ever go on vacation?"

"My parents would have spent our vacation worrying about what was going on back home."

"Camp?"

"Went once, hated it. I always preferred the company of women, the result of spending so much time with my mother."

"You haven't answered my question: why the beach?"

"I've never been to the beach. My mother feared I'd get sunburned and drowned. I wanted you to ask me to come along with your family."

"You would have gotten a sunburn and drowned."

"With any luck, Margo would know mouth-to-mouth."

"She does."

"Secretly, I wanted to be a part of your family. The first time I saw you, I was riding my bike past the Mount. You, Rosaria, and Mae were standing by the side of the road next to a car with the hood up. I saw Margo coming down the street with a man carrying a jug of water; the car must have overheated. I pretended I was the guy with the water. You girls were so happy I had come to your rescue. You asked, no begged me to come along in case the car gave you any more trouble, and Margo thought I was cute. I said I'd have to ask my mother, and you said, 'Screw the old lady, get in the car.'"

"I remember that vacation. Rosaria had just gotten her driver's license. We were heading to Falmouth to catch the ferry to Martha's Vineyard." Colleen paused, not knowing if she should reveal the details of a night she and her sisters swore never to speak of. "Poppy was a kind, caring man with a heart of gold, but one night, I don't know what brought it on, if he was very drunk or had the DTs, but he turned violent. Ma and Mae tried to restrain him. He swore and spat on my mother, took a swing at Mae, I mean, he decked her. We were locked in one of the bedrooms for our own safety. Poppy pounded on the door, calling us names, saying things I knew he didn't mean. We watched from the window as he was taken away in a straitjacket. We thought we'd never see him again."

Lee's eyes teared. "I had no idea."

"We were instructed never to speak of the episode, not even with one another. I convinced myself that it never happened. Poppy's drinking left a lasting effect on the three of us. Rosaria enabled men. Margo never trusted men. And I regarded them as objects of ridicule, to be dominated and bullied the way my mother treated my father." Colleen wiped away a tear and nervously smiled up at Lee. "So, off we went to the Vineyard. My days were spent beating up boys, my nights frosted in Noxema.

"Poor Rosaria, her father let her down, her sister abandoned her for a boy, and in a couple of years, she wouldn't be walking. Rosaria would have given up all hope of having a normal life, being loved by a man, if it hadn't been for Aaron. He made her feel attractive, worthy of a busy young doctor's time. Mae would say, there was someone out there waiting for her. Aaron made her believe there was. It's true what they say about the other man's grass. I would have loved to have come home to a quiet, predictable environment, to be asked if there was homework I needed help with, not shooed away like a pest."

"Why didn't you ask the teacher for help?"

"Pride. Afraid of being ridiculed. I figured at some point they'd give up on me, leave me alone, write me off. That's why I was caught off guard when you offered to help me pass math. I thought, 'This kid is nuts.' So, I tested you. Pushed every button, exploited every weakness, I swore, spat, punched, kicked, did my 'Miracle Worker' routine, but you didn't give up on me."

"And I never will. Happy New Year."

***

"Get up," Colleen whispered.

"What... what time is it?" Lee mumbled.

"Someone is at the door, listen." It was a soft, muffled knock one would use to check for inhabitants, not to gain entry. "Hear it?"

Lee kicked off the blankets. "I'm going to see what this guy wants."

"Don't!"

"What are you so worked up about?"

"It's Ronny, he's come to kill Margo."

467

The door rattled. "That does it."

Colleen followed him into the living room. "Look," she said, pointing to the shifting light under the threshold. "He's leaving."

The footsteps moved on. Without unlatching the lock's chain, Lee was allowed a limited view of the hallway. "It's okay. He went into the apartment across the hall. It's New Year's Eve, the guy is probably drunk and forgot his apartment number."

Colleen rested her head on Lee's shoulder. "My hero."

***

Lee lightly glided his finger down a sleeping Colleen's spine, giving her the sensation of an army of bedbugs feeding on her flesh.

"Stop, that tickles."

"You don't strike me as the ticklish type."

"This is how I strike you." A power-packed swing of a feather-filled pillow landed Lee on the bedroom floor along with a Tiffany table lamp.

"Look what you did!"

"You swung the pillow."

"You took the fall!"

Lee bent over the shattered shade. "Let's have a look, it may be salvageable." Turning his back left him open for the cranial collision with a pillow. "Fowl," he yelled, shaking off feathers from the split pillow. Colleen collapsed in laughter.

"What's so funny?"

"You. You're covered in feathers."

Lee held his arms out. "Come fly with me." Flesh to flesh, the two twirled around the feather-filled room. "Where is your tiara, my Queen?"

"Where's your crown, Your Majesty?"

"I'm not a king, remember?"

"I'll tell you what you are, an Emperor without clothes."

"How observant, Lady Godiva."

The fairytale spell was broken by invaders outside the castle door. "Boston Police."

Lee hopscotched into his underpants. "You're over eighteen, right?"

Colleen picked feathers out of his hair. "Someone may have reported a raid on their chicken coop."

Sliding the lock's metal latch, Lee came face to face with two uniformed officers, one leaning cross-legged against the door frame. The other, with an open notepad like a waitress prepared to take a breakfast order.

"I'm sorry to..." The officer paused; his eyes ricocheted around the room. "...interrupt you. I'm Officer Gleason."

The scribe introduced himself as Robinson. Colleen shuffled out of the bedroom in Margo's pink satin robe and high-heeled slippers.

"Lee, look out the window, the street is crawling with cops." Her eyes met Gleason's. "What's going on?"

"I was about to ask you the same question," the officer said, eyeing the carelessly clad couple. "But that can wait."

"Honey, this is Officer Gleason and Robinson."

"Your names?" Robinson asked, not bothering to look up from his notepad.

"Leon Hirsch. That's H-i-r-s-c-h." Robinson pointed his pen at Colleen.

She hesitated. "Colleen..."

"Hirsch?"

"Not yet. It's Colleen Ronan, for now."

"Which one of you lives here?" Gleason probed.

"Neither," Lee answered. "It belongs to Nuala Hirsh. H-i-r-s-h."

"Your wife?" The officer asked, wearing a gotcha smile.

Colleen jumped in to set the record straight. "She's my sister, Margo. She's...was married to Lee's brother, Dr. Aaron Hirsh."

"Let's go over this again." The officer's summary was cut off by a raspy voice over a walkie-talkie.

"Victim's been transported to City Hospital. The post-mortem will be conducted this afternoon. The landlord has been informed."

"Victim!"

"There's nothing to be afraid of," Lee assured Colleen with a hug.

"Your brother-in-law or whoever is right, don't upset yourself. Were the two you here all last night?"

"Yes," Colleen answered. "Who was killed?"

Her question was ignored. "Did either of you hear anything last night? An argument, some kinda ruckus?"

Colleen looked down at the pink, fluffy feathers on Margo's slippers. "No."

Lee agreed with a headshake. Gleason sensed Colleen's ambivalence. "Ma'am, you got something to add?"

"Well... there was this knock on the door around oneish, but we didn't answer it. After a minute or so, he went away."

"What did he say?"

"Nothing."

"Then how ja know it was a man?"

"At first, I thought it was my sister's old boyfriend. He's been calling her home. She's recently separated and feared he may know she has an apartment in the city. It turned out to be a drunk who mistook this apartment for his."

"What apartment would that be?"

"Across the hall, Six B, Lee saw him."

"You saw him?"

"I poked my head out, saw him go in."

"Both of you, get dressed. You're coming with us; we'll need a statement."

Colleen covered her mouth. "She was strangled?"

"Lady, all I can tell ya is, not opening this door was the smartest thing you've ever done."

***

Located a few blocks from the crime scene, Boston Police Headquarters served as a toilet bowl for the city's New Year's hangover. A woman had been murdered. Party's over. Gleason directed the couple to a scuffed wooden bench unworthy of the station's marble hall. "Wait here."

Raising his eyes to the ceiling, Lee shook his head. "I came to town 48 hours ago, met up with you, and wouldn't you know it, I'm being held for questioning in a murder. And I want to be a part of this family? I must be sick!"

"I feel sick knowing we were fooling around while the woman across the hall was being strangled."

"Take a seat. I'm Lieutenant Bowdoin." The couple held hands at the interrogation table.

"I'll be taking a statement from you, it's routine, you're not suspects."

A crew cut and light complexion allowed Bradlee Bowdoin to "pass." He'd been raised from the age of four by his grandmother in a toney white suburb after his father took off and his mother died with a needle in her arm. His hazel eyes were fixed on Lee. "Seems you're the only person to get a look at our suspect. Can you describe the man you saw entering Apartment Six B?"

Lee cleared his throat. "He, um, well, I didn't get a very good look at him; his back was to me. He kinda tilted his head when he opened the door, giving me a glimpse of his profile."

"He opened the door. He wasn't let in?"

"He must have had a key, or it was unlocked."

"Can you describe him?"

"He was short."

"How short?"

"Not much taller than us," he said, referring to himself and the detective. Colleen closed her eyes and shook her head, knowing Bowdoin didn't appreciate being compared to Lee in stature. "He was wearing one of those green jackets servicemen wear."

"You think he was a vet?"

"No. That's the weird part; he had long dark hair in a ponytail. His pants and boots were black."

"Gloves?"

"I didn't notice."

"He was wearing them," Colleen added.

"You said you didn't see him." Bowdoin challenged with a squinty eye.

"I didn't, but his knock was muffled, like his hand was covered."

The interrogation door was opened without an apology. "Lieutenant, there's a nutty blond out here, name's Margo Hirsh."

Bowdoin looked at Lee. "Another wife?"

"She's my sister," Colleen explained. "She's Nuala."

"Let her in," Bowdoin said. "She may know the victim."

Margo bolted into the room, her eyes on Colleen, her finger pointed at Bowdoin. "Do not speak to that man without a lawyer. Did he give you water? A phone call? I heard about the murder while driving from the airport. When I reached the apartment, you were gone. You think I'm crazy now? When I was told you had been hauled off, I jumped back in my car and hit the gas. I must have been going over 70. That's what the cop who pulled me over said." Without invitation, Margo plopped into a chair next to Bowdoin and lit a cigarette. "Can you fix a traffic ticket?"

"I'm the one asking the questions, Mrs. Hirsh, now shut up."

Margo put her hand on her chest. "The nerve." Springing to her feet, Margo pointed at Colleen's finger.

"Where did you get that ring?"

"Lee gave it to me. We're engaged."

Margo stomped her feet and flapped her hands like a chicken hearing the farmer's truck backfire. Coming around the table, she kissed the couple. "Big wedding? Let's shoot for July."

Bowdoin grew impatient. "Can we get back to the subject at hand? Not the hand of the subject?"

Margo lowered her head and tiptoed back to her seat. "Sorry."

"Mrs. Hirsh, did you know the woman living in Apartment Six B?"

Deaf to the question, Margo cupped her hands around her mouth and whispered across the table. "I can get you a deal on a dress."

Margo turned back to Bowdoin. "What were you saying?"

"Did you know the victim?"

"No. I don't spend much time there, so I'm not acquainted with the other tenants."

"So, you never met Miss Lingard, never saw her in the lobby, or shared an elevator?"

"Lingard... Lingard..."

Bowdoin handed her the missing piece to the puzzle. "Lillian Lingard. She was some kind of fashion model back in the day."

"Lillian Lingard! I rented next to Lilly the Lips!"

Colleen cocked her head. "I never heard of her."

"You're too young, she did lipstick ads for Max Factor. When I think of what that woman could have done for my career. Did you get a look at the body? I bet she had a facelift."

Bowdoin wiped his hands down his face as if to erase his features. "Ladies, a woman is dead; show some respect."

Margo squirmed in her seat. "May I go now?"

"No, Mrs. Hirsh, you may not. I have a few questions for you."

"Me? I was out of town. Those two were at the murder scene."

"You can start by telling me about your old boyfriend." Margo slowly turned her head to Colleen.

"I told him it couldn't be Ronny."

"Detective Bowdoin, Ronny did not have a hand in this."

"Sister says he was harassing you."

474

"I admit we had a stormy relationship, but he wouldn't mistake me for Lippy. Christ, the woman was on the far end of sixty."

"Fifty-four. We like to be thorough. No harm in talking to him, if his story checks out, we let him go."

"You can't! He'll kill me! "Margo caught herself, "Not kill me. Kill me."

"I get your drift. Look, if he gives you any grief, call us and we'll pick him up. Now what's his name?"

"Conrad Ronald Kilday Junior."

"The real estate magnet?"

"More like real estate maggot."

"You are aware he owns that building?"

"No. It was a sublet. My husband took over the lease last year."

"Let me get this straight. Kilday owns the building, knows you live there, wants you dead, and has the keys to your apartment. Yeah, it's time to talk to your old flame."

***

Bowdoin sized up the pissed-off landlord seated across the table. The kid sister was right, Kilday didn't fit the description. He did what insincere people do—lay it on thick. Ronny tightened his lip to cool his temper. Bowdoin took note.

"I can't believe that murdering scumbag was in one of my buildings. Wouldn't I like to get my hands around the bastard's neck? These women shouldn't live alone, especially the pretty ones."

"What type of security system do you have in the building?"

"They have to be buzzed in."

"Ring enough bells, someone's bound to buzz you in."

"Look, I just purchased the property a couple of months ago. I was looking into one of those speaker phone systems."

"But as it stands, the tenants only have a simple slide lock to keep predators out."

"Awe come on! They let a stranger in, and I'm responsible? Christ, half the residential buildings in this town don't have a security system."

"They will now. Who besides yourself has keys?"

"The super, but he had the holiday off."

"So, the building was unattended."

"If there's a problem, they know what number to call, and I get someone out there. And that someone isn't a babysitter."

"Lillian Lingard couldn't use the phone; the cord was twisted around her throat."

"Like I gotta hear that."

Bowdoin leaned forward in his chair. "And you gotta see that cuz we're taking you to the morgue. By the way, where were you last night?"

"Dining with friends at the Statler. You can check with the manager; I know you won't take my wife's word for it."

"Did you have your keys with you?"

"Yeah, I have them. If it were me, why would I have to be let in?" Ronny jiggled the loaded keyring in Bowdoin's face. "I can let myself in."

***

Freida's hair was no longer wrapped around her crown in a tight woven braid. She wore it short, artificially-colored and curled, looking as though she belonged in her modern kitchen supplied with an automatic dishwasher, electric stove, and refrigerator.

Colleen squeezed Lee's hand as he led her to his pajama-clad father, seated at a table she recognized from Blue Hill Ave. It hadn't aged, Oscar had. "Do you remember me?" Colleen pensively asked. Oscar's slack mouth stretched into a smile.

"Dad's smiling because you're a pretty girl. He grows tired of looking at my mother all day."

"Leon!" Both women scolded.

"Get your father's robe. He's usually dressed," Freida apologized. "He didn't feel well this morning, so I thought maybe he should return to bed. You've grown into an attractive young lady."

"Thank you, Mrs. Hirsch."

"Suddenly you're bashful? Sit, eat."

"She can't keep this act up for long," Lee teased. Freida turned her attention back to Colleen.

"So, there's to be another Mrs. Hirsch."

"Lee told me you helped choose the stone."

"Helped! He wanted to buy an emerald. I told him emeralds are cold, Colleen is fiery, more suited for a ruby."

"Or a charcoal briquette," Lee joked.

Colleen didn't laugh; she'd never seen Oscar without a beard and glasses.

Freida detected Colleen's mournful expression. "He's not the man you last saw in Dorchester, such a shame. A great mind he had."

Lee stood behind Oscar's chair with both hands on his father's shoulders. "He was a very courageous man. I'll tell you sometime about his war experience. It's best he doesn't remember those dark days. But you remember Dorchester, don't you, Dad."

Colleen was reminded of Miss Pepperton's words. *"Home is not a place, it's a memory you'll always carry with you."*

477

"I don't think it's the four walls your father misses, but the family and friends that brought those walls to life."

Colleen bent down and clasped Oscar's hands. "It's going to be as it was back in Dorchester, we're all coming home."

His clouded eyes looked into hers. "Heimish."

Freida hastily swiped a tear. "Leon, bring your father into the living room; his shows are about to come on." Freida waved her hand. Cartoons he watches."

"My dad hated television, didn't want one in the house. 'Pick up a book if you want entertainment,' he'd say." Lee set up an aluminum TV table in front of his dad's recliner and rolled an ottoman next to it. "I'll help you with the soup," he offered while tucking a napkin under Oscar's deflated chin. His good deed was rewarded with a whack on the hand from a hot spoon. "I can do."

"Alright, already!"

Freida waved Lee back to the kitchen. "Eat at the table, we can see him from here."

The conversation stalled; it had to be asked. "Your mother, she knows of your plans?" Freida asked, keeping her eyes lowered over her soup.

"She likes Lee, and knows if it weren't for him, I wouldn't know how to add or subtract."

"He better teach you how to multiply. Both families are dying out." Colleen's face turned as crimson as the ring on her finger. "Margo, is she well?"

"My sister is resurrecting her fashion career as well as her charity work for the hospital. Her latest project involves a health center planned for Blue Hill Ave. They intend to buy property on the six hundred block, which includes your building; the city will pay above the market value."

Lee took his soup and joined his father in front of the television. "You'll love this cartoon, Dad. It's the one where the Road Runner sticks a rocket up Wile E. Coyote's ass."

Freida shook her head. "Grown men. You were saying?"

"My mother's house wasn't on the chopping block, but Margo is trying to persuade the powers that be to take the property. Margo believes the house is haunted. I never bought into her theory, but she may be on to something. We've had four family members fall to their deaths on the staircase."

Lee returned to the kitchen. "You never told me any of this. I know about your grandmother. Who else?"

"My grandfather, great-grandfather, as well as my uncle, who took a header over the balcony last year."

Lee held up his palm. "Hang on, you're saying the house has been in your family for generations?"

"Apparently. I only know what Margo told me; it's a long story."

Lee pulled up a chair. "I've got time, let's hear it."

"Grandma Rourke, that's my mother's mother, claimed her husband Ambrose was run over by a trolly car the day he got off the boat, but his headstone listed his death as two years prior to my mother's birth. We were told the date was a stonemason's error. The plot thickens!" Colleen said with wide eyes, rubbing her hands over the soup as if to warm them.

"Margo met a Mrs. Zeigler, who is helping to finance the health center. Seems Mrs. Zeigler grew up in the area and remembers the original owner, Mr. Lindsey, who fell to his death on the staircase, one he'd stolen out of the house of a friend. His son Robert met the same fate after ending an affair with the Irish housemaid who gave birth to his twins, Robere and Roberta. The maid, Nuala, was dismissed. The boy was sent to France; the girl remained with Nuala."

"Did Margo tell your mother?" Lee asked.

"What's the point? Margo doesn't have any documentation. In my mother's eyes, Grandma was a saint. Besides, the Lindseys were Jewish; that would be a tough pill to swallow. Some things are best left unsaid."

Lee's jaw hung open. "Why didn't you tell me any of this?"

"I just found out myself," Colleen answered with a shrug, concentrating more on her soup than the bombshell bigger than the one sending Wile E. Coyote rocketing around the desert. "Margo will get to the bottom of it."

A car horn put an end to the conversation. "That's Margo now. I'm keeping her company. She's afraid to be left alone."

"Tell her there's no bad blood. She's always welcome."

"Thank you, Mrs. Hirsch. She'll appreciate that." Colleen kissed Freida's cheek and Oscar's head.

Lee held Colleen's coat open. "I'll see you to the door."

He returned to the kitchen wearing a wide grin. Freida raised her brow. "Something you find funny?"

"Berta had a Bubbie."

***

The apartment door was unlocked. Her first impulse was to run, but Margo was no longer fearful; she was fed up. Ronny heard her come in, yet remained seated at the edge of her bed perusing through lingerie.

"What are you doing here?" Margo directed him to the door with her head. "Get out."

"You've gone up a size, tut-tut," Ronny said, holding up a shear slip.

"I don't know why you're here or what you want, nor do I care. Now get out."

Ronny continued to fondle the fabric. "Cops said one of my tenants got a look at the killer, so I checked my records, and what da ya know, Nuala Hirsh rents apartment Six A. I think to myself, how many Nualas are out there?"

"Ronny, I swear I didn't bring your name up."

Twisting a silk stocking around his knuckles, he advanced toward her. "Cops think I'm the strangler."

Margo held her hands out. "Don't come any closer."

Ronny looked up at the ceiling and laughed. "What are you going to do? Beat me to death with a stiletto? I'm your landlord. I've come to check your pipes. Everything seems to be in order, so I'll be on my way." Reaching for his overcoat at the foot of the bed, Ronny spun around, wheeling a foot-long metal pipe, cracking the side of Margo's head, sending her to the floor. "Get up... I said Get up."

She was pulled to her feet by her hair. "I'm stalking you?"

Tears swam in her eyes; she snorted blood through her swollen nose. "Please don't."

"You're the one stalking me."

"I didn't know you bought the building."

"Sh, sh, look, babe, I'm sorry your husband left you. I truly am, but you gotta back off, I'm a happily married man, two kids. You want to see a picture of them? I would have liked to have gotten a look at my other kid, but it ended up in a bucket with other organs fed to an incinerator. Not only did you kill my kid, but the guy you were with. And I'm the murderer?"

"Those were rumors."

"Girls, so catty. They fill in missing information with cruel assumptions, like the stories you spread about Abby. Me, I can understand, but what did my sister ever do to you?" Ronny yanked Margo's hair from behind, pressing the pipe tight against her throat as he spoke. "You destroyed her marriage. Told that woodpecker freak where he could find her. You sabotaged my wedding, making a fool out of my wife. Now you finger me for a murder. You've accused me of every crime but the one I'm guilty of. Why's that?"

Margo shook her head from side to side like a baby refusing strained pears. "I'm sorry, I didn't know."

"I'll tell you what you did know. You knew what your mother's reaction would be when you lied and told her I called Rosaria a pathetic cripple. Odd, your mother would believe I'd say such a cruel thing, but you knew she'd never believe I raped you. She knows you're a slut. You were asking for it, wanted it. You still do, ain't that right, Margo? Admit it, every time you fuck you think of me. Let's refresh your memory." With a shove, Margo's body hit the bed. "Take your clothes off."

"I'll kill you, Ronny, I swear I'll see you dead."

The pipe landed hard against her ribs. The blow left her curled in a ball, unable to exhale. "You want it the way I gave it to you in the park? You want me to, what's the word? Ravish. That's it. You want me to ravish you? You're not the innocent young virgin you once were, so it won't be as exciting for me as it will be for you."

***

"She won't kill you, "Colleen assured Lee as she tugged him up the front steps.

"I'm not afraid," he said, shadow boxing around Colleen. "Bring her on." He jumped at the sound of the oak door slamming shut behind him.

"Ma! We're here!" Colleen called out in a house accustomed to loud voices.

Berta surfaced from the basement. "That furnace won't see another winter. Don't tell your sister." Her complaint was hijacked by her eyes that shot from Lee to Colleen and back. "Mother of God, what happened to you?"

"Grew up, I guess."

"You guess? Where did your sandy curls go?"

"Washed out to sea. They return on rainy days."

"It needs to be cut. You resemble your brother, only you're good-looking."

He knew the remark was a commentary on Aaron's personality. Not his appearance. "Thank you, I think."

After putting Lee's overcoat in the closet and the kettle on, Colleen returned to share the sofa with her future husband. "Like it?" she asked, wiggling the red stone under her mother's nose.

"Yes, I noticed it when you came in. I don't pretend to know much about jewelry, but it's very pretty."

"That's the tea." Colleen rushed to answer the kettle's call. She wondered if her mother's blood had also come to a boil. Voices weren't raised, doors weren't slammed, it was safe to return to the living room with a tray.

"Lee tells me his father is failing."

"Oh, Mom, he's so frail."

Berta poured the tea. "Your poor mother, a sick husband, a son out of the country, now you take up with this one," Berta said, jerking her head at Colleen.

Unfamiliar with Berta's dry humor, Lee cordially smiled. "This is the one bright spot in my mother's life. She's looking forward to the marriage and only wants the best for us. "

"Marry if you must, but I can't give my blessing. Don't roll your eyes at me, Missy. You're a poor representation of the faith, you and that fan-dancing sister of yours."

Lee squirmed in his seat. Colleen took a stand. "I won't fight Margo's battles."

Berta composed herself. "I apologize, Lee. Now is not the time nor the place for an argument. I expected Colleen to run off with a Hell's Angel, or some hippie, you're neither. You're a good, honest, decent young man."

"Thank you, Mrs. Ronan, you have no idea how relieved I am to know you approve of me."

Colleen poured herself a second cup of tea. "We're on our way over to Margo's apartment; she's moving out."

"She wasn't renting in the building where that murder took place?"

"She never uses it, sees no point to keeping it."

"Staying in Chestnut Hill, is she?"

"For the time being."

"You'll be moving out that way?"

"Brookline Village," Lee answered. "I'll be going back to school. Wherever I find work will determine where we'll eventually settle."

"What about you? Are you quitting school?" Berta asked, eyeing her daughter's belly. Colleen turned her head ever so slightly from side to side, mouthing the word, "No."

***

The '58 Lincoln sloshed along Storrow Drive, turning off at the Back Bay exit.

"Who would have thought we'd be driving around in the same car we took to the prom?"

"If you take care of a vehicle. You'll get ten years out of it, but this rock salt is rotting the undercarriage."

"You prefer black ice?"

"I prefer black coffee."

"I told Margo to wait; we'd go over to the apartment together. I've got a bad feeling."

"The killer wouldn't go back to the same building he'd just committed a murder," Lee assured her as he turned down Margo's block.

"Good, there's a spot on the street."

"Colleen, there's a snow emergency, we'll be towed. I'll swing around the block."

"Let me out here."

"What are you freaking out about? Okay, okay, I'll leave the car here."

Winded, he caught up to Colleen, relentlessly pushing the elevator button. The door rattled open; its fluorescent light flickered with each jolting chug to the sixth floor. "Margo!" Colleen cried as she pounded on the door with both fists.

"Use your key," a breathless Lee puffed.

"I tried; it's latched from the inside. I'm pulling the fire alarm."

"Step aside." One kick and he was in. "Oh God, oh Christ!" Colleen pushed past him, removing the gag from Margo's mouth.

She didn't scream.

"No one is out there," Lee said, looking out the open window to the fire escape. Returning from the kitchen with a steak knife, he sliced through the rough twine that bound her blue and bleeding wrists to the bedposts. Once free, she slumped into Colleen's arms. "Speak to me, Margo, was it him? Was it Ronny?"

On a mouthful of blood, Margo spit out a name. "AARON! Aaron, you did this, you left me. You knew he'd come back, but you didn't care. You promised to protect me, that I'd never have to be afraid again. But you didn't care, nobody cares."

***

Lieutenant Bowdoin met Colleen in the emergency ward. "Let me make something clear. She was told not to return to the apartment. We had no indication Kilday was violent."

Colleen poked her finger in his face. "You met him, you knew he had a temper. You wanted him to attack her to justify arresting him for the Lingard murder." She wanted to slap him but was anxious to see her sister.

"They won't let me look in the mirror. They said I'm too hysterical. How bad is it?" Margo mumbled.

Colleen gulped back tears. "You look like the rest of us now."

"That bad?"

Removing a hairbrush from her handbag, she attempted to brush her sister's knotted hair. "OUCH!" Margo whimpered. "He pulled my hair out by the roots. He was waiting for me like the night in the park."

"What park?"

"Sagamore Park. I wasn't mugged, I was raped. Ronny dragged me into the park, beat me, raped me, and left me for dead."

"Why didn't you tell someone?"

"Who? You? Ma? It would have been a tough sell to the police. I was advertising myself, Ronny wasn't a stranger, we dated. It probably wasn't our first time. It was, but not the last. They were both rapes. Violent men want to kill me; intelligent men discard me once I've lost my physical appeal."

"Ronny raped you because he's a sick, powerless, drunk. Aaron left you because he's a selfish, vain, coward, not worthy of you."

"Not only do I get what I want, I get what I deserve." A soft knock on the exam room door stunted Colleen's reply.

"May I come in?"

"I'm leaving," Colleen said, brushing past Bowdoin.

"Please stay. I have a question for you both. After all that's occurred, do you still maintain Kilday didn't murder Miss Lingard?"

"As much as I want to see him strapped to the chair, he's not your man," Margo mumbled through stitched lips. "I'll see he's punished, humiliated, bankrupted, dead."

"Please, Mrs. Hirsh, don't take the law into your own hands."

"You had him in yours and let him go."

Margo picked at her brittle nails. An approaching voice stopped her short of tearing off a cuticle.

"Mrs. Hirsh, I'm Officer Wales." She wasn't the masculine matron Margo envisioned. The spunky streetwise officer looked as if she were in costume, not in uniform.

Margo tugged on her johnny. "You wouldn't know where they put my clothes? I sent my sister to look for them."

"She'll have to bring you something to wear from home. Your clothes are evidence. "

Margo's nose tingled with the scent of menthol. "You wouldn't have a cigarette?"

"Newport, okay?"

"I'll smoke anything." Margo threw her head back, exhaling her first drag.

Officer Wales eyed Margo's bruised neck. "He got you good."

"Collapsed trachea."

"Maybe a cigarette's not a good idea." Ignoring the advice, Margo continued to puff.

"Mrs. Hirsh, according to the test results, they only found trace evidence of a sexual assault. Nonetheless, we have enough to charge Mr. Kilday with attempted murder. Even if the rape charge is thrown out, he'll be sent away for a long time."

"I wouldn't count on it. He's a very wealthy man, charming at times."

A deep voice interrupted the interview. "Officer Wales, I'd like a word with you. "

Alone, Margo puffed out smoke and grumbled, "Not enough evidence."

The officer returned. "Mrs. Hirsh, I've got great news. They're charging Mr. Kilday with assault, rape, and murder."

"Murder?"

"Lillian Lingard."

___

Chapter Thirty-One

Bowdoin lumbered into the interrogation room. Clipboard in hand, he slid it across the table to Ronny.

"You need a pen?"

Ronny looked up from the document, "What's this?"

"A confession," Bowdoin stated flatly. "Sign it."

"Yesterday I was the 'Boston Strangler,' today I'm the 'Boston Rapist,' and Margo's the accuser. Who's a jury gonna believe? Me, a successful, law-binding businessman, or a woman half the city has seen on TV with a rainbow flying out of her ass?"

"That's for a jury to decide if you choose to go that route."

"Darn right I do. I wanna tell ya..." A rattling knock stopped Ronny mid-sentence.

"Sorry, stuck in traffic. I'm Kevin Davidson, Mr. Kilday's attorney."

"Thank you for being here. We want to do everything by the book." Bowdoin said with a handshake. "You don't mind if I ask your client a few questions before he signs his confession?"

"Ronny, don't sign anything."

"This is a joke," Ronny said with a smirk, tossing the clipboard back at Bowdoin.

"You share a history with Mrs. Hirsh."

"Ronan was the whore's name when we dated, a real Eva Perón she is."

Kevin came to his feet. "This interview is over."

"No, Kev, I'm setting the record straight. Sure, I dated her, me and every other guy in Dorchester. I come from wealth; money has always been Margo's priority. My parents pegged her as a gold digger, but I was young, horny, and Margo gave out. My mother, God rest her soul, put an end to the romance. So, Margo gets her hooks into a rich Jewish doctor. He wises up and leaves her. Now she's back to her old tricks and I ain't one of them. I don't need some desperate broad from my past chasing me, wanting to pick up where we left off."

"She was chasing you?"

"Darn right. With her husband gone, she does her homework, finds out I bought the building, and figures she'll rekindle the romance. First, it was drafty windows, then the plumbing, the electric, rodents. She said the Super can't handle it, she needs me to come over, like I'm gonna fall for that. I just bought the building; it was inspected, no violations. I wanted to get rid of her, but she had a lease. I spurred her advances, so she claims I'm snooping on her, making hang-up calls, and breaking into her house in Chestnut Hill. That's another thing. Why would a woman with a big house in an affluent community rent in a seedy part of town?"

Bowdoin glared at Ronny. "Commonwealth Ave, seedy?"

"Ask Albert DeSalvo, he fancied the neighborhood."

"You can ask him yourself; you'll be sharing a cell."

Kevin gave Ronnie a disapproving look. "Are you done questioning my client?"

"No. Mrs. Hirsh claims you sexually assaulted her back in '64."

"Oh yeah, Sagamore Park. Some spook roughs her up, rapes her. You cops know what they're like when they see a White woman; she doesn't even have to be good-looking. They'll rape the ugly ones. Is there a police report? A hospital record? No."

"If the two of you had broken up, how did you hear about it?"

"She sought me out, needed a shoulder to cry on, called me her rock, pleaded with me to take her back. I'd met my wife by then. Margo was damaged goods; the box had already been opened."

"You know a Teddy Harbell?"

"Should I?"

"You hired him."

"I hire lots of people."

"We picked Theodore up at the Pine Street Shelter. He took a swing at one of the workers, so we brought him in. He fits the description of the man entering Six B."

"Then you got your man."

"Yeah, I got my man. I'm look'n at him. You have the keys to the building with you?"

"I got them. Why?"

"I think you'll find the key to Six B missing," Bowdoin said, daggling the key in Ronny's face.

Kevin grabbed Ronny by the arm to keep him from lunging at Bowdoin.

"Teddy claims he was given a key, told to "have a go" at the blonde in Six A. He tried the key, but it didn't work. He figures he heard you wrong. Tries it in Six B, the

490

door opens, and there's a blonde, a feisty one. Amazing what a junkie will tell ya when he needs a fix."

***

"Home sweet home," Mago said as she entered her once-showplace house.

"I'm staying with you," Colleen insisted.

"What about Lee?"

"He's going back to Chicago to pack up." Colleen headed for the kitchen. "You want coffee?"

"No. I'd have to drink it through a straw," Margo answered as she sorted through mail.

"You know Ma is going to hear about this when it goes to trial."

"Good. She wanted me to marry that murdering rapist."

"You know as well as I do, he didn't kill Miss Lingard."

"Bowdoin thinks so."

"Bowdoin hates Ronny. He'd send him to the chair for jaywalking." Colleen used her eyes to point to the ringing phone.

"That's probably Ma now." Margo brushed her hair behind her ear and walked the phone into the bedroom. Colleen saw no point in listening to a one-way conversation.

"Yes, I understand, thank you for letting me know before it appears on the news." Margo strolled out of the bedroom. "That was Bowdoin. Ronny made bail."

"He better provide you with police protection."

"That won't be necessary. Ronny's car was found in the State Forrest. He was behind the wheel with a rifle between his legs, and his head in the backseat."

Colleen's hands shot to her mouth. "His poor wife."

"Poor? She inherits his vast fortune. She won't be in black for long."

"What happens now?"

"Case closed. No trial, no publicity."

"You must be relieved."

"Bet your ass. I was afraid a jury wouldn't convict him."

"Why wouldn't they?"

"Because he didn't rape me."

"You framed him!"

"Not exactly. He did attempt it, but he was drunk, couldn't keep it up."

"But there was evidence."

"On the bedding, not in me. That blessed discharge wasn't Ronny's. You two rabbits mustn't have had time to tidy up before the police hauled you away. But the lamp. I loved that lamp."

"I can't believe you'd sink this low!"

"What was I supposed to do?"

"Tell the truth!"

"Not in my nature. I wanted Ronny dead. I always get what I want."

**

"This reminds me of prom night," Colleen reminisced. "We're all dressed up with my foot on the wheel."

Lee slapped her toes. "There will be none of that nonsense, Mrs. Hirsh." Colleen rested her head on her husband's shoulder.

"Too bad Aaron couldn't have been there for the ceremony."

"Aaron wouldn't have come even if he were in town. My brother is a complicated guy. He never warmed up to my dad—downright hates him. I never told you my family's history, have I?"

"Bits and pieces, I never felt it was my place to ask."

"As of today, you're a part of the story. My father is Prussian, a strict disciplinarian. All the characteristics Aaron hates in my dad, he developed himself. Uncle Izzy was jovial, easy-going. He immigrated to America in the early teens, got a job cutting meat at the old stockyard. That's where he met Aunt Nelda. They married, saved their money, and bought the building on Blue Hill Ave. They wanted children but couldn't have them.

My father left Germany after the First World War, settling in Palestine. An ardent Zionist, he joined the Haganah and fought to oust the British. When the Second World War broke out, his hatred for the Nazis trumped his contempt for the Brits. Dad volunteered his services to The Crown. Being fluent in Slavic languages, he was placed in the intelligence service stationed in the Soviet Union. My mother said he was a secret agent; Dad claims he was no more than an interpreter. My grandparents ran a market in Yerusalymka. Dad wandered in. To hear him tell it, it was love at first sight. Aaron's father was in the Red Army; no one knows what became of him. Aaron must have told all this to Margo."

"He may have, but if Margo doesn't hear her name in the first sentence, she stops listening,"

Lee continued, "Knowing it was just a matter of time before the Germans reached her town, Dad arranged for Mom and Aaron to escape to England. From there, they were to board a ship bound for Boston to live out the war with Izzy. My mother was an only child; she didn't want to leave her parents behind, so Aaron made the journey with my mother's cousin Jacob, who, on reaching England, took off, leaving Aaron to make the voyage alone. By the time my dad learned the switch, there wasn't much he could do. All but a handful of people in my mom's village had been massacred. Somehow Mom survived the camp. At war's end, Dad worked for the Red Cross as an interpreter. He located my mother in one of their hospitals. You wouldn't know to look at her now, but she weighed under 40 pounds; that's why she's consumed with feeding everyone.

"It was presumed Aaron's parents were dead, so Izzy was free to adopt him. No longer Ari Zdorvyak, Russian orphan, he was Aaron Hirsh, American. When my parents finally arrived in Boston, Aaron resented them. He thought my mother stayed behind to be with Dad. My parents lived on the first floor while Aaron lived upstairs with Izzy and Nelda. He may hate my dad, but if it weren't for him, the only brains Aaron would be cutting into would be cows. Aaron played sports and chased girls. Dad stepped in and forced Aaron to buckle down, study hard, get into Harvard, become a doctor, and a linguist. Funny, now Aaron's in Israel, living out Dad's dream."

Colleen shook her head. "Wow." Her attention turned to his driving. "Slow down."

"We've been married for less than four hours, and you're already nagging me. We can't miss our flight."

"We shouldn't leave town without seeing Margo."

"Call her from the airport."

"That's so unfair. My family was left out."

"Your mother wouldn't attend, and Margo's still recuperating."

"Please?"

"Ten minutes, Colleen. I mean it."

***

"Married! You got married and didn't tell me? I would have postponed my doctor's appointment." Margo wiggled Lee's cheeks like a washerwoman scrubbing a shirt collar. "Details, details."

"No time. No time."

Colleen waved Lee off. "Don't listen to him, our plane doesn't leave for two hours."

"Hey! What happened to love, honor, and obey?"

"We're so beyond that," Colleen kidded.

"Where are you going? And please don't say you're moving to Chicago."

Lee put his arm around his wife's waist. "Just honeymooning."

Margo frowned. "I don't like that dress. Why didn't you wear the cream-colored Nina Ricci suit I bought you?"

"Because I didn't know today would be my wedding day."

"I have champagne in the fridge, let's have a toast."

"Oh no," said Lee. "A toast with you now will turn into toast with you at breakfast."

Colleen fired off the day's events. "We got the marriage license the day after New Year's but hadn't set a date. Last night Lee told me they're holding a birthday party for his father at the senior center."

"It really is my dad's birthday. Someone once told me, to tell a convincing lie, start with the truth."

Colleen's voice was rapid with excitement. "The hall was decorated with balloons and streamers. All the old folks are eating and listening to music when Lee clinks his glass to get their attention."

"They were all hard of hearing; what I needed was a cowbell," he joked.

"A rabbi came out, and I think it's for a birthday blessing. Lee asks me to come up on stage. I see Freida bawling her eyes out, that's when I knew we'd be leaving the hall as man and wife."

"It was my mother's idea. She figured there wasn't much family and no friends to speak of."

"Speak for yourself!"

"I wish you had let me in on it," Margo pouted.

"With those stitches in your face, you'd look like the bride... of Frankenstein."

"Better than getting married in that dress. You didn't have to get married?" Margo asked, giving Lee "the eye."

"Yes, we did. It was destined from the day we met; all that was needed were the vows."

Margo squinted and twisted her threaded lips. "Hum, a wedding gift, I could give you the silver handcuffs Aaron gave me for our wedding, but Houdini left town with the key... I know." She returned from her bedroom with a small bag bearing The Holy See's coat of arms. "I picked these up at the Vatican. I intended to give them to Patsy and Salina, but killing their mother wasn't a gift-giving occasion, so I tucked them away. They were blessed by the Pope," she informed Lee as he opened the small box containing a medal on a gold chain. "That's Saint Christopher," Margo explained. "He's the patron saint of travelers. He can't stop your plane from crashing, but if it does, you'll survive." Margo ceremoniously clasped the gifted chain around his neck. "You have travelled a long road to find your way home to us. You always had a brain, but it was your heart that brought you home to us. As for you, Missy," Margo said in her mother's witchy voice. "I haven't forgotten you." From a tissue-filled bag, Colleen lifted out a long white mantilla. The newlyweds laughed.

"What's so funny?"

Colleen kissed her sister's cheek. "Just what Lee wanted."

***

"How long must we wait in line?" Colleen whined.

Lee looked at his watch. "Now you know why I wanted to get to the airport early."

"I need to go to the bathroom."

"Come right back. They won't hold the plane for us."

"Yes, dear," Colleen said with a hint of sarcasm.

Never having been to an airport, it was time to explore. Logan didn't possess the romance of the railway, but it did have a chapel. Taking the mantilla from her handbag, Colleen veiled her head, genuflected, made the sign of the cross, and slid

496

into a pew. A priest entered from a side door. Colleen rose from the kneeler and approached the chapel's tiny altar. "Father."

"Yes?" answered the priest with a welcoming smile.

"May I ask a favor of you?"

"Of course, you may."

"Will you marry me?"

"I've already taken a vow."

Colleen ribbed the priest. "You kidder. What I mean is, will you marry my husband and me?"

"If there's a husband, there's been a marriage."

"We weren't married in the church but plan to," Colleen quickly added. "My husband is leaving on the next flight to Chicago. I know you can't perform a sacramental marriage, but if anything should happen to him..." Colleen wiped away rented tears. "I want us to have stood before God, have him recognize our love for each other."

"All I can do is give a blessing, nothing more."

"That's all we need. I'll be right back." Colleen raced from the chapel to the spot she swore to return to.

"Where have you been?"

Colleen took hold of Lee's hand and yanked him out of line. "Yell at me later, right now we have to get to the chapel."

She abruptly halted her sprint to wiggle the wedding ring from his finger. "What are you doing!"

"We're going to get married again," she announced, handing him her band. Lee stopped at the chapel's entrance.

"I'm not going in there."

"Scaredy cat."

"I can't kneel at the altar or make the sign of the cross."

"Can't you pretend to be a Catholic for 10 minutes?"

Displaying the Saint Christopher medal on the outside of his shirt, he was marshalled down the aisle. "Father, this is my husband, Leon."

"Thank you for obliging us," Lee said, wearing a weak smile.

"Your wife is a very persuasive woman, Mister..."

Colleen jumped in. "He's Mister Right." The couple stood facing one another at the foot of the altar.

The priest began. "Dear Lord, this man, and this woman, come to your house asking your blessing as your loving servants bound by a bond only you can break. In your goodness and mercy, guide them through a long and fruitful marriage. A vow was taken for them at baptism; they come to you now to renew that vow not only to love you, but each other in holy matrimony."

The priest looked up from his text. "Would you care to make that vow to one another?"

Colleen spoke first. "Leon, I was an angry, lonely girl the day you took my hand so many years ago. Once again, I give my hand to you, not with suspicious curiosity but as a woman who spent her life looking for someone who loved and understood a girl who didn't love or understand herself. I never left the schoolyard knowing one day you'd return for me." Colleen returned the ring to his finger.

"We've made a full circle, one powered by love."

Lee took her hand. "Colleen, you showed me a world I never knew existed. Introduced me to people who are passionate and protective, who fight for one another, love as deeply as they hurt. You allowed a boy to grow into a man and celebrate the love, and rewards manhood brings. Bring that magic into our marriage and into the lives of our children who will be loved by their father, protected by their mother, and blessed by God."

The priest placed his hands on the couple's heads. "In the sight of God, and in the cloak of perpetual love, I bless this union."

Lee stroked the lace mantilla. "Put this in a safe place, you're right, it is sacred, it's my wife's wedding veil."

Chapter Thirty-Two

There was no need to hike her skirt, but she did, just enough for his eyes to detect the color change at the top of her stockings, but not the garters that secured them. A leg man would know they weren't pantyhose. Margo would never trade her silks for nylon. In the words of her sister, "Pantyhose were invented so Siamese twins could rob banks."

The mayor thanked his audience of Boston businessmen for sharing their thoughts on the impact his downtown revitalization project will have on the business community, which only served as background music with lyrics they had heard before but never danced to.

"Excuse me, miss." The apology came from a suited young man who bore a strong resemblance to the speaker.

"The mayor would like a word with you." Margo was led to the wavy-haired politician who needed no introduction but liked hearing his name. "What an honor to meet you, Mayor Bullard," Margo gushed. "I deserve to be dressed down, but I mistakenly wandered into the wrong room. Witnessing your commanding presence, hearing you speak with such unbridled passion, I felt compelled to take what may be my only opportunity to be in the presence of a true Boston legend. You're a busy man, and here I am behaving like a schoolgirl."

"A Democratic stalwart." Bullard remarked, looking to either side for his "yes-men" to join in the laughter. His stalking eyes drifted down to Margo's breast under the guise of reading her handcrafted name tag strategically placed on her white satin blouse that shifted across a lace brassiere with each exaggerated movement. "I'm Margo Hirsh," she said, stroking the tag. "I'm here on behalf of the Peter Bent Brigham Hospital. I was en route to a conference down the hall before trespassing."

"A nurse?"

"Not my calling. I'm in public relations. We may have an occasion to cross paths again. I have a hand in bringing a health center to my native Dorchester."

"Native is a good description," Bullard chuckled.

"I've hit a snag in bringing the project to fruition. We'll need the city's cooperation."

"If there's anything my office can do to assist you, let me know."

"Actually, there is, but this is neither the time nor the place." Margo extended her hand. "Thank you for allowing me to bend your ear." She counted out her steps. *"One, two, three, come on, four, five."*

"Mrs. Hirsh," Bullard said, consulting his watch. "If you're free later today, we could go over your plans at length. I'll have my secretary pencil you in for three."

"Three it is," Margo repeated.

***

Leaning back in his chair that bore the city's seal on its headrest, Mayor Bullard tapped a pen on his lips, obliging Margo to pitch a project he had no interest in. Margo unfurled a blueprint scroll across the conference table. "This is the proposed site. There's a need for additional parking. I've been trying in vain to purchase this vacant lot." Her reach pulled the buttons on her satin blouse taut.

Margo's eyes followed his to her lace-covered cleavage. "You are familiar with this area?" she asked, fondling the pearls running across her throat.

"Yes, I grew up not far from there."

"Then you know how congested the streets are. We'll need the parcel behind the lot as well."

"You're saying the city is standing in the way of the purchase?"

"The hospital never propositioned, I mean, partitioned, the city... but I am."

"If the hospital hasn't any interest in making a purchase, there's little I can do."

"The property isn't on the market; the city will have to take it. My mother's house sits on that lot."

"Let me get this straight. You want the city to take your mother's house?"

"She refuses to move out of the parish. The poor dear lives alone. I fear for her safety. When my Aunt Mae died, I assumed Mother would sell. Mae would say, "Berta, you're as stubborn as a mule.""

Bullard threw his head back in laughter. "I know that ass! Your mother is Berta Rourke."

"But of course, Mae worked here. What a dear you are to remember her. My mother and I agree on little. Still, I don't want to break her heart. I've spent many sleepless nights envisioning the harm that may befall my poor, helpless mother."

"If she's the Berta I knew, she can take care of herself. What do you want me to do?"

"Insist that more parking be made available. A bus runs along Blue Hill Ave. You wouldn't want the M.T.A. to risk having an accident due to the influx of additional street traffic. Here's the clincher: you donate money for the project. A great photo opportunity, you handing a check to a board member."

"You Rourke women and your check giving. You've got your aunt's good looks and your mother's moxie. I'm not at liberty to grant your request directly. That would spark an investigation. For all I know, you may be wearing a wire."

"The only wire I'm wearing is in my bra. Care to pat me down?"

"You'd make a great politician."

"I'm not looking for a job."

"I am. I'll put my money where your mouth is."

A notarized promise of eminent domain securely tucked in her coat pocket, Margo hurried across City Hall Plaza. A gust of wind sent her white beret sailing over the red brick walk. In the distance, a distinguished gentleman waved her hat like a marooned man flagging down a rescue plane. "Hey, Sunny! Sunny Shine!"

"Mac? Mac!" Margo ran to him, locking her arms around his waist in a vice grip.

"Ow, Ow, not so hard. I got into a dust-up with a young lady the other night, my balls took the brunt of it."

"Still hurts?"

"Wicked, but enough about my balls, for now. What brings you to City Hall?"

"I came to have my mother's house taken away from her."

"Mother's Day, or her birthday?"

"Valentine's Day. What better way to say 'I love you, Mom.' And you?"

"I'm trying to get out of jury duty."

"You can't serve on a jury; you must have a record."

"I have never run afoul of the law. My only crimes were against God and nature."

"You sold the station."

"My viewers had died or grown up. I made a bundle. I plan to enjoy what time I have left."

"Who would have guessed under all that scum lay a handsome man. The hair is cut and clean, shoes shined, and the suit, good quality, perfect fit, if I'm not mistaken, and I rarely am, it's a Brooks Brothers."

"I had to buy it for my father's funeral."

"You told me your father was dead."

"When I mentioned my mother was living, you hit me with a barrage of questions, so when you asked about my father, I said he was dead. Has Sunny married?"

"The sun has set on my marriage."

"Who ja dump him for?"

"He left me."

"Get out da here. I guess some guys ain't into bondage."

"He better be, because I'll have him tied up in court for years."

"I read about Kilday."

"What goes around."

"Seeing I'm no longer your boss or you my subordinate, unless you prefer that position, howz about we go to dinner and take in some porn for old time's sake."

"The Julian in the Rochambeau Hotel serves an early dinner; it's just around the corner."

"French it is. I hope they serve women."

"Willis explained that joke." There was an uncomfortable silence; Margo broke it. "Anyone ask why I left the station?"

"Lots of people, I told them someone threw acid in your face, so I had to let you go. I figured with you out of the picture, I could get a depicter on the cheap. As they say, you get what you pay for. I hired a girl and christened her Marshmallow Bunny; she had a harelip. The audience didn't warm up to her. I let her stick around for the Easter forecast, then I told her to beat it, or I'd bite her ears off."

The two walked across the hotel's opulent lobby. "Wait here." Mac strutted to the registration desk. Margo took the opportunity to inspect him from behind, a view she'd spent years avoiding. In the past, she'd found him sexually disturbing, yet somehow the suit made him perversely palatable.

Mac returned wearing a roguish grin and a key dangling from his index finger. "I booked us a room."

"I can't believe you got a room!"

"Me neither. But the guy at the desk is new, and nobody recognizes me in a suit."

"You expect me to drop everything and spend the night with you holed up in a hotel room?"

"Aw, come on," Mac said, giving Margo a folksy slap on the back. "Build up the old white blood cells. It's here or the rat ranch."

"You still live in that dump?"

"Sure do, but I don't want you over there. You may come to like the place, want to move in, hang curtains, and put a flowered wreath on the door. You're not a Leo, are you?"

"No, why?"

"Two Leos in the same bed," Mac flung his fingers out. "Spontaneous combustion."

"You dabble in astrology?"

"No. A pyromaniac tipped me off."

One of only a handful of diners, the two laughed while reminiscing about their days at W.H.B.N. If Aaron could see her now, in a five-star restaurant, raising brows and drawing disapproving stares. She now understood why feelings of jealousy surfaced while watching Colleen and Clay laughing at the fundraiser, unconcerned about how they appeared to those around them. It wasn't that Colleen found a wealthy man, but a friend. Colleen always had someone in her life to share a laugh with. Now Margo had someone.

Without breaking his gaze from hers, Mac snapped his fingers over his head to summon their waiter.

Margo shielded her eyes. "Must you?"

Giving the check a mere glance, Mac shut the leather-bound check presenter on a fifty-dollar bill for their twenty-five-dollar dinner. "Thank you, sir!" the wide-eyed waiter exclaimed.

"You earned it." He'd come a long way from a dollar fourteen.

***

"A little man is pounding his anvil in my brain," Mac groaned.

"I can hear the echo on this side of the bed. What you have is a caffeine headache. Call room service and order breakfast," Margo suggested as she got out of bed.

"Where are you going?"

"To the bathroom."

"I better not hear that shower; I like the way I smell on you. I may bottle the scent. I'll name it, Mac Godfrey's Number Two. Give old lady Chanel some competition."

Lying back, Mac squeezed his eyes shut the way children do when pretending to be asleep. Margo returned to bed.

"Mac, may I ask you a question?"

"No, there's your answer."

"Pleeeze?"

Mac dragged out a long sigh. "Since you've fulfilled all my perverted fantasies, I'll make this one exception."

"Why do you disguise the fact you're a well-bred, well-educated man?" Mac opened one eye. "What makes you think I have a brain?"

"You knew which fork to use, you didn't need the menu explained, and had we ordered wine, I've no doubt you would have known the proper vintage."

"What alcoholic doesn't?"

"I overheard you speaking to the concierge in French."

"I once dated a classy fille de joie. I picked up more from her than the clap, or was it Chickmunga?"

"After I left the station, I delved into your past."

"Oh boy, here it comes."

"You're a college graduate, Yale '55."

"Yale is a four-letter word, one I don't employ."

"You hold a degree in music, of all things. Frat boy to Fagin-what gives?"

No reply.

"Now that I know there's a civilized man lurking under that greasy facade, I'll exhume him."

"No, you won't. I like who I've become. So do you."

"My mother pegged you as an educated baboon."

"Got to get up pretty early in the morning to pull one over on Mom. I'm what's known as a Renaissance man."

"Neanderthal would have been my guess."

"Don't let the overhanging forehead fool ya. Since we're going down this road, I never bought into your dumb blonde act."

"It wasn't an act. I was dumb!"

Mac spoke in a falsetto tone. "'Gee wilikers, Mister Mac Godfrey, why are those people wrestling with their clothes off? Move the film forward, no going back again.' Christ, Sunny, it was porn, not the Zapruder film."

"You haven't answered my question."

"My father made his fortune in railroad stock. He took a shellacking in the crash of '29 but had the foresight to know we were entering the communication age. He took what little money he had and opened a radio station in Altoona, that's where I was raised. When television came along, he got in on the ground floor. After I graduated, he put me to work at the Toledo station. I wasn't cut out for television. You know why the station failed?"

"Because I left?"

"No. It failed because, deep down, I wanted it to fail. I was a fool not to follow my heart and do what I was put on earth to do. Now look at me, thirty-eight and the laughingstock of Boston."

"Thirty-eight, I still can't believe that's all you are."

Mac rolled over, turning his back to Margo. "Go on, Sunny, laugh. I not only tell jokes, I am one."

"You're crying."

"Yeah, I'm crying over a wasted life."

Margo rested her head against his back. Reaching over, she braided her fingers into his. It felt more intimate than their lovemaking. "You're still young, kinda. You can start over; your father did. Is there something you always wanted to pursue but never had the opportunity?"

"Who doesn't? I had this pie-in-the-sky dream; don't laugh, Sunny."

"I won't," she whispered.

"Ever since I was a little tyke, I wanted to be a pimp."

Margo ripped her hand from his. "You bullshit artist!"

"I know it sounds crazy, but tell that to a lonely little boy. By golly, back then, I believed I could make it in the exciting world of drugs and prostitution. I guess you could say I was bit by the bug."

"Crabs?"

"Probably. Everyone knew me as the little boy with the big dream. Folks would point me out and say, "That's the kid who wants to be a pimp." I'd smile and wave as I rode past them on my tricycle, knowing one day I'd return to that sleepy little town and make'm proud." Mac pounded his right fist into his left palm. "Damn it, Sunny. I could have made a difference." Mac lay back, staring up at the ceiling. "That lonely kid stuff wasn't a joke. I threw money around like birdseed to attract friends. Willis was the only pigeon to take the bait. He liked me for me. Sunny, let's clear the air. I was upset; Willis was loyal, a great guy. You're not to blame. He couldn't see for shit. I shouldn't have scared you off when I needed you most. Let's put it behind us. Why, I bet Willis is looking up at us and saying- 'Enough about me. You two go back to doing it.' We have the room for three more hours; let's go for it."

***

The Jag purred into the Brookline home's driveway. The two-family was no longer a rental but a wedding gift from one Mrs. Hirsh to another.

"I knew I'd find you here," said Margo, pushing aside boxes of books with her foot.

Colleen greeted her sister with a hug. "Thank you for letting us live here."

"I told you, the house is yours. I've no doubt Aaron would approve."

Colleen purse stringed her lips and narrowed her eyes. "You've been keeping yourself scarce. I've been calling you for the last two days. Ronny may be dead, but I still worry,"

"Worry no more. I went to City Hall. Ma should receive the eviction notice in a few weeks. She won't have to move right away."

"Gosh, I hoped it wouldn't come to this."

"I know it sounds harsh, but she's seen the writing on the wall. The house is empty. Why would she want to stay?"

"Memories."

"She can take them with her."

"Where will she go?"

"Where the goblins go. Irena is alone now and has an extra bedroom. She only lives 20 minutes from here."

Colleen wagged her finger. "You've been in New York to see that married doctor."

"Stan? Heavens no."

"You're seeing someone."

"If you must know."

"Oh, I must."

"I've spent the last two days holed up in a hotel room experiencing the most delicious sex I've ever dreamed of. He did things to me the ancient Romans never thought of."

"Do tell."

"You'll love him. He's wealthy, witty, totally irreverent, and has a libido that's off the charts."

Colleen backed away. "Please, God, not Mac."

"You've got it."

"No, you've got it. See a doctor. That dirty, demented relic is still alive? He must be in his seventies."

"Thirty-eight. I don't care what you think. He gives me all I ever wanted from a man."

"Herpes? From now on, bring your own utensils. When are you going to tell Ma about him?"

"I'm not. Mac may be an ideal lover, but he's not the marrying kind. I had a good husband, and he left me. Mac and I may never marry, but wherever he goes, I'll be at his side."

"Send me a postcard from the leper colony."

***

"Happy Saint Valentine's Day!" Colleen and Lee sang into the phone. "Are you excited?" Colleen asked.

"Petrified. Mac is sending a driver for me."

"Who are you wearing, darling?"

"Saint Laurent, darling."

"He'll destroy it. Where is he taking you?"

"He asked where I'd like to dine; I told him The Ritz. He's been throwing money around to impress me. I wouldn't be surprised if he gave me a gem."

"It's pronounced 'germ.'"

Margo gasped. "There's the bell. You two enjoy a quiet evening at home playing Mahjong with Freida."

"Miss Ronan?" asked the little man in an overcoat, looking like a ventriloquist dummy. "I'm Rupert. Mister Mac sent me." Reaching into his coat pocket, he removed a black sash. "He wants you to wear this."

"You needn't kidnap me; I'll go willingly."

"Mac's orders."

Margo squatted, allowing Rupert to cover her eyes and lead her to a limo. "Mind if I smoke?"

"Mister Mac won't like it."

Margo slid into the backseat. "Let me handle Mister Mac. Wearing a blindfold and smoking a cigarette, I feel like I'm about to face a firing squad."

Ten minutes into their journey, the car slowly turned a corner. Margo tensed at the sound of crackling glass under the tires and a distance howling. "Please tell me that's a cat."

Without answering, Rupert led her up wooden stairs to a loading dock. Margo slid the scarf down past her nose.

"Seen enough, take me home."

"I have orders. You must go into the freight elevator. Press the button for the 3rd floor."

"Aren't you coming?"

"No, ma'am. This is where I leave you."

Margo rolled her eyes. "Oh, all right."

Wearing only a T-shirt and yellowed boxer shorts, Mac parted the elevator's heavy metal doors and lifted the grate.

"Sunny! Welcome to my humble abode," he announced, shoving a bouquet in her hands before she could object.

"Flowers for me, lady. Orchids and tulips-get it?" Taking Margo by her elbow, Mac gently led her into the dark dungeon he called home. "You love it, I can tell. I call it my little piece of heaven."

Margo curled her lip. "More like The Boulevard of Broken Wet Dreams."

Mac patted his unmade bed's exposed, stripped mattress. "Take a seat."

Margo closed her eyes as she spoke. "I'm not sitting on that filthy thing." She pointed to a small lamp on a rickety night table, its shade veiled by a sheer scarf, giving the room a cheap, eerie ambiance.

"That's a fire hazard, and what are those things?"

Mac lifted a small pair of metal spurs off the nightstand. "I picked these babies up in Juarez, Mexico, home to the cockfighting hall of fame. I popped into the gift shop on my way out and couldn't resist them. The spurs are wrapped around the cock's feet, the intent being to slice their opponent to death." Mac dangled the souvenirs in Margo's face. "Ya want'em? Make a great pair of earrings, a real conversation starter. Interesting place, Juarez. I've got to take you down there sometime. I stay at a hotel off the beaten path, only the locals know about. It's called The Hotel Juarez My Wallet."

"I don't want to go to Mexico. I want to get out of this filthy rathole and go to dinner."

"If you think this place is dirty, you're welcome to come over in that French maid costume. That was my favorite forecast- 'We're expecting a dusting of snow during the overnight.'" His humor wasn't up to par, sophomoric at best. Margo lit a cigarette. "There's no smoking at the rat ranch."

"Fine," Margo defiantly snuffed the cigarette out on a piece of greasy cardboard from a snack cake package.

"Your husband, the doctor, he let you smoke?"

"Of course not. You know how doctors are."

"No, but I know how I am. It's not because I'm a clean freak. I want you to stop for the same reason he did."

Margo walked over to Mac, who sat on the bed looking down at his shaking leg. "Are you detoxing?"

"No, Sunny, I don't drink or use drugs. I chase broads; that's my only vice. You're going to love this story. It's about the time I came across an old, bearded man lying dead on the side of the road next to the carcass of a rotting deer. It really messed me up because I was only four years old at the time."

"Stop. This is sick."

"Listen, it has a happy ending. My father lied to me. It wasn't Santa Claus but a bum from the next town over. Someone must have hit him, and a deer then sped off. We got to keep the meat... the deer."

"You're nervous; you tell stories when you're ill at ease." Margo sat on the bed next to Mac. "You're in love with me... huh?

"You'd like that."

"I expect that. If you won't say it, sing it." Margo leaned into his ear. "I remember you."

"I'll kill that dead bastard. I ever tell ya about the time I was trapped in a meat locker with Hildegarde? The one time she forgot her gloves."

"Heard it."

"I know you haven't heard this one; it's about the time I was mistaken for Wink Martindale. It was the first name to pop into my head when I was asked to step out of the vehicle. That's when Betsy Palmer took off into the woods. I don't know why she was still wearing a blindfold; she'd guessed Wink's line back at the bar."

"You're running out of stories. Say it, Mac, say- 'I love you, Sunny.' Always have."

Mac drew a deep breath. "When you started working at the station, you were sweet, sexy, and innocent. I looked forward to being around you; I had so much fun at your expense. I like that in a woman."

"Why didn't you tell me how you felt?"

"It wouldn't have worked out. You'd always be looking for a younger, richer, handsome guy, and you would have found one. You started playing the game of love before you learned the rules. See, ya always want the one that didn't want you. You say to yourself, 'Good, she's probably a lesbo, who needs her?' Years later, you run into her. She's old, bitter, jaded, but you want her just so you can dump her, even the score."

"Are you dumping me?"

"We never got that far into the game, never will."

Margo wrapped her arms around Mac's neck. "We're a lot alike; you thought people only liked you for your money. I thought they only liked me for my body."

"They do."

"You sound like my mother."

"Quite a gal, your mother." Standing, Mac pulled Margo off the bed and to his lips. "Tell you what, if you quit smoking, I'll give up broads."

Margo walked to the toilet, plopped her pack of Salems into the bowl, and pulled the box's chain.

"Jesus Christ! Don't flush that toilet!"

"I just did."

"Grab that bucket under the sink, the one with the wrench in it. We've got to get downstairs before that ceiling caves in."

"Who lives down there?"

"No one."

"Then why do you care?"

"I own the damn building."

The laughing couple staggered back upstairs, holding one another up. "Look at me!" Margo cried in a fit of laughter. "Do you have any idea what this dress costs?"

"You earned your merit badge. Tell ya what we'll do, you take a whore's bath in the sink while I call Rupert."

"Where will we dine on such short notice?"

"The Plaza."

"On Valentine's Day? Don't tell me you own The Plaza."

Mac's mouth ripped into a sardonic smile. "No, but I own the manager. A few years back, he was caught having sex with a fourteen-year-old. I refused to broadcast the story; he's forever in debt to me. Come on, let's get out of this dump," Mac said, shutting out the lights and closing the door behind them. "Funny, I didn't think a Great Dane could live to 14. Go figure."

Chapter Thirty-Three

"I'm in Mae's room," Colleen called down to her sister.

"These stairs are killing me," Margo puffed.

"Lose weight."

Margo put up her dukes. "Those are fighting words."

"It's easier to lose weight than to quit smoking. I'm proud of you. "

Margo sat on the cedar hope chest that housed her aunt's mementos. "This is the first time I've been in this room since Mae died. What strange twists and turns our lives have taken. I was supposed to be the prom queen, not you. I was going to have the big wedding, not Rosaria. The outline of our lives was drawn at birth; it was left up to us to color it in. We all got what we were searching for. Rosaria found love, I got money, and you have a friend. The road we took to get here isn't the one we planned to take. Mae made those dreams come true. Love, money, and friendship were her gifts to us. Think about it: Mae was the one to convince Rosaria to go to the Christmas party, where she met Patsy. She got Patsy his job at City Hall, where he met Angie. She even arranged for Lee to ask you to the prom."

"I thought Freida orchestrated that plot."

"Think again. We were all in on it, even Ma."

"What about you? Did Mae deposit money in your account?"

"No, but she deposited Mac into my life, and he's a very wealthy man. He moved in with me. The rat ranch has been condemned. I get a kick out of seeing him in Aaron's pajamas. I hit the jackpot. I found love, money, and a friend."

***

The door flew open before Colleen had put her key in the lock. "Where have you been?" Lee breathlessly asked.

"The dentist. I was stuck in traffic; the bridge was up. The one on the boulevard, not in my mouth."

Lee stood wringing his hands. "Margo called. Call her back. I'll get my coat.

***

"Where's Mac?" Colleen asked, cradling her weeping sister.

"Gone to get drunk and laid. He said it was my own fault."

Lee came to Mac's defense. "The news came as a shock. He's blowing off steam; he'll be back."

Margo pointed to the opposite wall. "He threw a paperweight at me."

Lee inspected the punctured plaster, sliding his fingers into the crack as Saint Thomas had into the side of the risen Jesus.

"Christ, he's nuts!"

"You doubt me?"

"What's the game plan?" Colleen asked.

"The surgery is booked for Tuesday," Margo answered between gulps. "It's a very aggressive form of cancer. Colleen, I can't do this. It's not losing my breast, honest it isn't. I don't think there's any point to living."

"Do I deserve to lose another sister?"

"You have Lee and a future."

"And you're going to be a part of it. We're survivors, you and me."

Margo's shoulders slumped in resignation. "I'm prideful, and God is taking away my femininity."

"That's not where your beauty lies."

"God always gets his pound of flesh."

"Let him have the pound, not your life."

**

The IV sedative dripped like tears into her veins; her neck lost the strength to hold up her head. "Where's Ma?" Margo asked with half-closed eyes. Colleen was livid but tried not to show it. "She went to Mass; she'll be here when you wake up."

Colleen covered her face and wept as Margo was wheeled away. "I hate them all. Where are they? Look at this place," she said, waving her arms around the empty waiting room. "They all flocked around her when she was healthy, with a smile on her face and a buck in her pocket, willing to share both. When Rosaria was hospitalized, a round-the-clock vigil was held. Aaron was at her beck and call. Margo's not worth it? Aaron has a new life, Patsy has a new family, Mac's run off, and God only knows where my mother's broom took her."

"You need sleep."

"I'm not leaving."

"She won't be out of surgery for hours. We live five minutes away, and you haven't slept in days. I'm taking you home."

**

Colleen raced down the hospital's freshly waxed corridor. "Hurry up!"

"Slow down. She's not going anywhere."

519

Colleen placed her hand and ear against the door. "Wait," she whispered. "My mother's in there. Let's go for coffee."

Rooted to her mother's side, Margo softly whimpered. "I'm frightened, Mama, I'm frightened," she puffed out in broken syllables like a steam engine departing the station.

"We'll have none of that."

"I'm a coward, a self-centered coward."

"Who put that nonsense in your head?"

"You."

"I said many things I shouldn't have." Berta's pounding heart flushed out all the emotions that clogged her arteries.

"The doctor said you'll make a full recovery. I agree."

Margo forced a smile and nestled her head under her mother's chin. "Been a long time since we shared a bed."

"Or a civil word," Berta added.

"Mom, I don't care what I look like. God took back the gift I abused." Berta held Margo's face in her hands and wiped away a tear with her thumb. "God almost took back the gift he gave me, one I abused, but you're here, I'm here."

"God took Rosaria. He took Mae."

"They weren't of this world; they were on loan to us from God. You're a fighter, you survived many a battle with me."

"If I can beat you. I can beat cancer."

"I never said you beat me; I always won the day. You're a lot like your grandmother. That's why I gave you her name. She was impulsive, made poor choices, always got her way, even at the detriment to herself and others."

At that moment, Margo knew her mother wasn't ignorant of her parentage. How she wanted to tell her mother she was the product of love, not rape.

Holding her daughter in her arms, Berta felt the warmth of Fredrik's body lying next to her. Nuala was the vessel housing his spirit; his blood ran through her veins, he'd hear Berta's words, through their daughter's ears, see her through Margo's eyes.

"Do you remember your father?"

"Vaguely. Tell me about Daddy."

"Did you know he was a Lutheran?"

"NO!"

"Neither did your grandmother." The two giggled like teenagers gossiping at a slumber party.

"He promised to convert. They all do."

"How did you meet?"

"Mae and I would go to the dance clubs. On this particular night, we went to the Delmont. In walks the handsomest man you ever did see. All eyes were on him, but his were on Mae, who was on the dance floor with a fellow she was dating. Fredrik asked me to dance. The very nerve of him, he said, "Let's dance over to that blonde, she'll be mine by the end of the night." By God, if I ever heard one of you girls use the language that came out of my mouth, I'd rip your tongue out. Do you know what he did?"

"No, what?"

"He laughed at me."

"He didn't!"

"You know how I feel about that."

"Do I ever! What did you do then?"

"I stomped on his foot with the heel of my shoe. Again, he laughs. So, I took out his other foot.

"Dance over to her now, Astre, I said." Berta deeply sighed. "Lovely to look at, he was."

"Was his body ever recovered?"

"Yes."

"Where was he buried?"

"Idaho. He was an only child; his parents wanted his body. I didn't."

"Why not?"

"I was angry with him. He'd abandoned me."

"He didn't abandon you. He was off serving his country. You should be proud. He was a hero."

"Far from it. Your father wasn't killed in the war or in the service. Having a wife and two children, he was exempt from the draft."

Margo tilted her head. "Why did you lie?"

"Lies, secrets, they protect us from hurt."

"How did Daddy die? The truth."

"It was a bitterly cold night. He promised to take me to a swanky nightclub for our wedding anniversary. I borrowed Mae's fur coat for the occasion. I felt like a movie star on the arm of a handsome leading man. The club was packed, wall to wall. We were seated at a small table in a dark corner. The waiter was slow getting to our table, so your father went to the bar for drinks. I saw him standing by the exit, chatting up a pretty girl. Angry, I got up to leave." Berta's eyes pooled with tears. "There were screams, I smelled smoke, that's when the lights went out."

Margo placed her hands over quivering lips. "You're talking about The Coconut Grove."

"I crawled along the floor; a burning beam fell from the ceiling onto my back. I was trapped and trampled; the scar tissue, not arthritis, makes it difficult to bend. If it weren't for the thickness of Mae's coat, God knows if I'd be alive today. Marty located me at City Hospital, but there was no sign of Fredrik. The Southern Mortuary is next to the hospital, and I insisted that Marty take me there.

The place stank, the entire city stank. People filed into the room in silence. The victims, hundreds of them, were lying on sheets covering a tiled floor. Now and then, the silence would be broken by a howl when a loved one was recognized. I saw school chums, couples whose names I never knew, but I'd seen regularly at the dance clubs. The women were in gowns, like mannequins, remnants of a department store fire, their faces coated in soot and terror. But not your father's. Fredrik was easy to identify. The inferno had incinerated his lungs, not his face, that beautiful, beautiful, face.

I never forgave him for abandoning me, leaving me to find my own way out. I destroyed any pictures I had of him, but you are the picture of him. Whenever I'd look at you, I was reminded of him, his cowardice. I took my anger at him out on you. But you're not like him, you're the brave one, the hero of this story, not your father."

"Oh, Ma, how could you think such a thing? He was standing by the exit; he would have been one of the first to escape. He ran into the inferno to get you; he wants you to know that."

Berta wiped her nose. "Who better to tell me. Looking back on it, I never told him I loved him, how proud I was to be his wife, and bear his children. But I'm telling you. I love you, Nuala, and I'm blessed to be your mother. You shouldn't have to lose a breast to find your mother."

"I'd gladly sacrifice the other to keep you."

Berta got up off the bed and tucked the sheet snugly around Margo's body. "You know what I think?"

"What?"

"I think your aunt is looking down on us, and she's smiling."

Colleen sat at the hospital coffee shop counter, tearing off pieces of her Danish, rolling its soft dough between her index finger and thumb.

"Eat it, don't play with it," said her exhausted husband.

"We ought to get back up there," she abruptly announced.

Lee nodded at the newspaper rack. "Now we know where Patsy is: in jail."

Squinty-eyed and hunched over, Colleen gasped. "My mother is going to flip." Lee dropped a dime in the newspaper dispenser. Colleen read the article aloud. "Councilor Pasquale Patsy Travella led demonstrators protesting Logan Airport's expansion project, which would result in the leveling of East Boston's Wood Island neighborhood. Travella, along with soon-to-be displaced residents, blocked Neptune Road, preventing bulldozers from entering the close-knit Italian neighborhood."

Colleen tucked the paper under her arm. "Margo will get a kick out of this. My nerves are shot, and I'm sick to my stomach. I'll go to the ladies' room and meet you at the elevators."

Lee stood looking into the gift shop window. *"Hum, roses or mums? Nix the mums, too obvious, but the roses look sicker than she does."* Roses in hand, his name sailed across the crowded lobby. "Leon!"

"Aaron!" Bearded with strands of silver framing his tanned face, a shade one develops from farmwork, not sunbathing, Aaron flashed a dimpled smile. Lee stood stiff, too shocked to share in Aaron's embrace. "When? How? I mean, we had no way to get in touch with you."

"Stan, let me know."

Colleen ran across the lobby with open arms. "I can't believe you're really here!"

"She's my wife. She's sick, I'm a doctor."

"Now you resurface?"

Aaron held up his hand. "No fist fights in the hospital. We'll settle this outside after I have a word with my brother."

Colleen kissed Aaron's full beard. "I'm leaving, I have some unfinished business in the restroom."

As Colleen walked off, Aaron again embraced his brother, who detected a faint sniffle. "Let's sit over here."

Aaron suddenly spun Lee in the opposite direction. "That's Mrs. Clarkson over there. She was a patient of mine. I can't believe she's still alive. I'm a better surgeon than I thought."

"I doubt that's possible."

"Come, we'll duck into the chapel."

The brothers sat in silence as Aaron gathered his thoughts. "I'm sorry, Leon. I'm in need of your forgiveness."

"That's not necessary."

"It is. I wasn't there for you when you needed a brother. I knew you had a troubled adolescence, and I had a responsibility to help you get through it, but I was self-absorbed. After Izzy and Nelda died, I wanted nothing to do with that place; I hated going over there.

"Any conversation I had with Oscar would turn into an argument. In my eyes, you were Oscar's son, not my brother. That's inexcusable."

"There wasn't much you could have done for me."

"Sure, there was. I could have got you involved in sports."

"What sport? I'm too blind for baseball, too short for basketball, and too Jewish for hockey."

"Could have got you laid."

"I'm happy with the way my life has turned out."

"No thanks to me. Strange," Aaron reflected, "All these years, I felt there was a hole in my soul I couldn't fill. No matter what I bought, whom I seduced, or what professional achievements I was awarded, I couldn't fill the void. Now I know what I was missing.

A home. I was homesick. I remember life in Ukraine, before the war, the village, the music, the food. We weren't wealthy but happy with our lot. We were family. The spirit I remember as a child exists in Israel." Aaron looked up at the altar's stained-glass image of the Holy Family. "I found my home, my family."

There were so many questions Lee wanted to ask, but knew it best not to interrupt this cathartic moment. Aaron leaned on the pew, burying his head in his folded arms. "I never saw the pictures, never felt the need. That was the past, the war is over, America is a new country, move on." Aaron lifted his head. "But I knew one day I would have to confront the past.

"I visited Yad Vashem, more as a tourist than a Jew. There was a picture of four boys in the camp looking out from behind a barbed wire fence. They were the same age I would have been at the time, but looked like old men, their bodies dying, their spirit dead, their haunting hollow eyes looking out at me. They weren't asking, 'Why are we here?' but 'Why aren't you?'

I wasn't in that picture because Oscar kept out of it, sent me to a country people spoke of, but I didn't believe could truly exist. I love America, and I took advantage of all this country had to offer. Whatever I desired was given to me, or I earned it. And how did I treat the man who sent me here? With contempt. Oscar was the Mitzvah that saved me from being the fifth boy behind the wire." Aaron flashed a sly smile. "I was always jealous of you."

"ME?!"

"When you were born, I watched Mamushka fall in love with you. She loved her parents enough to stay behind, loved Oscar enough to survive the camp. Me she sent away. I felt any love she showed me was out of guilt. I didn't want that kind of love, so I sought it elsewhere."

Aaron rested his head on his brother's shoulder, the way lovers do in a dark theater. "I would have been successful in any field I chose. I chose medicine because I like people." Anticipating his brother's skepticism, Aaron lifted his head. "I swear I do! I pretend to be all-powerful, all knowing, but behind the confident façade is a homesick boy who could have gone to his death if someone hadn't loved him." Smiling, Aaron looked skyward. "There is a God, I'm not him."

"You believe in God?" Lee questioned.

"I believe in God because He believes in me." Aaron ruffled his brother's hair. "A married man!"

"Baby on the way. She hasn't told me yet."

Colleen walked through the chapel's swinging doors like a gunslinger entering a saloon. "I thought I'd find you here. Wouldn't my mother love to see this, the Hirsch brothers seated before the Eucharist."

"How is your mother?" Aaron asked.

"See for yourself, she's up there. She'll probably think you came to put a pillow over Margo's face."

Aaron kissed her cheek. "I'll see you up there."

Colleen slid into the pew next to Lee, whose eyes were glued to the altar. "Until a few minutes ago, Aaron and I never had a conversation. I don't ever remember being alone with him; he never touched me until today."

"You both missed out."

"The only reason I liked him keeping a room in my parents' apartment was so I could sneak a peek at his pornography collection. He had a deck of playing cards with pictures of naked women in different poses. The three of diamonds looked like you. I took her out of the deck because I didn't want him looking at her. I always kept the card with me, living in fear of the day he'd come out of that room and yell, "Who stole my three of diamonds!"

"Are you telling me Aaron isn't playing with a full deck? Let me have a look at her."

"I left her in Chicago; I no longer need her. I married the Queen of Hearts."

"I'm carrying your child."

"Our child."

"It depends on who it looks like."

"It had better be a boy or our daughter is going to be one mean, ugly Math teacher."

"This news will cheer Margo up more than those crummy flowers."

Lee handed the wilted roses to Colleen. "They're for you."

Colleen wacked the blimp bouquet over his head. "Three of Diamonds."

***

A soft voice laced with guilt breezed into Margo's ear. "Sunny?"

Margo opened her eyes to a familiar face speaking in an unfamiliar tone.

"I went to the wrong room, you shoulda seen the look on that poor woman's face. That wasn't the first time I've been mistaken for Jesus. I ever tell ya about the time..."

"Mac, save the stories."

"I don't blame you for hating me; I hate myself."

"I don't hate you; I'm done hating."

"You've got a group of devoted fans on the other side of that door; they all want to see me dead."

"No, they don't."

"Mom's pack'n."

Margo managed to smile, watching Mac nervously scratch his unwashed scalp. "I didn't get drunk. After all these years, they still have a picture of me over every bar in Boston with the caption, "Do not serve this man." The whorehouses post the same notice."

"Don't make me laugh, it hurts."

"Then I'll be serious. I love you. That's why I ran, but I won't get far without you by my side. Sunny, Nuala, Margo, I don't care what you want to be called as long as I can call you my wife. I plan on having the biggest wedding this town has ever seen. I even have Mom's blessing as long as we marry in that church she goes to."

"Saint Regina's?"

"Yeah, that's the one.

"We can't marry in a church. You're not Catholic."

"Not yet. I promised Mom I'd convert as long as it doesn't involve a circumcision. She told me I'd have to confess my sins to a priest. I hope those guys work in shifts. I ever tell ya about the time Willis and me tried to perform an exorcism? Willis heard about this wacko broad who was possessed by demons. Originally, we had other plans for her, thus the term, Devil's Delight. Anyway, Willis gets this brainstorm, he says, "Why don't we have the demons driven out of her on live TV? It will be a ratings bonanza." We conned some Polish priest, Father Wojamakolit from Our Lady of Canonized Kielbasa, to perform the exorcism. When I ran the promo for the show, and I get a call from a doctor at Holy Shit Hospital. He said the woman is a patient of his, she's epileptic and has that swearing disease. It cost my old man a bundle. I knew we shoulda gone with plan A. That house on The Jamaica Way you wanted to buy, it's yours."

"That's a big house for just two people."

"We'll get a maid; an ugly one, I promise."

"Or...we could have my mother move in with us."

"Whoa- when I said your mother belongs in a home, I didn't mean ours."

"She can have her own wing."

"I'll give the buzzard two wings, and she can fly off."

"Please, Mac? I need her."

"I've done some stupid things in my day, but this tops them all. If that's what you want, but she'll have to pick up a part-time job, we can't live on her social security check alone. I used all the money I received from the sale of the station to buy the house; the rest of my vast fortune I spent on this."

"A diamond!"

"I would have bought a more expensive ring, but there isn't one. I shit a brick when the jeweler told me the price."

"Watch your mouth, there won't be any swearing when my mother moves in."

"Dagnabit."

"You have all these grandiose plans, yet you haven't properly asked for my hand."

"Let me start over. Sunny, I love you. I didn't know I had a heart until I broke yours. I'm going to spend the remainder of my short life making it up to you. You're not only my sun, but my world, a crazy world, but one I want to share with you. Sunny, will you marry me?"

"Yes, you pig." Margo placed her finger to her lips as Mac moved in to kiss her. "Let me make this perfectly clear: I can't have children."

"Good. I hate kids. That's not to say if one was trapped inside a burning building, I ...who am I kidding? That's what firemen are for."

***

"Are you another doctor?" Margo asked, responding to a light tap on her open door.

"It's your husband," Aaron answered.

Her eyes tightened. "Aaron?" she questioned in a strained, hoarse voice.

"I got past your mother, I thought I'd try my luck with you. You're too weak to throw that potted plant at me."

"That's not the pot I want to throw."

530

Aaron kissed her hand. "Nice diamond." Margo slid her right hand out from under the sheet; its ring finger was dressed with an opal.

"I'll always wear it. The day you gave me this ring was the happiest day of my life. How did you find out?"

"Stan."

"Stan? You know what I'm going to do to that bastard?"

"Rip his head off, hollow it out, and leave it in a playground."

"How sweet of you to remember."

"Your mother was civil to me. She probably didn't want to cause a scene in front of her boyfriend."

"That peculiar-looking man is my fiancé. I'll have you know, he's younger than you, but unlike you, I knew he was a whoremaster when I met him."

"For an intelligent man, I've done some stupid and cruel things. I apologize for making a fool of you when we met and a fool of you when I left."

"But in between, you made me feel worthy to be the wife of one of the greatest minds in medicine. I'm still in love with you."

"You're on some strong meds. I want you to know I never loved Magdala. What I loved was her spirit. She was the catalyst that led me to the place I belong. In Israel, I live a simple life free of all the trappings wealth brings."

"You've overcome your addiction to fast cars and slow women?"

"I only have one car, a Maserati. You need one over there."

"A car or a Maserati?"

Aaron lay his head on Margo's stomach. "What I need is you. I'd occasionally call the house to see if a man would answer."

"That was you!"

"I don't know why we fought."

"Make up sex."

"There was that."

Margo ran her fingers through Aaron's thick hair. "You're my hero, you always were, always will be. I want to make love to you, to once more feel your arms around me, your breath on my neck, your sweat on my chest. You made me feel safe. I knew as long as I had your love, no harm would come to me. The only other person who gave me that sense of security was my mother, and I drove you both away. I want to die in your arms, with your name on my lips. There is nothing, nothing, I wouldn't do for you."

"Come with me to Israel."

"Fat chance."

"Hey! What happened to dying in my arms with my name on your lips?"

"That's the drugs talking."

"Israel is not your home; your future is on the other side of that door."

"I'm going to live, right?"

"You'll live. Not because I say so, but because you're Margo Ronan, whatever Margo wants, Margo gets."

Her voice thinned. "I'm tired."

"Sleep, I'll come back tomorrow." Her hand slipped from his; he kissed it.

Sticking his head out the door, Aaron looked in both directions as if attempting to cross a freeway. Berta was rejoicing with the expecting parents. For a fleeting moment, he was back in the apartment on Blue Hill Ave, looking on as Izzy and Nelda hovered over his mother with her new son. Once more, he felt like an outsider. He turned and headed for the stairwell.

"Aaron."

Hearing Berta speak his name without his title sounded unnatural, uncomfortably intimate. He'd lured her daughter away from her family and her faith only to abandon her. Karma had come to call. Taking a deep breath, he spun on his heels, prepared to be reprimanded.

"I want a word with you." The two walked to a bank of windows that granted a view of the Blue Hills. "I'm sorry," Berta said, looking into Aaron's questioning eyes.

"Sorry? Whatever for?"

"The Tim business, if I hadn't gotten in the way, you could have saved him. I made him sick, then prevented you from making him well."

"It would have happened whether or not I was there."

"Will Nuala live? I told her she would, but I'm not a doctor."

Aaron took Berta's hand into his. "I wouldn't leave if I thought otherwise."

"You're returning to that Godforsaken country?"

"As a matter of fact, we could use a woman like you over there."

"I'd put an end to that nonsense-homeland my ass."

"On second thought, you have battles to fight here at home."

"That I do. How long will you be in town?"

"A few weeks. I have fences to mend with Oscar... my dad." Aaron looked over at Mac. "Margo found herself a great guy."

"Him? He's a horse's ass. But he makes her laugh; they say laughter is the best medicine. You may have heard the city is stealing my house. Nuala asked me to move in with her. I'm not sold on the idea, but she has her heart set on it, and that man is mentally ill."

"I may be living in another country, but thanks to my brother, I'll always be a part of the Ronan family."

"You became a part of our family the day you sent Rosaria home to us, walking."

"If you're heading back to Dorchester, I can give you a ride."

"Me? In one of your sporty cars? You are hell bent on doing this family in. Stay safe, Aaron."

"Take care of her," he said, kissing Berta on her cheek.

"Shave that beard. You look like a rabid rabbi."

***

Wet leaves clung to the attic's cupola, blocking the sun that bleached the century-old wallpaper and yellowed a pile of news clippings announcing the end of war in Europe, Queen Elizabeth's coronation, the Kennedy assassination, and the moon landing. Knowing her mother's bad knee prevented her from climbing to the third floor, Colleen was free to cry as she looked out the turret's windows.

To the east, the checkerboard Boston Gas tank stood watch over Dorchester Bay. To the north, Boston's ever-changing skyline. To the west, Lee's old neighborhood. In a few short years, the tank would wear a rainbow, the city would sprout a 60-story glass tower, and Mishkan Tefila, Boston's Stadt Shul, would serve as an African-American Arts Center. Her castle walls would crumble, but the Mount would remain. The three sister crops would continue to rotate from maize, to barley, to soybean. The harvest would vary, but the field would continue to be fruitful.

The remaining contents of the twelve-room house barely took up half the space in the U-Haul attached to Colleen's Datsun. Berta foraged for items she didn't need or want, but would justify the rental. "I never realized how much junk there is in this house. If you girls had taken your crap with you when you moved out, it wouldn't be left to me to get rid of it."

"Over 20 years' worth," Colleen commented from the butler's pantry.

Berta rubbed her stiff spine. "I'm going out back to burn some papers in the barrel. I don't trust the trashmen; they'll have my personal papers flying all over the park, everyone on the Mount will know how much I paid to bury your father."

"I'll come with you; there may be something in the carriage house worth saving."

The Duryea was no longer in residence. The carriage house echoed Colleen's cough. From the cobweb-covered window, she watched her mother standing over the rusty barrel's open flame, tearing pages from a thin ledger. One by one, Berta held each page until the flame was within an inch from her fingertips; only then would she surrender them to the pyre. *"How strange,"* Colleen thought, *"for a woman who spent her adult life in mortal fear of fire to risk her fingers to destroy worthless papers."*

Berta lifted a bucket of standing rainwater, dousing the cremated remains of her parents' dark past. Pushing her jaw forward, she puffed a stray hair off her forehead. "Good riddance."

Crossing the lawn in triumph, Colleen held up the old rake, its claws clinging to the remnants of last October's foliage. "We won't need this."

"Leaves don't fall in Brookline? Take it." Berta looked over at the swing. "I never thought the house would come down before that branch. If trees could talk."

The second-floor linen closet had been emptied. For the first time, Berta could see the corner of a photo crammed under the cracked linoleum. Colleen craned her neck over her mother's shoulder. "What ja looking at?"

"An old photograph, no one we know."

Colleen studied the creased image of a young man in uniform. "I bet that's Mrs. Lindsey's son Robert."

Berta wore a skeptical expression. "How would you know?"

"Grandma mentioned him."

"Did she?"

Colleen wondered if her mother was aware of the striking resemblance. A smile came to Colleen's lips, knowing her mother was seeing her father's face for the first time... or was she? Had Grandma taken their daughter along on her rendezvous with Robert?

Was her mother scouring her memory bank for a match to the familiar face staring back at her? Berta handed the picture over her shoulder to Colleen.

"Throw it out, he's nothing to us."

"I'm keeping it."

"Do as you please."

"Ready to go?" Colleen asked in an upbeat voice.

"Come sit with me," Berta said, taking a seat on a staircase step. Yesterday I went from room to room recalling our years here.

Rosaria coming down these stairs in a wedding gown, you in a prom dress, your father in a straitjacket. Tim was a simple man whom I treated as a simpleton. He didn't expect much out of life and never got it. His joy came from the happiness of others; if he had a hand in it, all the better. When I think of all the times I yelled up to your sisters to turn down that rock'n roll music. I should have let them go on that dance program. Kids would come from miles around to watch them dance, yet their mother wouldn't climb a flight of stairs to witness what others would pay to see. My hardwood floors be damned, they'll be a pile of splinters by week's end. They should knock this house down with me under it."

Colleen squeezed her mother's hand. "No Monday morning quarterbacking. They say God gives us the parents we need to accomplish our mission here on Earth. I was sent to the right address."

"Had I known that I would have stamped 'return to sender' on your forehead."

"Hey! That was a compliment!"

The day was darkening, Colleen was cold, eager to leave, yet her mother remained seated.

"Last New Year's Eve, I sat on this step recalling the first time I was alone in this house. It was November, dark and cold. Your father and Mae were at work, and Grandma was nursing Marty's injured back. It was left to me to wait here for the Edison man to turn on the utilities. I was eight months pregnant with you.

As I sat here, I thought, how lonely it must have been for Mrs. Lindsey living alone in this elaborate mausoleum. Now here I am in the same tomb."

Getting to her feet, Colleen held her hands out. "We are going to leave this house the way we came in, you pregnant with me, now I'm pregnant and with you." Berta buttoned her blue coat. Catching her reflection in the darkened glass pane of the dining room's French doors, she stroked the wool now glossy with age.

"Oh, Ma."

"Don't 'oh Ma,' me. If it weren't for this coat, you wouldn't be here."

Standing on the front porch, Berta deeply inhaled the autumn air. "Everyone thought I wouldn't leave the Mount because living here was my dream, but the dream belonged to your grandmother. Your father and I wanted to shop around, look at other houses on the market, but my mother wouldn't hear of it, so we relented. I was told the house was haunted. Never believed it, still don't. Departed souls live within its walls, that I know to be true. The Lindseys, Grandma, Mae, Tim, and Rosaria watched over us; that's not haunting. Destroying the house won't snuff them out. I packed them away in my heart; they're coming with me. I'm glad the house is being torn down; that ours was the only family to have lived in it."

"Were the Lindseys family?"

Berta looked over at the park as if the answer lay hidden among the trees. "My mother would say- "We're like fallen leaves, no matter where the wind carries us, a maple is a maple, a chestnut, a chestnut, but together we make autumn."

"That's beautiful!"

"The woman was illiterate yet; she could weave magic with the twist of her tongue. Never believed a word that came out of that woman's mouth. But she was right, we are unique, from different trees, but together we make a family."

"We can't postpone autumn."

"God knows I've tried." Colleen reached into her handbag for her house keys, laughing, realizing there was no point in locking the door. Winding up her arm, she threw the keys across to the park as though she were throwing out the first pitch at a Red Sox game.

The two women locked arms as they walked down the front steps. "Are you sure you want to live with your mother-in-law?"

"Lee's close to his mother. Freida will be a help when the baby arrives."

"Suit yourself, but I know... when to keep my opinions to myself." Both women laughed at Berta's phony admission.

Colleen nudged her mother, "I never thought I'd live to see the day you and Mac would share a roof."

"Stranger things have happened."

"No, they haven't."

"Mac's a good egg. Repeat that and I'll call you a liar. He needs looking after, and Nuala will be traveling to promote her mastectomy fashion line. She's calling it Nualawear. Always liked that name, Nuala. It means white shoulders in Gaelic."

"What does Colleen mean?"

"Fat ass in plain English. That girl was given the gift of beauty; now she's making other women feel her equal. I'm very proud of her."

The slam of Colleen's car door set off a farewell sonata from the piano Clay had silenced. Berta clutched her daughter's arm. "Let's get out of here. That house is haunted!"

Colleen yanked the seatbelt across her ripe belly. "The obstetrician thinks I'm having a girl."

"He's a doctor, what the hell does he know? I never thought Nuala would become a successful businesswoman, and you a conventional housewife and mother."

"I can work."

"At what?"

"I'm a writer, remember."

"Ah, yes, you write. And what will you write about?"

"I'm going to write about you, Ma, I'm going to write about you."